Windows Server 2019 Cookbook

Second Edition

Over 100 recipes to effectively configure networks, manage security, and administer workloads

Mark Henderson

Jordan Krause

BIRMINGHAM—MUMBAI

Windows Server 2019 Cookbook
Second Edition

Copyright © 2020 Packt Publishing

Commissioning Editor: Vijin Boricha
Acquisition Editor: Meeta Rajani
Senior Editor: Rahul Dsouza
Content Development Editor: Alokita Amanna
Technical Editor: Sarvesh Jaywant
Copy Editor: Safis Editing
Project Coordinator: Neil Dmello
Proofreader: Safis Editing
Indexer: Pratik Shirodkar
Production Designer: Shankar Kalbhor

First Edition: November 2016
Second Edition: July 2020

Production reference: 1200720

Published by Packt Publishing Ltd.
Livery Place
35 Livery Street
Birmingham
B3 2PB, UK.

ISBN 978-1-83898-719-0

www.packt.com

"To Angela, Levi, and Sophie: You supported me with much patience, understanding, and love during the countless afternoons, evenings, and late nights I spent on this book. For that I will always be grateful. Thank you."

– Mark Henderson

Packt.com

Subscribe to our online digital library for full access to over 7,000 books and videos, as well as industry leading tools to help you plan your personal development and advance your career. For more information, please visit our website.

Why subscribe?

- Spend less time learning and more time coding with practical eBooks and Videos from over 4,000 industry professionals

- Improve your learning with Skill Plans built especially for you

- Get a free eBook or video every month

- Fully searchable for easy access to vital information

- Copy and paste, print, and bookmark content

Did you know that Packt offers eBook versions of every book published, with PDF and ePub files available? You can upgrade to the eBook version at packt.com and as a print book customer, you are entitled to a discount on the eBook copy. Get in touch with us at customercare@packtpub.com for more details.

At www.packt.com, you can also read a collection of free technical articles, sign up for a range of free newsletters, and receive exclusive discounts and offers on Packt books and eBooks.

Contributors

About the authors

Mark Henderson is a Site Reliability Engineer. He has worked for companies such as Take 2 Games and Stack Overflow. He has a bachelor's degree in information systems and over 13 years of experience in Windows administration, focused on internet-facing applications and scaling enterprise applications. He works daily with containers, Azure, Amazon Web Services, Active Directory, IIS, SQL Server, and .NET. He lives in a quiet, peaceful beach town in Australia with his family, but has been working with small, medium, and large American companies since 2015.

> *I'd like to acknowledge Tom Limoncelli for convincing me that everyone has at least one book in them. Thanks to my Dad, John Henderson, for leading by example with a strong work ethic and beliefs. Finally, thanks to Jordan Krause for all his work in providing a great foundation for this edition of the book.*

Jordan Krause is a six-time Microsoft MVP, currently in the Cloud and Datacenter Management category. He has the unique opportunity of working daily with Microsoft networking and remote access technologies. Jordan specializes in Microsoft DirectAccess and Always On VPN. Committed to continuous learning, Jordan holds Microsoft certifications as an MCP, MCTS, MCSA, and MCITP Enterprise Administrator, and regularly writes articles reflecting his experiences with these technologies. Jordan lives in beautiful West Michigan (USA), but works daily with companies around the world.

About the reviewer

David Moravec is currently working as a Technical Expert for Microsoft Azure in EmbedIT. Prior to that, he was working as an architect and a leader of a cloud team at one of the top Czech consulting companies. His projects have won Microsoft Partner of the Year a few times. He started his IT journey 20 years ago as a helpdesk guy and, after a year, moved to the configuration management domain. At that time, his passion for the automation of server environments began. In 2006, he fell in love with PowerShell and later became a PowerShell MVP. He has reviewed books on various topics, such as PowerShell, Python, Docker, and Kubernetes.

I'd like to thank Míša for her patience with my sleepless nights. And to Kilian and Amálka for charging my batteries for these nights.

Packt is searching for authors like you

If you're interested in becoming an author for Packt, please visit `authors.packtpub.com` and apply today. We have worked with thousands of developers and tech professionals, just like you, to help them share their insight with the global tech community. You can make a general application, apply for a specific hot topic that we are recruiting an author for, or submit your own idea.

Table of Contents

2

Core Infrastructure Tasks

3
Networking

4

Working with Certificates

5
Internet Information Services

6

Remote Access

7

Remote Desktop Services

8

Monitoring and Backup

11

File Services and Data Control

12

Server Core

13
Working with Hyper-V

14
Containers and Docker

15

Desired State Configuration and Automation

16

Hardening Your Infrastructure

Other Books You May Enjoy

Index

Preface

Windows is, and will probably always be, the leader in server software for businesses. In any data center in the world that supports desktop Windows computers, you will find Windows Server. You will also find Windows powering one of the world's largest cloud environments – Microsoft Azure. Businesses have been relying on Windows and Windows Server for almost 25 years, and not without reason! Windows Server 2019 continues the long-standing tradition of providing all the core functionality from previous versions of Windows Server along with many enhancements and improvements new to this version of Windows.

Windows has seen a substantial shift in the past 10 years towards remote management. Where once upon a time you had to log into individual servers, now almost everything can be done from the comfort of your Windows 10 desktop. Many remote management GUIs are available, and for those who like scripting and repeatability there's a large focus on PowerShell. Windows Server 2019 is no exception, and for the first time in the *Windows Server* cookbook series we'll be looking at this extensively.

When I was approached to continue the excellent work of Jordan Krause, who wrote the previous editions of the book, I was excited at the idea of being able to educate readers on many of the common mistakes I see made in Windows environments around the globe. I've seen more badly named Active Directory domains than well-named ones. I've seen so many web servers that were meant to be identical but where one or two have been configured differently. I see companies that don't have the right tools in place to be able to reconstruct a security incident after the fact. I saw this edition of this book as my chance to share the knowledge I've built up over the past 15 years. Windows Server 2019 has so many wonderful features that are woefully under-utilized. Desired State Configuration is one particular example that, if used properly, could have saved a lot of the heartache I've seen.

You may be asking yourself why this book even exists – isn't everything moving to the cloud? Why do I need to learn all this? The simple answer is that most of the things you learn here are still relevant to the cloud! The cloud isn't some magic wand that you can wave over your infrastructure and make it all just work. There's still management that needs to be done. Servers still need configuring, users need administering, file servers still need anti-virus. There are also a lot of workloads that are not moving to the cloud yet. Any medium to large business probably has at least one or two Windows servers sitting in a rack in each office. And let's not forget that cloud services only work well if you have a solid, high - bandwidth, low - latency internet connection. For countries where internet bandwidth is limited or expensive, then on-premises hardware will surely always win. So, whether or not your company is going all-in on the cloud, you will still need a good, fundamental, solid understanding of Windows Server 2019.

A book about Windows Server can't just focus on the new fancy pieces. It also needs to lay a good foundation to get you to a point where you can use these new features with confidence. That's why a lot of the recipes early on in this book cover doing things two ways: once via the GUI and a second time via PowerShell. As we get into the more advanced chapters of the book, the GUI will be seen less and less, and we'll be in PowerShell a lot more. As your skills in PowerShell improve, my hope is that you can take the foundations found in this book and maybe one day you can write your own book about your adventures in Windows administration. Maybe you will take over the reins of the Windows Server cookbook series!

Who this book is for

This book is for system administrators and IT professionals that may or may not have previous experience with Windows Server. The ideal target is desktop administrators wanting to get into the server world, and developers hoping to better understand the infrastructure upon which their applications run. The target readers may also have some experience in previous versions of Windows Server but be interested in some of the new 2019 features or wants to know how to manage servers remotely. All will benefit from the information provided here. Anyone hoping to acquire the skills and knowledge necessary to manage and maintain the core infrastructure required for a Windows Server 2019 environment should find something interesting in this book.

What this book covers

Chapter 1, Learning the interface, takes you on a journey of working with Windows Server 2019 as we figure out how to navigate through the new look and feel of this new operating system, and gain some tips and tricks to complete our daily chores efficiently.

Chapter 2, Core Infrastructure Tasks, takes us through configuring and working with the core Microsoft technology stack. The recipes contained in this chapter are what I consider essential knowledge for any administrator who intends to work in a Windows network.

Chapter 3, Networking, runs through many common network configurations and useful tools that you'll need to know to configure a Windows network.

Chapter 4, Working with Certificates, starts to get us comfortable with the creation and distribution of certificates within our network. Public Key Infrastructure is an area that administrators increasingly need to use and operate, but many administrators have not yet had an opportunity to work hands-on with it.

Chapter 5, Internet Information Services, brings us into the configuration of a Windows Server 2019 server as a web server in our network. We will start to tie in the earlier chapters of this book – we'll be using network configuration, core infrastructure tasks, and certificates in this chapter. We'll also be looking at a certificate authority called Let's Encrypt.

Chapter 6, Remote Access, digs into using Windows Server 2016 as the connectivity platform that brings your remote computers into the corporate network. We discuss DirectAccess and VPNs in this chapter.

Chapter 7, Remote Desktop Services, encourages you to look into using Server 2019 as a virtual session host or VDI solution. Remote Desktop Services (RDS) can be an incredibly powerful tool for anyone interested in centralized computing.

Chapter 8, Monitoring and Backup, covers some of the capabilities included with Windows Server 2019 to help keep tabs on the servers running in your infrastructure. From monitoring system performance and IP address management to backing up and restoring data using the tools baked into Windows, these recipes will walk you through some helpful tasks related to monitoring and backup, and checking for viruses.

Chapter 9, System Insights, covers a new feature in Windows Server 2019 that allows large-scale analysis and predictions of server health and capacity. We look at how we can use this for capacity planning, and how you might integrate it into an existing monitoring system. We also do a lot of work in the new Windows Admin Center.

Chapter 10, Group Policy, takes us into the incredibly powerful and far-reaching management powers contained within Active Directory that are provided out of the box with Windows Server 2019.

Chapter 11, File Services and Data Control, provides us with information and step-by-step recipes on some of the lesser - known ways that data can be managed on a Windows server. We will cover technologies such as DFSR, iSCSI, and Windows Server 2019 Work Folders. We also look at building a scale-out file server.

Chapter 12, Server Core, encourages us to shrink our servers! Most of us automatically deploy our servers with the full graphical interface, but often we could make our servers more efficient and more secure by using a headless interface. Let's explore these capabilities together to see where they can fit into your environment.

Chapter 13, Working with Hyper-V, takes a look into the backend interface of our virtualization infrastructure. Many server administrators only ever access their virtual machines as if they were physical servers, but there may come a day when you need to get into that backend administration and create a new VM or adjust some settings. We also look at another brand-new Windows Server 2019 feature: nested resilience.

Chapter 14, Containers and Docker, takes us into one of the most exciting technologies since virtualization became mainstream. It's an entirely new way of deploying server applications. Most of the talk regarding containers has been about Linux, but did you know that Windows supports containers too? Docker is the most popular container platform, and Windows Server 2019 supports it! You'll learn the basics of how Docker works with Windows and we'll build a Minecraft server while we're at it.

Chapter 15, Desired State Configuration and Automation, teaches a new tool for ensuring that your servers are consistently configured. This allows you to easily deploy dozens, hundreds, or thousands of identically configured servers (for example, a web server tier), update their configuration by updating a single file, and undo any changes that might have been made by other services. DSC integration is also provided by other tools, such as Puppet; however, Microsoft's preferred DSC management method is with Azure.

Chapter 16, Hardening Your Infrastructure, takes a look at the most secure version of Windows Server yet. Windows Server 2019 is more secure out of the box than any Windows version previously. However, you cannot just stop at the defaults. Every environment is different. In this chapter, you will learn about the tools and processes you need to ensure that you can secure your Windows servers in the ways that are the most appropriate for you.

To get the most out of this book

All the technologies and features that are discussed in the recipes of this book are included with Windows Server 2019! As long as you have access to the operating system installer disk and either a piece of hardware or a virtualization environment where you can spin up a new virtual machine, you will be able to install the operating system and follow along with our lessons.

Software/Hardware covered in the book	OS Requirements
Windows Server 2019	A downloaded ISO or an installation DVD of Windows Server 2019. An accessible internet connection.

Many of the tasks that we are going to accomplish together require a certain amount of base networking and infrastructure to be configured in order to fully test the technologies that we are working with. The easiest method for working through all of these recipes will be to have access to a Hyper-V server upon which you can build multiple virtual machines that run Windows Server 2019. With this available, you will be able to build recipe upon recipe as we move through setting up the core infrastructure tasks, and then build upon those same servers in the later recipes.

Building a baseline lab network running Server 2019 for the Microsoft infrastructure roles such as Active Directory, DNS, DHCP, certificates, and web/file services will help you tremendously as you move throughout this book. If you are not familiar with building out a lab, do not be dismayed. Many of the recipes included here will help with building the structure of the lab.

If you are using the digital version of this book, we advise you to type the code yourself or access the code via the GitHub repository (link available in the next section). Doing so will help you avoid any potential errors related to the copying and pasting of code.

Download the example code files

You can download the example code files for this book from your account at www. packt.com. If you purchased this book elsewhere, you can visit www.packtpub.com/support and register to have the files emailed directly to you.

You can download the code files by following these steps:

1. Log in or register at www.packt.com.
2. Select the **Support** tab.
3. Click on **Code Downloads**.
4. Enter the name of the book in the **Search** box and follow the onscreen instructions.

Once the file is downloaded, please make sure that you unzip or extract the folder using the latest version of:

1. WinRAR/7-Zip for Windows
2. Zipeg/iZip/UnRarX for Mac
3. 7-Zip/PeaZip for Linux

The code bundle for the book is also hosted on GitHub at https://github.com/PacktPublishing/Windows-Server-2019-Cookbook-Second-Edition. In case there's an update to the code, it will be updated on the existing GitHub repository.

We also have other code bundles from our rich catalog of books and videos available at https://github.com/PacktPublishing/. Check them out!

Code in Action

Code in Action videos for this book can be viewed at (https://bit.ly/3eu4Boy).

Download the color images

We also provide a PDF file that has color images of the screenshots/diagrams used in this book. You can download it here: http://www.packtpub.com/sites/default/files/downloads/9781838987190_ColorImages.pdf.

Conventions used

There are a number of text conventions used throughout this book.

Code in text: Indicates code words in text, command, folder names, filenames, file extensions, server names, dummy URLs and user input. Here is an example: "Restart-Computer is a PowerShell command that does the same thing as shutdown /r /t 0 – but is much easier to remember."

A block of code is set as follows:

```
Write-Host "Hello! Here is the current date and time:
$(Get-Date)"
Write-Host "The name of your computer is: $(hostname)"
```

Any command-line input or output is written as follows:

```
hostname
shutdown /r /t 0
```

Bold: Indicates words that you see onscreen. For example, words in menus or dialog boxes appear in the text like this. Here is an example: "Now, when you click on **Shut down** or **Restart**, you are asked to supply a reason why you are restarting."

> **Tips or important notes**
> Appear like this.

Sections

In this book, you will find several headings that appear frequently (*Getting ready*, *How to do it...*, *How it works...*, *There's more...*, and *See also*).

To give clear instructions on how to complete a recipe, use these sections as follows:

Getting ready

This section tells you what to expect in the recipe and describes how to set up any software or any preliminary settings required for the recipe.

How to do it...

This section contains the steps required to follow the recipe.

How it works...

This section usually consists of a detailed explanation of what happened in the previous section.

There's more...

This section consists of additional information about the recipe in order to make you more knowledgeable about the recipe.

See also

This section provides helpful links to other useful information for the recipe.

Get in touch

Feedback from our readers is always welcome.

General feedback: If you have questions about any aspect of this book, mention the book title in the subject of your message and email us at customercare@packtpub.com.

Errata: Although we have taken every care to ensure the accuracy of our content, mistakes do happen. If you have found a mistake in this book, we would be grateful if you would report this to us. Please visit www.packtpub.com/support/errata, selecting your book, clicking on the Errata Submission Form link, and entering the details.

Piracy: If you come across any illegal copies of our works in any form on the Internet, we would be grateful if you would provide us with the location address or website name. Please contact us at copyright@packt.com with a link to the material.

If you are interested in becoming an author: If there is a topic that you have expertise in and you are interested in either writing or contributing to a book, please visit authors.packtpub.com.

Reviews

Please leave a review. Once you have read and used this book, why not leave a review on the site that you purchased it from? Potential readers can then see and use your unbiased opinion to make purchase decisions, we at Packt can understand what you think about our products, and our authors can see your feedback on their book. Thank you!

For more information about Packt, please visit packt.com.

1
Learning the Interface

In an effort to become familiar with the look and feel of Windows Server 2019, in this chapter, you will learn how to navigate through some daily tasks using the graphical interface.

Windows 8 and Server 2012 brought us a drastic change in the way that we interfaced with the Windows operating system, and most of us didn't think that change was for the better. By now, I assume you have seen, used, and are hopefully deploying Windows 10 on your client computers, which brings some relief with regard to the user interface. With Windows 10, we have kind of a mix between Windows 7 and Windows 8, and it fits the needs of most people in a better way. Just like the last couple of rollouts of the Microsoft Windows operating systems, the Server platform follows on the heels of the Desktop version. Beginning with Windows Server 2016 Microsoft, went back to the basics and returned with the look and feel of Windows 10. Thankfully, Windows Server 2019 keeps this interface.

If you have been using Windows 10, you already have a good head start if you wish to successfully interface with Windows Server 2019. However, if you are still using older equipment and haven't had a chance to really dive into the latest and greatest operating systems, these big changes in the way that we interact with our servers can be a big stumbling block to successfully utilizing the new tools. Many differences exist when comparing Server 2019 to something like Server 2008, and when you are working within three levels of **Remote Desktop Protocol (RDP)**, bouncing from one server to another, all of these little differences are compounded. It suddenly becomes difficult to know which server it is that you are working on or changing. Let's have a show of hands – how many of you have mistakenly rebooted the wrong server? Or, even more likely, how many of you have rebooted your own computer while you were trying to reboot a remote server? I know I have! And not just once.

Hope is not lost! I promise you that once you learn how to manage the interface rather than letting it manage you, some of these changes may start to seem like good ideas. They can increase productivity and help make accomplishing tasks easy – we just need some pointers on making the best use of the new interface.

We're also going to start making use of PowerShell to do a lot of administrative tasks. First introduced in 2006, PowerShell is Microsoft's command-line interface and it's one of the ways Microsoft really wants new administrators like yourself to work. After 13 years of constant development and work, PowerShell is an excellent tool for managing Windows. But if you really love your mouse and GUI, then don't fret – we're going to include both methods where possible!

The recipes in this chapter are dedicated to helping you find your way around the basic Windows Server 2019 interfaces. Let's work together to gain a better understanding of why the interface was built the way it is and learn to take advantage of these new screens and settings.

Let's look at the list of recipes in this chapter:

- Shutting down or restarting the server
- Launching Administrative Tools
- Using *WinKey* + *X* for quick admin tasks
- Using the search function to launch applications quickly
- Managing remote servers from a single pane with Server Manager
- Using PowerShell to accomplish any function in Windows Server

- Installing a role or feature

- Administering Server 2019 from a Windows 10 machine

- Managing your servers through the Windows Admin Center

- Identifying useful keyboard shortcuts in Server 2019

- Setting up your PowerShell execution policy

- Building and executing your first PowerShell script

- Searching for PowerShell cmdlets with `Get-Help`

Shutting down or restarting the server

I just couldn't resist starting with this one. Yes, this seems trivial. Silly even. However, the number of times that I have watched a simple server restart consume more mouse clicks than creating a domain controller has convinced me that this needed to be in this book. Perhaps the shutdown and restart options were hidden away purposefully, because once your system is up and running, there is not often a need to accomplish either of these tasks. When first configuring the box, though, it is very common to have to reboot a couple of times or shut down a machine to move it to another location. Let's face it, it doesn't seem to matter how many years computers have been around – sometimes, the magical reboot process is still the fix.

Getting ready

To complete this recipe, you will need a Windows Server 2019 system online. There are no other prerequisites.

How to do it...

Let's take a look at three different ways to shut down or restart your system. The first is going to be the most commonly employed. The second is still being used by quite a few folks who had to work hard at getting this strange location in their heads during the Windows 8 rollout, and they have continued to use it from that point forward. The third is less commonly known but is by far my favorite when tasked with restarting a remote server.

Using the Start menu

The first option, thankfully, is in a location that makes sense to anyone using Windows 10. We can simply click on the **Start** button, and see right there, near the bottom, that we have **Power** control options available to us:

Figure 1.1 – Power control options in the Start menu

Now, when you click on **Shut down** or **Restart**, you will be asked to supply a reason why you are restarting. Common sense tells us that if you are manually clicking on the **Restart** button, there is a pretty good chance you are actually intending to restart the server, right? A planned occurrence? But what is the default option that presents itself? **Other (Unplanned)**. Alas, this default option is certainly going to cause us log files full of unplanned restarts, even though all of those restarts were actually planned. Because let's be real – nobody takes the time to change that drop-down menu before they click **Continue**:

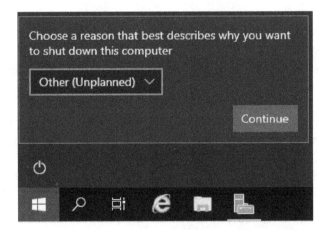

Figure 1.2 – Shut down/Restart prompt, asking users to choose a reason for shutting down or restarting

The second method to accomplish shutting down or restarting is by right-clicking on the **Start** button. We will discuss this little menu that is presented when right-clicking on Start in our next recipe, but for the sake of a quick shutdown or restart, you can simply right-click on the **Start** button and then choose **Shut down or sign out**:

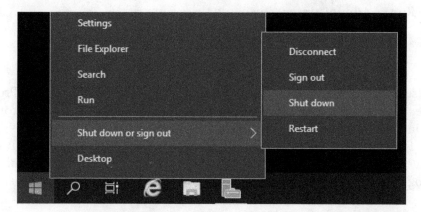

Figure 1.3 – The shutdown or sign out prompt in the Start menu

These two examples run the risk of rebooting the wrong system. Depending on how many layers of remote connections, such as RDP, you are using, it is fairly easy to reboot your own computer or the wrong server instead of the server you intended to reboot. This is because it is fairly easy to click on the **Start** button of a different system than the one you intended in the first place. One of the most fool-proof ways of restarting your server is at the Command Prompt. Doing this gives you the opportunity to double-check that you are manipulating the correct machine.

Using the Command Prompt

Open a Command Prompt (make sure you are selecting **Run as Administrator**) and run a quick hostname check to make sure you are restarting the one you really intend to. Then, utilize the shutdown command to take care of the rest. This process can be especially helpful when you're logged into remote servers using RDP. Use the following commands to perform the explained operations:

```
hostname
shutdown /r /t 0
```

If you were to simply type shutdown, the server would shut itself down in 60 seconds. Using /r indicates a restart rather than a shutdown, while /t 0 is a timing flag that indicates the number of seconds the server should wait before restarting. Specifying zero here tells it to wait for zero seconds before initiating the restart.

Using Windows PowerShell

The Command Prompt is very 2003. As mentioned in the introduction, we're going to start doing things the **PowerShell** way. So, instead of opening a Command Prompt, we'll open PowerShell instead (you will need to right-click on PowerShell in the **Start** menu and choose **Run as Administrator**). Then, run these commands:

```
hostname
```

```
Restart-Computer
```

As you can see, the first line, `hostname`, is the same as it was in our Command Prompt from before. That's because almost any command that works in the Command Prompt also works in PowerShell. However, our second command is different. `Restart-Computer` is a PowerShell command that does the same thing as `shutdown /r /t 0` but is much easier to remember. As a bonus, you can also restart other servers without having to log onto them at all with that command using the `-ComputerName` parameter:

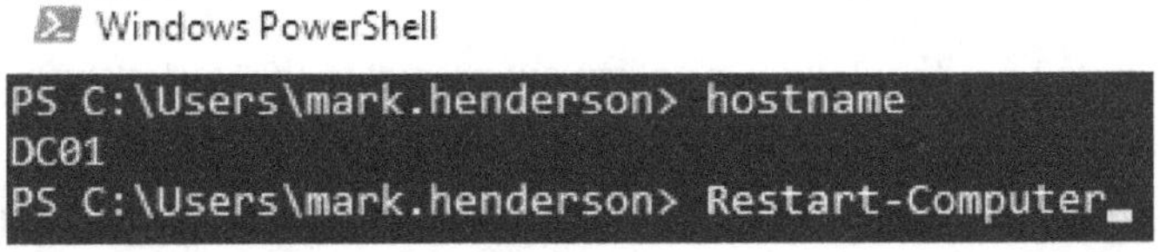

```
Windows PowerShell
PS C:\Users\mark.henderson> hostname
DC01
PS C:\Users\mark.henderson> Restart-Computer_
```

Figure 1.4 – An example of the output of using the hostname command in Windows PowerShell

Windows also has a `Stop-Computer` command, which you can use if you wish to shut down a server instead of restarting it – but be aware that once the machine is shut down, you will be unable to use PowerShell to start it back up!

> **Tip**
>
> PowerShell has a feature called "tab completion". If you write the first few letters of a command and then press *tab* on your keyboard, PowerShell will try to finish the command for you. Try just typing the letters "Restart" and press *tab*. PowerShell should auto-complete this to `Restart-Computer` for you.

How it works...

Shutting down or restarting a server doesn't require a lot of explanation, but I hope that this small recipe has got you thinking about creative ways to perform regular tasks. As you will see throughout this book, you can accomplish anything in Windows Server 2019 through the use of commands, scripts, and PowerShell. You could easily turn the `Restart-Computer` command, which we explored in the last example that we tested in this recipe, into a script file, and place it on the desktop of each of your servers as a quick double-click option for accomplishing this task.

However, I work with RDP windows inside RDP windows very often. When bouncing around between a dozen servers that all have the same background image, I found that the only sure-fire way to make sure you are restarting the correct device is to do a quick hostname check before you initiate the restart. If you are interested in discovering all of the available flags that are available in PowerShell for restarting your server, make sure to type in `Get-Help Restart-Computer` sometime to take a look at all of the available options. We'll look at this in more detil in the *Searching for PowerShell cmdlets with Get-Help recipe*.

> **Tip**
> Using PowerShell is also an easy way to log off a server. Let's say you are layers-deep in RDP and want to log off from a single server (not all of them). Are you sure you clicked on the **Start** button of the right server? Instead, open PowerShell and simply type `logoff`.

Launching Administrative Tools

Earlier versions of Windows Server placed all of the Administrative Tools in a self-named folder right inside the **Start** menu. This was always a quick and easy place to visit in order to see all of the Administrative Tools installed on a particular server. This location for the tools disappeared as of Server 2012 because of the infamous Start Screen. I am glad to say that a more traditional-looking **Start** menu returned in Windows Server 2016 and has stayed in 2019. Once again, this is a link to **Windows Administrative Tools**. However, as you also know, there is this thing called Server Manager (and later, we'll learn about the new Admin Center), which loves to present itself every time that you log into a server. Since Server Manager is already on your screen most of the time anyway, it is actually the fastest way to launch the Administrative Tools that you need to utilize so often. Let's take a look at launching your commonly used infrastructure tools right from inside the Server Manager interface.

Getting ready

All you really need is a Windows Server 2019 machine online. The more roles and services that you have running on it, the more options that you will see on your screen as we navigate these menus.

How to do it...

To launch Administrative Tools from your Desktop, perform the following steps:

1. Open up Server Manager. In fact, if you just logged into the server, it's probably already open for you.

2. You will probably see a message that tells you about the Windows Admin Center. Feel free to check the box that says "**Don't remind me again**" and close that window. We'll look at the Windows Admin Center in more detail in the *Managing your servers through the Windows Admin Center recipe*.

3. Click on **Tools** in the upper-right corner.

There you go – a full list of all Administrative Tools installed on that server. Heading into this list is also a quick way of taking a look into what a particular server is doing, which you can take an educated guess at based on what roles and services are installed. Your server may not look exactly like the one shown in the following screenshot – this screenshot was taken before any roles and services had been installed. It is important to note that your server may also be running components that do not show up in this list. For example, if you install a role via PowerShell and do not enter the parameter to also install the management tools for that role, it is possible that you could have a server where the role is up and running, but the management tools simply have not been installed. In that case, those tools would not show up in this list:

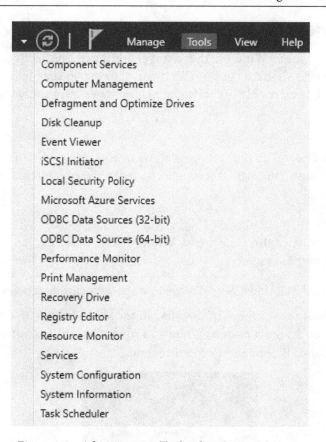

Figure 1.5 – Administrative Tools tab in Server Manager

How it works...

Since Server Manager likes to open automatically when we've logged in, let's make quick use of it to open the tools that we need to do our jobs. Another way to have easy access to your tools from the desktop is to create shortcuts or to pin each of them to your taskbar. Sometimes, this isn't as easy as it sounds. In the past, these tools were all grouped together in the **Administrative Tools** folder, so you didn't have any reason to memorize the exact names of the tools. While you can access them that way again in Server 2019, that folder may or may not appear inside the **Start** menu, depending on how the server is configured, because it appears as one of the live tiles. If you click on the **Start** button, you can try using the search function to find the tool you are looking for, but its name may not immediately come to you. If you're a consultant working on someone else's server, you may not want to pin anything to their desktop anyway. I like to stick with launching Administrative Tools from Server Manager since it always exists, and the tools will always be available inside that menu.

Using WinKey + X for quick admin tasks

There are some functions in Windows that a server administrator needs to use all the time. Instead of making shortcuts or pinning them all to the taskbar, let's get to know this hidden menu, which is extremely useful for launching these commonly used admin tools.

Getting ready

A running Windows Server 2019 machine is all we need to highlight this one. In fact, this menu also exists on any Windows 10 computer, so make use of it often!

How to do it...

There are two ways to open this little menu. While you are in the Server 2019 desktop, you can perform either of these steps:

1. Hold down your Windows key (*WinKey*) on the keyboard and press *X*.

2. Hover your mouse over the Windows flag in the lower-left corner of the Desktop – over the **Start** button. When you right-click on that button, you will see a menu, as shown in the following screenshot:

Figure 1.6 – The right-click menu for the Windows Start button

How it works...

This little quick-tasks admin menu is very easy to open and is very convenient for launching programs and settings that are accessed often. I won't talk too much about what particulars are in the menu as it's pretty self-explanatory, but I use this menu multiple times per day to open up the **System** properties and **PowerShell**, as it has an option to open an administrative PowerShell prompt right from the menu.

> **Tip**
> Look at that, you can also shut down the server from here!

Using the search function to launch applications quickly

Windows 10, and therefore Windows Server 2019, have moved back to a more traditional **Start** menu. Ever since Windows 7 was released, I have been using the **Start** menu for one critical function in my daily workflow: searching. Let's explore the search capabilities of Server 2019, which can be accessed with a single press of a button.

Getting ready

For this recipe, you will need a Windows Server 2019 system online.

How to do it...

There are two ways to search inside Server 2019, but they both do exactly the same thing. One is to click on the little magnifying glass next to the **Start** button, while the other one is to just click the **Start** button itself. The only difference is that the magnifying glass brings up the search box automatically, while with the **Start** button, you have to start typing first:

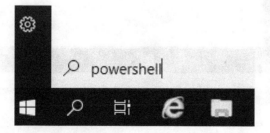

Figure 1.7 – Using search to open PowerShell on the taskbar

You can see here that I've started searching for the PowerShell prompt. It's not immediately obvious, but I have just pressed the **Start** button and just typed in the word powershell. That's it. I didn't click on anything or move my mouse. I just pressed the **Start** button on my keyboard and then typed in the word.

Search results are presented at the top of that screen, and you can choose what you are looking for accordingly. This is a quick, easy search. I employ this method of opening applications all day, every day. This way, I don't have to pin anything to the task bar, I don't have to create any shortcuts, and, most importantly, I don't have to use my mouse in order to launch applications:

Figure 1.8 – Using the Start menu search feature to open PowerShell

How it works...

From the **Start** menu, we can search for anything on the server. This gives us the ability to quickly find and launch any program or application that we have installed. This includes Administrative Tools. Rather than moving into Server Manager in order to launch your administrative consoles from the **Tools** menu, you can also search for them using the **Search** menu and launch them from there. It also gives us the ability to find files or documents by name. Another powerful way to use the search function in Windows Server 2019 is to open any kind of setting that you might want to change. In previous versions of Windows, you had to either memorize the way to get into the settings that you wanted to change or you had to open up the **Control Panel**, where you had to poke and prod your way around until you stumbled upon the one that you were looking for. Now, it is a very simple matter of pressing the Windows key, typing the first few characters of the setting or program you want to launch, and pressing *Enter*.

Another common task to perform from the **Search** screen is to right-click on the application that you are trying to launch and pin it somewhere. When you right-click on a program from the **Search** screen, you will see the option to pin the program to either your **Start** menu or to the taskbar. This will create a quick-launch shortcut on either the main **Start** menu or on the taskbar of the Desktop mode, giving you easier and faster access to launch those applications in the future.

Managing remote servers from a single pane with Server Manager

If you've used a much older version of Windows Server (say, Server 2003), you may have noticed that Server Manager has changed significantly over the past couple of versions of Windows Server. Part of these changes are a shift in mindset, where the emphasis is now placed on the *remote* management of servers. Server Manager in Windows Server 2019 can be used to manage and administer multiple systems at the same time, all from your single pane of glass – the monitor that you are sitting in front of.

Server Manager makes use of the **Windows Remote Management (WinRM)** tools to remotely manipulate servers. Historically, most of us who administer Windows Servers make extensive use of RDP, often having many windows and connections open simultaneously. This can cause confusion and can lead to tasks being accomplished on servers for which they are not intended. By using Server Manager from a single machine to manage multiple servers in your network, you will increase your administrative efficiency, as well as minimize human error by having all the management processes happen from a single pane of glass. In this recipe, you are going to learn how to manage both the local server we are logged into as well as a remote server from the same Server Manager window.

Getting ready

For this recipe, we need two servers. One is the machine we are physically logged into. The other is a server on the same network that we can contact from our primary server so that we can manage it from our local Server Manager.

How to do it...

To manage a local as well as a remote server from the same Server Manager window, perform the following steps:

1. Log in to your primary server and launch **Server Manager**. You will see in the upper-left corner that the only server you have listed is the **Local Server** that we are logged into:

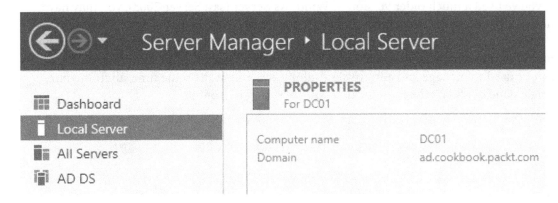

Figure 1.9 – Local Server open on Server Manager

2. Now, head over toward the top-right of **Server Manager** and click on the **Manage** button. In this menu, click on **Add Servers**:

Figure 1.10 – Using Add Servers in Server Manager

3. If your servers are part of a domain, finding remote machines to manage is very easy. Simply select them from the default **Active Directory** tab. If they are not yet joined to your domain, you can simply click over to the tab labeled **DNS** and search for them from that screen:

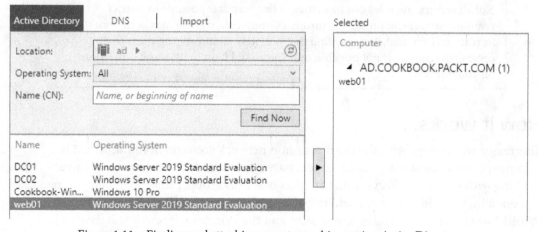

Figure 1.11 – Finding and attaching remote machines using Active Directory

4. After adding the servers that you want to manage, if you go ahead and click on
    All Servers in the left window pane, you will see the additional servers listed that
    you have selected. If you double-click or right-click on those remote server names,
    you will see that you have many options available to you to remotely manage those
    machines without having to log into them:

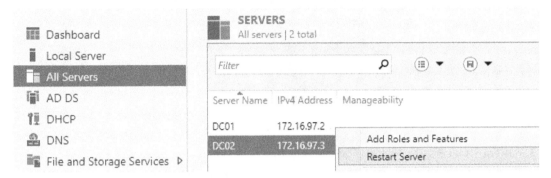

Figure 1.12 – Using All Servers to manage servers

> **Tip**
> Not all servers and roles can be managed this way. It is possible to restrict
> remote management on servers through Group Policy. If that has been done
> in your environment, you may find that remotely administering them from a
> centralized console is not possible, and you would have to lift those restrictions
> on your servers.

How it works...

This recipe was written with the most common network scenario in mind, which is
a domain environment where both servers have been joined to the domain. If you are
working with standalone servers that are part of a workgroup, rather than being joined
to a domain, you will have some additional considerations. In the workgroup scenario,
WinRM will need to be enabled specifically, and the Windows Firewall will have to be
adjusted in order to allow the right ports and protocols for that WinRM traffic flow to
happen successfully. In general, though, you mainly will be working within a Microsoft
domain network, in which case these items are not necessary.

See also

- *Administering Server 2019 from a Windows 10 machine*

Using PowerShell to accomplish any function in Windows Server

As you may have seen earlier in this chapter, an incredibly powerful tool in Windows Server 2019 is PowerShell. Think of PowerShell as a Command Prompt on steroids. It is a command-line interface from which you can manipulate almost anything inside Windows. Better yet, any task that you may wish to accomplish can be scripted out in PowerShell and saved as a `.ps1` script file so that you can automate large tasks and schedule them for later or at regular intervals. In this recipe, we'll open up PowerShell and run some sample commands and tasks just to get a quick feel for the interface. In most subsequent chapters of this book, we will do some more specific tasks with PowerShell to go even deeper into the technology.

Getting ready

To start using PowerShell, all you need is a server with Windows Server 2019 installed. PowerShell is installed and enabled by default.

How to do it...

To get a feel for using PowerShell, perform the following steps:

1. Our first step to working in PowerShell is finding it. Thankfully, Microsoft has begun the process of phasing out the Command Prompt and PowerShell is now accessible in more places than ever before. The most common methods are pressing *WinKey + X* and choosing **Windows PowerShell (Admin)**, or typing `PowerShell` into the **Start** menu, right-clicking it, and choosing **Run as administrator**:

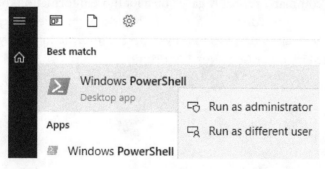

Figure 1.13 – Searching in the Start menu for PowerShell

2. Test out some commands that you are familiar with from using the Command Prompt, such as `dir` and `cls`. These still work! Since you are able to make use of these familiar commands, PowerShell can really be your one and only command-line interface.

3. Now, let's try some of PowerShell's secret sauce; that is, one of its cmdlets. These are special commands that are built into Windows and allow us to do all kinds of information gathering, as well as manipulate server components. We will be using many of these commands later on. Let's start by pulling some data. Maybe take a look at what IP addresses are on the system with `Get-NetIPAddress`:

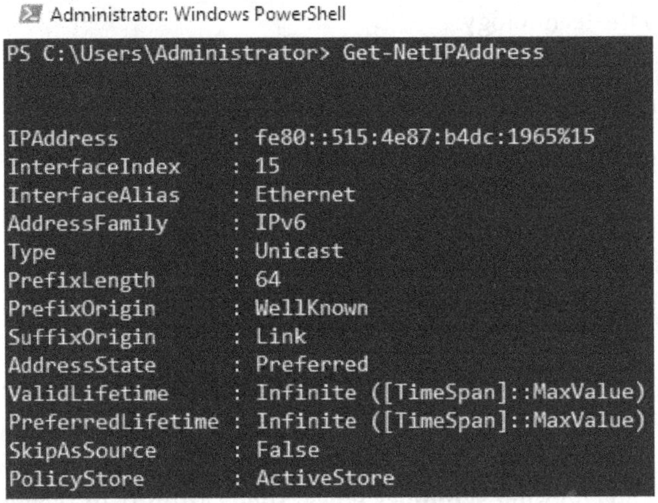

```
Administrator: Windows PowerShell

PS C:\Users\Administrator> Get-NetIPAddress


IPAddress          : fe80::515:4e87:b4dc:1965%15
InterfaceIndex     : 15
InterfaceAlias     : Ethernet
AddressFamily      : IPv6
Type               : Unicast
PrefixLength       : 64
PrefixOrigin       : WellKnown
SuffixOrigin       : Link
AddressState       : Preferred
ValidLifetime      : Infinite ([TimeSpan]::MaxValue)
PreferredLifetime  : Infinite ([TimeSpan]::MaxValue)
SkipAsSource       : False
PolicyStore        : ActiveStore
```

Figure 1.14 – Using Get-NetIPAddress to look at IP addresses on a system

4. The previous command probably gave you a lot more information than you needed, since a lot of companies don't make use of IPv6 inside their network yet. Let's whittle this information down to the IPv4-specific information that you are most likely interested in. Enter `Get-NetIPAddress -AddressFamily IPv4` to attain it:

Figure 1.15 – Refining your IP address search using –AddressFamily IPv4

5. That's more useful! But if you have a lot of data, this would be very difficult to read. PowerShell supports what's called "pipelining" of requests. This means that the output of one command can be directly sent into a second command. PowerShell comes with commands for making output more human readable, and we can use them with pipelining. One very useful command that I use every day is `Format-Table`. Type `Get-NetIPAddress | Format-Table` into PowerShell:

Figure 1.16 – Using Format-Table to organize an output

Tip

PowerShell has a lot of shorthand aliases, which makes typing out commands much easier. For example, you can just use `ft` instead of typing out all of `Format-Table`. You can get a list of aliases by running `Get-Alias`.

How it works...

We just got a feel for some of the many PowerShell commands and cmdlets by launching the program and pulling some data with this particular recipe. There are thousands of `Get` commands that can be used to query information from the server and, as you have seen, those cmdlets have various parameters that can be appended to the cmdlets to pull more specific data to meet your needs. To make things even better, it also gives us `Set` cmdlets, which will allow us to make use of the PowerShell prompt to configure many aspects of the configuration on our server, as well as remote servers. Almost every recipe in this book from here on will also show you how to do what we'll be covering in PowerShell.

Installing a role or feature

If you've got this far, you have a working Windows Server 2019 operating system. Great! Now what? Without adding roles and features to your server, it just makes for a great paperweight. We're going to take the next steps here together. Let's install a role and a feature into Windows so that we can start making this server work for us.

Getting ready

As long as you have Windows Server 2019 installed and running, you are ready to install roles and features onto that machine.

How to do it...

To install a role and a feature into Windows, perform the following steps:

1. Open **Server Manager**. In the middle of the screen, you'll see a link that says **Add roles and features**. Click on that link:

Figure 1.17 – Server Manager showing the Add roles and features link

2. Click **Next** on the first summary screen. You will come to a choice on the second page. For most roles and features, we want to leave it set at the top bullet, which is **Role-based or feature-based installation**. If we were configuring Remote Desktop Services, which we will discuss in *Chapter 7*, *Remote Desktop Services* then we would choose the second option:

Figure 1.18 – Selecting the installation type

3. Now, we choose where we want to install a new role or feature. This is a neat page as we can choose from any server that we have added to our Server Manager, or we can even choose to install a role or feature into a virtual hard disk. I am running the **Add Roles Wizard** from DC01, but I want to install the IIS role onto WEB01. Rather than having to log into WEB01 to accomplish this task, I will do it right from here. In the following screenshot, you can see WEB01 listed as a server that I can install a role onto, even though I am opening this console on the DC01 server:

Select a server or a virtual hard disk on which to install roles and features.

- ◉ Select a server from the server pool
- ○ Select a virtual hard disk

Server Pool

Filter:		

Name	IP Address	Operating System
DC01.ad.cookbook.packt.com	172.16.97.2	Microsoft Windows Server 2019 Standard
DC02.ad.cookbook.packt.com	172.16.97.3	Microsoft Windows Server 2019 Standard
web01.ad.cookbook.packt.com	172.16.97.5	Microsoft Windows Server 2019 Standard

3 Computer(s) found

Figure 1.19 – Selecting a server

4. Scroll down and choose the role that you want to install. For WEB01, I am choosing the **Web Server (IIS)** role. Then, click **Next**.

> **Tip**
> You can install more than one role or feature at a time. Some roles require additional components to be installed for them to work properly. For example, when I chose to install the IIS role and clicked **Next**, I was prompted to install some management tools. Simply click on the **Add Features** button to automatically add the items that it needs to operate correctly.

5. Now, choose any features that you would like to install. For example, in order to do some network connectivity testing later, go ahead and select **Telnet Client** from the list.

6. Read and click **Next** through the informational messages that are displayed. These messages will vary, depending on which roles and features you have installed.

7. The final screen is your installation summary. If everything looks correct, go ahead and click on **Install**.

After your roles and features have finished installing, the server may or may not have to reboot. This depends on whether or not the role installation requires it. Following installation, or following the reboot, if your new role needs any additional configuration or setting up to be completed, you will be notified at the top of the Server Manager screen:

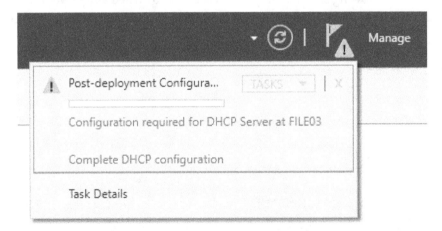

Figure 1.20 – The post-deployment configuration alert

As mentioned in the previous recipes, I'm going to show you how to do the exact same task via PowerShell. In this case, we're going to install IIS and the Telnet Client on the same web01 server, even though I am running this PowerShell from the DC01 server:

```
Install-WindowsFeature -Name Web-Server, Telnet-Client
-ComputerName web01 -IncludeManagementTools
```

This command installs the IIS role and the Telnet Client onto the web01 server. If you wish to check if these roles are installed on a server, you could also run the following command:

```
Get-WindowsFeature -Name Web-*, Telnet-Client -ComputerName
web01 | Where-Object Installed
```

As you can see, it's a lot less clicking, and you only need to memorize two very small, simple commands (Get-WindowsFeature and Install-WindowsFeature):

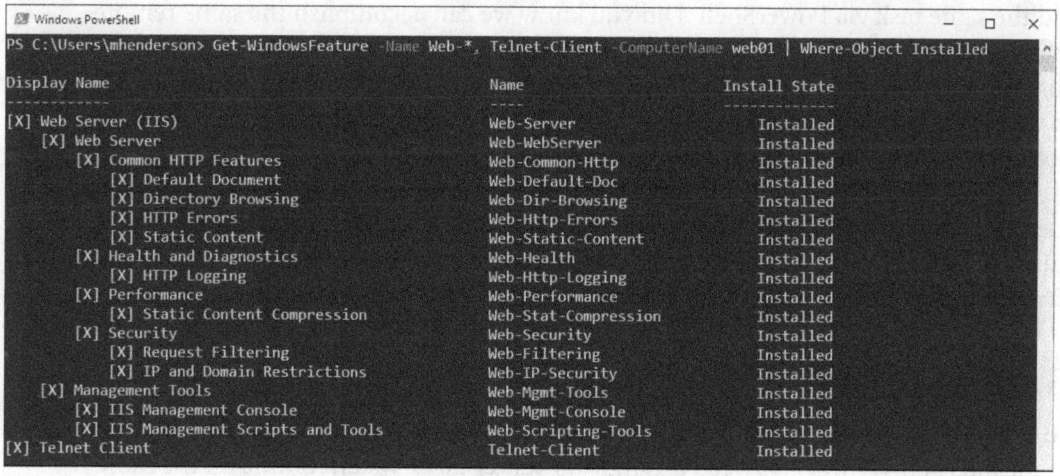

Figure 1.21 – Using Get-WindowsFeature in PowerShell

How it works...

Adding roles and features to a Windows Server is something that every administrator will have to do sooner or later. These items are necessary to turn on the functions in the server that will perform tasks that need to be performed in your environment. Adding roles is quite straightforward, whether you do it via the Server Manager or via PowerShell. However, it is interesting to see the options that are available to add more than one role or feature at a time. Moreover, the ability to remotely install these items for servers in your network that you are not logged into is incredibly useful.

Administering Server 2019 from a Windows 10 machine

In the *Managing remote servers from a single pane with Server Manager* recipe, we discussed remotely administering another server by using Server Manager. We also did the same task via PowerShell. Did you know we can accomplish the same remote management (including using PowerShell) by using our day-to-day Windows 10 computer? We will install and use the **Remote Server Administration Tools** (**RSAT**) to take even more advantage of Server 2019's remote management ideology. It's worth noting, however, that although having the RSAT tools installed locally is very useful and highly recommended, Microsoft is in the process of retiring Server Manager and some of the RSAT tools – many of them have been around since Windows 2000! We will look at this new tooling more in the following *Managing your servers through the Windows Admin Center recipe.*

Getting ready

To test out these RSAT tools, we will need a Windows 10 client machine that is connected to the internet. We will also need a Windows Server 2019 system online on the same network that we can remotely control and manage.

How to do it...

To remotely manage a server using RSAT, follow these instructions:

1. First, we need to download and install the RSAT tools. Prior to October 2018, the RSAT tools had to be downloaded from the Microsoft website. Thankfully, now, there's a simpler way: Click **Start** and type **Manage Optional Settings**. Once you are on the **Manage Optional Settings** screen, click **Add A Feature**. In the feature list, you will see a list of tools beginning with **RSAT**. Which precise set of tools you require will depend on what roles you need to manage. For now, we'll install Server Manager. You will want to install the RSAT tools for any relevant Windows features you intend on using:

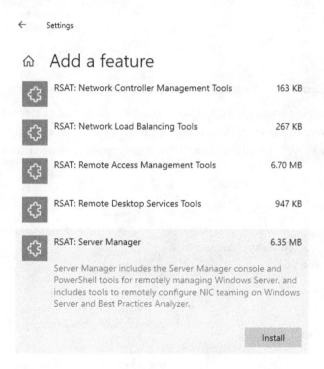

Figure 1.22 – Installing RSAT – Server Manager

2. Once the server manager has been installed, launch it from the **Start** menu. For this recipe, I have the machines we are working with joined to a domain, so we will take a look at adding servers that are part of the domain. Click the **Manage** menu, then **Add Servers**. This is the same step we undertook in the *Managing remote servers from a single pane with Server Manager recipe*.

3. Click on the **Find Now** button. You will see a list of server names that are remotely manageable:

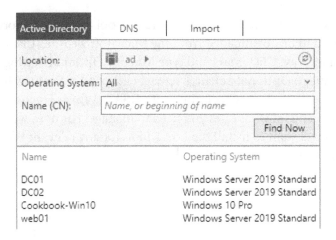

Figure 1.23 – Searching for a server through Active Directory

4. Click on the server names that you want to administer and click on the arrow to move them over to the right-hand side of the screen. Upon clicking on **OK**, you will see these new servers listed and ready for management inside your **Server Manager** console:

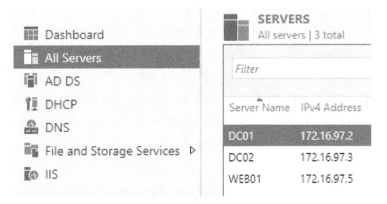

Figure 1.24 – Server DC01 highlighted in the All Servers tab

How it works...

Server Manager in Windows Server 2019 is a powerful tool that can be used for the management of not only the local server but also remote servers that you want to manage. If we take this even a step further and install the RSAT tools on a Windows 10 computer, this gives us the ability to launch and use Server Manager from our everyday Windows 10 computer. In doing so, we enable ourselves to add roles, view events, and restart servers, all from our own desk. Managing servers using these tools will increase productivity and decrease errors because your entire infrastructure of servers can be available within a single window. This is much more efficient than using the RDP client to connect to many different servers, all in different windows. If you've never tried using RSAT to manage servers, give it a try!

See also

- *Managing remote servers from a single pane with Server Manager*
- *Managing your servers through the Windows Admin Center*

Managing your servers through the Windows Admin Center

You may have noticed that every time you open Server Manager, you see a little prompt telling you about the new Windows Admin Center. Microsoft are pushing this new Admin Center as their replacement for Server Manager and their traditional RSAT tools that we just installed. The Windows Admin Center does not cover all aspects of Windows Server management, which is why we still need the old tools; however, some new Windows Server features are only accessible via the Windows Admin Center. As a bonus, if you deploy the Windows Admin Center on its own server, you may be able to make it available to everyone and not just yourself. The Windows Admin Center is a web-based replacement for the Server Administrator and a complimentary tool to many of the RSAT components.

Getting ready

To test out the Windows Admin Center, we will need a Windows 10 client machine. We will also need a Windows Server 2019 system online on the same network that we can remotely control and manage.

How to do it...

1. The Windows Admin Center does not ship with Windows by default, so we need to download and install it. On your Windows 10 machine, visit `https://aka.ms/WACDownload` – your download should start automatically. Once the download completes, install it like you would any other software. Pay close attention to the screen asking you to select a port – if you change that port, you will need to remember it. By default, it is set to `6516`. Also, pay close attention to the message you receive after the install is finished!

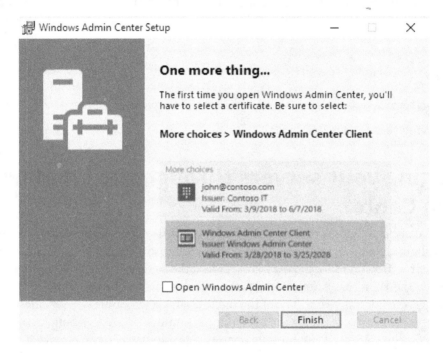

Figure 1.25 – Selecting Windows Admin Center Client in the Windows Admin Center Setup window

2. Once the Windows Admin Center has installed, click on the **Start** menu and find Windows Admin Center. It should launch `https://localhost:6516/` in your web browser. Feel free to browse the tour.

3. Once the Windows Admin Center has loaded, under **All connections**, click **Add** and choose **Servers**:

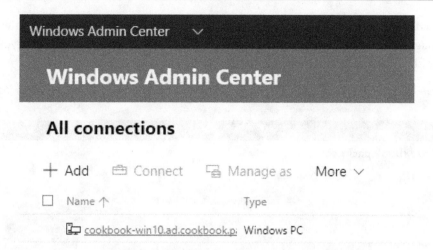

Figure 1.26 – Windows Admin Center

4. Click the menu for **Search Active Directory** and search for *. This will show you
    every server in your domain. Put a checkmark next to the servers you wish to
    manage and click **Add**:

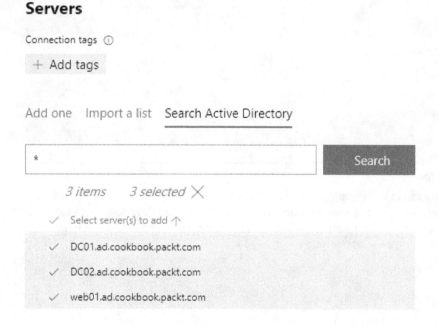

Figure 1.27 – Searching Active Directory

5. Once the servers have been added, click on the hyperlink for the server you want to manage. Windows Admin Center will then connect to that server and give you a full list of things you can manage on that server:

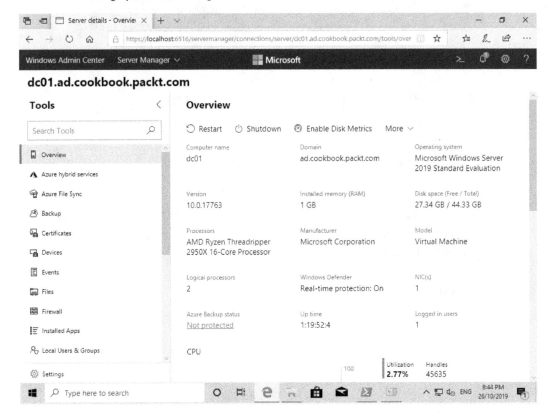

Figure 1.28 – Overview of the selected server

> **Tip**
> Instead of installing the Windows Admin Center on your own Windows 10 computer, you can install it on any server on your network, such as an existing web server. Then, you can access it over the network without having to install anything on your computer!

How it works...

The Windows Admin Center is designed to be a replacement for Server Manager and allows you to control many more aspects of the server in a single place. Take a look – you can probably manage the remote servers firewall, view its event log, manage its certificates, and connect it to hybrid Microsoft Azure cloud solutions. You can even get a remote PowerShell console if you are on a computer that doesn't have PowerShell. The Windows Admin Center is the most powerful GUI administration tool Microsoft has ever produced and does away with the need for many of the old RSAT tools. Note that Windows Admin Center is not a complete replacement for RSAT, though – in Microsoft's own words, this tool is complimentary to the existing RSAT.

The Windows Admin Center can be used to manage Windows Server 2016, 2012 R2, 2012, and 2008 R2 hosts as well (although with limited functionality in some cases).

Identifying useful keyboard shortcuts in Server 2019

I prefer using a keyboard over a mouse any day, for almost any task. There are numerous keyboard shortcuts and tips and tricks that I employ on a daily basis and I want to test them out with you in this recipe. Some of these shortcuts have been around for over 30 years and will work with multiple versions of Windows Server; some are much more recent. They will all be useful to you as you start working with servers in your network.

Getting ready

We are going to run these commands and keyboard shortcuts while logged into a Windows Server 2019 machine.

How to do it...

- *Windows key*: Opens the **Start** menu, where you can immediately start typing to search for programs.

- *Windows key + X*: Opens the **Quick Links** menu.

- *Windows key + I*: Opens the **Windows Settings** options.

- *Windows key + D*: Minimizes all open windows and brings you back to the desktop.

- *Windows key + R*: Opens the **Run** box. Launching applications this way is often faster than using the **Start** menu, if you know the executable name of the application you are trying to launch.

- *Windows key + M*: Minimizes all windows.

- *Windows key + E*: Opens **File Explorer**.

- *Windows key + L*: Locks the computer.

- *Windows key + Tab*: Takes you into the new **Task View** options.

- *Window key + Ctrl + D*: Creates a new virtual desktop from Task View.

- *Windows key + Ctrl + F4*: Closes the current virtual desktop.

- *Windows key + Ctrl + Left or Right Arrow*: Moves you between different virtual desktops.

- *Windows key + 1* or 2 or 3 or…: Launches applications that are pinned to your taskbar, in order. So, the first application pinned to the taskbar would open with *WinKey + 1*, for example.

- *Alt + F4*: Exits the program you are currently working in. This is especially helpful in full-screen app such as those from the Windows Store where it is not always obvious how to exit the program with your mouse.

- *Alt + Tab*: Displays a list of open programs so you can hop between them.

- *Shift + Delete*: Holding down *Shift* while pressing *Delete* deletes files without placing them in the Recycle Bin.

- Using *Tab* inside Command Prompt or PowerShell: When you are working inside PowerShell, if you type the first letter of a command or a file or folder that exists in the directory where you are working in and then press the *Tab* key, it will auto-populate the rest of the command or filename. For example, you may be trying to launch a Microsoft update file with a filename that is 15 characters long and comprises a mix of numbers and letters. There's no need to type out that filename! Let's say the file starts with KB. Simply navigate to the folder where your installer exists, type in KB, and press *Tab*. The full filename is populated inside the prompt and you can press the *Enter* key to launch it. If more than one file is matched and you get the wrong one, keep pressing *Tab* until you get the right one.

How it works...

Keyboard shortcuts can greatly increase productivity once you are fluent with them. This is not an extensive list by any means – there are many more key combinations that you can use to launch apps, minimize and maximize windows, and do all sorts of other functions. This is a list to get you started with the most common ones that I employ often. Start using these with your daily tasks and I bet your mouse will start to feel lonely.

If you are interested in exploring more of the Windows Server 2019 key combinations available, this website is a great place to start, at `http://technet.microsoft.com/en-us/lib rary/hh831491.aspx`.

Setting your PowerShell Execution Policy

As you've hopefully already seen, Windows PowerShell can be an extremely powerful tool for server management. Windows and PowerShell are fully intertwined, and PowerShell can be useful for so many tasks on your servers. However, the ability to run PowerShell scripts is disabled by default on many machines. The first stumbling block that many new PowerShell administrators bump into is the execution policy. It's quite simple: in order to allow PowerShell scripts to run on your server, the execution policy must be adjusted to allow that to happen. Let's introduce our first task in PowerShell by using some commands in this recipe that will set this policy for us.

This is also a good introduction to the idea of the verb-noun syntax that PowerShell utilizes. For example, we are going to make use of cmdlets called `Get-ExecutionPolicy` and `Set-ExecutionPolicy`. The `Get` and `Set` verbs are very common across all facets of cmdlets available in PowerShell. Wrap your mind around this verb-noun syntax and you will be well on your way to figuring out PowerShell on your machines.

Getting ready

We will be working within a PowerShell prompt on our Windows Server 2019 server.

How to do it...

Follow these steps to set the PowerShell execution policy:

1. Right-click on the PowerShell icon and choose **Run as administrator**:

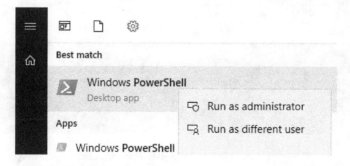

Figure 1.29 – Running PowerShell as administrator

2. Type `Get-ExecutionPolicy` and press *Enter* in order to see the current settings for the PowerShell execution policy:

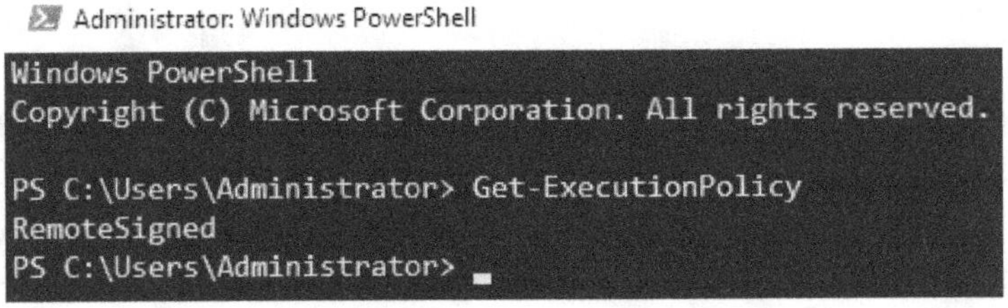

Figure 1.30 – Running Get-ExecutionPolicy

3. You can see that the current execution policy is set to **RemoteSigned**. Here is a short description of the different options for the policy:

    Remote Signed: This is the default setting in Server 2019 and allows PowerShell scripts that are locally created to run. If you try running remote scripts (for example, downloaded from the internet), they must be signed by a trusted publisher in order to execute successfully.

    All Signed: With this setting, all scripts will only be allowed to run if they are signed by a trusted publisher.

    Restricted: With this setting, PowerShell is locked down so that scripts will not run.

    Unrestricted: This setting will allow PowerShell to run scripts with or without signing.

4. For the purposes of our recipe and to make sure the scripts will run for us as we progress through these recipes, let's set our execution policy to unrestricted. Go ahead and use this command:

```
Set-ExecutionPolicy Unrestricted
```

The following is the output:

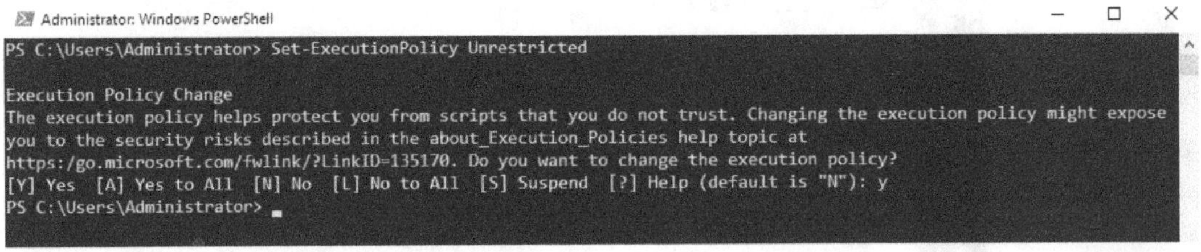

Figure 1.31 – Output of Set-ExecutionPolicy

How it works...

The PowerShell execution policy is a simple setting and easy to change, but can make a world of difference when it comes to running your first scripts. If configured to be more restrictive than you intend, you will have trouble getting your scripts to run and you may think that you have mistyped something, when in fact the issue is only the policy. On the other hand, in an effort to make your servers as secure as possible, on machines where you don't need to execute PowerShell scripts, it makes sense to restrict this access. You may also want to read some additional information on the signing of scripts to see whether creating and executing signed scripts would make more sense in your own environment. There are some in-built server functions that rely on a certain level of security with your execution policy. Setting your policy to **unrestricted** on all your servers could result in some functions not working properly, and you may have to increase that level of security back to **remote signed**.

Building and executing your first PowerShell script

PowerShell is a great interface for acquiring and configure information about our servers. Most of us are familiar with creating some simple old-fashioned batch files that are driven by the Command Prompt, essentially programming out small tasks within these batch files to automate a series of commands. This saves time later as we do not have to type out the commands line by line, especially for common tasks or for items that we need to run during login.

PowerShell has a hugely increased level of functionality in this regard, but the ability to write out multiple lines of PowerShell into a script file is the most basic of them. We can then launch this script file as we would a batch file, automating tasks while taking advantage of the additional features that PowerShell brings to the table over the Command Prompt. These PowerShell scripts are put together inside `.ps1` files; let's build a simple one together to get a feel for running these scripts.

Getting ready

Our work with PowerShell today will be accomplished from a Windows Server 2019 machine. PowerShell is installed by default with Windows, and there is nothing further that we need to install.

How to do it...

Follow these steps to build and execute your first PowerShell script:

1. Open the **Start** menu, type `Windows PowerShell ISE`, and click the desktop app to open it. Do not choose the one ending in (x86) – for some reason, Windows thinks this is a good choice. It isn't. You may need to look further down your Start menu to find the correct one. **Windows PowerShell ISE** is an editor for PowerShell scripts that is much more useful than opening a simple text editor such as Notepad in order to build our script:

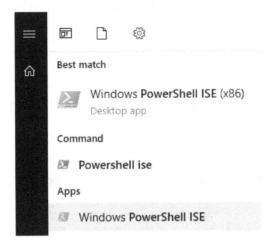

Figure 1.32 – Locating Powershell ISE in the Start menu

2. Navigate to **File | New** from the menus in order to open a blank `.ps1` script file.

3. In your first line, type the following:

```
Write-Host "Hello! Here is the current date and time:"
```

4. From the toolbar menu, click the green arrow that says **Run Script**. Alternatively, you can simply press the *F5* button. When you run the script, the command and output are displayed in the lower portion of the ISE window:

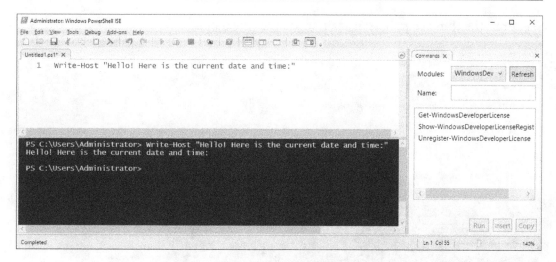

Figure 1.33 – Using Windows PowerShell ISE

Cool? Not really. So far, it's pretty lame – it's just reflecting the text that we told it to echo, but it worked. It didn't even actually tell us what the time is. But that is the nice thing about using the ISE editing tool rather than a generic text editor – you have the ability to quickly test run scripts as you make modifications.

5. Now, let's add some additional lines to our script so that we get the information we are looking for. You can see a list of available commands on the right-hand side of the screen (you may have to switch your **Modules** to **All**) if you would like to browse through what is available, but for our example, simply change your script so that it includes the following:

```
Write-Host "Hello! Here is the current date and time:
$(Get-Date)"
```

```
Write-Host "The name of your computer is: $(hostname)"
```

6. Press the **Run Script** button again to see the new output:

Figure 1.34 – Using Windows PowerShell ISE

7. Now, navigate to **File | Save** and save your new .ps1 PowerShell script.

8. Let's test this script by launching it from within a real PowerShell command window. Go to your Start menu and run PowerShell.

9. Browse to the location where you just saved your script file – you can use the old DOS cd commands for this. Then, launch the script by inputting .\filename. In my case, I used .\GetTime.ps1. Don't forget that you don't need to type the entire filename – in my case, I could just type *G* and press *Tab* and have PowerShell auto-complete:

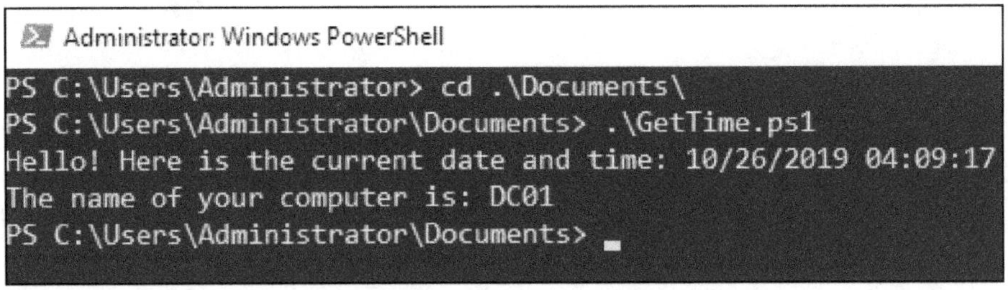

Figure 1.35 – Running the script file

> **Tip**
>
> The PowerShell ISE comes with Windows by default, but you can write PowerShell scripts in any code editor. Visual Studio Code is a free editor provided by Microsoft that is cross-platform and has excellent support for PowerShell scripting. I have written tens of thousands of lines of PowerShell in Visual Studio Code. Check it out on your Windows 10 machine at `https://aka.ms/vscode`.

How it works...

In this recipe, we created a very simple PowerShell script and saved it on our server for execution. While, in practice, getting time and date information from your server may come faster by using the standalone `Get-Date` cmdlet, we provided this recipe to give you a small taste of the ISE and to get your scripting juices flowing. Expanding upon the ideas presented here will start to save you valuable time and keystrokes as you identify more and more ways to automate the tasks and information gathering processes that are part of your daily routines. The possibilities of PowerShell are practically limitless, so make sure that you open it up and start becoming familiar with the interfaces and tools associated with it right away!

> **Tip**
>
> Windows Server 2019 comes with PowerShell 5, which only works on Windows. However, if you upgrade to PowerShell 6 or 7, these run on Linux and OSX as well – so if you wanted to, you can have PowerShell on all your servers, not just your Windows ones! Be careful, though: if you have existing scripts, some things have changed in PowerShell 6 and above, so you will want to check that they still work. With Visual Studio Code and PowerShell 6 or above, you can write *and* run PowerShell from Windows, Mac, or Linux.

Searching for PowerShell cmdlets with Get-Help

With this recipe, we'll spend a minute using **Get-Help** inside PowerShell in order to, well, get some help! I see both new and experienced PowerShell administrators going to the web a lot in order to find commands and the parameters of those commands. The internet is great, and there is a ton of data out there about how to use PowerShell, but in many cases, the information that you are looking for resides right inside PowerShell itself. By using the `Get-Help` cmdlet combined with the functions you are running or searching for, you might not have to open that web browser after all.

Getting ready

We will be running some commands from inside PowerShell on a Windows Server 2019 machine.

How to do it...

To use the Get-Help function inside PowerShell, run the following steps:

1. Launch a PowerShell prompt.

2. Type Get-Help.

3. You may be asked to run Update-Help to download the latest help from the internet – you can do this if you wish (although it can sometimes take a while).

4. You're finished! No, I'm just kidding. Using Get-Help by itself will present you with some helpful data about the Get-Help command, but that's not really what we are looking for, is it? How about using Get-Help with a search parameter, like this:

```
Get-Help Computer
```

The following is the output:

Figure 1.36 – Running Get-Help Computer

Cool! That searched the available cmdlets and presented us with a list of the ones that contain the word `Computer`.

5. Now, what if we wanted to find out some more particular information about one of these cmdlets – maybe about `Restart-Computer`, which we used earlier? Use the following command:

```
Get-Help Restart-Computer
```

The following is the output:

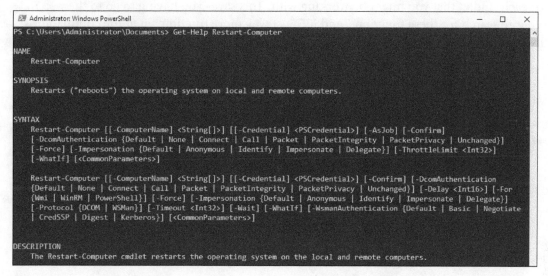

Figure 1.37 – Running Get-Help Restart-Computer

Now we're really cooking! This is wonderful information.

There are many sections of help in the `Get-Help` output, and you may not see them all by default. Try running `Get-Help Restart-Computer -Full` to see all of them! This is basically what you would find if you were looking for information about the `Restart-Computer` cmdlet and went searching on TechNet for it.

How it works...

The Get-Help cmdlet in PowerShell can be used with virtually any command in order to find out more information about that particular function. I often use it when the specific name of a cmdlet that I want to use escapes my memory. By using Get-Help as a search function, it will present a list of available cmdlets that include the keyword you specified. This is a brilliant function in PowerShell and is just another example of why PowerShell should replace your usage of the Command Prompt.

Also included with the Get-Help files are all the special syntax and parameter options for each cmdlet that you might be working with. This saves you having to go to the web in order to search for these functions, and it is just way more fun doing it at the command line than in a web browser.

2

Core Infrastructure Tasks

There are a number of technologies in Windows Server 2019 that you *need to know* about if you plan to ever work in a Windows environment. These are technologies such as **Active Directory Domain Services (AD DS)**, **Domain Name System (DNS)**, and **Dynamic Host Configuration Protocol (DHCP)**. If you haven't noticed already, everything in the Windows world has an acronym. In fact, you may only recognize these items by their acronyms, and that's okay. Nobody calls DHCP by its full form anyway.

But do you know how to build these services and bring a Windows Server infrastructure online from scratch, with only a piece of hardware and a Windows Server 2019 installation disk to guide your way? This is why we are here today. I would like to instruct you on taking your first server and turning it into everything that you need to run a Microsoft network.

Every company and network is different and has different requirements. Some will get by with a single server to host a myriad of roles, while others have thousands of servers at their disposal and will have every role split up into clusters of servers, each of which has a single purpose in life. The Windows Hyper-V role makes this very simple (you can read more about this in *Chapter 13, Working with Hyper-V*). Whatever your situation, this will take us back to the basics of setting up the core infrastructure technologies that are needed in any Microsoft-centric network.

In this chapter, we will cover the following recipes:

- Configuring a combination domain controller, DNS server, and DHCP server
- Adding a second DC
- Organizing your computers with OU
- Creating an A or AAAA record in DNS
- Creating and using a CNAME record in DNS
- Creating a DHCP scope to assign addresses to computers
- Creating a DHCP reservation for a specific server or resource
- Pre-staging a computer account in Active Directory
- Using PowerShell to create a new Active Directory user
- Using PowerShell to run commands on another server

Configuring a combination Domain Controller, DNS server, and DHCP server

The directory structure that Microsoft networks use to house their users and computer accounts is called **Active Directory (AD)**, and the directory information is controlled and managed by **Domain Controller (DC)** servers. Two other server roles that almost always go hand-in-hand with Active Directory are DNS and DHCP, and in many networks, these three roles are combined on each server where they reside. A lot of small businesses have always made do with a single server containing all three of these roles, but in recent years, virtualization has become so easy that almost everyone runs at least two DCs for redundancy purposes. And if you are going to have two DCs, you may as well put the DNS and DHCP roles on them both to make those services redundant as well. But I'm getting ahead of myself. For this recipe, let's get started building these services by installing the roles and configuring them for the first time: the first DC/DNS/ DHCP server in our network.

Getting ready

The only prerequisite here is an online Windows Server 2019 that we can use. We want it to be plugged into a network and have a static IP address assigned so that as you add new computers to this network, they have a way of communicating with the domain we are about to create. Also, make sure to set the hostname of the server now. Although domain controllers in Windows Server 2019 can be renamed, it's best to get them right from the start.

How to do it...

Let's configure our first DC/DNS/DHCP server by performing the following set of instructions:

1. Add the roles all at once. To do this, open up **Server Manager** and click on the link to add some new roles to this server. Now, check all three, that is, **Active Directory Domain Services**, **DHCP Server**, and **DNS Server**:

Figure 2.1 – Service listings in the Add a Role wizard

2. When you click on some of these items, you will be prompted regarding whether you want to install some supporting items. Go ahead and click on the **Add Features** button to allow this:

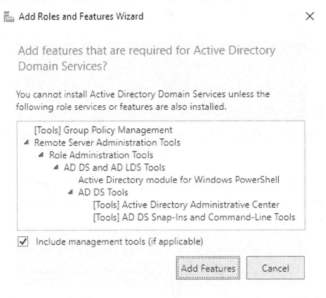

Figure 2.2 – Confirmation screen for new services being added

3. Click **Next** through the following few screens. We don't have to add any additional features, so you can read and click through the informational screens that tell you about these new roles.

4. Once satisfied with the installation summary, press the **Install** button on the last page of the wizard.

5. Following installation, your progress summary screen will provide a window with a couple of links on it. These are **Promote this server to a domain controller** and **Complete DHCP configuration**. We are going to click on the first link to promote this machine so that it's a DC:

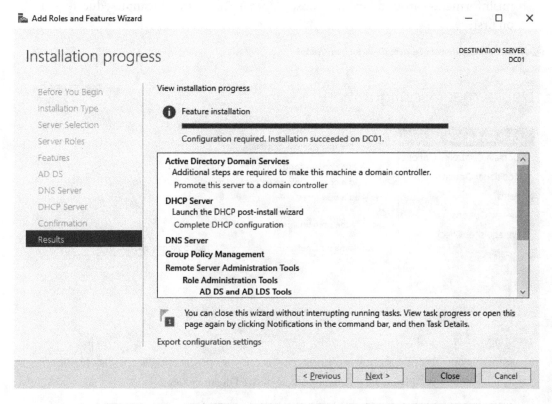

Figure 2.3 – An in-progress installation of selected Windows features

After this, we are taken into the configuration of our DC. Since this is the very first DC in our entire network, we will choose the **Add a new forest** option. At this point, we must also specify a name of our root domain. Please read the *There's more…* section of this recipe before choosing your domain name. There is a lot of misinformation around how to choose a domain name that I want to educate you on first!

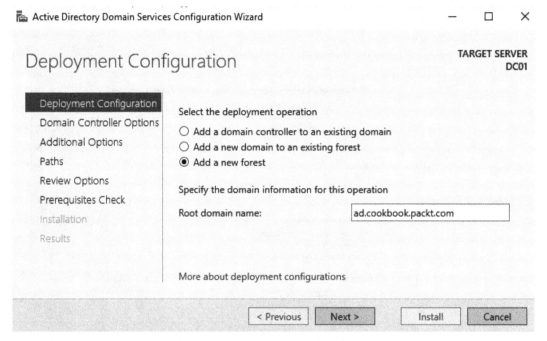

Figure 2.4 – Creating a new Active Directory forest

> **Tip**
> It is very important that you choose a root domain name that you like and that makes sense for your installation. Whatever you enter here will more than likely be your domain name forever and always.

6. On the **Domain Controller Options** screen, you can choose to lower the functional level of your forest or domain, but this is not recommended unless you have a specific reason to do so. One thing to note is that Windows Server 2019 does not introduce any new functional levels, so you will still have this set to 2016. You must also specify a DSRM password on this screen in case it is ever needed for recovery. You will receive a **DNS Options** warning message on the next page. This is normal, because we are turning on the first DC and DNS servers in our environment.

7. The following two screens are for **NetBIOS** and **Paths**. You can leave **Paths** alone, but pay close attention to the NetBIOS name. This is very difficult to change later, so make sure it's something sensible. If you are using a subdomain of a real domain, it might default to something like CORP or AD. In this book, I have renamed this to COOKBOOK as it's more meaningful than the default AD.

8. Once you have reviewed the installation plan, go for it! You should see a green check mark telling you **All prerequisite checks passed successfully**, which means you are ready to proceed. There might be some scary-looking warnings, but for a fresh new domain that you do not intend to connect old NT4 or Windows 2000 servers to, you can ignore them. When the server has finished being promoted to a DC, it will have to be restarted:

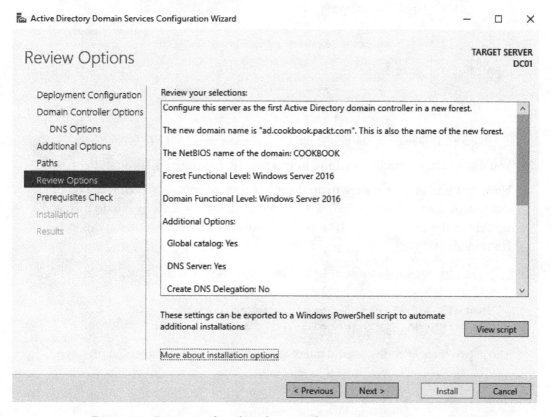

Figure 2.5 – Reviewing the selected options for your new Windows forest

9. Following the restart, you will have noticed that you are now forced to log into the server as a domain account. Once a server has been promoted to a DC, it no longer contains local user accounts on the system. All logins to the server from this point forward will have to be user accounts within the domain. Your old Administrator password is now the Domain Administrator password, and you will need to use this to log in.

10. Inside Server Manager, you will have a notification up top to **Complete DHCP configuration**. Go ahead and click on that:

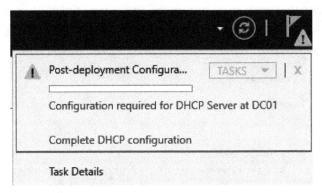

Figure 2.6 – Reviewing the post-deployment requirements for the DHCP feature

11. You don't have to specify anything in this wizard. Simply click through the steps.

12. Now, that was a fair few steps to go through – but, of course, you can also do the exact same steps via PowerShell, and it's an awful lot less clicking. To do this, you would use the `Install-ADDSForest` cmdlet. For this book, I used this exact command:

```
Install-WindowsFeature AD-Domain-Services, DNS, DHCP
-IncludeManagementTools
Install-ADDSForest -DomainName ad.cookbook.packt.com
-DomainMode WinThreshold -DomainNetbiosName COOKBOOK
```

Those two lines of code are equivalent to the previous 12 steps of clicking:

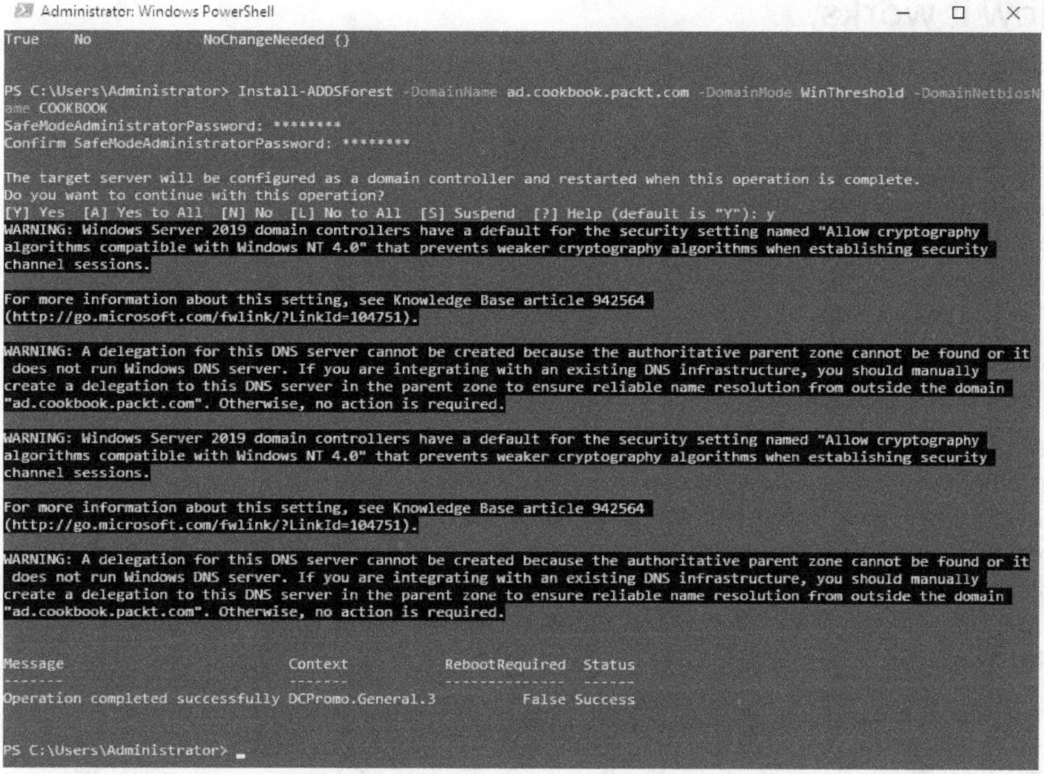

Figure 2.7 – The output of the Install-ADDSForest command

> **Tip**
>
> Because your domain controller is not a server you typically log onto, it has excellent remote management tools for all its features. You might want to try using Windows Server Core. You can read more about this GUI-less version of Windows Server in *Chapter 12*, *Server Core*.

How it works...

Configuring your first DC is essential to having a successful Microsoft Windows network. We now have roles installed for AD, DNS, and DHCP. This means we have the core infrastructure in place to start joining computers to the domain, adding users to the network, and shuttling around some network traffic. Each of these technologies has enough depth to warrant their own book, so there is no way that we can cover everything here. I hope that this tutorial has got you comfortable with enabling these system-critical functions in your own network. Having the ability to create a network properly from scratch is priceless ammunition to a server administrator.

There's more

Before we conclude this recipe, this might be a good opportunity to explore some definitions and explanations. You can think of a **forest** as the top level of your Active Directory structure. Within that forest, you are setting up a **domain**, which is the container within your forest that contains your user, computer, and other accounts that will be joined to the domain. You can contain multiple domains within a forest, and multiple forests can share information and talk to each other by using something called a **trust**.

I'm going take this opportunity to discuss what you should name your root domain. There is more than one school of thought on this, so I'm going to refer to what Microsoft officially recommend. Unfortunately, Microsoft have violated their own recommendations in the past (their Small Business Server unfortunately started many bad practices that continue to this day). I will be summarizing Microsoft's advice from `https://social.technet.microsoft.com/wiki/contents/articles/34981.active-directory-best-practices-for-internal-domain-and-network-names.aspx`.

Firstly, you should name your Active Directory using a real domain name that you or your company own. A lot of people recommended using a fake domain name, such as `mydomain.local`, as your domain name. This turned out to be a mistake because `.local` is now a real internet routable top-level domain and is no longer fake. However, you also shouldn't use the exact domain you run your website on. If your company website is `example.com`, then your domain name could be a subdomain such as `ad.example.com` or `corp.example.com`. This way, you can ensure that you retain ownership over your domain forever. Alternatively, you could register a whole new domain name just for your Active Directory, such as `example.net`. Domain names are cheap – just remember to renew it every year!

Now, I know what you might be thinking – 'I want my users to be able to use their email address as their username. How can I do that if our domain is `corp.example.com`? Won't that make it `username@corp.example.com` or `CORP\username`? I'll never be able to train them to remember that!' Nope. The part of the username that comes after the @ sign is called the **UPN suffix**. You can have more than one to choose from, and it can be *anything you want*. As for the `CORP` name, that's called the **NetBIOS** name for your domain and it does not need to be related to your UPN suffix at all.

In this book, I have chosen `ad.cookbook.packt.com` as the domain name. I chose it pretending that my company site was `cookbook.packt.com`, and `ad.cookbook.packt.com` is a subdomain that this fictional company can control as long as they own `packt.com`.

Adding a second DC

AD is the core of your network. It has ties to everything! As such, it makes sense that you would want this to be as redundant as possible. In Windows Server 2019, creating a secondary DC is so easy that you really have no reason not to do it. Can you imagine rebuilding your directory by following a single server hardware failure where you have 100 user accounts and computers that are all part of the domain that just failed? How about with 1,000 or even 10,000 users? That could take weeks to clean up, and you'll probably never get it back exactly the way it was before. Additionally, while you are stuck in the middle of this downtime, you will have all kinds of trouble inside your network since your user and computer accounts are relying on AD, which would then be offline. In this recipe, we'll go through the steps you need to follow to take a second server into your network and join it to the existing domain that is running on the primary DC to create our redundant, secondary DC. The larger your network gets, the more domain controller servers you are going to have.

Getting ready

Two Server 2019 machines are needed for this. We will assume that the first one is running Active Directory and DNS already, like the one we set up in the previous recipe. The second server is online, on the same network, and has been named `DC02`.

How to do it...

To create a redundant secondary DC, perform the following steps:

1. Open **Server Manager** on DC02 and click **Add roles and features**.

2. Click **Next** a few times until you get to the **Server Roles** screen. Let's choose both **Active Directory Domain Services** and **DNS Server**. It is very common for each DC to also run DNS so that you have redundancy for both services. Both of these roles will prompt for additional features, so make sure you press the **Add Features** button when it prompts you to allow the installation of those extra components:

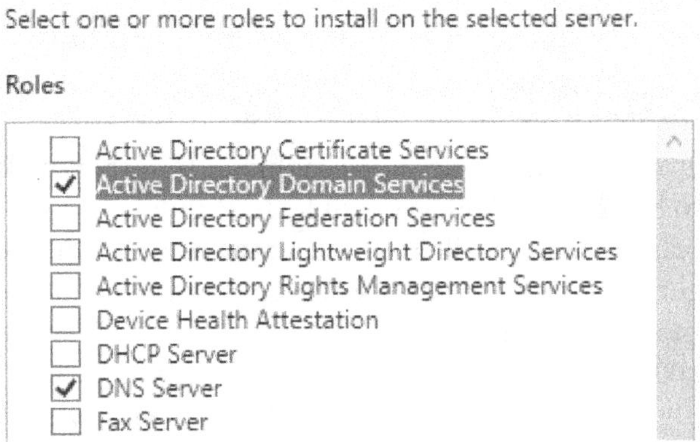

Select one or more roles to install on the selected server.

Roles

- ☐ Active Directory Certificate Services
- ☑ Active Directory Domain Services
- ☐ Active Directory Federation Services
- ☐ Active Directory Lightweight Directory Services
- ☐ Active Directory Rights Management Services
- ☐ Device Health Attestation
- ☐ DHCP Server
- ☑ DNS Server
- ☐ Fax Server

Figure 2.8 – Service listings in the Add a Role wizard

3. We do not require any other features, so click **Next** through the remaining screens and then click on **Install** on the last page.

4. Once the installation is finished, you have a link to click on that says **Promote this server to a domain controller**. Go ahead and click on that link:

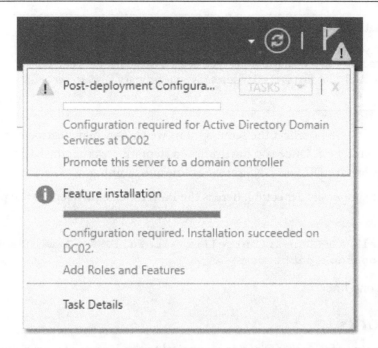

Figure 2.9 – Reviewing the post-deployment requirements for the ADDS feature

5. For this second DC, we are going to choose the **Add a domain controller to an
    existing domain** option. Then, in the **Domain** field, specify the name of the domain
    that is running on your existing DC. You must also specify a domain administrator
    account in the credentials field to validate against the domain:

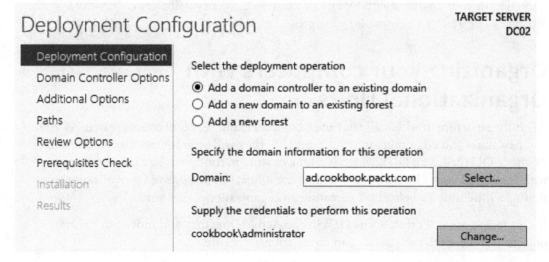

Figure 2.10 – Adding an additional domain controller to an existing forest

> **Information Box**
>
> If you receive an error message saying that a DC for the domain could not
> be contacted, you probably haven't specified a DNS address in your TCP/IP
> settings. Add your first DC's IP address as your primary DNS server and it
> should work.

6. The rest of the steps reflect the same options we chose when creating our first DC in
    the previous recipe. Once you have finished stepping through the wizard, you will
    have a secondary DC and DNS server online and running.

7. As you are hopefully expecting, here is the PowerShell equivalent of the process we
    just did:

```
Install-ADDSDomainController -InstallDNS -DomainName
ad.cookbook.packt.com
```

Another one-liner!

How it works...

Creating redundancy for Active Directory is critical to the success of your network.
Hardware fails, we all know it. A good practice for any company is to run two DCs so
that everyone continues to work in the event of a server failure. An even better practice is
to take this a step further and create more DCs, some of them in different sites perhaps,
and maybe even make use of some **Read-Only Domain Controllers (RODCs)** in your
smaller, less secure sites. See the following link for some additional information on using
an RODC in your environment: `http://technet.microsoft.com/en-us/
library/cc754719(v=ws.10).aspx`.

Organizing your computers with Organizational Units

AD is the structure in which all your user, computer, and server accounts reside. As you
add new users and computers into your domain, they will be automatically placed into
a generic OU (called an OU), which is a type of storage container. You could get away
with leaving all your objects in their default locations, but there are a lot of advantages to
putting a little time and effort into creating an organizational structure.

In this recipe, we will create some **OUs** inside Active Directory and move our existing
objects into these OUs so that we can create some structure.

Getting ready

We will need a DC online for this recipe, which is a Server 2019 machine with the Active Directory Domain Services role installed. Specifically, I will be using the DC01 server that we prepped in the *Configuring a combination Domain Controller, DNS server, and DHCP server* recipe.

How to do it...

Let's get comfortable working with OUs by creating some of our own, as follows:

1. Open **Active Directory Users and Computers**. This can be launched from the **Tools** menu inside Server Manager. As you can see, there are some pre-defined containers and OUs in here:

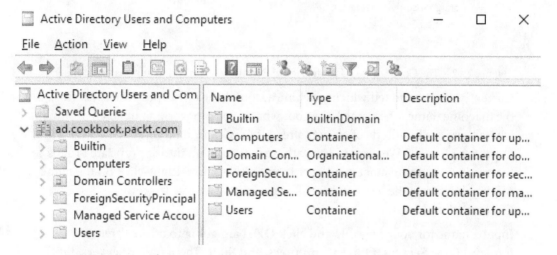

Figure 2.11 – The Active Directory Users and Computers management console

> **Tip**
> Alternatively, you can also open **Active Directory Users and Computers** by running dsa.msc from Command Prompt or the Start screen.

2. We can already see that the DC servers have been segmented off into their own OU. If we look in our **Computers** folder, however, we can see that, currently, all the other systems we have joined to the domain have been lumped together:

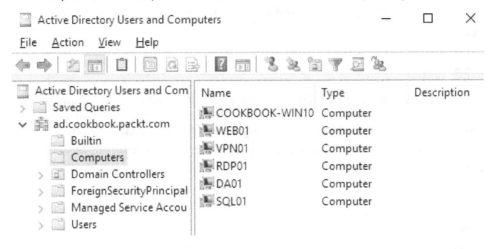

Figure 2.12 – The Computers OU in the Active Directory Users and Computers console

3. Currently, it's hard to tell which machine accomplishes what purpose apart from the machine name. The name helps, but what if you are working in an environment where there are hundreds of objects already? Or if your naming scheme were a lot more complicated? We want to break these machines up into appropriate groups so that we have better management over them in the future. Right-click on the name of your domain in the left-hand window pane and navigate to **New | Organizational Unit**.

4. Input a name for your new OU and click **OK**. I am going to create three new top-level OUs: **Servers**, **Office Computers**, and **Staff**. Then, under **Servers**, I'm going to create **Remote Access**, **Database**, and **Web Server**. Under **Staff**, I'm going to create **Sales**, **Marketing**, **Executives**, and **Sysadmins**. We're not going to use the Staff OU right now, but it will come in handy later:

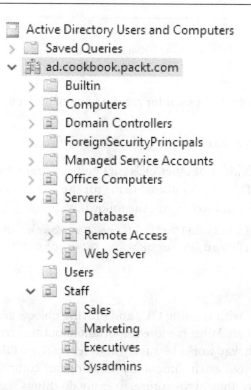

Figure 2.13 – Showing the new OUs that have been created

5. Now, for each object that you want to move, simply find it, right-click on it, and then click on **Move...**:

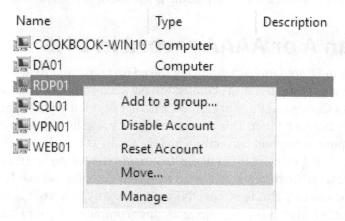

Figure 2.14 – An example of moving a server to a different OU

6. Choose which OU you would like this object to move into and click **OK**.

> **Tip**
> You can also drag and drop objects between OUs instead of right-clicking and choosing **Move....**

The PowerShell command I used for creating one of my new top-level OUs is as follows:

```
New-ADOrganizationalUnit -Name Servers
```

Creating OUs as children of other OUs isn't quite as straightforward as it requires you to know the LDAP distinguished name for the group you want to create it under. In this example, I would run the following:

```
New-ADOrganizationalUnit -Name Database -Path
'OU=Servers,DC=ad,DC=cookbook,DC=packt,DC=com'
```

How it works...

The actual work involved with creating OUs and moving objects around between them isn't complicated at all. What is more important about this recipe is prompting you to think about which way works best for you to set up these OUs to make the best organizational sense for your environment. By breaking our computer accounts out into pinpointed groups, we are able, in the future, to easily do things such as discover how many web servers we have, or do some quick reporting on how many user accounts we have in the sales group. We could even apply different Group Policy settings to different computer sets based on what OU they are contained within. Both reporting and applying settings can be greatly improved upon by making good use of OU inside AD.

Creating an A or AAAA record in DNS

Most folks working in IT are familiar with using the `ping` command to test network connectivity. If you are trying to test the connection between your computer and another, you can ping it from Command Prompt and test whether or not it replies. The PowerShell equivalent is `Test-Connection`. This assumes that the firewalls in your computers and network allow the ping to respond correctly, which generally is true. If you are inside a domain network and ping a device by its name, that name resolves to an IP address, which is the device's address on the network. But what tells your computer which IP address corresponds to which name? This is where DNS comes in. Any time your computer makes a request for a name, whether it is you pinging another computer or your Outlook email client requesting the name of your Exchange Server, your computer always reaches out to your network's DNS servers and asks, 'How do I get to this name?'.

DNS contains a list of records that tell the computers in your network what IP addresses correspond to what names. By far the most common type of DNS record is called a **host record**. When the host record resolves to an IPv4 address, such as 192.168.0.1, it is called an **A record**. When the host record resolves to an IPv6 address, such as 2003:836b:2:8100::2, it is called an **AAAA record**. This is usually pronounced **quad A**.

The DNS system is also where Active Directory stores a lot of information about your network and is used for service discovery, request routing, and many other important Active Directory features.

Understanding how to create and troubleshoot host records in DNS is something that every Windows server administrator needs to know. Let's take a minute to create and test one of these DNS records so that we can experience firsthand how this all works together.

Getting ready

We have a DC online, which also has the DNS role installed. This is all we need to create the DNS record, but we will also make use of a Windows 10 client computer.

How to do it...

To create and test a DNS record, perform these steps:

1. Most networks contain a router, which is a device that is normally not connected to an Active Directory domain at all. This means the only way to get a DNS record for it is to manually create one. We're going to call this device simply router. Open a PowerShell prompt and run Test-Connection router -Count 1. As expected, this command fails as we haven't created a DNS record for this yet. You could also use the ping router command if you are more used to the old tools:

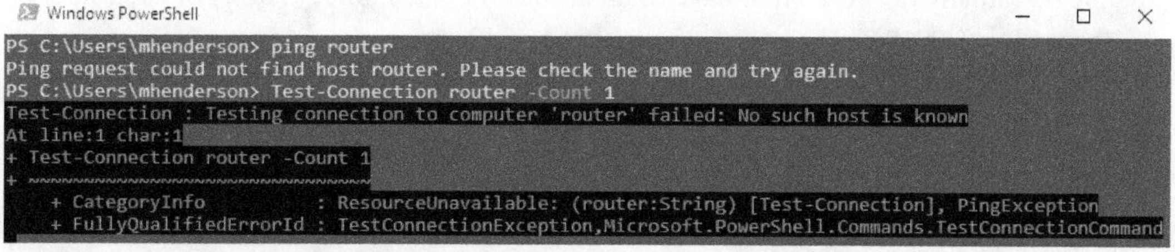

Figure 2.15 – The output of a failed connection to a non-existent DNS name

2. Now, head into the DNS server (if you're following all the recipes in this book, this will be either DC01 or DC02) and open the **DNS** console from the **Tools** menu. The nature of Active Directory and DNS means that it does not matter which DNS server you do this step on – your changes will replicate to all of them.

3. Inside **Forward Lookup Zones**, you should see your domain listed. Click on the name of your domain to see your existing DNS records:

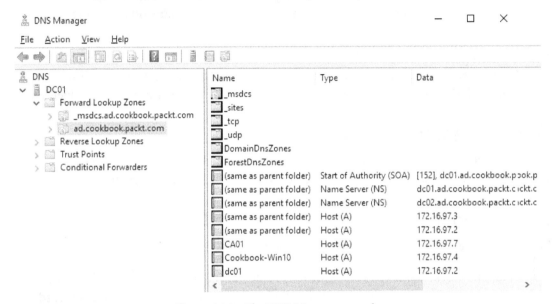

Figure 2.16 – The DNS Manager console

4. Right-click on your domain and click on **New Host (A or AAAA)….**

5. Input the server name into the top field and the IP address of your network router into the bottom field. Then, click **Add Host**. Not all routers are on a .1 address – I've seen many networks that have them at the end of a subnet (.254) or even in the middle (.160):

New Host   ✕

Name (uses parent domain name if blank):

router

Fully qualified domain name (FQDN):

router.ad.cookbook.packt.com.

IP address:

172.16.97.1

☐ Create associated pointer (PTR) record

☐ Allow any authenticated user to update DNS records with the
same owner name

Add Host   Cancel

Figure 2.17 – The New Host screen in the DNS Manager

Tip

If you are running IPv6 on your network and want to create an AAAA record
instead, you use this exact same process. Simply enter the IPv6 address into the
IP address field, instead of the IPv4 address.

6. Now that our new host record has been created, let's test it out! Going back to our
client computer, type Test-Connection router again (or ping router).
You will see your output, as shown in the following screenshot:

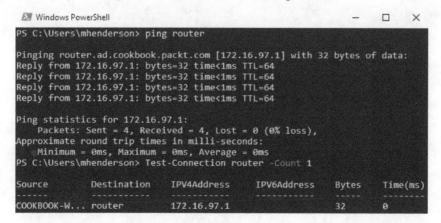

```
PS C:\Users\mhenderson> ping router

Pinging router.ad.cookbook.packt.com [172.16.97.1] with 32 bytes of data:
Reply from 172.16.97.1: bytes=32 time<1ms TTL=64
Reply from 172.16.97.1: bytes=32 time<1ms TTL=64
Reply from 172.16.97.1: bytes=32 time<1ms TTL=64
Reply from 172.16.97.1: bytes=32 time<1ms TTL=64

Ping statistics for 172.16.97.1:
    Packets: Sent = 4, Received = 4, Lost = 0 (0% loss),
Approximate round trip times in milli-seconds:
    Minimum = 0ms, Maximum = 0ms, Average = 0ms
PS C:\Users\mhenderson> Test-Connection router -Count 1

Source          Destination     IPV4Address     IPV6Address     Bytes     Time(ms)
------          -----------     -----------     -----------     -----     --------
COOKBOOK-W...   router          172.16.97.1                     32        0
```

Figure 2.18 – The output of a successful connection after creating a DNS record

This is also an excellent demonstration of the difference between a PowerShell cmdlet and the old tooling. Here, we can see that the result from `Test-Connection` is fully tabulated and contains even more information than the old `ping` command. You can then save or pipeline the output of `Test-Connection` into other cmdlets.

To create these DNS records via PowerShell, you need to import the `DNSServer` module and then use the `Add-DnsServerResourceRecordA` cmdlet:

```
Import-Module DNSServer
Add-DnsServerResourceRecordA -Name router -ZoneName
ad.cookbook.packt.com -IPv4Address 172.16.97.1
```

How it works...

Any time a computer in a domain network requests to communicate with a hostname, DNS is the party responsible for pointing it in the right direction. If you or your applications are having trouble contacting the servers they need, this is one of the first places you will want to look into. Understanding DNS host records is something that will be necessary when working with any networking technology. If you are working within an Active Directory-integrated DNZ, which you probably will be, then any time you add a computer or server to the domain, its name will be automatically added to DNS for you. In these cases, you will not have to manually create them, but it is still important to understand how that works in case you need to troubleshoot them later.

In this recipe, we have only talked about the most common form of DNS record, but there are others you may want to learn about and test as well. In fact, look at our next recipe for information on another useful type of DNS record, known as CNAME.

Note, however, that there are a couple of other name resolution functions in the Windows operating system that may cause resolution to happen before a hostname request gets to the DNS server. For example, if someone has created a static name and IP record inside a client computer's `host` file (which is located in `C:\Windows\System32\drivers\etc\`), it will resolve to the specified IP address, no matter what is in the DNS server. This is more common on Linux machines than Windows machines but is still very possible. This is because the host file has priority over DNS. Also, there is a special table called the **Name Resolution Policy Table (NRPT)** that is used by DirectAccess client computers, and it works in a similar way. Name resolution requests pass through the host file and through the NRPT before making their way to DNS. If one of the former tables has an entry for the name that is being requested, they will resolve it before the computer sends the request to the DNS server for resolution. There is also a mostly outdated but still in use protocol called **NetBIOS**, which the `ping` command is notorious for falling back on and bypasses DNS altogether. So, if you are troubleshooting a name that doesn't resolve properly, keep those additional terms in mind when looking for the answer to your problem.

Creating and using a CNAME record in DNS

Now that we are familiar with moving around a little bit inside the DNS management tool, we are going to create and test another type of record. This one is called a **CNAME** (which is short for canonical name), and it is easiest to think of this one as an alias record. Rather than taking a DNS name and pointing it at an IP address as we do with a host record, with a CNAME, we are going to take a DNS name and point it at another DNS name! Why would this be necessary? If you are hosting multiple services on a single server but want those services to be contacted by using different names, CNAME records can be your best friend. Some corporate naming schemes are also very unfriendly to being used by users (imagine getting your users to remember that `W19UE1WEB7` is the payroll server), and a CNAME allows us to assign a more memorable name for users to use.

Getting ready

We are going to make use of the same environment that we used to create our A records in the *Creating an A or AAAA record in DNS* recipe. There is a DC/DNS server online where we are going to create our records. We will also need WEB01 running, a server where we are hosting a website, as well as some file shares. We will also use a Windows 10 client to test out our CNAME records after they have been created.

How to do it...

To create and test a CNAME record, perform the following steps:

1. WEB01 is hosting a website and a file share. Currently, the only DNS record that exists for WEB01 is the primary A record, so users have to type in the WEB01 name to access both the website and the file shares. Our goal is to create aliases for these services by using CNAME records in DNS. First, we need to log into the DNS server and launch **DNS Manager**.

2. Once inside **DNS Manager**, expand **Forward Lookup Zones** and then your domain name so that we can see the list of DNS records that exist already.

3. Now, right-click on your domain and select **New Alias (CNAME)....**

4. We would like our users to be able to browse the website by typing in `http://intranet`. So, in our CNAME record, we want **Alias name** to be `intranet` and **FQDN for target host** to be `web01.ad.cookbook.com`, which is the server where the website is being hosted:

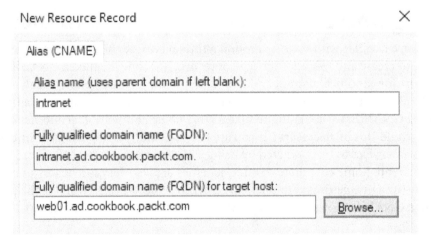

Figure 2.19 – The New Resource Record screen in the DNS Manager for creating a CNAME

5. We also want our file shares to be accessible by using `\\FILESERVER\SHARE` so that the actual name of the server hosting this share is not visible to the users. Create another CNAME record with the **Alias name** field as `FILESERVER` and the **FQDN for target host** field as `web01.ad.cookbook.com`.

6. Log into the test client machine and give it a try. Users are now able to open their web browser and successfully browse to `http://intranet`. They are also able to open File Explorer and access `\\fileserver\share`.

To create these CNAME records via PowerShell, you need to import the `DNSServer` module and then use the `Add-DnsServerResourceRecordCname` cmdlet:

```
Import-Module DNSServer
Add-DnsServerResourceRecordCName -Name intranet -ZoneName
ad.cookbook.packt.com -HostNameAlias web01.ad.cookbook.packt.
com
Add-DnsServerResourceRecordCName -Name fileserver -ZoneName
ad.cookbook.packt.com -HostNameAlias web01.ad.cookbook.packt.
com
```

How it works...

We have a server in our environment called **WEB01**. There is a website running on this server. It is also hosting a file share called SHARE. By creating a couple of quick **CNAME** records inside DNS, we can give users the ability to use some intuitive names to access these resources. By following this recipe, we have masked the actual server name from the users, making knowledge of that name unnecessary.

See also

- The *Creating an A or AAAA record in DNS* recipe

Creating a DHCP scope to assign addresses to computers

In the *Configuring a combination Domain Controller, DNS server, and DHCP server* recipe, we installed the DHCP role onto a server called DC01. Without some configuration, however, that role isn't doing anything. In most companies that I work with, all the servers have statically assigned IP addresses, which are IPs entered by hand into the NIC properties. This way, those servers always retain the same IP address. But what about client machines that might move around or even move in and out of the network? What about phones, tablets, and laptops that join your Wi-Fi networks? DHCP is a mechanism that clients use in order to obtain IP addressing information for the network that they are currently plugged into.

This way, users or admins don't have to worry about configuring IP settings on the client machine as they are configured automatically by the DHCP server. In order for our DHCP server to hand out IP addresses, we need to configure a scope to use.

Getting ready

We have a Server 2019 machine online with the **DHCP** role installed. We will also be testing using a Windows 10 client machine to ensure that it is able to acquire IP address information properly from the server.

It is important that you *do not do this recipe* if you are simply testing this out and are connected to a production network! If you are using a **virtual machine** (**VM**), make sure it is not connected to your work or home network – if you can isolate it to a lab network, that would be ideal. Doing this as a test while on a production network could upset many other services on your network.

How to do it...

Perform the following steps to create and configure a DHCP scope to assign addresses to client computers:

1. Drop down the **Tools** menu inside Server Manager and click on **DHCP**. This opens the DHCP management console.

2. Expand the left-hand pane, where the name of your DHCP server is listed. You will see sections for **IPv4** and **IPv6**. For our network, we are sticking with IPv4, so right-click on that and choose the option for **New Scope…**:

Figure 2.20 – The New Scope option in the DHCP Manager

3. Start the **New Scope Wizard** screen by creating a name for your scope. This can be anything you like.

4. Enter a range of IP addresses that you would like the DHCP server to hand out to computers. Typically, you would choose a range that is big enough to encompass all the client machines you expect, but small enough to allow room for static IP address either side. Often, the first 50 or 100 IP addresses in the network are set aside for static IP addresses and the following 200 or 150 addresses are used for DHCP. The **Subnet mask** field will likely populate automatically, but Windows often doesn't get this correct – just double-check to make sure it is accurate:

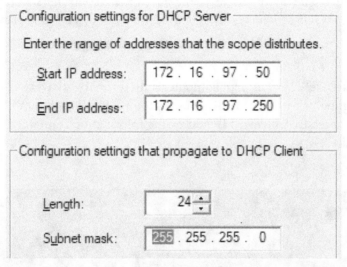

Figure 2.21 – The basic configuration options for a new DHCP range

5. On the **Add Exclusions and Delay** screen, if there are any IP addresses within the scope you just defined that you do not want handed out, specify them here. For example, if you are going to use .50 through .250, as in our example, but you already have a print server running on .75, you could exclude .75 on this screen so that DHCP doesn't try to hand out the .75 address to a client computer.

6. Now, set a time in your **Lease Duration** field. This is the amount of time in-between DHCP *refreshes* for a client computer. If a particular computer leaves the network and comes back within its lease duration, it will be given the same IP address that it had last time. The default is 8 days, which is probably fine for a corporate network of desktops and laptops but is far too large for a guest Wi-Fi network, which could see hundreds of machines coming and going throughout a given week. I generally drop this to 5 days for corporate networks and 2 hours for guest Wi-Fi networks.

7. Next, we will populate the rest of the IP information that the client computers need to receive on our network. Fill out the fields for **Router (Default Gateway)**, **Domain Name and DNS Servers**, and **WINS Servers**, if necessary. Make sure your Default Gateway is configured correctly for your network as DHCP clients will not get internet access correct for this. The DNS portion is equally important as without this, clients will not be able to look up any domain names (thus breaking most of the internet) and will not be able to access any of your company's resources! You should set this to be the IP addresses of your domain controllers. You probably do not have any WINS servers and can, in most likelihood, leave this blank.

8. The last item to choose is **Yes, I want to activate this scope now**. Now, we're in business!

9. As a quick test, let's boot a client computer onto this network whose NIC has not been configured with a static IP. If we take a look at its IP configuration, we can see that it has successfully received IP addressing information from our DHCP server automatically:

▓ Administrator: Windows PowerShell

```
PS C:\Windows\system32> ipconfig

Windows IP Configuration


Ethernet adapter Ethernet:

   Connection-specific DNS Suffix  . : ad.cookbook.packt.com
   Link-local IPv6 Address . . . . . : fe80::b9cf:f266:2032:f560%4
   IPv4 Address. . . . . . . . . . . : 172.16.97.51
   Subnet Mask . . . . . . . . . . . : 255.255.255.0
   Default Gateway . . . . . . . . . : 172.16.97.1
```

Figure 2.22 – Example ipconfig output

Configuring DHCP with PowerShell is slightly more complicated than the one-liner Powershell codes we've seen so far. To repeat these steps in PowerShell, you will need to import the DHCPServer module and then use the Add-DhcpServerv4Scope and Set-DhcpServerV4OptionValue cmdlets:

```
Import-Module DHCPServer
Add-DhcpServerv4Scope -Name Cookbook -StartRange 172.16.97.50
-EndRange 172.16.97.250 -SubnetMask 255.255.255.0
-LeaseDuration 5.0:0:0
Set-DhcpServerv4OptionValue -ScopeId 172.16.97.50 -DnsDomain
```

```
ad.cookbook.packt.com -DnsServer 172.16.97.2,172.16.97.3
-Router 172.16.97.1
```

If that looks complicated, it's probably just because of the sheer number of IP addresses we've had to type in – but given that DHCP deals with IP addresses, that's not surprising. Ultimately, there's two parts to this: first, we created the DHCP scope, and then we had to configure the optional DHCP components of the DNS Server in a second command.

> **Tip**
>
> You do not need to keep running the `Import-Module` command. I'm including it here for the sake of completeness, but once you've imported a module once, you're good to go for the rest of that PowerShell session without re-importing it. In fact, you may not need to call `Import-Module` at all due to PowerShell's module auto-loading, but I am including it for the sake of completeness.

How it works...

DHCP is one of the core infrastructure roles that almost everyone uses inside their networks. While we have only scratched the surface here of what DHCP is capable of, the ability to automatically hand out IP addresses to connecting client computers is DHCP's core functionality. Installing the role and creating a scope are our primary steps to make use of DHCP. Take a look at our next recipe for one of the most advanced functions that can be accomplished within your scope.

Creating a DHCP reservation for a specific server or resource

In a simple DHCP scope, any device that connects and asks for an IP address is handed whatever IP is next available within the scope. If you have a device that you always want to keep the same IP address for, you could manually configure the NIC properties with a static IP address. Otherwise, a more centralized way to assign a particular IP to the same device on a long-term basis is to use a **DHCP reservation**. Using a reservation in DHCP to assign an IP to a device makes a lot of sense because you can see that reservation right in the DHCP console, and you don't have to worry about keeping track of the static IP addresses that you have configured out in the field. Let's walk through configuring a quick reservation so that you are familiar with this process.

Getting ready

We will be using a Windows Server 2019 machine as our DHCP server where we will create the DHCP reservation. Additionally, we will use our WEB01 server as the recipient of this reservation by assigning WEB01 to IP address `172.16.97.84`.

How to do it...

To create a DHCP reservation for a specific server or resource, perform these steps:

1. Open the **DHCP** manager tool.

2. Expand the left-hand pane down into the DHCP scope that we created earlier. Under this scope, you will see a folder called `Reservations`. Right-click on `Reservations` and click on **New Reservation....**

3. Populate the fields. Your **Reservation name** field can contain anything descriptive. Fill out the **IP address** field with the IP address you want to reserve for this purpose. The last important piece of information is the **MAC address** field. This must be the MAC address of the device that you want to receive this particular IP address for. Since WEB01 is a Windows Server 2019 machine, we can get our MAC address by using `Get-NetAdapter` on WEB01:

Figure 2.23 – Output of the Get-NetAdapter command

4. You can see `MacAddress 00-15-5D-0F-05-28` in Command Prompt – this is our MAC address for WEB01. Use it to finish populating the DHCP reservation:

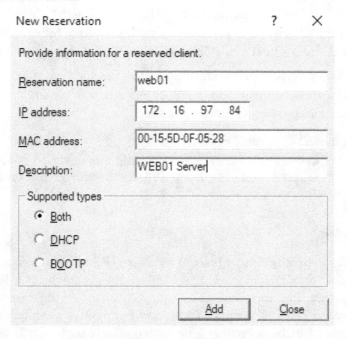

Figure 2.24 – Creating a DHCP reservation

> **Tip**
> You can take your PowerShell to the next level here! Instead of highlighting and copying the MAC address, or even worse, typing it out by hand, try using `(Get-NetAdapter).MacAddress | clip` – it will copy your MAC address to your clipboard for you.

5. Click on **Add**. You will see your new reservation listed in the **DHCP** management console.

6. Now, make sure that the network on WEB01 is set to **Obtain an IP address automatically**. A quick PowerShell command to set this would be `Set-NetIPInterface -InterfaceAlias 'Ethernet' -Dhcp Enabled`. When WEB01 reaches out to DHCP to grab an IP address, it will now always receive `172.16.97.84` because of the reservation, rather than getting whatever IP address is next available within the DHCP scope.

7. You can probably detect a pattern forming here when the PowerShell commands for this one. Again, it's the `DHCPServer` module and, this time, the `Add-DhcpServerv4Reservation` cmdlet:

```
Import-Module DHCPServer
Add-DhcpServerv4Reservation -IPAddress 172.16.97.84 -Name
web01 -ClientId '00-15-5D-0F-05-28' -Description 'WEB01
Server' -ScopeId 172.16.97.50
```

How it works...

Typically, whenever a client computer is set to obtain an IP address automatically, it reaches out and looks for a DHCP server that hands to the client whatever IP address is free and next in the list. This may cause an IP address to change if the lease has expired and another device has taken its previous IP address. For desktop computers, this is usually fine. In some cases, however, it is beneficial to reserve particular IP addresses for specific devices, thereby ensuring they always receive the same IP address. The most common example of this that I have seen is a printer changing IP addresses after it's been turned off for a while, causing everyone in the office to be unable to print. Creating DHCP reservations is a good practice for static devices on the network, such as print server boxes and telephony equipment.

> **Tip**
> DHCP clients renew their lease when there is 50% of the lease time remaining. This means that for a 12-hour, lease they will renew after 6 hours. If unsuccessful, it will try again after 3 hours, then 90 minutes, then 45 minutes. Once the lease has expired, it will continue to try and refresh, requesting the same IP address it had before. However, there is no guarantee that it will receive the same IP address if, say, the DHCP server has reissued that IP to someone else in the meantime.

Pre-staging a computer account in Active Directory

Joining computers to your domain is going to be a very normal task for any IT professional, enough that you are probably familiar with the process of doing so. What you may not realize, though, is that when you join computers or servers to your domain, they get lumped automatically into a generic `Computers` OU inside AD. Sometimes, this doesn't present any problem at all and all of your machines can reside inside this `Computers` OU forever. Most of the time, however, organizations will set up policies that filter down into the `Computers` container automatically. When this is the case, these policies and settings will immediately apply to all the computers that you join to your domain. For a desktop computer, this might be desired behavior. When configuring a new server, though, this can present big problems.

Let's say you are interested in turning on a new web server that is going to be running IIS. You have a domain policy in place that blocks inbound HTTP traffic for all computers that get added to the `Computers` container. In this case, if you turned on your web server and simply joined it to the domain, it would immediately apply the policy to disable blocking the traffic because it is no different than a regular client computer in your network. IIS requires the firewall to permit HTTP traffic (it is, after all, a web server) and so you have effectively broken your server before you've even finished configuring it! You would eventually realize this mistake and move the server into a different OU that doesn't have the firewall policy; however, this doesn't necessarily mean that all the changes the policy put into place will be reversed. You may still have trouble with that server on an ongoing basis.

The preceding example is the reason why we are going to follow this recipe. If we pre-stage the computer account for our new web server, we can choose where it will reside inside Active Directory, even before we join it to the domain. **Pre-staging** is a way of creating the computer's object inside Active Directory before you go to the actual server and click **Join**. When you do this, as soon as the request to join the domain comes in, Active Directory already knows exactly where to place that computer account. This way, you can make sure that the account resides inside an OU that is not going to apply the firewall policy and keep your new server running properly.

Getting ready

We will use the **Active Directory Users and Computers** tool to pre-stage the computer account. This can be done on the domain controller itself, or on a Windows 10 machine that has the appropriate RSAT tools installed. Following this, we will use a second server that we are going to join to our domain, which we plan to turn into a web server in the future.

How to do it...

To pre-stage a computer account so that it resides inside AD, perform the following steps:

1. Open **Active Directory Users and Computers**

2. Choose a location where you want to place this new server. I am going to use the OU we created earlier, that is, `Servers\Web Server`.

3. Right-click on your OU and navigate to **New | Computer**.

4. Enter the name of your new server. Make sure this matches the hostname you are going to assign as you build this new server so that when it joins the domain, it matches up with this entry in AD. Note that, on this screen, you also have the ability to determine which user or group has permission to join this new machine to the domain, if you want to set a restriction here:

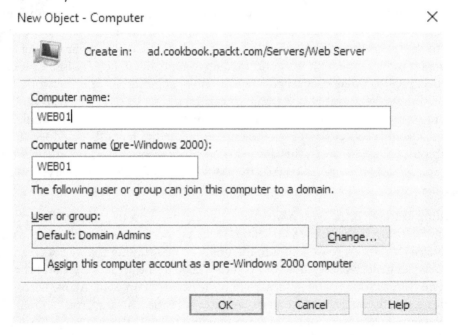

Figure 2.25 – Creating a new Computer object in the Active Directory Users and Computers console

5. Click **OK**, and that's it! Your object for this new server has been entered into AD, waiting for a computer account to join the domain that matches the name.

6. The last step is building the `WEB01` server and joining it to the domain, just like you would with any computer or server. When you do so, it will utilize this pre-existing account in the `Web Servers` OU, instead of placing a new entry into the generic `Computers` container.

7. The PowerShell for this one requires the `ActiveDirectory` module and will use the `New-ADComputer` cmdlet:

```
Import-Module ActiveDirectory
New-ADComputer -Name WEB01 -Path 'OU=Web
Server,OU=Servers,DC=ad,DC=cookbook,DC=packt,DC=com'
```

As in the previous PowerShell commands that involves OUs, you will need to know your LDAP Distinguished Name for the OU you wish to use.

How it works...

Pre-staging computer accounts in Active Directory is an important function when building new servers. It is sometimes critical to the long-term health of these servers for them to steer clear of the default domain policies and settings that you apply to your regular computer accounts. By taking a quick 30 seconds prior to joining a new server to the domain to pre-stage its account in AD, you ensure the correct placement of the system so that it fits your organizational structure. This will keep the system running properly as you continue to configure it for whatever job you are trying to accomplish.

Using PowerShell to create a new Active Directory user

Creating new user accounts in Active Directory is pretty standard stuff, but doing it the traditional way requires a lot of mouse clicks. Since we know that PowerShell can be used to accomplish anything within Windows Server 2019, but not many people actually employ it regularly, let's implement this common task as a recipe to be accomplished with PowerShell rather than the GUI.

Getting ready

We will use PowerShell on any Windows machine that is either a DC or has the Active Directory RSAT tools installed.

How to do it...

Follow along to create a new user account in Active Directory by using the PowerShell Command Prompt:

1. Launch a PowerShell Command Prompt as an Administrator.

2. Enter the following command in order to create a new user account with very simple parameters:

```
Import-Module ActiveDirectory
New-ADUser -Name 'John Smith' -UserPrincipalName 'jsmith@
cookbook.packt.com ' -SamAccountName 'jsmith'
```

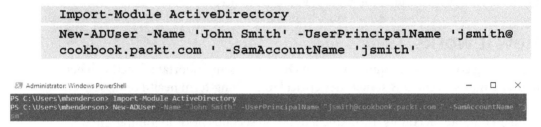

Figure 2.26 – Output of the New-ADUser PowerShell command

> **Tip**
> You may have noticed that this account's User Principle Name is *@cookbook.packt.com* – not *@ad.cookbook.packt.com*. This is because I have added an additional UPN suffix to my domain to make my Active Directory usernames match the user's email address.

3. If you open up the GUI for **Active Directory Users and Computers**, you will see that **John Smith** has now been created as a **User** account. There aren't many properties that exist within this account as it is pretty simple, but it will work in order to get a new user up and running:

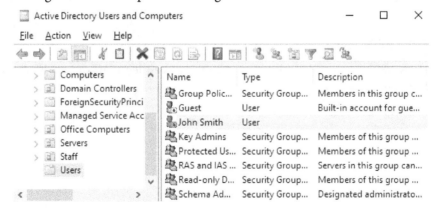

Figure 2.27 – Showing the default Users OU in Active Directory Users and Computers

4. Now, let's create another new user, this time adding some additional parameters to our code in order to populate more of the typical user information. You may have also noticed that our new **John Smith** user account is currently disabled – this happens automatically when you create a new user account but do not populate a password. So, we will add some more information, up to the first name and surname. We will also specify a couple of additional parameters in order to make sure the account is enabled and to require that the user changes their password during their initial login:

```
New-ADUser -Name 'Jase Robertson' -UserPrincipalName
'jrobertson@cookbook.packt.com ' -SamAccountName
'jrobertson' -GivenName 'Jase' -Surname 'Robertson'
-DisplayName 'Jase Robertson' -AccountPassword (Read-Host
-AsSecureString 'AccountPassword') -ChangePasswordAtLogon
$true -Enabled $true
```

This results in the following output:

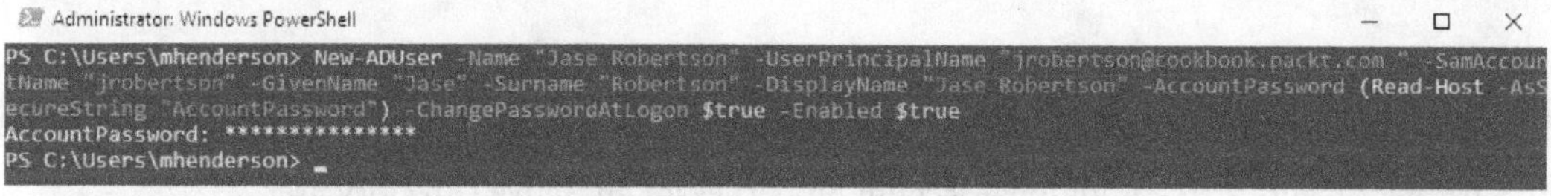

Figure 2.28 – Output of the New-ADUser command with optional additional user configuration

5. Open **Active Directory Users and Computers** again and take a look at our new **Jase Robertson** user account. You will see that the account is enabled and ready for use and that is also has much more information populated:

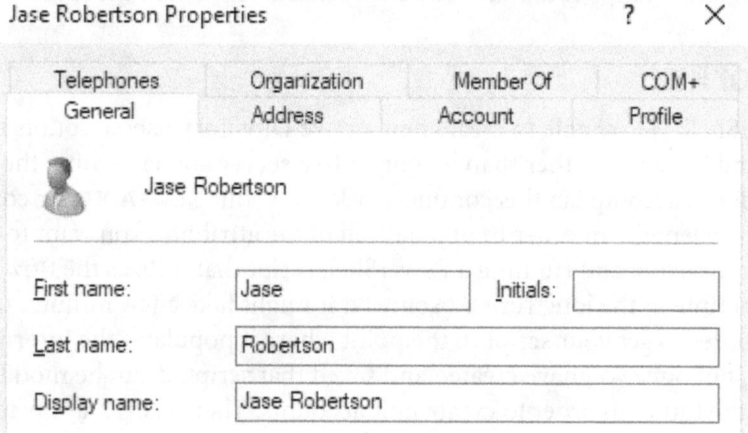

Figure 2.29 – General properties for an Active Directory user

6. Move over to the **Account** tab. You will also see that box for **User must change password at next logon** is now checked, just like we specified in our PowerShell command:

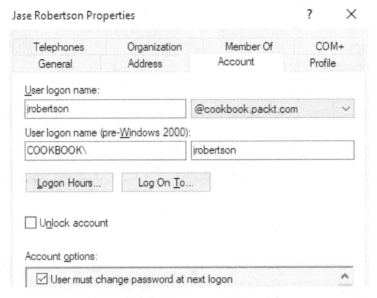

Figure 2.30 – Additional account properties for an Active Directory user

Using this small PowerShell cmdlet, you could take things a lot further if you wanted. For example, if your HR department was to email you an Excel spreadsheet of all the new hires starting next week, you could save that spreadsheet as a CSV and use PowerShell's Import-CSV cmdlet to read the spreadsheet and create all the new users for you automatically. A small script could save you many hours of work in the future.

How it works...

By using PowerShell, we are able to create new Active Directory user accounts right from a command interface, rather than logging into a server and launching the graphical interface in order to accomplish this common task. Can your New-ADUser commands become extremely lengthy in order to populate all of the attributes you want to include? Yes. However, can saving and running a PowerShell script that utilizes the New-ADUser cmdlet save you time in the long run? Absolutely! It might take a few minutes of thought and testing in order to get your script to the point where it populates the information that you would like, but once you have created and saved that script, it can be modified and run quickly in the future in order to create new accounts. There is even a way to utilize the New-ADUser cmdlet to copy properties from an existing user account while it sets up the new one, which may also help save you some time and energy on new user account creations.

See also

Make sure to check out the following TechNet link. This page lists all of the possible parameters and syntax that you might want to run alongside your `New-ADUser` cmdlet script. There are a ton of options:

- `http://technet.microsoft.com/en-us/library/ee617253.aspx`

Using PowerShell to run commands on another server

If you find yourself constantly having to log onto various servers to perform maintenance tasks, you may eventually run into something that can't be done by the Windows Admin Center, Server Manager, or any of the RSAT tools. You might need to delete a file or adjust a firewall rule. In the past, we would have fired up Remote Desktop, typed in our username and password, waited for the desktop to load in, then started Command Prompt, Windows Explorer, or any number of other mundane maintenance tasks.

With PowerShell, however, there is often no need to jump through the RDP hoops to access a server. In the same way that you can `ssh` into another server to run commands with Linux, PowerShell has `Enter-PSSession`, `Invoke-Command`, and other commands that can be used to configure servers remotely. In this recipe, we'll go through some of these commands to show you how they can save you time in the future.

Getting ready

We will be using a Windows 10 computer to connect remotely to our Windows Server 2019 domain controller DC01.

How to do it...

Let's run through three common scenarios: when you need to browse around on the remote server, when you just need to run a single command, and when you have a cmdlet that has built-in support for remoting. We'll do the same thing three times – check what time our server was last booted:

1. On your Windows 10 computer, launch a PowerShell prompt as Administrator.

2. Run the `Enter-PSSession DC01` command. This may take a moment to connect, but after, your Command Prompt should be prefixed with [DC01] (or whatever server name you chose to connect to). Every command you type now is going to be executed on your remote server, not yours.

3. To make sure this is the case, run `hostname`. You should see the remote computer's name show up – not yours.

4. Let's check what time the server was last booted. Run the following command:

```
(Get-CimInstance Win32_OperatingSystem).LastBootUpTime
```

This results in the following output:

```
Administrator: Windows PowerShell                                          —    □    ×
PS C:\Users\mhenderson> Enter-PSSession DC01
[DC01]: PS C:\Users\mhenderson\Documents> hostname
DC01
[DC01]: PS C:\Users\mhenderson\Documents> (Get-CimInstance Win32_OperatingSystem).LastBootUpTime

Saturday, 2 November 2019 10:38:50 AM
```

Figure 2.31 – Demonstrating the Enter-PSSession PowerShell command

5. That was pretty cool – but if you just have a small script or a one-liner to run, you do not need to use `Enter-PSSession` at all! Run `exit` to get out of your remote session and back to your local computer's PowerShell prompt.

6. Now, run this:

```
Invoke-Command -ComputerName DC01 -ScriptBlock {
(Get-CimInstance Win32_OperatingSystem).LastBootUpTime }
```

7. What we've done now is run the exact same command that we typed out on DC01, but we did it without ever having to get an interactive session on the server. The `-ComputerName` argument here can take more than one name, so we could run this command against multiple servers if we wanted to.

> **Note**
>
> If you get different `LastBootUpTimes` when running these commands, this will be due to timezone differences between your server and your local computer. The first command was presented in the servers timezone, while the second command was presented in your timezone.

8. That's still a bit cumbersome, though, but we're in luck. The `Get-CimInstance` cmdlet also supports the `-ComputerName` argument directly, so we don't need to wrap the command in the `Invoke-Command` cmdlet. Try this:

```
(Get-CimInstance -ComputerName DC01 Win32_
OperatingSystem).LastBootUpTime
```

9. The result should be exactly the same as what we got with the previous code we ran. And like the previous code, `-ComputerName` takes more than one computer name, so we could also run the following:

```
(Get-CimInstance -ComputerName DC01,DC02 Win32_
OperatingSystem).LastBootUpTime
```

The following is the output:

```
PS C:\Users\mhenderson> (Get-CimInstance -ComputerName DC01,DC02 Win32_OperatingSystem).LastBootUpTime

Sunday, 3 November 2019 7:53:44 PM
Sunday, 3 November 2019 4:46:31 AM
```

Figure 2.32 – Running a PowerShell command against multiple computers remotely

How it works...

In this recipe, we looked at three different ways of running commands on a remote server. `Enter-PSSession` gives us full control over PowerShell on the remote computer, allowing us to do virtually anything we need to. `Invoke-Command` is a great way to execute small scripts that you may need to run on multiple servers. And finally, we saw that some cmdlets have built-in remote capabilities with `-ComputerName`. Most of the Windows RSAT cmdlets support this `-ComputerName` functionality. You can see a full list of which ones by running `Get-Command -ParameterName ComputerName`.

This remoting ability can make your tasks so much simpler, especially once you start to integrate them into some of your scripts. You may never need to remote desktop into a server ever again – and, in fact, if you are running Server Core (which we will cover in *Chapter 12, Server Core,* you will need to use this functionality as there is basically no remote desktop!

3
Networking

A server is not particularly useful unless it's connected to a network. Modern networks range from a simple single connection to having multiple connections with different subnets. Every network is different in its own way, so we need to understand how to make Windows Server work effectively on each different network. Many network administrators will require certain rules to be enforced on your firewalls.

We're going to look at some of the common networking tasks that will help you out in your day-to-day work. With these recipes, you will start to dig deeper into some of the features that Windows Server 2019 offers, and hopefully, it will have you thinking deeper about the different ways that Windows Server 2019 can be used and deployed.

In this chapter, we'll cover the following recipes:

- Using Windows Firewall with Advanced Security to block unnecessary traffic
- Multi-homing Windows Server 2019
- Adding a static route to the Windows routing table
- Using dynamic BGP routing in your Windows routing table
- Using telnet and `Test-NetConnection` to test a connection and network flow
- Using the `pathping` command to trace network traffic
- Setting up NIC Teaming
- Renaming and domain joining via PowerShell

Using Windows Firewall with Advanced Security to block unnecessary traffic

I encounter far too many networks with policies in place that disable the built-in **Windows Firewall with Advanced Security** (**WFAS**) by default on all their machines. Usually, if I ask about this, the reason is either unknown or 'It's always been that way.' I think this is a carry-over from the Windows XP/Server 2003 days, or maybe even older, when Windows Firewall was less than desirable. WFAS in today's operating systems is very advanced, stable, and beneficial – a far cry from the days of Windows XP. If you want to stop unnecessary or malicious traffic from getting to your server, look no further than this built-in tool.

Getting ready

We are going to use two Windows Server 2019 machines for this task. We will test connectivity between the two to set our baseline and then create a rule that blocks the functions we just tested. Next, we will test again to ensure that our changes did what we expected them to, blocking the traffic that we attempt to generate. It is important to set up a baseline of tests and run those same tests following each change to ensure the rules are working exactly as you want them to.

How to do it...

If you want to stop unnecessary traffic from getting to your server, execute the following instructions:

1. First, we want to test the existing connectivity. Log into your DC02 server. From there, I execute `Test-Connection web01` in PowerShell and get a successful connection. I can also open up File Explorer and browse to `\\WEB01` and see a folder shared there. This baseline test tells me that both ICMP (ping) traffic and file access are currently open and allowed by WFAS on WEB01. For the sake of this exercise, we will stop these functions from happening:

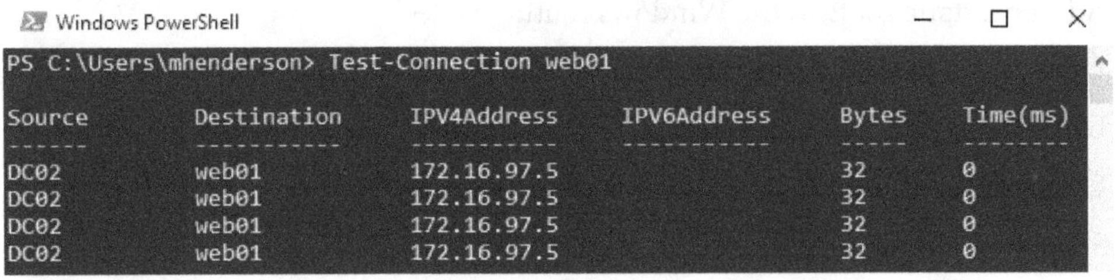

Figure 3.1 – A successful connection to web01

2. Log into WEB01 and open **Windows Defender Firewall with Advanced Security**. You can open this either from the **Start** screen and typing it in, or by opening a **Run** prompt and typing wf.msc.

3. Inside WFAS, your two best friends when trying to control traffic are the **Inbound Rules** and **Outbound Rules** sections on the left. You need to think of inbound and outbound from the server's perspective. Inbound rules manipulate traffic that is flowing in toward your server, while outbound rules handle traffic flowing out of your server toward the rest of the network. If you click on **Inbound Rules**, you will see the list of preconfigured rules that exist already:

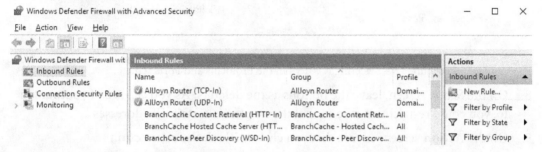

Figure 3.2 – The Inbound Rules screen of Windows Defender Firewall

4. First, let's make a rule to stop the ability to ping the server. Some archaic security models require this, so it's a common enough thing to implement (even if it provides little actual security). Right-click on **Inbound Rules** and click on **New Rule…**.

5. On the first screen, choose **Custom**. Other, more straightforward rules can be done using some of the other options on this page, but we're going to go through all the screens for now.

6. Leave the default **All programs** option selected and move onto the next screen.

7. In the **Protocols and Ports** screen, under **Protocol type**, choose `ICMPv4`:

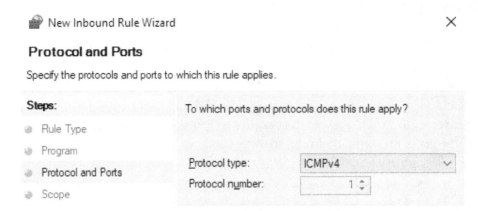

Figure 3.3 – Selecting ICMPv4 in the Protocols and Ports screen

8. On the **Scope** screen, leave the options as the defaults. As you can see, if you wanted to, you could restrict this rule so that it only affects certain IP addresses.

9. On the **Action** screen, ensure that you choose **Block the connection**:

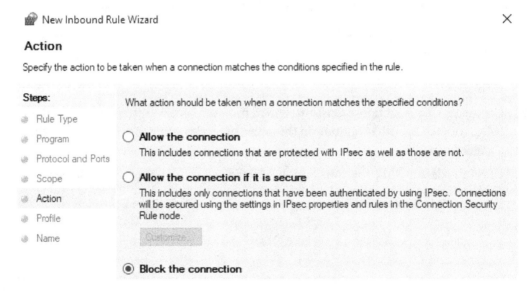

Figure 3.4 – Block the connection on the Actions screen

10. For the **Profile** screen leave these as the defaults.

11. On the **Name** screen, give your rule a descriptive name such as `Block ICMP`.

12. You did it! You will see that the new rule exists and that it is immediately put into action. If you head back to your other servers, you will see that Test-Connection web01, which we ran in *Step 1*, now fails.

Windows Firewall can also be used to restrict which connections your server can make itself – not just which servers can connect to it. We can do this on the **Outbound Rules** screen. Another common rule that security teams like to enforce is to block servers from using any other DNS servers than the ones that they control. Thankfully, this is also fairly easy to implement:

1. On WEB01, go back to **Windows Defender Firewall with Advanced Security** but this time, choose **Outbound Rules** and then **New Rule…**.

2. For **Rule Type**, select Custom.

3. Leave the default **All programs** selected and move onto the next screen.

4. For **Protocols and Ports**, select the TCP protocol. For **Remote port**, enter 53 (this is the port that DNS operates on):

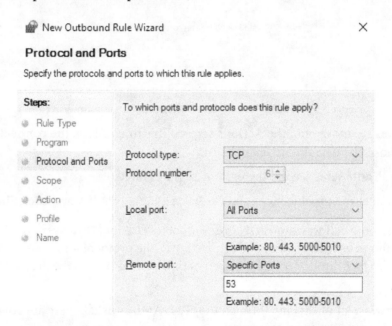

Figure 3.5 – Setting the remote port to 53 in an outbound security rule

5. On the **Scope** screen, for **Which remote IP addresses does this rule apply to?**, choose **These IP addresses** and then click **Add…**.

6. Choose **Predefined set of computers** and then select **Internet**. Click **OK**:

Figure 3.6 – Setting the predefined set of computers to Internet

7. Click **Next** to move onto the **Actions** screen. This time, **Block the connection** has been chosen by default. Leave it like this.

8. For the **Profile** screen, leave the options as the defaults.

9. Give another memorable name such as `Block DNS (TCP)` and click **Finish**.

However, we're only half way done. DNS runs on both TCP *and* UDP over port 53. The firewall only allows us to select either TCP *or* UDP as the protocol – not both. So, you will need to repeat *steps 1* through *9* again – but this time setting UDP as the protocol in *steps 4* and *9*.

As usual, that was a lot of clicking through the GUI. And, as usual, there are PowerShell one-liners that can do the exact same work:

```
New-NetFirewallRule -DisplayName 'Block ICMP' -Direction
Inbound -Protocol ICMPv4 -Action Block
```
```
New-NetFirewallRule -DisplayName 'Block DNS (TCP)' -Direction
Outbound -Protocol TCP -RemotePort 53 -RemoteAddress Internet
```

```
-Action Block
New-NetFirewallRule -DisplayName 'Block DNS (UDP)' -Direction
Outbound -Protocol UDP -RemotePort 53 -RemoteAddress Internet
-Action Block
```

How it works...

We used Windows Defender Firewall with Advanced Security to create a couple of simple rules that many security departments require. These rules are put into place immediately and are very easy to generate. What is even greater is that our WFAS rules can be created centrally by making use of Group Policy so that you don't even have to touch the individual servers to apply connection rules to them. WFAS is very different than the Windows Firewall of 10 years ago, and if you are not making use of it, I seriously recommend that you reconsider your stance.

Multi-homing Windows Server 2019

Historically, there haven't been many scenarios that require Windows servers to have a connection to more than one network. This is because most of the roles that they were accomplishing were done on whatever single network they were plugged into. There was no need for a server to have direct connections to multiple networks because that was the router and switch's job, right? In today's Windows Server world, there are numerous roles that can take advantage of multi-homing, which simply means having multiple network cards connected to different networks at the same time. There are some proxy roles that can use multiple NICs; Remote Access roles such as **DirectAccess** and **VPN** recommend a dual-NIC setup, and you can even use a Windows Server as a general router if you want to.

If you work a lot with DirectAccess, you will find many multi-homed servers with incorrect network configurations. This recipe is a collection of points that need to be followed when configuring a Windows Server with multiple NICs that are connected to different networks to make sure it behaves and flows traffic as you expect it to.

Getting ready

You just need a Windows Server 2019 instance online for this recipe. We have two NICs installed on this server and they are plugged into different networks. I am prepping a Remote Access server that will sit on the edge, so I have one NIC plugged into the corporate internal network and the other connected to the internet.

How to do it...

To configure a Windows Server with multiple NICs, perform the following process:

- **Only one Default Gateway**: In your NIC properties, you need to make sure that you only have a Default Gateway identified on one of your NICs. This is the most common mistake that I find in the field. If you have two NICs, it would seem logical that you would simply populate their IP address settings just like you would with any server or computer, right? Nope. The purpose of a Default Gateway is to be the fallback or the route of last resort. Whenever your server tries to send out network traffic, it will search the local routing table for information on how to send out that traffic. If it does not find a specific route that corresponds to the IP address that you are sending to, then it will default that traffic over to the Default Gateway address. Therefore, you only ever want to have one Default Gateway assigned on a server, no matter how many NICs are connected. On all other NICs installed on the system, simply leave the Default Gateway field unpopulated inside the TCP/IP properties. By the way, for a DirectAccess server or for pretty much any other server that faces the internet, the Default Gateway needs to be on the external NIC, so I will be leaving that field empty in the properties of my internal NIC.

- **Limit your DNS servers**: Another common configuration that I have seen is to have DNS server addresses defined for every network adapter installed on the system. While this doesn't usually break anything like multiple Default Gateways can, it does cause unnecessary slowness when the system is trying to resolve DNS names. Try to have DNS server addresses configured on only one NIC. Once again, using our example DirectAccess server setup, I will be configuring DNS server addresses on my internal NIC because that is necessary for DA to work. I will not be putting my public DNS server specifications into the external NIC; instead, I will leave those fields empty.

- **Use static IP addresses**: The roles and functions you may perform on a Windows Server that require multiple NICs will be best served by having static IP address information assigned to those network cards. If you let one or more of the NICs pull information from DHCP, you could easily create a situation where you have too many DNS servers defined, or where you have multiple Default Gateways on your system. As we already know, neither of these scenarios is desirable.

- **Prioritize the NIC binding**: It is a good practice to set a priority for your NICs so that you can place the card that you expect to have the most network traffic as #1 in the list. For our DirectAccess server, we always want the internal NIC to be placed on the top. In earlier versions of Window Server, this could be done via the GUI. However, in Windows Server 2019, the only way we can do this is via PowerShell.

- Follow these steps:

1. Open PowerShell as Administrator.

2. Run `Get-NetIPInterface -AddressFamily IPv4`. You will receive a list of network connections that are available on your server. The fields we're interested in are **InterfaceAlias** and **InterfaceMetric**:

```
Administrator: Windows PowerShell                                                    —   □   ×
PS C:\Users\mhenderson> Get-NetIPInterface -AddressFamily IPv4

ifIndex InterfaceAlias                AddressFamily NlMtu(Bytes) InterfaceMetric Dhcp     ConnectionState PolicyStore
------- --------------                ------------- ------------ --------------- ----     --------------- -----------
25      External                      IPv4                  1500              15 Enabled  Connected       ActiveStore
4       Internal                      IPv4                  1500              15 Disabled Connected       ActiveStore
1       Loopback Pseudo-Interface 1   IPv4            4294967295              75 Disabled Connected       ActiveStore
```

Figure 3.7 – Example Get-NetIPInterface showing internal and external connections

3. If your internal network has an `InterfaceMetric` value lower than your external network, then you can stop here. However, if the `InterfaceMetric` value of the external interface is the same or lower than your internal interface, then it needs to be renumbered with `Set-NetIPInterface -InterfaceAlias 'External' -InterfaceMetric 20`, where `External` is the name of your external
adapter and `InterfaceMetric` is higher than `InterfaceMetric` of your internal adapter:

```
Administrator: Windows PowerShell                                                    —   □   ×
PS C:\Users\mhenderson> Set-NetIPInterface -InterfaceAlias "External" -InterfaceMetric 20
PS C:\Users\mhenderson> Get-NetIPInterface -AddressFamily IPv4

ifIndex InterfaceAlias                AddressFamily NlMtu(Bytes) InterfaceMetric Dhcp     ConnectionState PolicyStore
------- --------------                ------------- ------------ --------------- ----     --------------- -----------
25      External                      IPv4                  1500              20 Enabled  Connected       ActiveStore
4       Internal                      IPv4                  1500              15 Disabled Connected       ActiveStore
1       Loopback Pseudo-Interface 1   IPv4            4294967295              75 Disabled Connected       ActiveStore
```

Figure 3.8 – Demonstrating how Set-NetIPInterface has reordered the external interface

- **Add static routes**: A couple of minutes ago, you probably started thinking 'Hey, if I don't have a Default Gateway on my internal NIC, what tells the server how to get packets into the subnets of my internal network?' Great question! Because you only have one Default Gateway, when you need to send traffic out one of the other NICs, you need to make sure that a static route exists in the Windows routing table. This ensures that the server knows which interface gets traffic for each subnet. Make sure to check out the next two recipes for specific information on how to add those routes.

How it works...

Anybody can multi-home their server by simply plugging two NICs into two different networks. The tricky part is making sure that you configure those NICs and the operating system appropriately so that network traffic flows in the right directions at the right times. Following this list of rules will give you a solid foundation so that you can build out these types of scenarios and know that you are doing so in the correct fashion. Deviating from these rules will result in unexpected behavior, which sometimes is not immediately obvious. This can make for some very frustrating troubleshooting down the road.

See also

- *Adding a static route to the Windows routing table*
- *Using dynamic BGP routing in your Windows routing table*

Adding a static route to the Windows routing table

This recipe follows right on the heels of our previous recipe, *Multi-homing your Windows Server 2019*. If you have never worked on a server that is making use of more than one NIC, then you have probably never had a reason to poke around in the Windows routing table. The minute that you are tasked with setting up a new server that needs to be connected to multiple networks, or you get thrown into a situation where you need to troubleshoot such a system, this suddenly becomes critical information to have in your back pocket.

On a server that is connected to multiple networks, you only have one Default Gateway address defined. This means any subnets that need to be reached by flowing through one of the other NICs – the ones that do not contain the Default Gateway – need to be specifically defined inside the routing table. Otherwise, Windows simply does not know how to get to those subnets and it will attempt to push all traffic through the Default Gateway. This traffic will never make its way to its destination and communications will fail.

Today, we are setting up a new VPN server. This server has a NIC plugged into the internet where remote clients will come in, and another NIC plugged into the internal network so that the client traffic can make its way to the application servers that the users need to access. In this scenario, the Default Gateway must be populated on the external NIC. There will be no Default Gateway address defined on the internal NIC, and without some assistance, Windows will have no idea how to properly route traffic toward the servers inside the network.

For our example, the internal NIC is plugged into the 172.16.97.x network. Since it has a direct physical connection to this network, it is automatically able to properly contact other servers that reside on this subnet. So, if the VPN server was 172.16.97.5 and we had a Domain Controller running on 172.16.97.1, we would be able to contact that Domain Controller without any additional configuration. But most companies have multiple subnets inside their network. So, what if our VPN users needed to contact a web server that is sitting on the 172.16.120.x network? When traffic comes into the VPN server looking for a destination of 172.16.120.10 (the web server), the VPN server will check its local routing table and find that it does not have an entry for the 172.16.120.x network. Since it doesn't know what to do with this request, it sends it to the Default Gateway, which sends the packets back out the external NIC. Those packets don't have a valid destination to reach through the external NIC, which is plugged into the internet, and so the traffic simply fails.

We need to define a static route in the routing table of our VPN server so that when VPN clients request resources inside the 172.16.120.x network, that traffic makes its way to the destination network successfully. We need to bind this route to our internal NIC so that the VPN server knows it must send these packets through that physical network interface.

Getting ready

We are setting up a new Windows Server 2019 VPN server. This server has two NICs installed: one plugged into the internet and the other plugged into the internal network. Inside our corporate network, there are two subnets: 172.16.97.x (/24), which our internal NIC is plugged into, and 172.16.120.x (/24), where our web server resides. There is, of course, a router between the two internal subnets, which is how traffic physically flows between the two. The IP address of that router is 172.16.97.1. If we were able to configure a Default Gateway on the internal NIC of our VPN server, it would be set to 172.16.97.1, and all traffic would work without any further input. However, since our VPN server is multi-homed and there can only be a Default Gateway configured on the external NIC, we need to tell the server that it must push 172.16.120.x traffic through 172.16.97.1 by using the internal NIC.

How to do it...

We need to do the following to create a static route in our VPN server:

1. Identify the subnet that we want to contact. In our example, this is `172.16.120.0`.

2. Identify the subnet prefix length, which is `24` (equivalent to the subnet mask of `255.255.255.0`).

3. Identify the IP address of the router that will get us to that network, which is `172.16.97.1`.

4. Identify the Interface ID number of the physical NIC that needs to carry this traffic. You can determine this by running `Get-NetIPInterface -AddressFamily IPv4` and looking at the `ifIndex` field. This could be different for every server, but for this example, it is 4.

5. We now have all the information needed to put our route statement together and bind it to our internal NIC. The command we would run for our example route is as follows:

```
New-NetRoute -DestinationPrefix '172.16.120.0/24'
-InterfaceIndex 4 -NextHop 172.16.97.1
```

The non-PowerShell equivalent would be as follows:

```
route add -p 172.16.120.0 mask 255.255.255.0 172.16.97.1
if 4
```

See how cryptic the non-PowerShell command is versus the nicely labeled PowerShell command? Note that the PowerShell command will look like it is outputting the new route twice. This is because the route is actually added twice, but to two different parts of the system (the currently active routing table and the routing table that is loaded when the server reboots). You can verify that it was added correctly with the `Get-NetRoute` command:

```
Administrator: Windows PowerShell                                                    —   □   ×
PS C:\Users\mhenderson> New-NetRoute -DestinationPrefix "172.16.120.0/24" -InterfaceIndex 4 -NextHop 172.16.97.1

ifIndex DestinationPrefix                        NextHop              RouteMetric ifMetric PolicyStore
------- -----------------                        -------              ----------- -------- -----------
4        172.16.120.0/24                         172.16.97.1                  256 15       ActiveStore
4        172.16.120.0/24                         172.16.97.1                  256          Persiste...


PS C:\Users\mhenderson> Get-NetRoute

ifIndex DestinationPrefix                        NextHop              RouteMetric ifMetric PolicyStore
------- -----------------                        -------              ----------- -------- -----------
25       255.255.255.255/32                      0.0.0.0                      256 20       ActiveStore
4        255.255.255.255/32                      0.0.0.0                      256 15       ActiveStore
1        255.255.255.255/32                      0.0.0.0                      256 75       ActiveStore
25       224.0.0.0/4                             0.0.0.0                      256 20       ActiveStore
4        224.0.0.0/4                             0.0.0.0                      256 15       ActiveStore
1        224.0.0.0/4                             0.0.0.0                      256 75       ActiveStore
25       172.16.200.255/32                       0.0.0.0                      256 20       ActiveStore
25       172.16.200.220/32                       0.0.0.0                      256 20       ActiveStore
25       172.16.200.0/24                         0.0.0.0                      256 20       ActiveStore
4        172.16.120.0/24                         172.16.97.1                  256 15       ActiveStore
```

Figure 3.9 – Example of adding a new route and reading the existing routing table

How it works...

With a multi-homed server, only one NIC will have a Default Gateway. Therefore, any subnets that we need to access through the other interfaces have to be specifically defined. Before we added this new route, the server was completely unable to contact the 172.16.120.x network. This is because the routing table did not have any information about this subnet, so any traffic trying to get there was being sent out the Default Gateway, which is on the external NIC plugged into the internet. By adding a static route to our server, we have now defined a routing path for the server to take whenever it has traffic that needs to get to 172.16.120.x.

If you have many subnets in your network, you may be able to cover them all with a blanket route statement. A blanket route is also known as an aggregate or supernet route. This could save you the time of having to set up a new route statement for each and every one of your networks. For example, if we had many *172.16.something* networks and we wanted to flow all of them through our internal NIC, we could do that with a single route statement, as follows:

```
New-NetRoute -DestinationPrefix '172.16.0.0/16' -InterfaceIndex
 4 -NextHop 172.16.97.1
```

This route would send any 172.16.x.x traffic through the internal NIC. Whether you aggregate your routes like this or set each one up individually doesn't make a difference to the server, as long as its routing table contains information about where to send the packets that it needs to process.

The other option, which we will look at in the next recipe, is that your server can learn these routes from the actual router itself if the router has been configured to permit this.

Using dynamic BGP routing in your Windows routing table

In the previous recipe, we added a single route to the routing table. For a lot of networks, this would be sufficient. However, in more complex networks, there might be dozens, hundreds, or even thousands of routes that would be beneficial to learn – especially if your server is acting as a VPN server or a remote gateway.

Thankfully, Windows does have a way to learn these routes from other routers on the network. The **Border Gateway Routing** (**BGP**) protocol has been in use since 1989 and is one of the key technologies that allows the internet to work. Because of this, with the cooperation of your networking team, you may be able to have your Windows server learn everything it needs to know about available routes from your corporate routers.

Getting ready

We have a Server 2019 server that will learn the routes. We will also need a network router that has BGP configured and has your server whitelisted to read its routes. Although out of scope for this book, there are virtual machines you can download to act as a pretend router so that you can experiment with BGP. Your network administrator may be able to assist you with this.

Before we can begin, we need to collect some information about the network's BGP configuration. Every network will be different. The details we are going to be using for this example are as follows:

- The BGP router's IP address. Ours is `172.16.97.1`.

- The BGP router's **Autonomous System Number (ASN)**. Ours is `64999`.

- Your local IP address that is on the same subnet as your router. Ours is `172.16.97.5`.

How to do it...

To add our first BGP peer, follow these steps:

1. First, we need to install the `RemoteAccess` windows feature. Run `Add-WindowsFeature Routing,RSAT-RemoteAccess-PowerShell` in an **administrator** PowerShell window. This will install the `RemoteAccess` Windows feature.

2. Now, we need to enable BGP routing. To do this, run `Install-RemoteAccess -VpnType RoutingOnly`.

3. Next, we need to create a virtual router on our Windows system. We do this with `Add-BgpRouter`. `BgpIdentifier` should be your internal IP address, while `LocalASN` should be the same as the BGP router's AS number. So, in our case, this will be `Add-BgpRouter -BgpIdentifier 172.16.97.5 -LocalASN 64999`.

4. Run the `Add-BgpPeer` command using the details we collected earlier. In our example, this will be `Add-BgpPeer -Name router -LocalIPAddress 172.16.97.5 -PeerIPAddress 172.16.97.1 -PeerASN 64999`.

In a simple environment, that should be it – we should now be learning routes from our router. As the router becomes aware of new networks, they will automatically be added to our routing table as well. We can verify that we're receiving routes using the `Get-BgpRouteInformation` command:

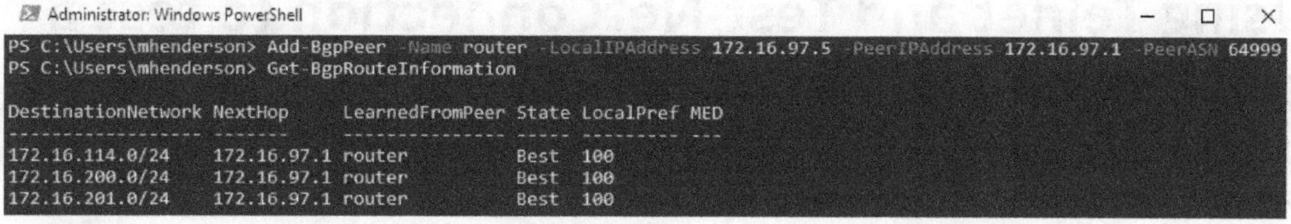

```
Administrator: Windows PowerShell                                                            —  □  ×

PS C:\Users\mhenderson> Add-BgpPeer -Name router -LocalIPAddress 172.16.97.5 -PeerIPAddress 172.16.97.1 -PeerASN 64999
PS C:\Users\mhenderson> Get-BgpRouteInformation

DestinationNetwork  NextHop        LearnedFromPeer State LocalPref MED
------------------  -------        --------------- ----- --------- ---
172.16.114.0/24     172.16.97.1 router            Best  100
172.16.200.0/24     172.16.97.1 router            Best  100
172.16.201.0/24     172.16.97.1 router            Best  100
```

Figure 3.10 – Showing the routes that Windows Server has learned via BGP

That might have all been a bit hard to follow, so for the sake of completeness, every command that was run from beginning to end goes as follows:

```
Add-WindowsFeature Routing,RSAT-RemoteAccess-PowerShell
Install-RemoteAccess -VpnType RoutingOnly
Add-BgpRouter -BgpIdentifier 172.16.97.5 -LocalASN 64999
Add-BgpPeer -Name router -LocalIPAddress 172.16.97.5
-PeerIPAddress 172.16.97.1 -PeerASN 64999
```

You can repeat the last command, `Add-BgpPeer`, for as many different routers as you need to.

How it works...

Adding lots of routes to your server by hand can be a pain. And if they ever change or go offline, you would need run commands to keep them up to date. BGP takes away the pain of having to manage all this by learning from the networks the server is connected to.

The Windows BGP routing ability is basic by many standards – a proper router from Cisco, Juniper, or Mikrotik can do a lot more. However, for the purposes of a typical Windows server, its BGP implementation is more than sufficient. In more advanced situations, such as if your server is a VPN or remote access server, you can also provide BGP routing information back to your core network routers so that you can share information about your servers' networks as well.

Just remember that using BGP generally requires the assistance of your network administrator, and may not be suitable for all networks.

See also...

- The MSDN reference for BGP on Windows at `https://docs.microsoft.com/en-us/windows-server/remote/remote-access/bgp/border-gateway-protocol-bgp`

Using Telnet and Test-NetConnection to test a connection and network flow

The `ping` (or `Test-Connection`, in PowerShell) command has always been an IT person's best friend to do quick network connection checks. How many of you are the family and neighborhood go-to guy to fix anything with buttons? I'm guessing most of you. And as such, if someone told you they were having trouble accessing the internet from their laptop at home, what is the first thing you would do when you showed up? Try to ping their router, a website, or another computer in their network. You know you would! This has always been a wonderfully quick and easy way to test whether you have network traffic flowing between two endpoints. The same troubleshooting procedure exists in all workplaces and corporations. I have seen many monitoring tools and scripts utilize the results of whether a ping replies to report on whether a service is up and running. If you get a ping reply, it's working, and if it times out, it's down, right?

Not necessarily. The problem we are here to address today is that more and more networks and routers are starting to block ICMP traffic by default. ICMP is another protocol like TCP or UDP and is used by a lot of network troubleshooting tools. In the Windows world, a ping is ICMP traffic (on Unix and Linux, this is not always true – but this is a book on Windows Server, after all!). This means that you can no longer take your ping test results to the bank. If your network connection traverses a router or firewall that blocks ICMP, your ping test will time out, even if the service is up and running. Earlier in this book, we created a Windows Firewall rule to block ICMP as an example. If you bring a new server online in your network and give it an IP address, you may notice that attempting to ping that new server results in timeouts. There is nothing wrong with the server, and it is capable of sending and receiving network traffic, but the local firewall on that server is blocking the incoming ping request.

I have only laid out this information to let you know that `ping` is no longer the best tool for determining a connection between machines. Today's recipe will introduce a tool that has been around for a long time, but that I don't find many administrators taking advantage of. This is Telnet Client, which I use on a daily basis. I hope that you will too! We'll also take a look at some of the different parameters of `Test-NetConnection` that can achieve a similar outcome.

Getting ready

We have a Server 2019 web server that has a website running. It is also enabled for RDP access and file sharing, but ICMP is being blocked by the local Windows Firewall. We are going to run some tests with a client machine against this server to try to determine which services are up and running.

How to do it...

To start working with Telnet Client, have a look at these instructions:

1. First, just to prove our point here, let's open a prompt on our testing client machine and try to ping WEB1 using the `ping web01` command. Because ICMP is being blocked by the firewall, all we get is a series of timeouts:

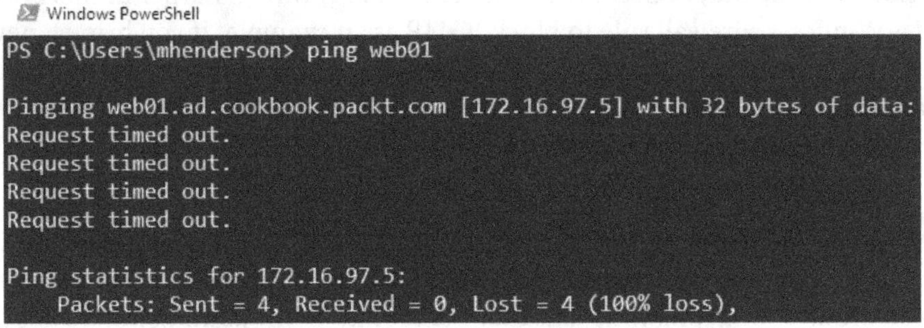

```
Windows PowerShell
PS C:\Users\mhenderson> ping web01

Pinging web01.ad.cookbook.packt.com [172.16.97.5] with 32 bytes of data:
Request timed out.
Request timed out.
Request timed out.
Request timed out.

Ping statistics for 172.16.97.5:
    Packets: Sent = 4, Received = 0, Lost = 4 (100% loss),
```

Figure 3.11 – A failed ping test between two machines

2. Now, let's use the `telnet` command to accomplish some more intuitive digging into whether WEB01 is online and functional. Note that Telnet Client is not available inside the Command Prompt by default; it is a Windows feature that must be installed. On the client machine we are using to test, head into **Control Panel | Programs | Turn Windows features on or off** (or **Server Manager**, if your testing machine is a server) and choose to **Add roles or features**. We want to install the feature called **Telnet Client**. Alternatively, you can install the **Telnet Client** feature with a simple PowerShell command.

   On Windows Server, run the following command:

```
Install-WindowsFeature Telnet-Client
```

   On Windows 10, the command to install Telnet Client is different:

```
dism /online /Enable-Feature /FeatureName:TelnetClient
```

3. Now, we have the `telnet` command available to use inside the Command Prompt. The general format of the command is `telnet <server> <port>`. When you run this command, you are effectively saying 'Let's try to create a connection to this server name, on this particular port.'

4. Even though we cannot ping WEB01, let's try to use `telnet` to open a connection to port `80`, which is the website that we have running. The command for this is as follows:

```
telnet web01 80
```

5. When we press *Enter*, the Command Prompt window changes to a flashing cursor. This is your confirmation that Telnet was able to open a successful connection to port 80 on the WEB01 server. Press *Control + C* to exit the Telnet session:

Figure 3.12 – A blank telnet screen, indicating a successful connection

6. Now, try using the `telnet web01 3389` command. This also results in a flashing cursor, indicating that we successfully connected to port `3389` (RDP) on our WEB01 server. You could have also used an IP address instead of the name WEB01 here.

7. And finally, how about `telnet web01 53`? This one results in a timeout, and we do not see our flashing cursor. So, it appears that port 53 is not responding on the WEB01 server, which makes sense because port `53` is commonly used by DNS, and this is a web server, not a DNS server. If we were to query one of our Domain Controllers that is also running DNS, we would be able to make a successful telnet connection to port `53` to one of those.

> **Tip**
> Telnet queries work with TCP traffic, which covers most services that you will be polling for. Telnet does not have a connector for UDP ports.

I don't blame you if you found that all a little bit confusing – it's OK. A blank screen indicates a valid connection? Strange, but true! However, PowerShell has a command that provides us with some more human-readable output. Let's try those tests again, but this time using PowerShell:

1. To replace our first test, which was checking for an active web server, run the following command. Notice that you do not need to remember which port HTTP runs on, as this command has a short list of commonly tested ports to choose from if you can't remember:

```
Test-NetConnection web01 -CommonTCPPort HTTP
```

You should be presented with a short report that indicates whether the test was successful:

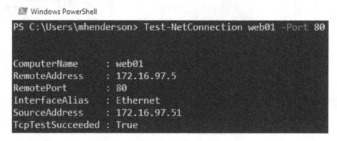

Figure 3.13 – Test-NetConnection showing a successful connection

2. Next, let's reproduce our test of the RDP server. You should see a similar outcome:

```
Test-NetConnection web01 -CommonTCPPort RDP
```

3. And finally, let's test a non-common port, such as 53 for DNS, as in our previous examples. This time, we won't use CommonPort; we will use a specific port:

```
Test-NetConnection web01 -Port 53
```

You will receive the following output:

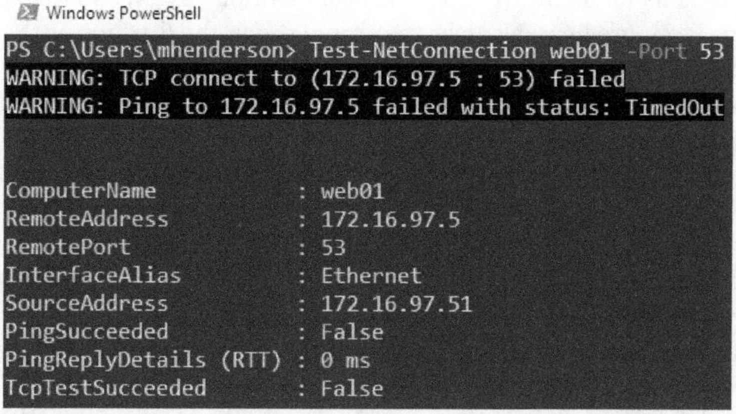

Figure 3.14 – A failed Test-NetConnection command

How it works...

Telnet and its partner, `Test-NetConnection`, are simple but powerful commands that can be run to query against ports and services on your servers. When trying to determine whether a service is available, or when trying to troubleshoot some form of network connectivity problem, it is a much more reliable tool than using a simple `ping` request. If you have been thinking about building a script that programmatically reaches out and checks against servers to report whether they are online or offline, consider using `Test-NetConnection` rather than `ping` so that you can query the individual service that the system is providing by using its particular port number.

Using the pathping command to trace network traffic

When building or troubleshooting a network connection, it is often very beneficial to be able to watch the path that your packets take as they make their way from source to destination. Or perhaps they never make it to the destination, and you want to figure out how far they travel before stopping so that you can focus your work efforts in that area.

One command that has been used by network admins for years is traceroute (`tracert`), but the output contains some information that is often unnecessary, and the output is missing one large key ingredient. Namely, traceroute shows the first hop as the first router that you traverse and does not show you what physical NIC the packets are flowing out of. Granted, many times, you only have one NIC, so this is obvious information. But what if you are working with a multi-homed server and you are simply checking to make sure packets for a destination are flowing out the correct NIC? What if we just want to double-check that some route statements we added are working properly? Cue `pathping`. This command has been around for a long time but is virtually unknown. It shows the same information that `tracert` does, except it saves the information about the time between hops and some other details until the end of the output. This allows you to focus on the physical hops themselves in a clear, concise manner. More importantly, it shows you our key ingredient right away – the NIC that your packets are flowing out of! Once I discovered this, I left `tracert` behind and have never looked back. `pathping` is the way to go.

Getting ready

There's not much to get ready for this recipe. All we need is a server with a network connection and a Command Prompt window. `pathping` is a command that is already available to any Windows Server; we just need to start using it.

How to do it...

The following two steps get you started with `pathping`:

1. Open a prompt on your server.

2. Type `pathping <servername or IP>`. Your output will be as follows:

```
 Windows PowerShell

PS C:\Users\mhenderson> pathping dc01

Tracing route to DC01.ad.cookbook.packt.com [172.16.97.2]
over a maximum of 30 hops:
  0  Cookbook-Win10.ad.cookbook.packt.com [172.16.97.51]
  1  DC01 [172.16.97.2]

Computing statistics for 25 seconds...
            Source to Here   This Node/Link
Hop  RTT    Lost/Sent = Pct  Lost/Sent = Pct  Address
  0                                            Cookbook-Win10.ad.cookbook.packt.com [172.16.97.51]
                              0/ 100 =  0%   |
  1   0ms     0/ 100 =  0%    0/ 100 =  0%  DC01 [172.16.97.2]

Trace complete.
```

Figure 3.15 – The output of using the pathping command

How it works...

`pathping` is a networking tool that allows you to watch the path that your packets are taking as they make their way to the destination. Like traceroute, it is much less commonly known but can give a better layout of the same data. It is a command that should be added to your regular toolbox and vocabulary, right alongside `ping` and `telnet`. There is no PowerShell equivalent of this tool yet.

Setting up NIC Teaming

Teaming your network cards basically means installing two NICs onto the same server, plugging them both into the same network, and joining them together in a *team*. This gives you NIC redundancy in case of a failure, and redundancy is always a great thing! Sounds simple, right? Well, with Windows Server 2019, it actually is. This seemingly easy task has been challenging to put into practice with previous versions of the operating system, but with 2019, we can do this properly from a single interface and actually count on it to work as we expect it to.

Getting ready

We are going to set up a NIC team on a Windows Server 2019 machine. There are two NICs installed on this server, neither of which have yet been configured.

How to do it...

With the following steps, we can start teaming up:

1. Open **Server Manager** and from the left-hand pane, go ahead and click on **Local Server**.

2. Near the middle of the screen, you will see a section marked **NIC Teaming**. Go ahead and click on the word **Disabled** in order to launch the **NIC Teaming** screen, as follows:

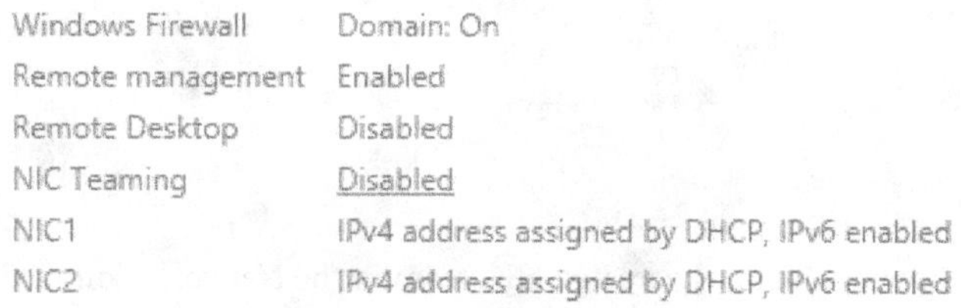

Windows Firewall	Domain: On
Remote management	Enabled
Remote Desktop	Disabled
NIC Teaming	Disabled
NIC1	IPv4 address assigned by DHCP, IPv6 enabled
NIC2	IPv4 address assigned by DHCP, IPv6 enabled

Figure 3.16 – Server Manager showing the NIC Teaming option

3. Down in the **TEAMS** section, drop down the **TASKS** menu and click on **New Team**:

Figure 3.17 – The New Team option in the NIC Teaming window

4. Define a name for your new team and choose the two NICs that you want to be a part of it:

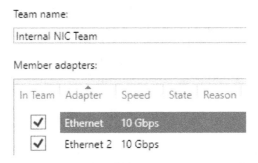

Figure 3.18 – Adding two new NICs to a NIC team

5. That's it! NIC1 and NIC2 are now successfully joined together in a team and will work in tandem to make sure you are still connected in the event of a failure.

6. If you make your way to the regular **Network Connections** screen, where you define IP address information, you will see that you now have a new item listed beneath your physical network cards. This new item is the place where you will go to define the IP address information that you want the server to use:

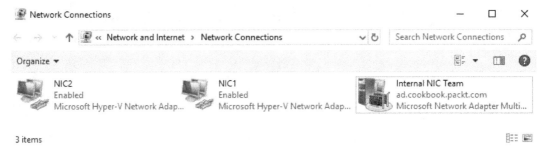

Figure 3.19 – Showing the newly created NIC team in the Network Connections panel

> **Tip**
> You can create more than one team on a server! When setting up a multi-homed server with two network connections, you could easily make use of four NICs and create two teams, each containing two physical network cards.

How it works...

Creating NIC teams is a pretty easy process that you should practice as time permits. This option for redundancy has never been very popular, partly because it used to require the input of the network administrators to configure switch settings as well. Now that we have Windows Server 2019 available to us, and the process to configure it is so straightforward, I fully expect that NIC Teaming will become a standard procedure for administrators as they build every new server.

Renaming and domain joining

Every server that you build will need a hostname, and most likely will need to be joined to your domain. We are all likely familiar with doing these things with the mouse using system properties, but have you ever thought of using a command interface to do these tasks quickly? Let's work together to discover how PowerShell can, once again, help make these necessary tasks more efficient.

Getting ready

We have just finished turning on a new Windows Server 2019 machine. Immediately following the mini-setup wizard in order to get logged into Windows, let's use PowerShell to set our hostname and join the system to our domain.

How to do it...

Follow these steps to rename and domain join this new server with PowerShell:

1. Open a PowerShell session as an administrator.

2. In order to rename our new server WEB02, input the following command. Using the -Restart flag will ensure that our server reboots following the name change:

```
Rename-Computer -NewName WEB02 -Restart
```

You will receive the following output:

Figure 3.20 – The Rename-Computer command

3. That's it for renaming! Now that our WEB2 server has rebooted, open PowerShell again and use the `Add-Computer` command in order to join it to our domain:

```
Add-Computer -DomainName ad.cookbook.packt.com
-Credential cookbook\Administrator -Restart
```

4. Since we specified an account to use as credentials when joining the domain, we are prompted to supply the password. As soon as you enter the password, the server will be joined to the domain and will immediately restart to complete the process:

Figure 3.21 – A credential request prompt

5. If you wanted to rename your computer and join it to the domain in a single step instead of rebooting in between, you can do that with the following command:

```
Add-Computer -NewName web02 -DomainName ad.cookbook.
packt.com -Credential cookbook\Administrator
```

6. Following the reboot, in system properties, you will be able to see that our server is now appropriately named and domain joined:

Computer name, domain, and workgroup settings

Computer name: web02

Full computer name: web02.ad.cookbook.packt.com

Computer description:

Domain: ad.cookbook.packt.com

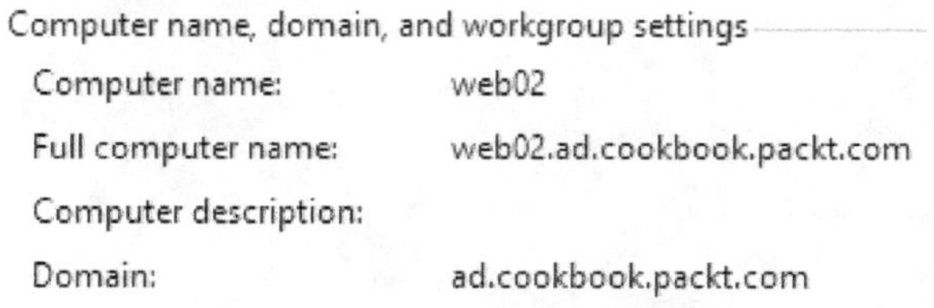

Figure 3.22 – System properties showing the renamed and domain joined server

How it works...

Through a couple of quick PowerShell cmdlets, we can rename computers and join them to our domain. In fact, these functions are even possible without ever logging into the console of the server. There are parameters that can be added to these cmdlets that allow you to run them remotely. For example, you could run the PowerShell commands from a local desktop computer, specifying that you want to run them against the remote server's IP address or name. By performing the functions this way, you never even have to log into the server itself in order to name and join it. See the links in the following section for additional information on these parameters.

See also

Take a look at the following links for even more detailed information about the Rename-Computer and Add-Computer cmdlets that we used in this recipe:

- http://technet.microsoft.com/en-us/library/hh849792.aspx
- http://technet.microsoft.com/en-us/library/hh849798.aspx

4
Working with Certificates

Understanding certificates used to be something that many people avoided. For many facets of IT, you can avoid dealing with them. They were for the networking team, not anybody doing development or desktop support. However, times have changed, and a solid understanding of the common certificate types is quickly becoming an ability that anyone in support should possess. More and more, security has become focused on certificates and with the exponential increase in the amount of applications that are served via the web, understanding the certificates that protect these services is more important than ever.

Almost anyone who has set up a website has dealt with SSL certificates from a public **Certification Authority (CA)**, but did you know that you can be your own CA? That you can issue certificates to the machines in your network, right from your own CA server? Follow along as we explore some of the capabilities of Windows Server 2019 while running as a CA server in our network.

Together, we are going to build a **public key infrastructure (PKI)** environment inside our network and use it for some common certificate issuing tasks. By the end of this chapter, you should be comfortable with creating a PKI in your own environment, which will prepare you for any requirements you may encounter when working with certificate-based technologies.

This chapter will cover the following recipes:

- Setting up the first Certification Authority server in a network
- Building a subordinate Certification Authority server
- Creating a certificate template to prepare for issuing machine certificates to your clients
- Publishing a certificate template to allow enrolment
- Using MMC to request a new certificate
- Using the web interface to request a new certificate
- Using PowerShell to request a new certificate
- Configuring Autoenrollment to issue certificates to all domain-joined systems
- Renewing your root certificate
- Revoking a certificate

> **Important Note**
>
> You may have seen the acronyms **Secure Socket Layer (SSL)** and **Transport Layer Security (TLS)** used before and wondered what the difference is. In practice, these are two names for the same thing, and they both use certificates (the proper name for certificates by the way is X.509, but nobody uses that either). After the SSL v3 protocol was released, it was followed by the TLS v1 protocol. The current correct name is TLS, but a lot of people are unfamiliar with this term. So, for this book, we're going to use the phrase SSL, but know that this also means TLS.

Setting up the first Certification Authority server in a network

The first hurdle to overcome when you want to start certificate work is putting the server into place. There are many valid questions to be answered. Do I need a dedicated server for this task? Can I co-locate this role on an existing server? Do I need to install an Enterprise or standalone CA? I've heard the term offline root, but what does that mean? Let's start with the basics and assume that you need to build the first CA server in your environment.

In an AD domain network, the most useful CA servers are of the Enterprise variety. Enterprise CA servers integrate with AD, making them visible to machines in the network and automatically trusted by computers that you join to your domain. There are differing opinions on the matter of best practices when setting up a series of CA servers. For example, there is a good test lab guide (referenced at the end of this recipe) that have been published by Microsoft that walks you through setting up a standalone Root CA, a subordinate Enterprise CA, and then taking the standalone root offline.

An advantage of this is that certificates are issued from the subordinate, not directly from the root. If certificate keys are somehow compromised in the environment, the root CA is completely offline and unavailable so that it cannot be compromised. In this situation, you could wipe out the subordinate and the certificates it has published . Then, you can bring up the offline root, build out a new subordinate, and be back in business, publishing certificates without having to regenerate a new root CA server.

Given the preceding best practice, or as defined by some anyway, it is surprising that I quite rarely see offline root CAs in the field. Almost never, in fact. And in some of the cases where I have, the existence of an offline root CA has caused problems. Just as an example, when deploying a DirectAccess infrastructure with **one-time-password (OTP)** capabilities in a customer environment, it was discovered that in order to make the OTP work correctly, the offline root CA had to be brought back online.

This wasn't in the best interests of the way the PKI had been established. Due to this, we had to implement a second certificate environment as a standalone root with two intermediaries. This enabled us to maintain an online root CA for the purpose of the OTP certificates. This caused big delays in the project as we had to build three new servers just to get the certificates published in the correct way. This created a more complex certificate infrastructure to support afterward.

If the preceding description confused you, good – it's kind of a messy setup. If the company had instead been running on the online root CA server in the first place, none of this extra work would have been necessary. I'm not advocating that an Enterprise root CA that remains online all the time is the best way to do certificates. However, it will cause you the fewest problems. In fact, many companies operate their production CA environments in exactly this way.

Another field observation is that most small- or medium-sized companies do not take the offline root CA approach. In fact, I find that many small businesses need to co-host servers in order to save resources. This includes them having their CA role installed onto a server that is also performing some other task. Many times, the CA role is installed on a Domain Controller. While at the surface level this appears to make sense, because the Enterprise CA services are so tightly integrated with AD, this is actually a bad idea. Microsoft recommends that you never co-host the CA role on a Domain Controller, so stay away from that scenario if you can. That being said, I have seen dozens of companies that do exactly this and have never had a problem with it, so I suppose it's just your call on how closely you want to adhere to the *Microsoft way*. Make sure that you do some reading by taking a look at the links provided at the end of this recipe, as they should provide you with information that will help you make the right decisions about which certificate server setup is best suited for your network.

Getting ready

I have created a new Windows Server 2019 named CA01. We are going to do all our configuration from a Windows 10 computer with all the RSAT tools installed so that we can use some of the skills we learned in previous chapters for remote management. If you want to, you can create your CA as a Windows Server Core (more on this in *Chapter 12, Server Core*).

How to do it...

To install Active Directory Certificate Services onto your server, use the following set of instructions:

1. On your Windows 10 machine with RSAT installed, open **Server Manager**. Make sure your new CA server is in your server list and click the **Add roles and features** link.

2. Walk through the steps provided, choosing the default settings. When you come to the **Select Destination Server** screen, make sure you choose your CA server:

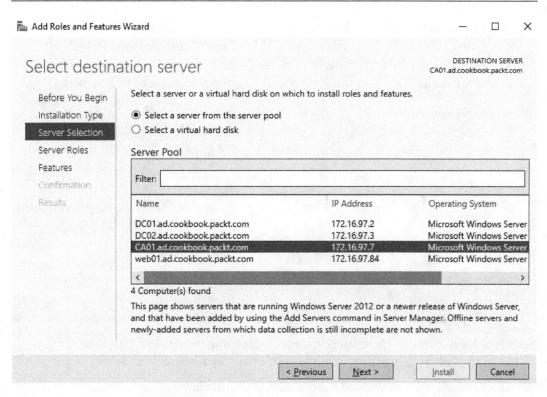

Figure 4.1 – The Select destination server screen and selecting the CA server

3. On the **Server Roles** screen, select **Active Directory Certificate Services**.

4. Click **Next** a couple of times until you come to the **Role Services** screen. Here, you will see a few different options that can be used on your CA server.

5. Since we would like to be able to request certificates from a web interface on the CA, I am going to check the additional box for **Certification Authority Web Enrollment**. After selecting this box, you will receive an additional pop-up box, asking you to add features. Make sure you allow those features to be installed:

Figure 4.2 – Selecting the Certification Authority Web Enrollment role

6. Click **Next** through the remaining screens until you reach the last page, where you need to click on the **Install** button to start installing the role.

7. Once completed, you will see a link inside your installation summary screen that says **Configure Active Directory Certificate Services on the destination server**. You can click either on this link or on the Server Manager yellow exclamation mark near the top of the Server Manager screen in order to continue configuring the CA role.

8. On the first configuration screen, the wizard may auto-insert the username of the currently logged-in user. If it doesn't, click **Change** and enter your credentials. As stated in the text on that screen, make sure the user you are logged in as has Enterprise Admin rights on the domain, as we are planning to set this CA server up as an Enterprise root CA.

> **Tip**
> You can click on **More about AD CS Server Roles** at any time to read more information about the different types of CA roles and features available. For the purposes of this recipe, we will not discuss them all, but rather focus on creating our Enterprise root CA.

9. To get certificate services rolling on our server, go ahead and check the top two options used to configure **Certification Authority** and **Certification Authority Web Enrollment**:

Figure 4.3 – Selecting the roles to configure for the CA server

10. Choose **Enterprise CA**.

11. Choose **Root CA**; because this is our first CA server, we need to implement a root before we can think about a subordinate.

12. Choose **Create a new private key**.

13. On the **Cryptography** screen, you can choose the kind of cryptography options you will provide on your CA server. Typically, the default options will work best if you're unsure of these settings. Just make sure that the **Key length** field is set to **2048** as a minimum. This is the industry standard for the minimum key length. Similarly, hash standards have changed recently to SHA256, so you should no longer be using SHA1 for any of your certificates:

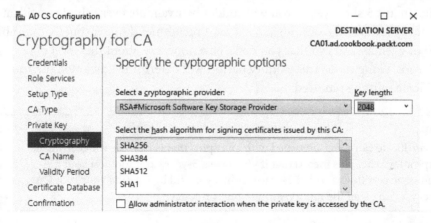

Figure 4.4 – CA cryptography options for the new private key

14. If desired, you may modify the **Common name for this CA** option. Keep in mind that this does not have to match the hostname of the server in any way and that it can never be changed. It is usually a good idea to not use the server name in this field as you may move the CA role to a different server many years down the line and then have a mismatched certificate/server name. This name will show up inside Active Directory, as well as inside the certificates that you issue from this CA. Typically, I find that admins leave the **Distinguished name suffix** field alone:

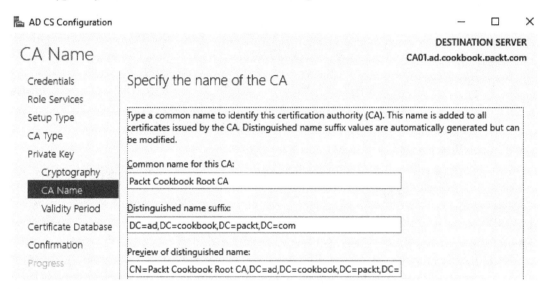

Figure 4.5 – The CA common name has been changed to a more generic name

15. Change the **Validity Period** section of your root certificate if desired. Often, admins blow through this screen and leave it set at the default 5 years, but that means in just 5 short years, you will suddenly invalidate every single certificate that you have ever issued from this CA server. I recommend increasing that number to 10 or even 20 years so that you don't have to worry about this level of certificate expiry for a long time. This validity period will determine how often the root certificate must be renewed.

> **Tip**
> A certificate can never be issued with an expiry that is past the root certificate expiration date. This means that if you have a 5-year expiration on your CA and issue certificates with a 2-year validity, you will be rotating your root CA every 3 years – all the more reason to make it longer.

16. Continue through the remaining screens, leaving the default options set in place. When the wizard has finished, your CA server will be live:

Figure 4.6 – A successful AD CA configuration

That was a fairly complex process, and not one that you're going to repeat very often. Because of this, you may not want to bother going through this process via PowerShell as the GUI is honestly no more difficult. However, the relevant documentation, should you wish to explore this is, can be found in the *See also* section of this recipe.

How it works...

In this recipe, we installed our first CA server in our network. As we discussed, you will want to make sure you read over some of the following links to help determine how many CAs you require and where they should be installed. This is one of those answers that can be different for every organization, so I cannot make any blanket statements here that will apply for everyone.

You may decide that your primary root CA should be standalone rather than Enterprise, and that is fine if it fits your needs. We also installed the web services piece of the role onto our root CA because we plan to use this in upcoming recipes to issue certificates. If you are building an environment with multiple CA servers, you might determine that your root authority doesn't need the web interface. Maybe only a subordinate CA will do that job for you. There are numerous ways that our design could play out, but through this recipe, I hope that enough information has been provided so that you are comfortable with the actual process once those decisions have been made.

There are a couple of items that we did not cover in this recipe that should be pointed out. Following the preceding steps will get you a CA server up and running that is ready to issue certificates. The remainder of the recipes in this chapter reflect CAs that have been built in the same way they've been built here. However, there are additional steps that can be taken in order to further customize your CA settings if you have the need. If you plan to issue SSL certificate for websites, especially if you plan to install these certificates on web servers that are facing the internet, you need to familiarize yourself with the **Certificate Revocation List** (**CRL**).

Whenever a certificate is accessed, the client computer checks in with the CRL in order to make sure the certificate is still valid. If the certificate is not valid or is fraudulent in some way, the CRL check will identify that compromise and disallow the connection. Particularly when publishing websites to the internet that use certificates issued by your internal PKI, you will need to plan when to publish your CRL so that external client computers can access it in a clean, secure fashion. Here is a great link to get you started with CRL: `https://docs.microsoft.com/en-us/previous-versions/windows/it-pro/windows-server-2008-R2-and-2008/cc771079(v=ws.11)`.

There's more...

The `CAPolicy.inf` file can be populated with various customization settings for your CA server. These include the following:

- The validity period of your root certificate

- Information about your CRL

- Whether you want the default certificate templates to be loaded during CA role installation

If any of these settings are of interest to you, do the following:

1. Simply create a `CAPolicy.inf` file with the appropriate configurations.

2. Place it inside `C:\Windows` on your CA server prior to role installation.

The role installation wizard will then utilize the settings inside this file during role installation and incorporate your customizations. If you do not use one of these files, that is fine; the role will be installed with some default settings in place, just like we did in this recipe. But if you are interested in changing some of them, check out this link for more detailed information on the `CAPolicy.inf` file: `https://docs.microsoft.com/en-us/previous-versions/windows/it-pro/windows-server-2012-R2-and-2012/jj125373(v=ws.11)`.

Neither of these options, that is, tweaking the CRL or using a `CAPolicy.inf` file, are required in order to get a certificate environment up and running. Thus, they are not included in the step-by-step configuration of the recipe itself. But I am always a fan of having all knowledge available on a particular subject, so I strongly encourage you to read over the additional links that have been provided so that you round out your understanding of possible functionality.

See also

To install and configure the CA via PowerShell, you will need to read up on the `ADCSDeployment` module:

- `https://docs.microsoft.com/en-us/powershell/module/adcsdeployment/?view=win10-ps`

Here are some links that make for good additional reading on this subject. In order to make an informed decision about what sequence of CA servers is right for your environment, I encourage you to do as much reading on the subject as possible before proceeding in the production network:

- `https://docs.microsoft.com/en-us/previous-versions/windows/it-pro/windows-server-2012-R2-and-2012/dn786443(v=ws.11)`

- `https://docs.microsoft.com/en-us/previous-versions/windows/it-pro/windows-server-2012-r2-and-2012/dn786436(v%3Dws.11)`

- `https://docs.microsoft.com/en-us/previous-versions/windows/it-pro/windows-server-2012-r2-and-2012/hh831348(v%3Dws.11)`

Building a subordinate Certification Authority server

Subordinate CAs aren't built for redundancy, just like many other kinds of servers. They are meant for performing specific tasks that you may want to process on a subordinate CA rather than a root CA. If you issue a lot of certificates or different kinds of certificates, you may want to differentiate between CA servers when issuing. Perhaps you want machine certificates that are used for IPsec to be issued from IPSEC-CA, but the SSL website certificates that you issue should show as being issued from WEB-CA. Rather than building out two independent root CAs that both have top-level rights, you should consider creating a single root CA, maybe called ROOT-CA, and placing these two CA servers in a subordinate role under the root CA in the chain. This can also be useful for geographically dispersed networks that have subordinate CA servers dedicated to assigning certificates for different offices or regions.

As we discussed in the previous recipe, there are certainly some best practice standards that would suggest you should only utilize subordinate CAs to accomplish your certificate issuance. I don't always find that this is feasible for companies, particularly smaller ones, but it is a good idea if you can. With subordinate CA servers online, you have the option of taking your root CA offline and using the subordinates to issue all your certificates.

Getting ready

We are inside a domain network and have a single Enterprise root CA online and running. We now require an additional server that will be joined to the CA environment as a new subordinate CA.

How to do it...

To implement our new subordinate CA server, the process will be very similar to the *Setting up the first Certification Authority server in a network* recipe. However, there are a few key differences, and that is where we will focus. Some of the specific steps may be shortened here; please refer to the previous recipe for more detailed information on the specific steps and settings with regards to installing the role:

1. Make sure our subordinate CA has been added to Server Manager on our Windows 10 machine and then follow the steps provided to add the Active Directory Certificate Services role to this server.

2. When we implemented our root CA server, we chose to install the necessary web services. This will enable us to request and issue certificates from a browser inside our network. You have the option of installing these web services on the new subordinate CA, which you would do if you planned on using an offline root CA. For our situation, we are not going to do this. We will stick with only **Certification Authority** in our list of available role services:

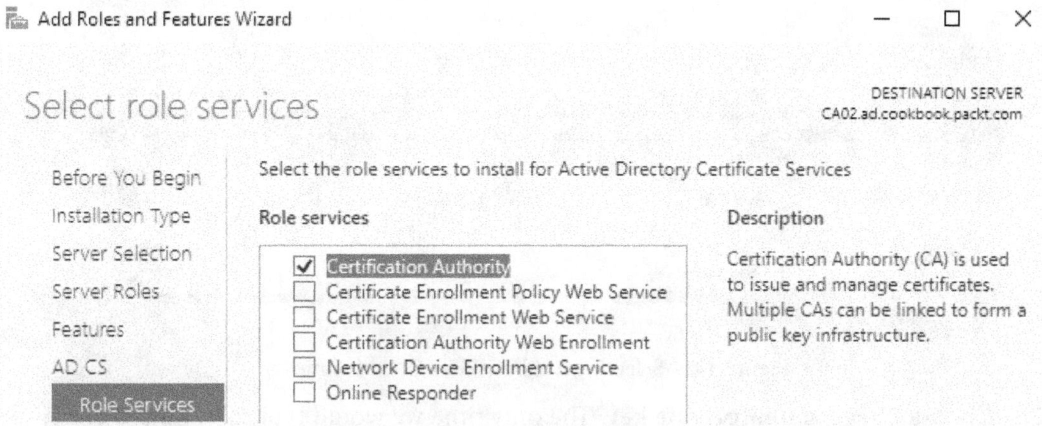

Figure 4.7 – Only selecting the Certification Authority role

3. After the role has finished installing, go ahead and click on your link for **Configure Active Directory Certificate Services on the destination server**.

4. Input the credentials as needed and choose the only option we have in the list to configure, **Certificate Authority**.

5. Here is where we start to detour from the path that we took with our root CA creation. We are still choosing to set up an **Enterprise CA** because we still want it to be domain integrated.

6. However, instead of choosing to install a new root CA, we are going to choose the option for **Subordinate CA**. In fact, it was already chosen for us as the default because it recognizes that a root CA already exists in the network. We could install another root CA, but that is not the purpose of this recipe:

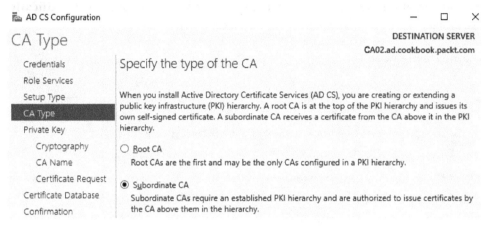

Figure 4.8 – Selecting a subordinate CA this time

7. Choose **Create a new private key**. The only time we would typically want to use an existing private key is when rebuilding a CA server.

8. Choose your cryptography settings. These are typically going to be the same as the ones you configured on the root CA.

9. Name your new subordinate CA appropriately. If you have a specific function in mind for this CA, it will be helpful to you to, in the future, name it accordingly. For example, I intend to use this subordinate CA to issue all the SSL certificates that I will need for internal web pages, so I have included *Web* in the name:

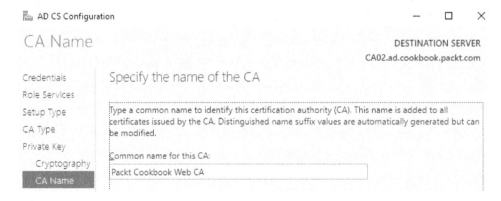

Figure 4.9 – As in the previous CA, give your CA a better name than default

10. Now, we come to a new screen. We need to acquire a certificate from our parent CA server in order to issue certificates from this new one. Choose the option for **Send a certificate request to a parent CA** and use the **Select...** button to choose your root CA:

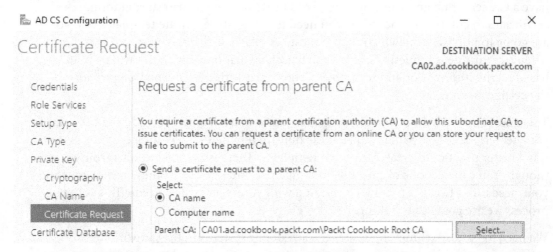

Figure 4.10 – Selecting the root CA to receive our subordinate CA certificate from

11. On the following screen, adjust the location of the certificate database files if required; otherwise, click **Next** and then **Configure**.

How it works...

Installing a subordinate CA server in a network is very similar to when we implemented our first root CA server. In our case, we simplified the installation by not having the requirement for the web services to run on the subordinate as we will do all those requests from the root CA.

We now have a root CA running and a subordinate CA running under it. For our installation, we are going to leave both online and running as we intend to issue certificates from both. We could easily run through this same process again with another new server in order to create another subordinate CA, maybe to issue a different kind of certificate or for a different division of the company to utilize.

See also

- The *Setting up the first Certification Authority server in a network* recipe

Creating a certificate template to prepare for issuing machine certificates to your clients

This recipe is the first hurdle that many new certificate admins bump into. You may have a CA server up and running, but what's next? Before you can start granting certificates to computers and users, you need to establish certificate templates that you are going to publish. You will configure these templates with particular settings, and when a certificate is requested against the template, that new certificate will be built based on the information in the template, combined with the information provided by the certificate requestor.

There are some built-in certificate templates that preinstall when you add the CA role to your server. Some companies utilize these built-in templates for issuing certificates, but it is a better practice to create your own templates. There is no need to start from scratch, though. You can take one of the built-in templates, find one that comes close to meeting your needs, and tweak it to do your bidding with your certificate's needs. This is the process we are going to be taking.

We need to issue machine certificates to each of our systems in the network to authenticate some IPsec tunnels. There are a few criteria we need to meet when it comes to these certificates, and the built-in Computer template comes close to checking all the options that we need. So, we will take that template, copy it, and modify it so that it meets our requirements.

Getting ready

This is a Server 2019 domain environment with a new CA server running in it. We will utilize the CA RSAT console on a Windows 10 machine to accomplish this recipe. The new template that we'll create will be automatically replicated with other CA servers in the domain.

How to do it...

The following steps will help you build a new certificate template:

1. Launch the **Certification Authority** management console from inside Server Manager or from the **Start** menu.

2. If you receive the error message stating **1060 ERROR_SERVICE_DOES_NOT_ EXIST**, that's OK – we just need to add the CA server. Right-click **Certification Authority (local)** and choose **Retarget Certification Authority....** Select **Another Computer** and enter the server name of your root CA. It may take a minute to connect:

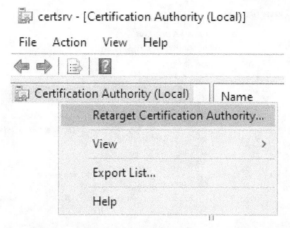

Figure 4.11 – Retarget Certification Authority

3. Expand the name of your CA and click on **Certificate Templates**. You will see a list of the built-in templates available to us.

4. Right-click on **Certificate** and choose **Manage**:

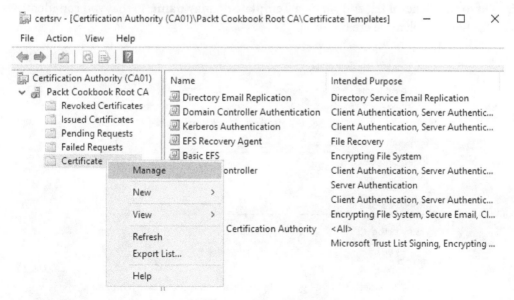

Figure 4.12 – Managing certificate templates on your root CA

5. Right-click on the **Computer** template and choose **Duplicate Template**:

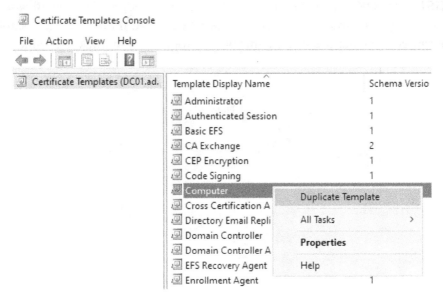

Figure 4.13 – Duplicating the Computer template

6. Now, we adjust the options within the certificate template. Any attributes that your certificates must have, you set here in the template properties. As an example, let's configure a few items that our new IPsec certificates must contain to be valid.

7. Go to the **General** tab and set up a **Template display name** so that you can identify this new template we are building:

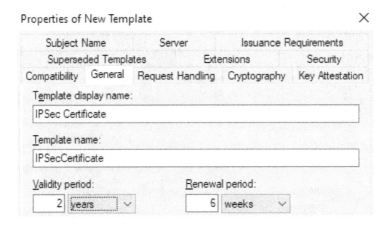

Figure 4.14 – Setting some general properties on a certificate template

8. On the same tab, adjust the field to 2 years.

9. Browse to and select the **Subject Name** tab and set **Common name** in the **Subject name format** field. This will cause the subject name of the certificate to reflect the hostname of the computer that is requesting the certificate. Using the DNS name as the alternate subject name is another requirement that we have been given for our new certificates. You can see it checked in the following screenshot. Since we used the built-in Computer template as our starting point, this checkbox, as well as other requirements that we needed to cover, were already taken care of for us:

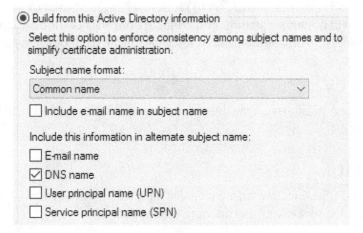

Figure 4.15 – The Subject Name tab

10. Click **OK**. There is now a brand-new certificate template in the list called `IPsec Certificate` (or whatever name you gave to yours).

How it works...

When installing any new technology that requires certificates to be issued, your first stop should be the certificate templates on your CA server. You need to make sure that you have a template configured with the appropriate settings and switches that you need in your new certificates. By duplicating one of the built-in templates that came with our CA server, we were able to build a new template without having to configure every single option from the ground up.

Publishing a certificate template to allow enrolment

One of the most common certificate troubleshooting issues that's encountered is figuring out why a particular certificate template is not available when the user or computer tries to request a certificate. Having created a new certificate template does not necessarily mean that you are ready to start issuing certificates based on that template. We also need to publish our new template so that the CA server knows that it is ready to publish to computers and users. There is also a security section of the template properties, where you need to define who or what has access to request certificates based on that template. In this recipe, we will find those settings and configure our new certificate template so that any domain-joined workstation can request a certificate from our new template.

Getting ready

We are going to use a Windows 10 machine to manage a Windows Server 2019 Certificate Authority.

How to do it...

In order to issue certificates based on a particular template, we need to take some steps to publish and adjust the security properties of that template:

1. Launch the **Certification Authority** management console from inside Server Manager or from the **Start** menu.

2. If you receive an error message stating **1060 ERROR_SERVICE_DOES_NOT_ EXIST**, that's OK – we just need to add the CA server. Right-click **Certification Authority (local)** and **choose Retarget Certification Authority....** Select **Another Computer** and enter the server name of your root CA. It may take a minute to connect.

3. Expand the name of your CA server in the left-hand tree.

4. Right-click on **Certificate Templates** and navigate to **New | Certificate Template to Issue**:

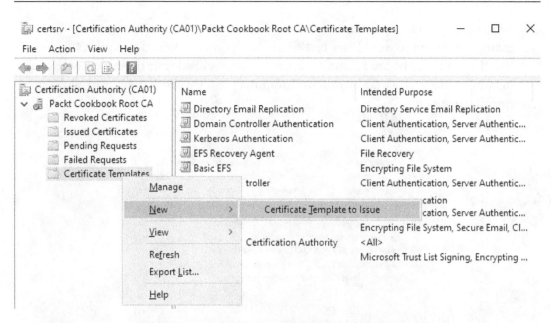

Figure 4.16 – Adding a new certificate template to Issue

5.   Select your new template from the list and click on **OK**.

The CA is now able to issue this certificate, but we have not configured any permissions or rules about who or what can use this certificate. So, let's continue and define some rules.

6.   Now, right-click on **Certificate Templates** and choose **Manage**.

7.   Find the template that you want to modify. For our recipe, we are modifying the new template called `IPsec Certificate`.

8.   Right-click on the template and choose **Properties**.

9.   Browse to the **Security** tab.

10. Now, we need to set up permissions according to our requirements. For our example, we want to issue IPsec certificates to all domain-joined computers so that they can later be used during IPsec negotiations inside our network. Therefore, in our permissions, we add **Domain Computers** and we check the box to allow **Enroll** permissions:

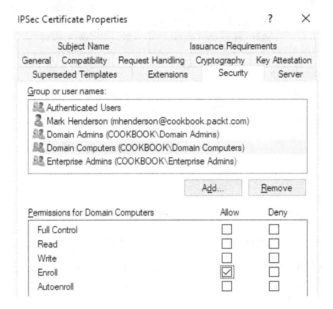

Figure 4.17 – Configuring the Enroll permissions for Domain Computers for a certificate template

How it works...

A new certificate template doesn't do us any good without us fulfilling a couple of extra steps to publish that template. We need to walk through the process of specifying our new template to be issued, which is a simple option to accomplish but one that isn't immediately obvious inside the CA management console. Also, we need to make sure that the permissions we have set on our certificate template line up with the purpose that our certificate is intended for. If your user accounts are going to be requesting certificates, then you will have to add users or user groups and grant them enroll permissions. If computer accounts are going to be the ones making the requests, then make sure that the appropriate groups are entered in there with enrolling rights as well.

Using MMC to request a new certificate

The most common way that I see administrators' interface with the certificates on their systems is through the MMC snap-in tool. **MMC** is short for **Microsoft Management Console**, and by using MMC, you can administer just about anything in the operating system. Though this is perhaps a greatly underutilized tool, I only generally see it being opened for a few select tasks. Requesting certificates is one of those tasks.

We are going to use the MMC console on a new server that we have in our network. There is a new certificate template that has been created, and we would like to issue one of these certificates to our new web server.

Getting ready

A Server 2019 Enterprise root CA server is online and running in our network. On it, we have configured a new certificate template called IPsec Certificate. The steps have been taken to publish this template so that it may be requested from computers in our network. We are now working from a brand-new web server that is also running Server 2019 and joined to our domain, where we are going to manually request a certificate from the CA server.

How to do it...

Follow these steps to request a new certificate using the MMC console:

1. Open the Command Prompt on our new web server and type mmc. Then, press *Enter*. Alternatively, you can open MMC from the **Start** screen.

2. Now, inside the MMC console, click on the **File** menu, and then on **Add/Remove Snap-in…**.

3. Choose **Certificates** from the list of available snap-ins and click on the **Add** button. This will open a new window with some more choices about the certificates snap-in.

4. First, we need to choose whether we are opening the user certificate repository or the Computer certificate repository. I don't generally see service accounts being used in the field. What you choose here will depend on what type of certificate you are requesting. For our example, we are looking for an IPsec certificate, which needs to go in the Computer container. Choose **Computer account** and click **Finish**:

> This snap-in will always manage certificates for:
>
> ○ My user account
>
> ○ Service account
>
> ◉ Computer account

Figure 4.18 – Selecting the computer account for the certificate manager

5. Leave the next option set to **Local computer** and click **Finish** again. Then, click **OK**.

There are also MSC launchers that can be utilized to bring you into the certificate stores even faster. You may have an entry in your **Start** menu called **Manage Computer Certificates** (although it is not always reliably accessible). Another option is to make use of some direct MSC launches by navigating to **Start | Run** or the Command Prompt and typing in the following commands:

a.CERTMGR.MSC opens user certificates

b.CERTLM.MSC opens computer certificates

Now, back to the certificate management process:

6. Inside the main MMC console, expand **Certificates (Local Computer)** and select the **Personal** folder. You will see that there are currently no certificates installed here.

7. Right-click on the **Personal** folder and navigate to **All Tasks | Request New Certificate…**:

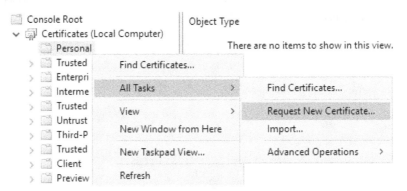

Figure. 4.19 – Selecting the Request New Certificate… option

8. Click **Next**.

9. On the **Select Certificate Enrollment Policy** screen, **Active Directory Enrollment Policy** is automatically selected. Simply click **Next** again to go to the next screen.

10. Now, we can see a list of certificate templates that are available to us. Check the boxes for the certificates that you want to request and click **Enroll**:

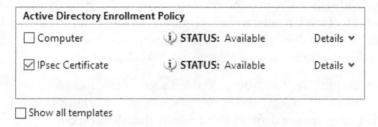

Figure 4.20 – Active Directory Enrollment Policy screen

> **Tip**
> If you are expecting to see a specific template here but it isn't in the list, click on **Show all templates**. This will display a list of all templates on the CA server and explain why it is not currently available. This can help for troubleshooting purposes.

How it works...

Utilizing the MMC console is a quick and easy way to request new certificates to be issued manually. In an Active Directory environment, any certificate template on the CA server that you have permissions to enroll will be visible and easy to enroll. This example displayed the enrollment process for a machine certificate that we are planning to use in the future for IPsec authentication. However, there are many cases where you may want to issue user-level certificates, rather than computer certificates. In those cases, you would want to snap in the user account certificates, where, in our example, we defined computer account certificates.

Using the web interface to request a new certificate

Sometimes, when requesting a new certificate, you may not have access to query certificate services directly by using a tool such as the MMC snap-in. Maybe you need to request a certificate for a non-Windows device by using a **certificate signing request (CSR)** that the device has provided. The CA web interface will allow us to do this. By enabling the web services portion of the CA role, we can turn on a website that runs on our CA server. This website can be accessed from inside the corporate network and could potentially even be published on the internet with a reverse proxy solution.

Because of its age and the fact that Microsoft don't seem particularly interested in maintaining the web interface, most of its functionality only works in Internet Explorer. However, Internet Explorer is a defunct web browser that shouldn't be used any more. As such, most of the functionality of the web interface (including this recipe in previous versions of this book) is no longer accessible. However, the most important function – the ability to request a certificate from a CSR – is still functional.

In this recipe, we'll access the web interface that is now running on the CA server where we installed the web services part of the CA role. We will use this website to request and acquire a certificate from a CSR.

Getting ready

Our Enterprise root CA is a Windows Server 2019 server that has the Active Directory Certificate Services role installed. When we installed and configured the role, we made sure to select the option for the web service so that we could make use of it to request a new certificate. We also need a CSR. Generally, a CSR is provided by a device or service that needs a certificate. For the purposes of this example, I have generated a dummy CSR from `https://csrgenerator.com/`.

How to do it...

We do not have to be logged into the CA server directly to complete this recipe. Here, we are logged into a Windows 10 machine in our environment. From this web server, perform the following steps:

1. Open Internet Explorer and browse to `http://<CAServerName>/CertSrv/`. In our case, it is `http://ca01.ad.cookbook.packt.com/CertSrv/`. You should be asked to log in with a username and password – use your domain username and password to log in:

Welcome

Use this Web site to request a certificate for your Web browser, e-mail client, or other program. By using a certificate, you can verify your identity to people you communicate with over the Web, sign and encrypt messages, and, depending upon the type of certificate you request, perform other security tasks.

You can also use this Web site to download a certificate authority (CA) certificate, certificate chain, or certificate revocation list (CRL), or to view the status of a pending request.

For more information about Active Directory Certificate Services, see Active Directory Certificate Services Documentation.

Select a task:
Request a certificate
View the status of a pending certificate request
Download a CA certificate, certificate chain, or CRL

Figure 4.21 – The default home page of the Windows CA web service

2. Click on **Request a certificate**, and then **advanced certificate request**.

3. For **Base-64-encoded certificate request**, paste your CSR. It should begin with the following:

```
-----BEGIN CERTIFICATE REQUEST-----
```

It should end with the following:

```
-----END CERTIFICATE REQUEST-----
```

4. Under **Certificate Template**, choose **Web Server**. Then, click **Submit**:

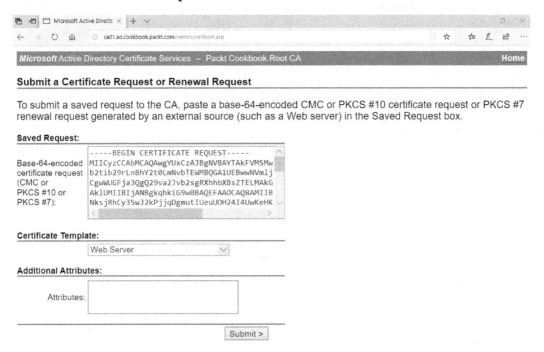

Figure 4.22 – An example CSR being submitted to the Certificate Authority

5. On the resulting page, you will be asked to download your new certificate. The format you want (**DER** or **Base 64**) will depend on the situation. Generally, the base64-encoded certificate is useful in more situations than the DER certificate.

Now, in your downloads folder, you should have a certificate that contains all the details about your CSR. You can determine that it's the certificate you requested by opening the resulting `certnew.cer` file that you just downloaded and looking at the different information tabs. You should see that the **Issued to** option is for your requested domain and that the **Issued by** option comes from the appropriate CA:

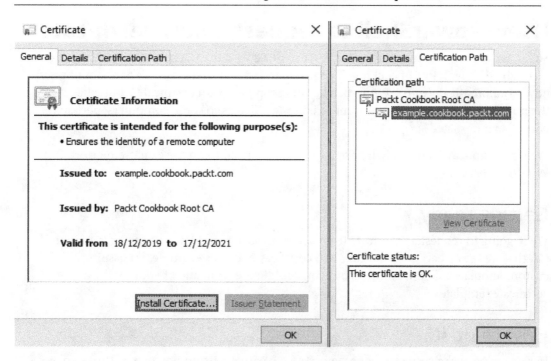

Figure 4.23 – Showing the details of the certificate and that it was issued by our AD CA

How it works...

Running the web service on your CA server can be beneficial because it allows another method of requesting certificates. In this recipe, we were able to quickly open our CA certificate requesting web page and walk through some simple steps. This enabled us to download a new certificate that we are planning to use with our web service.

Because our web server is inside the corporate network, we could have also accomplished this request right from the **Certificates MMC** console. However, if our web server had been in a different building separated by networking equipment and firewalls, this may not have been an option for us. Or if we were trying to acquire a certificate from another machine that didn't have MMC access for one reason or another, this web service is a nice way to accomplish the same task.

Using PowerShell to request a new certificate

So far, we've seen that most of the work we've done with the CA service has been done through GUIs with lots of clicking. This is fine for one-off tasks, and we're about to see how to automatically enroll entire batches of computers with certificates. But what about the middle ground – where you want to issue certificates to some computers, perhaps as part of an automated script?

Well, have no fear – PowerShell has all the tools we need to do the exact same work from Windows servers.

Getting ready

We're going to request a certificate from a Windows Server 2019 web server from our CA that we set up earlier for issuing web certificates. In this example, I'm issuing a custom template called WebECDH, but you could issue from any of your existing certificate templates.

How to do it...

In this recipe, we're going to request a certificate with a custom hostname. This is so we can use it on a custom website that's being deployed.

Let's start the process on the Windows machine that we want to generate the certificate for:

1. Open a PowerShell session as an administrator.

2. Issue the Get-Certificate -Template WebECDH -DnsName exampleservice.cookbook.packt.com -CertStoreLocation cert:\LocalMachine\My command, as follows:

Figure 4.24 – Requesting a certificate via PowerShell

That's it! You should have a certificate in your local certificate store that you can assign to a website:

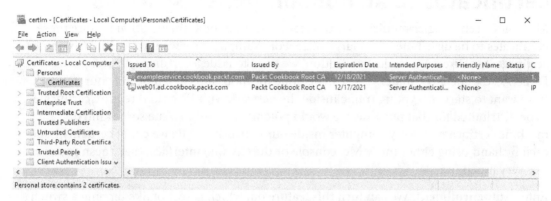

Figure 4.25 – The resulting certificate that we just received

How it works...

PowerShell is, as usual, your friend when it comes to doing simple tasks that are even simpler and easier than clicking through the GUIs. The Get-Certificate command can be embedded into scripts, rolled out in bulk via Invoke-Command, or even used by hand when a single one-off certificate is required.

There are additional arguments you can use with the command for specifying which CA to use (for example, you may wish to get your certificate from a subordinate CA instead). You can also use PowerShell to browse your certificate store if you need to – try this out with the cd cert:\ command.

See also...

- The MSDN documentation for Get-Certificate: https://docs. microsoft.com/en-us/powershell/module/pkiclient/ get-certificate?view=win10-ps

Configuring Autoenrollment to issue certificates to all domain-joined systems

Many new technologies requiring certificates to be used for authentication require those certificates to be distributed on a large scale. For example, if we want to use the Computer certificate for DirectAccess authentication, we need to issue a certificate to every DirectAccess client computer. This can be done for thousands of laptops in your network. If we want to start encrypting traffic inside the network with IPsec and require certificates to be distributed for that purpose, we would potentially need to issue some kind of machine certificate to every computer inside our network. While we could certainly issue each by hand using either the MMC console or the CA web interface, that doesn't sound like very much fun.

Enter **Autoenrollment**. We can turn this feature on, which is sort of like flipping a switch in Active Directory, and in doing so, we can tell AD to issue certificates automatically to the computers – even if we need to get them to every single domain joined the system. Let's work together through this recipe to turn on this option and test it out.

Getting ready

We are working inside a Windows Server 2019-based Active Directory domain. We also have a Server 2019 Enterprise root CA running in this network. The work that we will be accomplishing is a combination of the work we did on the CA server and the work we did inside the Group Policy Management console. This can be done on a Domain Controllers or on a Windows 10 machine with RSAT installed.

How to do it...

To enable Autoenrollment in your domain, follow these instructions:

1. Open the **Certification Authority** management pane. If you are on a remote Windows 10 computer, you will need to also connect to your CA, as we did in previous recipes.

2. Expand the name of your CA, then right-click on **Certificate Templates** and choose **Manage**.

3. Now, choose the certificate template that you want to be set up for Autoenrollment. I am going to use the certificate we created earlier (in *Creating a certificate template to prepare for issuing machine certificates to your clients*) called IPSec Certificate to be issued to every computer in my network. Right-click the template you wish to use and head into **Properties**.

4. Click on the **Security** tab. Here, you need to configure whatever users, computers, or other objects that you want to have Autoenroll permissions to this template. I am going to **Allow** the **Autoenroll** permission for all **Domain Computers** in my network, as shown in the following screenshot:

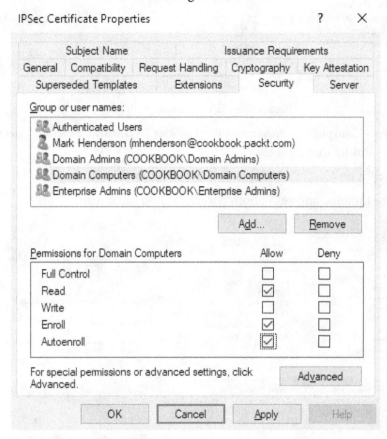

Figure 4.26 – Applying the Autoenroll permission to a certificate template

5. Click **OK**. Now, we need to head over to Group Policy. Open the **Group Policy Management Console** window (if you have been logged onto your CA server directly, you'll need to switch to a Domain Controllers).

6. I have created a new GPO for this task called **Certificate Autoenrollment Policy**. This new GPO is linked to the top of my domain so that it applies to all the machines that are joined to the domain. If you didn't need your policy to be so broad, you could, of course, filter down the access here by limiting the link or filtering associated with your GPO. We will go through Group Policies in more detail in *Chapter 10, Group Policy*.

7. Right-click on **Certificate Autoenrollment Policy GPO** and choose **Edit…**:

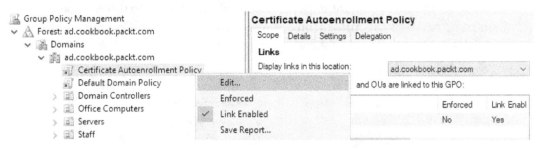

Figure 4.27– Editing Group Policy

8. Navigate to **Computer Configuration | Policies | Windows Settings | Security Settings | Public Key Policies**.

9. Double-click on **Certificate Services Client - Auto-Enrollment**.

10. Set this to **Enabled** and select both checkboxes on the screen:

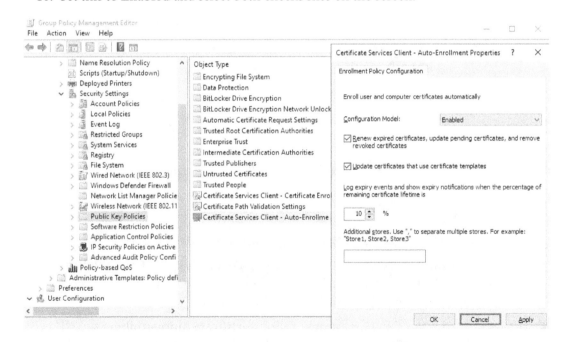

Figure 4.28 – Configuring autoenrollment in the GPO

11. As soon as you click **OK**, this new GPO will start taking effect. Machines will check in with Group Policy and realize they need these new settings from the GPO. Upon putting this new option into place, the computers will then check in with the CA server and ask it for a copy of any certificate for which it has autoenroll permissions. Since we configured all Domain Computers to have autoenroll permission to the IPSec Certificate template, our workstations and servers should immediately start receiving a copy of this new certificate.

How it works...

We make use of Group Policy in order to flip our autoenrollment on switch and immediately start the autoenrollment of certificates to our domain-joined systems. There are a couple of different ways that autoenrollment can be regulated. You can decide who gets the autoenrollment policy applied to them through Group Policy links and filtering, meaning that you can define in the GPO properties which users or computers are going to be subject to autoenrollment in the first place. Alternatively, or additionally, you can also specify permissions inside each certificate template on the CA server so that you can better determine which users or computers in your environment will receive copies of each template once autoenrollment is enabled.

Planning is essential for this task. You need to build a clear definition for what certificates you need to publish, and to which devices or people you need that certificate to roll itself out to. Follow these steps incorrectly and it may not work, or worse yet, you may end up with a thousand certificates being issued all over your network that you did not intend to be distributed. Group Policy is extremely powerful and tapping into that power comes with great responsibility.

After configuring these settings, if you reboot a few domain-joined machines in your network, you will notice that when they come back online, there will be a new certificate sitting in the computer's personal certificate store. If you sit back and wait a few hours, you will see that they will have rolled around to everybody automatically. If you don't like waiting for Group Policy to refresh, you can open the Command Prompt on some of those computers and issue the `gpupdate /force` command to manually refresh the policies and pull down the certificate.

Renewing your root certificate

Remember a few pages back, when we configured the first CA server in our environment – the Enterprise root? We left many of the default options in place, and that means that our root certificate is set automatically with a validity period of 5 years. This seems like a long time, but 5 years can flash by in an instant, especially if you have kids. So, what happens when that root certificate does finally expire? Bad things happen. You will definitely want to keep track of the expiration date on your root certificates and make sure to renew them before they expire!

Getting ready

We just built this new CA server, so we are not in danger of our root certificate expiring anytime soon. However, it is important to understand how to accomplish this task, so we are going to walk through the process of renewing the root Authority Certificate. We will accomplish this task right from our CA server itself.

How to do it...

To renew your CA's root certificate, take the following steps while logged into the CA itself. The GUI options are not available from the remote management tool (if you are running Windows Server Core and do not have a local CA tool, don't worry – we'll run through that later):

1. Open the **Certification Authority** management console on your CA.

2. Right-click on the name of your CA, navigate to **All Tasks**, and choose **Renew CA Certificate...**:

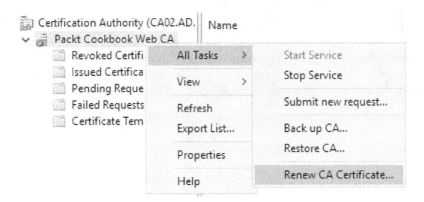

Fig 4.29 – Renewing a CA certificate

> **Tip**
> If you haven't stopped ADCS during this process, you will be prompted to do
> so. Go ahead and click **Yes** in order to stop the certificate processes temporarily.

3. On the **Renew CA Certificate** screen, you only have one option to worry about.
    You need to choose whether you want to generate a new key pair for the new root
    certificate or reuse the existing one. If you have published many certificates from
    this CA, it is generally easier to say **No** to this and let it reuse the existing key pair.
    As shown in the following screenshot, there are some situations where you would
    want to choose **Yes** and create a new key pair, so the correct answer to this question
    is going to depend on your situation and your needs:

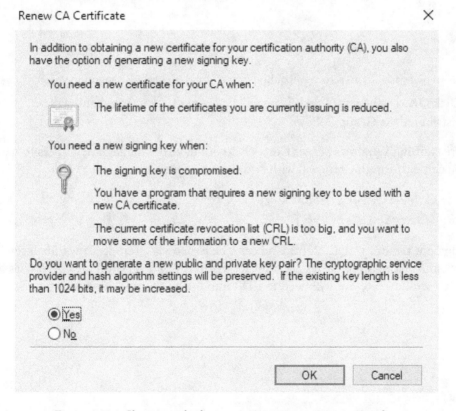

Figure 4.30 – Choosing whether or not to generate a new private key

4. If you are renewing a subordinate CA, you will be asked which CA to send your request to. This should be populated with the server that originally issued the request. If you are renewing a root CA, this screen will not appear:

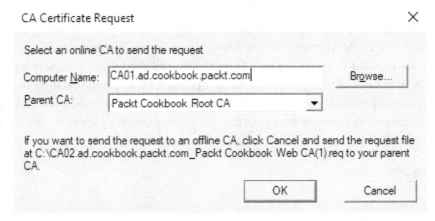

Figure 4.31 – This screen will only appear if you are renewing a subordinate CA

5. Click **OK**. The new root certificate will be immediately created and will be distributed via Group Policy.

If you are running Windows Server Core, or do not have the management tools to hand, then you can perform this renewal with two simple commands:

```
certutil -renewCert ReuseKeys
Restart-Service CertSvc
```

Unfortunately, the certutil command can't be issued via a remote PowerShell session due to various permissions issues and the fact that if this is a subordinate CA, it tries to load a GUI window. So, you will need to RDP into the box to run these commands.

How it works...

Your CA certificates are critical to the overall health of your PKI infrastructure. You can never issue a certificate with a length longer than these certificates, so unless you want to be issuing shorter and shorter certificates, they need renewing. Fortunately, renewing this root certificate is generally easy. Simply follow our steps and you'll be back in business for another 5 or 10 years. When you renew the root authority certificate, it places the new copy of that certificate into Group Policy's Trusted Root Authorities location. All systems joined to a domain keep this list updated automatically through Group Policy so that whenever you add a new CA server or renew an existing root certificate, the new trusts associated with that new certificate are automatically distributed to all your client machines and servers. Therefore, generally, all you have to do is renew the certificate and sit back and relax, because Group Policy will start pushing that new certificate into place all across your network.

However – and this is a BIG however – if you let your root authority certificate expire and you have issued certificates that are being used by clients and servers for network authentication, the root certificate expiry will cause those systems to no longer be connected to the network. You can easily renew the root certificate and get the backend up and running, but without having a valid way to authenticate to the network, your systems that are relying on a valid certificate to connect to that network will be dead in the water. You will need to figure out an alternative way to connect them to the network and update their Group Policy before they learn how to trust the newly refreshed root authority certificate. This warning comes to mind for me because I just helped a company combat exactly this issue. Their root certificate expired and they had whole offices worth of people who were connecting to the data center and the domain solely through the DirectAccess remote connectivity technology. DirectAccess relies on certificates as part of its authentication process, so those remote systems were completely unable to communicate with the network once their root certificate expired. We had to connect them to the network in a different way in order to pull down the GPO settings and a new copy of the new root certificate before they could start connecting remotely again.

Moral of the story: make sure you mark your calendars so that you renew your certificates BEFORE they expire!

Revoking a certificate

Individual certificates come and go. Most certificates last until they expire and are then renewed. Or maybe the service that was using the certificate is retired and has been turned off. But sometimes, a certificate is compromised. Maybe the private key for the certificate was uploaded to a public version control repository – in real life, this happens all the time. Maybe the private key was sent to the wrong person.

Once a certificate's private key has been compromised, that certificate can no longer be trusted. A malicious user could take that certificate and use it to 'man-in-the-middle' your previously secure SSL connection and intercept and read the sensitive traffic.

The way to limit the damage caused by this is to revoke the issued certificate. Most web browsers check something called a **Certificate Revocation List (CRL)** when establishing an SSL connection to check if a certificate has been revoked (in other words, blacklisted). What this means is that if a certificate is compromised, you can revoke the original certificate and reissue the certificate to a new private key, neutering the ability to use the old, compromised certificate.

Getting ready

In this example, we have a Windows Server 2019 IIS server with a certificate issued by a Windows Server 2019 CA installed on it. You can read more about how this can be configured in the next chapter of this book. We also have a Windows 10 computer to test the revoked certificate and do the revocation.

How to do it...

From your Windows 10 computer, follow these steps:

1. If you want to, check that the certificate you want to revoke is currently working. In this example, we're checking `https://revoked.ad.cookbook.packt.com/:`

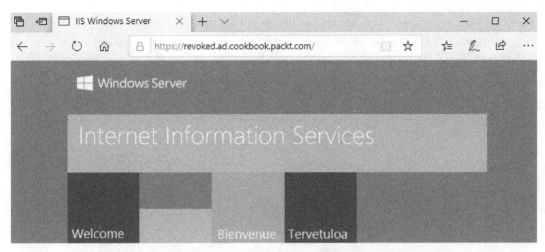

Figure 4.32 – The certificate we're about to revoke, currently working

2. Open the **Certification Authority** management pane. Connect to your CA if required. In this example, we are connecting to our subordinate CA, CA02.

3. Expand your CA name and go to the **Issued Certificates** folder.

4. Locate the certificate you wish to revoke. Right-click the certificate and choose **Revoke Certificate**. You can check the details of the certificate by scrolling to the right of the window and looking for **Issued Common Name**:

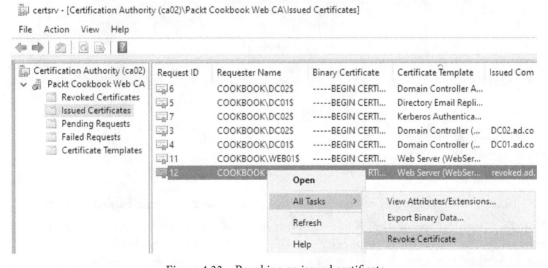

Figure 4.33 – Revoking an issued certificate

5. Fill in the reason why you are revoking this certificate. This will be helpful for future auditing. Set a date here if you want to revoke a certificate in the future (for example, if you want to cease this service in the future, but not immediately). *Make sure the certificate you are revoking is the correct one!*

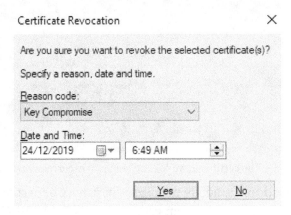

Figure 4.34 – The certificate revocation screen

6. The certificate has now been revoked. If you go to the **Revoked Certificates** folder in the CA, you should see the certificate in there:

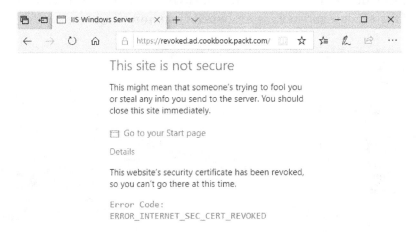

Figure 4.35 – Trying to browse a site using a revoked certificate shows an un-bypassable error

Note that certificate revocation is not always immediate – most operating systems and web browsers cache the certificate authority's list of revoked certificates and will not recognize the revocation until after the cache expires. You can check the revocation manually by running the following command:

```
certutil -f -urlfetch -verify .\certificate.crt
```

Here, `certificate.crt` is a local copy of the certificate to be checked. It should state that the certificate has been revoked:

```
Issuer: CN=Packt Cookbook Web CA, DC=ad, DC=cookbook, DC=packt, DC=com
NotBefore: 24/12/2019 6:26 AM
NotAfter: 19/12/2021 7:53 AM
Subject: CN=revoked.ad.cookbook.packt.com
Serial: 5f0000000caec16fc56b366184000020000000c
Template: WebServer
Cert: bb3cb031c7a81bd8175c36d8b9fd52758a03e78e
The certificate is revoked. 0x80092010 (-2146885616 CRYPT_E_REVOKED)
--------------------------------
Certificate is REVOKED
Leaf certificate is REVOKED (Reason=1)
CertUtil: -verify command completed successfully.
```

Figure 4.36 – Output of certutil showing the status of the certificate as revoked

How it works...

Each certification authority has a CRL. This CRL is published in a place that should be accessible by any domain-joined computer. By default, this is stored in a Windows AD LDAP location. These CRLs are then checked by web browsers each time it sees a new certificate. If the certificate matches a certificate in the revocation list, the connection to the service is denied.

Certificates should be revoked when they have been compromised or when a service is discontinued (to stop someone else from reusing that certificate and relaunching the service maliciously).

It is possible to publish your CRL to the internet, which would be a good idea if your computers are not all domain-joined or you intend to make many of your services publicly available using your internal CA certificates. However, the processes for doing this vary hugely and are dependent on your network and internet configuration.

See also...

One example of how you may be able to configure your CRL so that it can be published via the internet can be found here:

```
https://techcommunity.microsoft.com/t5/Configuration-Manager-
Archive/How-to-Publish-the-CRL-on-a-Separate-Web-Server/
ba-p/272748b.
```

5
Internet Information Services

Websites and web services are used for everything these days. With the evolution of cloud services, we are accessing more and more via web browsers than we ever have before. The cloud can mean very different things to different people, but what I see most commonly in Enterprise situations is the creation of private clouds. This generally means a collection of web servers that are being used to serve up web applications for the company's user population to work from. Sometimes, the private cloud is onsite in a company's data center; sometimes, it is in a colocated data center facility; and sometimes, it is a combination of a local data center and a true cloud web service provider such as Azure. Whatever defines a private cloud for you, one variable is the same: your cloud includes web servers that need to be managed and administered.

For any Microsoft-centric shop, your web servers should be running Windows Server with the **Internet Information Services (IIS)** role installed. IIS is the website platform in Windows Server 2019, and with it, we can run any kind of website or web service that we need. The hope for this collection of recipes is to give you a solid foundation to understand the way that websites work within IIS. Even if you don't normally set up new web services, you may very well have to troubleshoot one. Becoming familiar with the console and options, and just understanding the parts and pieces, can be hugely beneficial to anyone administering servers in a Windows environment.

If you have been reading through this recipe book from start to finish, you probably noticed that we utilize our new web server a lot when testing or rounding out tasks in our infrastructure. Our web server has a whole bunch of things on it that have been pushed down the path as a result of regular network tasks that we have done, but we aren't doing any actual web serving with it yet!

We are going to assume that for most of the tasks in this chapter, the role for IIS is already installed on the web server. This role is specifically called **Web Server (IIS)** in the list of roles, and there are numerous additional features that we can add to IIS. For all our recipes, we only need the defaults added – the ones that are selected automatically when installing the role. That role installation is the only thing a Windows Server 2019 box needs in order to serve up web pages to users, other than a little bit of knowledge of how to get the site doing what you want it to do. In order to get the role installed properly, make sure to stop by the *Installing the Web Server role with PowerShell* recipe in order to put that component into place. Now, let's get familiar with some of the common tasks in IIS.

In this chapter, we will cover following recipes:

- Installing the Web Server role with PowerShell
- Launching your first website
- Changing the port on which your website runs
- Adding encryption to your website
- Using a Certificate Signing Request to acquire your SSL certificate
- Using Let's Encrypt to acquire your SSL certificate
- Moving an SSL certificate from one server to another
- Rebinding your renewed certificates automatically
- Hosting multiple websites on your IIS server
- Using host headers to manage multiple websites on a single IP address

Installing the Web Server role with PowerShell

If you've been following this book from the beginning, you will hopefully know what's coming here. We've been showing the PowerShell methods for accomplishing tasks for a lot of previous recipes. If you haven't started using our PowerShell examples to accomplish some of your regular Windows Server tasks, then you can start now! PowerShell can be used in Windows Server 2019 to accomplish any task or configuration inside the operating system. I am a huge fan of using the keyboard instead of the mouse in any circumstance and saving scripts that can be used over and over to save time in the future.

In this recipe, we are going to explore the `Install-WindowsFeature` cmdlet, which can be used to add a role or roles to your Server 2019. Since we are discussing IIS in this chapter, we'll take our newly created web server and use PowerShell to place the Web Server (IIS) role onto it.

Getting ready

There is a new Windows Server 2019 web server in our environment called WEB02. Let's use PowerShell on this machine in order to install the IIS role.

How to do it...

To add the Web Server (IIS) role to WEB02 via PowerShell, follow these steps:

1. Log into WEB02 and open a PowerShell prompt; make sure to run it as an administrator.

2. All we need to do is run the proper cmdlet and specify the role name, but let's pretend that the specific name of our role evades us. This gives us a good opportunity to explore another command that will help us see a list of the available roles to be installed. Type in the following command to see the list of roles:

```
Get-WindowsFeature
```

You may recognize this command from much earlier in this book – back in *Chapter 1, Learning the Interface*, we experimented with this command.

3. Whoa! Here, there's a big list of all the roles and features that can be installed on this server. Scrolling up, I can see `Web Server (IIS)` in the list, and it looks like the role name is `Web-Server`. I am going to keep that name in mind, and since we can install multiple items at the same time, I am also going to take note of `Web-Common-Http` in order to install the common HTTP features when I install the role:

```
[ ] Volume Activation Services              VolumeActivation
[ ] Web Server (IIS)                        Web-Server
    [ ] Web Server                          Web-WebServer
        [ ] Common HTTP Features            Web-Common-Http
            [ ] Default Document            Web-Default-Doc
            [ ] Directory Browsing          Web-Dir-Browsing
            [ ] HTTP Errors                 Web-Http-Errors
            [ ] Static Content              Web-Static-Content
            [ ] HTTP Redirection            Web-Http-Redirect
            [ ] WebDAV Publishing           Web-DAV-Publishing
        [ ] Health and Diagnostics          Web-Health
```

Figure 5.1 – The output of Get-WindowsFeature showing the web server options

4. Now, we need to build out the PowerShell command to install these two items:

```
Install-WindowsFeature Web-Server,Web-Common-Http,Web-
Mgmt-Console -Restart
```

This will result in the following output:

```
Administrator: Windows PowerShell
PS C:\> Install-WindowsFeature Web-Server,Web-Common-Http,Web-Mgmt-Console -Restart

Start Installation...
  24%
     [oooooooooooooooooooo
```

Figure 5.2 – Installing the web server features with PowerShell

5. Installation succeeded! Just to double-check it for the sake of our recipe, if we navigate through the GUI to see the installed roles and features, we will see that the items we configured via PowerShell are fully installed:

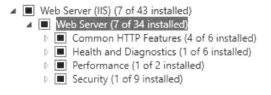

Figure 5.3 – Please add a figure caption

How it works...

We can use the `Install-WindowsFeature` cmdlet in PowerShell to easily add roles and features to our servers. This one can save a lot of time compared to running through these options in the graphical wizards. For example, if you had a group of new servers that all needed to accomplish the same task, and therefore needed the same set of roles installed, you could build out one single command to install those roles and run it on each server – no need to launch Server Manager at all!

See also

Here is a link to additional TechNet documentation on adding roles to servers, and specifically for the `Install-WindowsFeature` cmdlet. Make sure to familiarize yourself with all the available options. If there's one takeaway from this, it's that there are other ways to do things than using Server Manager!

```
https://docs.microsoft.com/en-us/windows-server/
administration/server-manager/install-or-uninstall-roles-role-
services-or-features#remove-roles-role-services-and-features-
by-using-windows-powershell-cmdlets
```

Launching your first website

This seems like a logical first step, so let's get a website started! You actually already have one, but it's pretty useless at the moment. As soon as you finished installing the IIS role, a standard website was started automatically so that you can verify everything is working as it should. Now, we want to replace that default website with one of our own so that we can make some real use of this new server.

Getting ready

We will be accomplishing all our work from our new Server 2019 web server. This one does happen to be domain-joined, but that is not a requirement. You would be able to launch a website on a standalone, workgroup-joined server just as easily.

How to do it...

Follow these steps to start your first website on this new IIS web server:

1. Open **Server Manager** and open the **Tools** menu. Then, click on **Internet Information Services (IIS) Manager**.

2. In the left-hand window, expand the name of your server and click on the **Sites** folder.

3. Right-click on **Default Web Site** and navigate to **Manage Website | Stop**. This will stop that automatically created website from running and getting in the way of the new website that we are about to create:

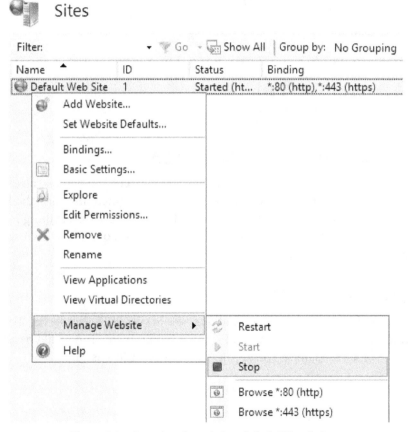

Figure 5.4 – Stopping the existing default IIS website

4. Before we create our new website, we will need to create an HTML web page file that will run when users browse to the new site. Let's leave IIS Manager open for a minute and switch over to File Explorer. Browse to `C:\inetpub`. This is sort of the home folder that IIS creates and can be a good starting point for building your website. You do not have to create your new page within this folder; you can certainly set one up in another location, or even on a different drive or network location altogether.

5. Create a new folder called `NewWebsite`, or whatever you want it to be called.

6. Inside this new folder, we are going to create a new file called `Default.htm`. To do this, I prefer to run the PowerShell `New-Item default.htm` command while in the directory we just created. However, whether you choose to do this doesn't matter, as long as we end up with that empty file:

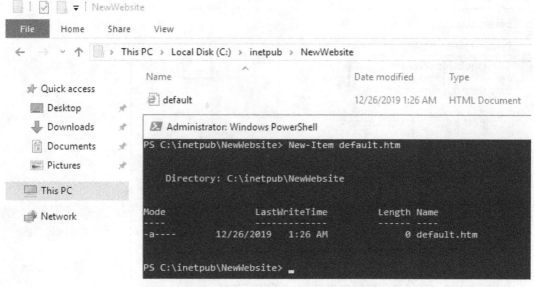

Figure 5.5 – Creating a new, empty default.htm file

7. Now, edit your new `Default.htm` file with Notepad or another text editing tool and enter some text. Thankfully, modern web browsers will properly display a page based on some plain text so, right now, we don't have to input valid HTML code. If you know how to program in HTML, even better! Maybe you have a preconfigured web page file or set of files from a software installation; you could place those into this folder as well. I am going to simply enter some text into that file that says, `Congratulations, you are viewing our new website!`.

8. Head back over to IIS. Now, let's get our site rolling. Right-click on the **Sites** folder and choose **Add Website…**.

9. Input a site name, which is just a descriptive name for your own purposes so that you can identify the site in IIS.

10. For **Physical path**, choose our new website location, which is C:\inetpub\ NewWebsite.

11. If you are running multiple IP addresses on this web server and want to dedicate this new site so that it only runs on a particular IP address, you can choose it from the **IP address** field. Otherwise, if you are running a single IP or if you want our new site to work on all IPs configured on this system, leave it set to **All Unassigned**:

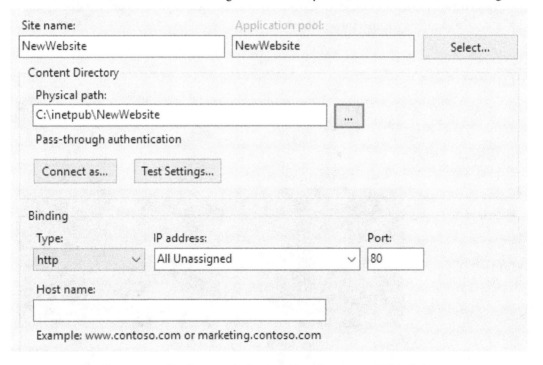

Figure 5.6 – Configuring the basic options for our new IIS website

12. Click **OK**. You may get a warning about the binding already being in use. This is fine – that's our default website that we stopped earlier. You can click **Yes** to that warning.

13. From another computer on the network, open Internet Explorer and browse to http://<webserver>. For our example, we will go to http://web02. ad.cookbook.packt.com:

Congratulations, you are viewing our new website!

Figure 5.7 – Viewing the new page we just created

Now, just there in the previous recipe, we were talking about how good PowerShell is, but we just went straight back into the GUI! Well, here's how we would do the same tasks via PowerShell. I'm going to show the entire code snippet, and then we'll break it down:

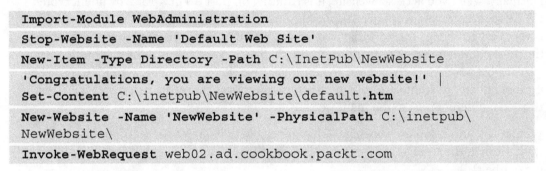

```
Import-Module WebAdministration
Stop-Website -Name 'Default Web Site'
New-Item -Type Directory -Path C:\InetPub\NewWebsite
'Congratulations, you are viewing our new website!' |
Set-Content C:\inetpub\NewWebsite\default.htm
New-Website -Name 'NewWebsite' -PhysicalPath C:\inetpub\
NewWebsite\
Invoke-WebRequest web02.ad.cookbook.packt.com
```

1. `Import-Module WebAdministration` loads the PowerShell module that provides the cmdlets that we'll use later.

2. The `Stop-Website` line stops the default website that ships with IIS so that we can create our new site to replace it.

3. `New-Item` creates the directory that we're going to use for the new site. I could have just as easily used the old `mkdir` command here as well.

4. The line containing `Set-Content` takes the text I passed it (`'Congratulations...'`) and writes it to our `default.htm` file in our new directory.

5. `New-Website` does what it sounds like – it creates our new website. We skipped every optional parameter, which meant it used the defaults for everything (which is fine for this example).

6. `Invoke-WebRequest` makes a web query to our new website. If the website has been set up correctly, you should see a response. The response `Content` property will contain what your browser would see.

How it works...

Starting a new website is perhaps the simplest task that can be accomplished in IIS, but it portrays the core functionality of this role. The purpose of running IIS in the first place is to publish websites. It is important to understand the location of this task and the places that you may have to reach inside the filesystem in order to modify or create websites of your own. Not everything is done from within IIS management.

Changing the port on which your website runs

Normally, when you access a website, it is running on port 80 or 443. Any unencrypted HTTP request travels over port 80, and the encrypted HTTPS uses port 443. Inside IIS, it is very easy to change the port that a website is listening on if you need to do so. Probably the most common reason to institute a port change on a website is to keep it hidden from a basic port scan. Maybe you have an administrative site of some kind and want to make it more difficult to stumble across or an **application programming interface** (**API**) that runs on a different port to the main website.

Whatever your reason for wanting to change the port that a website runs on, let's walk through the steps to accomplish this task so that it can be one more tool added to your belt.

Getting ready

We have a Windows Server 2019 server online that has the IIS role installed. There is already a website running on this server. Currently, it is using port 80 by default, but we want to change that port to 81 and test accessing it from a client computer.

How to do it...

Here are the steps needed to change your website listener port:

1. Open **Internet Information Services (IIS) Manager** from inside the **Tools** menu of **Server Manager**.

2. In the left-hand window, expand the name of your web server and click on the **Sites** folder.

3. Right-click on your website and choose **Bindings…**:

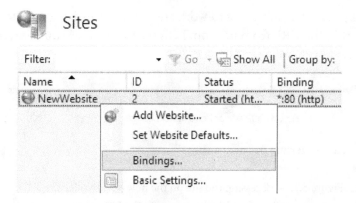

Figure 5.8 – Changing the binding of a website

4. Choose the **http** binding, which currently displays port 80, and click on the **Edit...** button.

5. Change the **Port** field to 81. This is just for our example, of course. You could enter any valid port number in this field that isn't otherwise in use on this server.

6. Click **OK**, then **Close**.

7. The port is immediately changed on your website. It is no longer listening on port 80. Let's test this by moving to a client computer on our network and opening Internet Explorer.

8. Try browsing to the old website address, that is, http://web02.ad.cookbook.packt.com:

Figure 5.9 – After changing the port binding, the site is inaccessible via its old URL

9. Whoops! I guess that isn't going to work anymore. Instead, we need to include our specific port in the URL from now on. Let's try `http://web02.ad.cookbook.packt.com:81`:

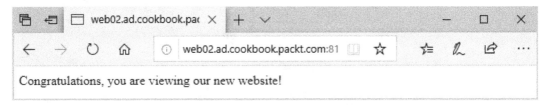

Figure 5.10 – Accessing the site on the new port. Notice the :81
at the end of the hostname in the URL bar

> **Tip**
> If you can't access the website at all after changing the port binding, you may need to allow the new port through Windows Firewall. There is a recipe *Using Windows Firewall with Advanced Security to block unnecessary traffic, in Chapter 3, Networking,* on configuring firewall rules.

Doing this via PowerShell is a two-step job. We have to remove the old web binding, as well as add the new one. You should add your new binding before removing the old one because if the site is left with no bindings, it will be stopped by IIS:

```
New-WebBinding -Name 'NewWebsite' -Port 81
Remove-WebBinding -Name 'NewWebsite' -Port 80
```

How it works...

We can easily adjust the port that is used to access a website inside IIS by making one simple change. After changing the port number in our website's bindings, the site immediately changes over to listening on the new port and is no longer active on the old port. Instead of changing the port, you could also add an additional binding to that same screen in order to get the website to respond from multiple ports at the same time. For example, if you wanted your website to run both HTTP for regular access and HTTPS for encrypted access to pages with sensitive information, you could create bindings for both port 80 and port 443. We will do this in the next recipe, *Adding encryption to your website.*

One thing to note when changing your website port is that doing so means your web links for accessing the website will now have to include that specific port number at the end. Also, if you are running firewalls in your network or on the web server itself, it is possible that you will need to adjust the settings on those firewalls to allow the new port safe passage.

Adding encryption to your website

Using websites to pass data around the internet is a staple of technology as we know it today. Installing even the simplest new tool or system will probably require you to download software or an update, or to register your information with a website. As an IT professional, I hope that you are familiar with HTTP versus HTTPS websites and the importance of distinguishing between the two. But now that we have a website running, how can we enable HTTPS on it so that we can protect this data that is traversing back and forth between our web server and the client computers?

It is typically the web developer's job to tell a website when to call for HTTPS, so you shouldn't have to worry too much about the actual content of the website. As the server administrator, however, you need to make sure that once HTTPS is called for on the website, your web server is capable of processing that traffic appropriately.

Getting ready

We are running a Server 2019 web server, from which we will accomplish this task. There is a simple website currently running inside IIS on this server. Part of this recipe will be choosing an SSL certificate that we want to run on our website, so this recipe assumes that the certificate is already installed on your server. If you need assistance with the acquisition of the certificate itself, please refer to the *Using a Certificate Signing Request to acquire your SSL certificate* recipe.

How to do it...

To configure your website for HTTPS traffic, follow these steps:

1. Launch **Internet Information Services (IIS) Manager** from the **Tools** menu inside **Server Manager**.
2. In the left-hand window, expand your web server name and click on the **Sites** folder.

3. Right-click on your website and choose **Bindings...**:

Figure 5.11 – Changing the binding of a website

Since it is a new website, you can see that there is only one binding listed currently. This binding is for port 80, which makes it an HTTP-only website. If you currently tried to access this site via HTTPS, it would fail. The port for HTTPS is 443, so we need to add a new binding that uses port 443. A mistake that I have watched new admins make is that they edit this existing binding and change it from 80 to 443. This will cause the website to only listen on port 443, or rather to only accept requests via HTTPS. This may be desirable in some instances, but not most. You generally want the website to respond to both HTTP and HTTPS requests:

1. Go ahead and click the **Add...** button.

2. Change the **Type** field to **https**. You will notice that the **Port** field changes to 443 automatically.

3. If you only want this new binding to work on a particular IP address, choose it now. Otherwise, leave it set to **All Unassigned** to cause this new listener to be active on all IP addresses that exist on our server. You will see some other options here, such as the ability to disable some HTTPS options. We're going to leave them as their defaults for now.

4. You can leave **Host name** blank for now. We're going to come back to this in a later recipe (*Hosting multiple websites on your IIS server*).

5. For **SSL certificate**, select the SSL certificate that you want IIS to use for authenticating requests to this website. HTTPS traffic is only encrypted and guaranteed to be safe from prying eyes because the tunnel is being validated by an SSL certificate that is specific to your website name. You must have an SSL certificate installed on the server so that you can choose it from the list here in order to create an HTTPS binding:

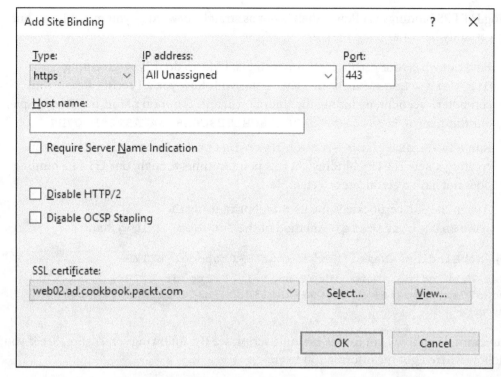

Figure 5.12 – The Add Site Binding options for HTTPS bindings

6. Click **OK**, and then click **Close**. Your HTTPS binding is now active on this website and it should be accessible via HTTPS:

Congratulations, you are viewing our new website!

Figure 5.13 – Viewing our site over HTTPS. Note the protocol in the URL bar and the visible padlock

Adding HTTPS bindings via PowerShell is not as straightforward as you might hope, but it can certainly be done:

1. Find out what your certificate thumbprint is. I like to do this by executing `dir Cert:\LocalMachine\My\` – this will show you all certificates in your computer's account, including the thumbprint and common name. In this example, our thumbprint is `75406C674A26138CB17E3C6B8E3ACA972AFD07B7`.

2. Run `New-WebBinding -Name 'NewWebsite' -Protocol HTTPS`, thus creating a new HTTPS binding. At this point in time, though, our HTTPS binding does not have a certificate selected.

3. Assign the SSL certificate using its thumbprint using the `.AddSslCertificate()` method of the `Get-WebBinding` item:

```
New-WebBinding -Name 'NewWebsite' -Protocol HTTPS

(Get-WebBinding -Name 'NewWebsite' -Protocol HTTPS).
AddSslCertificate('75406C674A26138CB17E3C6B8E3ACA972AFD07B7',
'my')
```

For an example of how I got to this example script, see the following screenshot. See if you can follow where I got the information from:

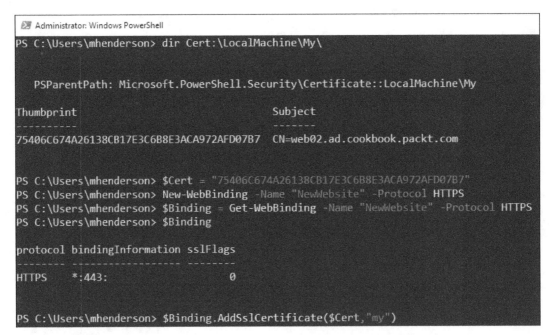

Figure 5.14 – The working out process for the sample script provided in this recipe.

It shows how the certificate thumbprint was discovered and then assigned to a new web binding.

How it works...

In this recipe, we used the IIS management console to add a second binding to our new website. This new binding is used to accept HTTPS traffic. We intend to run parts of this website as HTTP and some more sensitive pages as HTTPS. Therefore, we created a second binding, enabling both HTTP and HTTPS traffic to flow successfully to and from this site. During this recipe, we needed to choose the SSL certificate that the website was going to use in order to validate the HTTPS traffic that is coming in. Fortunately, there was already an SSL certificate installed on the server for our website; we simply had to choose it from the list.

Using a Certificate Signing Request to acquire your SSL certificate

When publishing a website to the internet, it is generally a best practice to use an SSL certificate on the website that you acquired from a public **Certification Authority** (**CA**). These are the big certificate issuing entities such as Entrust, Verisign, GoDaddy, and so on. It is possible to use your own internal PKI infrastructure to issue SSL certificates that can be exposed to the outside world, but it can be difficult to set up the certificate infrastructure appropriately and securely. As cheap as SSL certificates are, it is worth the investment to have the security of knowing that the certificate you are running on your website is the one and only certificate of its kind, and that nobody else has a chance to get their hands on a copy of your certificate and spoof your website. Modern browsers also have a pre-built list of the public CAs that they trust; this makes using a certificate from one of those public entities even more beneficial, because your user's browsers will automatically trust those certificates without any additional work having to be done on the client-side.

If you think back to *Chapter 2, Core Infrastructure Tasks*, we went into detail about how you need to choose your Active Directory domain name carefully. If you chose to use a real, dedicated domain (example.net) or a subdomain of your company name (ad.example.com), then the great news is that you can generate a certificate for your private website from a public CA. This is because most basic certificates are verified by an email from any parent domain – so a domain name of service.ad.example.com could be verified by an email to example.com, making verification easy.

It is easy enough to log into a CA's website and purchase a new certificate, but then comes the tricky part. Once purchased, you need to walk through some steps and enter information about your certificate. It may ask you for some company information and then it will ask for your **Certificate Signing Request (CSR)** and give you either a very large empty text box to paste it into or an upload function where you can upload your CSR directly to them. This is the place where I have watched many new admins struggle to find traction in their next step forward.

A CSR is a file that must be created on your web server. It contains information that the CA uses when it creates your certificate. When they do this, it binds the certificate to the information in the CSR, ensuring that your certificate is built specifically for your web server. Here, we are going to generate a CSR together so that you are prepared to handle that screen when you come across it.

Getting ready

We are going to use IIS, which is running on our Server 2019 web server, to generate a CSR. This server is the only piece of infrastructure that we need running for this task.

How to do it...

In order to request a new certificate from a public CA, you will need to generate a CSR on your web server. Here are the steps to do so:

1. Open **Internet Information Services (IIS) Manager**.

2. Click on the name of your server in the left-hand window.

3. Double-click on the **Server Certificates** applet. This will display the currently installed certificates on your server:

WEB2 Home

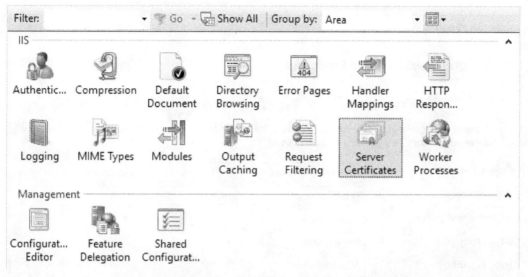

Figure 5.15 – The Server Certificates icon in the IIS manager

4. Click on the action to right of your screen that says **Create Certificate Request...**.

5. Populate **Common name** with the DNS name that your website will be running on. This is the name that users will type into their browsers in order to access this site; for example, `service.example.com`.

6. **Organization** is the name of your company or organization. Typically, this information needs to match whatever is on file with the CA, so take a minute to check another certificate that you might have already and make sure to type in the same information.

7. **Organizational unit** can be anything you desire. I often just type in the word `Web`.

8. Type in your **City/locality** and **State/province** to complete this screen. Make sure you spell out the whole word of your state; for example, California:

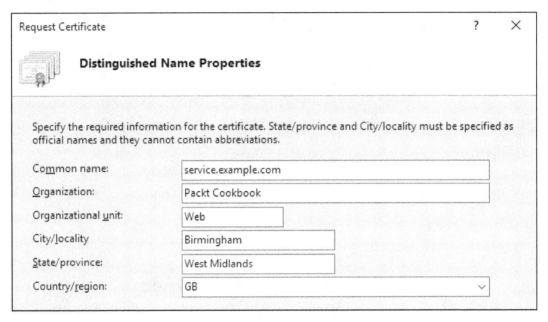

Figure 5.16 – An example Distinguished Name Properties screen in IIS

> **Tip**
> This CSR process was designed by a western system that forces you to build your addresses in this specific format. Many places in the world do not use the city/state/country style for addresses. If you live in one of these places, just do your best to make it fit. Unfortunately, every field does need to be filled in.

9. Click **Next**.

10. Increase your **Bit length** to at least **2048**. This is the minimum key length required for any certificate issued by a public CA:

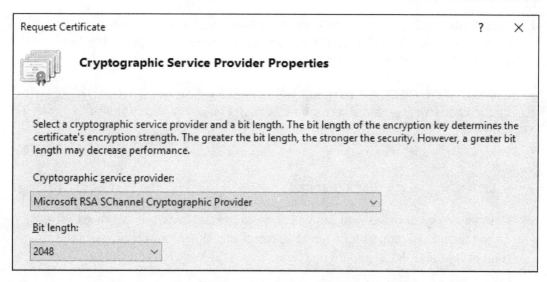

Figure 5.17 – Changing the bit length of the private key

11. On the next page, type in a location and name where you want to store your new CSR. Usually, you set this to a text (.txt) file. Make sure to specify the full filename, including the extension:

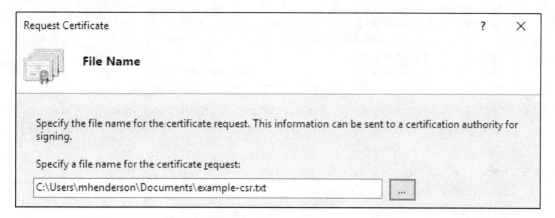

Figure 5.18 – Entering a filename to save the CSR to

12. Click **Finish** and open your new CSR file in Notepad. You should some base64-encoded data that looks like this (base64 is a way of encoding binary data in a text file):

```
-----BEGIN NEW CERTIFICATE REQUEST-----
MIIEfTCCA2UCAQAwfzELMAkGA1UEBhMCR0IxFjAUBgNVBAgMDVdlc3Qg
TWlkbGFu
...
Vw==
-----END NEW CERTIFICATE REQUEST-----
```

13. Now, you can proceed to your public CA's web interface and use this new CSR during the official request for a new SSL certificate. When prompted, paste the contents of the CSR file into their system. This is the last time you will need that CSR.

> **Tip**
> Each authority handles this process differently, but they are all generally done through a website with a series of steps that you walk through. Many CAs will allow you to generate a 15- or 30-day trial certificate so that you can test this without cost. Depending on the level of validation you have paid for, the CA may throw away some of the provided information in the certificate (such as company name). More expensive certificates that include company verification will include this information but cost more and take longer to issue.

14. After the CA has validated your request and your CSR, they will issue you a link where you can download your new certificate. Go ahead and download that file and copy it into your web server.

15. Once the certificate file is on your server, you need to import it into IIS. Head back into the **Server Certificates** section and, this time, click on **Complete Certificate Request…**.

16. Specify the newly downloaded certificate file and input the **Friendly name** field if you wish to. This is a descriptive name that you can give to this new certificate inside IIS so that you can easily identify it later when assigning it to a website binding. You typically want to store these certificates in the **Personal** store as this is set by default:

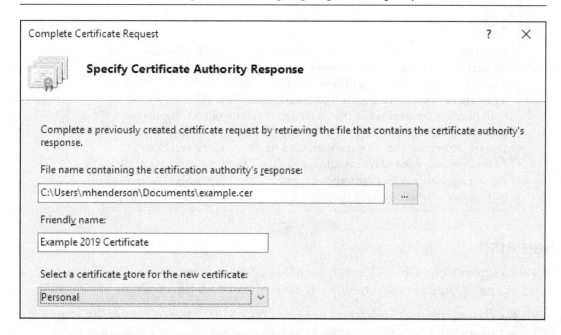

Figure 5.19 – Completing the CSR by installing the certificate

17. Click **OK**, and that's it! Your new certificate is installed and ready to use.

This would be an excellent place to now run you through this process in PowerShell. However, there is no good solution to this in PowerShell. Microsoft does have a utility called certreq that can achieve an CSR, but it's a process that is frankly more complicated than going through the GUI steps.

How it works...

In this recipe, we requested a CSR that we can submit to a public CA. In order to receive a certificate from them, we had to fill in some information about the certificate we wanted to issue. Once we have generated our CSR, we simply copy and paste it into the web interface for our CA entity and they give us a new certificate based on that CSR. Once downloaded, the new certificate file can be imported back into the web server, where it is ready for use by our own website.

> **Tip**
>
> Note that after you install the new certificate on your server, double-click on the certificate to open it up. You want to make sure that you have a message displaying on the main page of your certificate properties that says **You have a private key that corresponds to this certificate**. This will display near the bottom of the **General** tab of the certificate. If you do not see this message, something did not work correctly with the CSR and you will probably have to start the process over to request another new copy of the certificate (if the common name stays the same, you should not have to re-pay for it). Having a private key that corresponds to your SSL certificate is critical to getting your website working properly.

See also

- An explanation of the different types of SSL certificates you may be asked to buy: `https://serverfault.com/q/82039/7709`

- The certreq command reference: `https://docs.microsoft.com/en-us/windows-server/administration/windows commands/certreq_1`

Using Let's Encrypt to acquire your SSL certificate

In Chapter 4, *Working with Certificates*, and in the previous two recipes in this chapter, we've put a lot of time and effort into understanding, discussing, and implementing SSL certificates. You could be forgiven for thinking that SSL is more trouble than it's worth. However, the web browsers and search engines that govern how we design our websites are all putting more and more emphasis on HTTPS, which means that, at some stage, you are going to have to deal with these headaches.

Thankfully, you're not the only one who thinks the entire process is too difficult. That's where a non-profit organization called Let's Encrypt stepped in. They offer free SSL certificates that you can renew easily and automatically. There's no time delay as you wait for the administrator of your domain to approve the certificate via the WHOIS records or find out who has access to the admin@ email address at your company. Sound too good to be true? Well, it's not! The only main catch is that certificates are only valid for 90 days – but that's OK because the renewal is automatic; no human interaction is required.

Getting ready

We need to have a Server 2019 website operational. It needs to be connected to a real domain name and be accessible from the internet. This is because the Let's Encrypt servers need to be able to access your website to check its validity.

How to do it...

Because we have to use a real, internet connected domain for this process, I'm going to deviate slightly from my previous examples. In this book, you'll notice that I've been using cookbook.packt.com as part of my example domains. In this recipe, however, I'm going to be using a custom personal domain that I own that I can use for testing.

With that out of the way, let's begin:

1.   On another machine, download a program called win-acme from GitHub and transfer it to your web server. This is an open source program that integrates IIS with Let's Encrypt. You can download it from https://github.com/PKISharp/win-acme/releases. You will want to download the version ending in .x64.trimmed.zip (at the time of writing, the full download name is win-acme.v2.1.2.641.x64.trimmed.zip).

2.   Extract your downloaded ZIP file to C:\inetpub\win-acme\ (you may need to create this directory via Windows Explorer first, depending on your server's security settings):

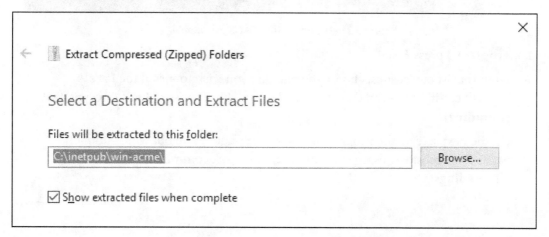

Figure 5.20 – Extracting the downloaded ZIP file

3. Browse to your extracted files and locate the program called wacs. Right-click this and select **Run As Administrator**:

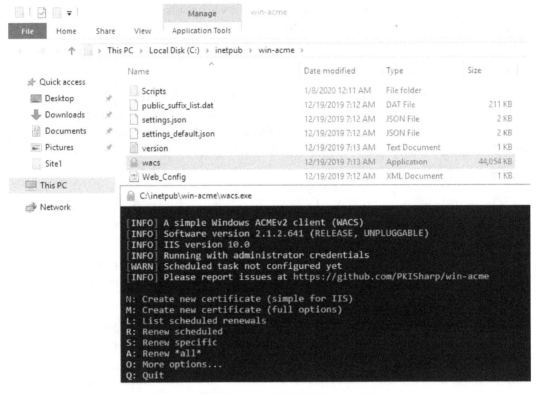

Figure 5.21 – Running the WACS executable

4. Type N and press *Enter*.

5. From the list of websites, choose the one that you wish to install the Let's Encrypt certificate for. In this example, I'm going to choose **6: Let's Encrypt Test (1 binding)**.

6. On the next screen, the program is going to try and figure out which domain name your website is using. The simplest (and most common) choice is **3: Pick * all* bindings**:

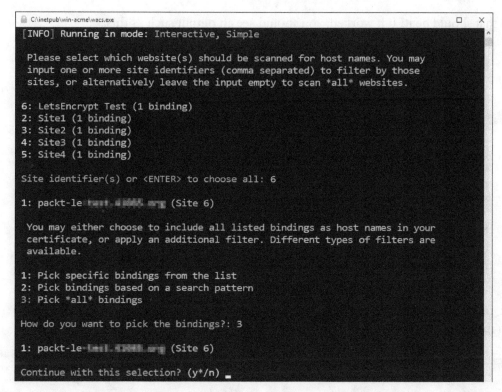

Figure 5.22 – The options I've chosen for my Let's Encrypt certificate

7. Enter **Y** if the settings look correct.

8. You will be asked to provide an email address. It's important that you provide a real, valid email address as Let's Encrypt will email you if there are any issues with your certificate (such as it not renewing).

9. You may be asked to review the Let's Encrypt terms and conditions. Answer these prompts as appropriate.

10. From here, the program is going to submit your certificate request to Let's Encrypt and then wait for Let's Encrypt to validate your site. This may take a few moments.

And that should be it! If it worked, you should see an output such as this:

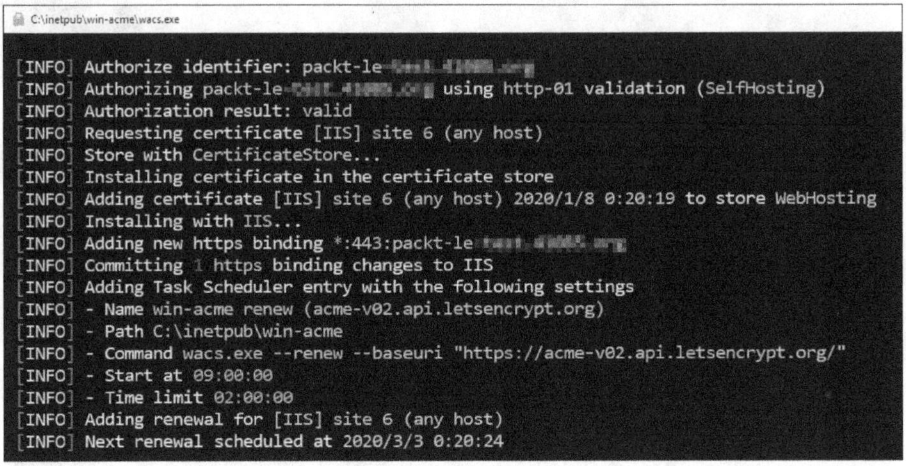

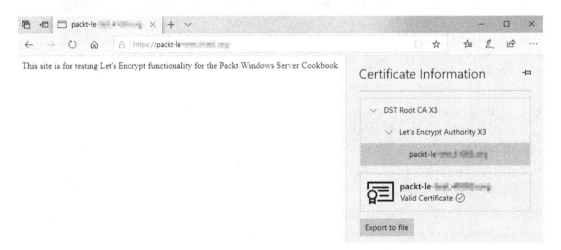

Figure 5.23 – A successful installation of a Let's Encrypt certificate

And, of course, you should validate in your web browser that the certificate has, in fact, been installed:

Figure 5.24 – Showing the Let's Encrypt certificate in use on our IIS website

How it works...

Let's Encrypt is a CA that is fully automated and does not charge for certificates. It does this by only communicating to you over their ACME protocol. This makes for a completely different process for installation than any other certificate provider. As you can see, it's generally much easier to use than going through the entire process of generating a CSR, submitting it to a CA, and then installing the certificates and managing the private keys.

However, there are some things to note, and there are also times when Let's Encrypt is *not* going to be an appropriate solution.

The first thing to note is that these certificates are short-lived. They have a 90-day expiry, which means that the server must renew them every few months. Normally, this is fine, but if anything goes wrong with the scheduled task that auto-renews them, your certificate can expire before you realise. If you entered a real email address during the certificate generation process, Let's Encrypt will email you to tell you your certificate has not been renewed and is going to expire.

The second thing to understand is how Let's Encrypt validates your domain. When the ACME protocol is being used for the certificate, it tells your server that you need to prove that you own that domain. The easiest way to do this is to put a specially named file in a special place on your web server. Let's Encrypt then checks for the existence of that file, and if it exists, it issues the certificate. This means that you may see some temporary files being created in your web folders.

You also need to understand when Let's Encrypt is not appropriate. It's fine for normal websites and it's probably fine for a website that runs an API. However, it is not suitable for any website that only lives inside your Active Directory domain. It is only for websites that are internet accessible. Additionally, it's probably not a good idea to use Let's Encrypt if the service is going to be accessed by old and inflexible devices such as IP desk phones as they often don't take kindly to regularly rotating certificates (and may not work with Let's Encrypt certificates at all). So, I would think twice before using this for Exchange web access if Unified Communications is in use.

See Also...

- The Let's Encrypt project: `https://letsencrypt.org/`
- The Win-Acme home page: `https://pkisharp.github.io/win-acme/`

Moving an SSL certificate from one server to another

There are multiple reasons why you may need to move or copy an SSL certificate from one web server to another. If you have purchased a wildcard certificate for your network, you are probably going to use that same certificate on a lot of different servers as it can be used to validate multiple websites and DNS names. Even if you are using singularly named certificates, you may be turning on multiple web servers to host the same site, to be set up in a load-balanced fashion. In this case, you will also need the same SSL certificate on each web server, as they could all potentially be accepting traffic from clients.

When moving or copying a certificate from one server to another, there is a right way and a wrong way of going about it. Let's spend a little bit of time copying a certificate from one server to another so that you can become familiar with this task.

Getting ready

We have two Server 2019 servers online in our environment. These are both destined to be web servers hosting the same website. IIS has been installed on both. The SSL certificate that we require has been installed on the primary server. We now need to export the certificate from there and import it successfully into our second server.

How to do it...

Follow these steps to copy a certificate from one server to another:

1. On your primary web server, launch **Internet Information Services (IIS) Manager** from the **Tools** menu of Server Manager.

2. Click on the name of your server in the left-hand window.

3. Double-click on the **Server Certificates** applet to view the certificates currently installed on this system.

4. For our example, I am using a wildcard certificate that has been installed on this server. Right-click on the certificate and choose **Export....** If you do not have this option, then the certificate may be restricted from being exported. This is common for a certificate issued by an Active Directory CA. In that case, your certificate *cannot* be exported in a way that makes it suitable for use on a different server. You will have to request an additional certificate for the additional servers:

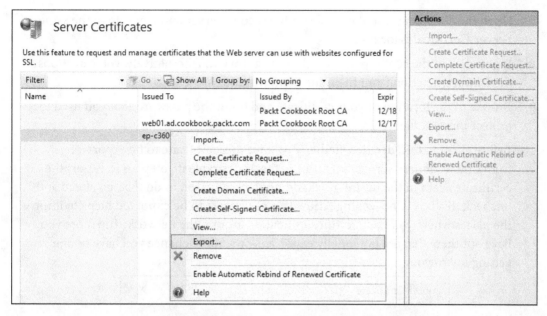

Figure 5.25 – Exporting the existing certificate

5. Choose a location where you wish to store this exported file and enter a password that will be used to protect the file:

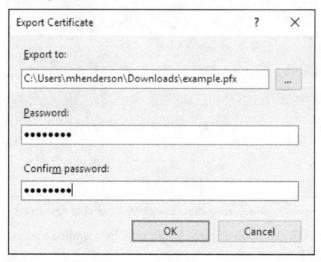

Figure 5.26 – Entering an export location and password for the PFX

6. Clicking **OK** will create a .PFX file and place it wherever you told it to. Now, copy this PFX over to your secondary web server.

7. Open the IIS Management console on the second server and navigate to the same **Server Certificates** location.

8. Right-click in the center pane and choose **Import...**. Alternatively, you can choose the **Import...** action from the right-hand window.

9. Browse to the location of your certificate and input the password that you used to protect the PFX file.

10. Before clicking **OK**, decide whether you want this certificate to be exportable from this secondary server. Sometimes, this is desirable if you plan to export the certificate again in the future. If you do not have a reason to do that, go ahead and uncheck this box. Unchecking **Allow this certificate to be exported** helps to limit the places where you have certificates floating around the network. The more you have out there that are potentially exportable, the more chance you have of one getting out of your hands:

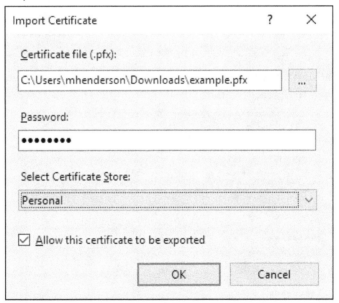

Figure 5.27 – Importing the exported PFX onto the new server

11. Once you click **OK**, your certificate should now be installed and visible inside the IIS window.

12. Double-click on the certificate and check the properties to make sure everything looks correct. Make sure that you see the message across the bottom that says **You have a private key that corresponds to this certificate**. If that message is missing, something didn't work properly during your export and the private key was somehow not included in the certificate export that you did. You will have to revisit the primary server and export it again to make sure that the certificate on the secondary server does contain private key information; otherwise, it will not work properly:

Valid from 12/18/2019 **to** 12/17/2021

🔑 You have a private key that corresponds to this certificate.

Figure 5.28 – The expiration date and private key notification for a certificate

Exporting and importing the certificate via PowerShell is something we can also do, as follows:

1. On your first server, you will need to know the thumbprint of your certificate. You can find this by looking in the cert:\ virtual drive:

```
dir Cert:\LocalMachine\My\
```

2. Once you have your thumbprint, you can generate the export via the Export-PfxCertificate cmdlet, passing it the certificate we just found:

```
Get-Item Cert:\LocalMachine\
My\39B9CC61BD1C6577C31CE8C058507796D88F55CE | Export-
PfxCertificate -FilePath export.pfx -Password (Read-Host
-AsSecureString -Prompt 'Password')
```

You will receive the following output:

Figure 5.29 – Exporting a certificate to a PFX via PowerShell

3. Once you have your certificate on your new server, you can run `Import-PFXCertificate` to get your certificate back in. Note the `-Exportable` flag – omit this if you do not want the certificate's private key to be able to be exported once it has been imported:

```
Import-PfxCertificate -FilePath .\export.pfx -Exportable
-CertStoreLocation Cert:\LocalMachine\My\ -Password (Read-Host
-AsSecureString -Prompt 'Password')
```

If we were scripting this out instead of running it from the console, you would replace the `Read-Host` section for the password with something else, such as pulling it from a password vault.

How it works...

We used both the IIS management console and PowerShell to export and import an SSL certificate, which is a simple task to do once you understand the process. The critical part is making sure that your export includes the private key information. If it doesn't, the certificate will not be able to validate traffic. You could also make use of the MMC snap-in for certificates to do the same task. If you use PowerShell or the Certificates MMC console, you will be able to choose whether to export the private key. The default option is set to **No, do not export the private key**. It is a common mistake to leave that setting in place and wonder later why the certificate doesn't work properly on other servers where you have installed it. You must make sure to select the **Yes, export the private key** option.

Rebinding your renewed certificates automatically

Certificates expire; this is just a simple fact of life. The longest a publicly issued certificate can be issued for is 2 years, and the trend is heading toward 90-day certificate expirations. This means that, on a regular basis, each certificate needs to be renewed. However, downloading a new copy of the certificate and installing it on your web server is not enough to make it continue working. Simply putting the new certificate into place on the server does not mean that IIS is going to start using the new one to validate traffic on your website. Even if you delete the old certificate, there is no action that has been taken inside IIS to tell it that this new certificate that suddenly appeared is the one that it should start using as the binding for your site. Previously, we have always had to make this additional change manually: every time you replace a certificate, you also go into IIS and change the binding on the website.

This seems particularly painful when you have the certificate renewal automated through something such as autoenrollment. You may mistakenly think that you are covered in the future and no longer must do anything to renew your certificates because they will be renewed at the server level automatically. But alas, this is not true: say hello to **certificate rebinding**.

The IIS team has made a simple but powerful feature to help this problem in the version of IIS that ships with Windows Server 2019. In fact, this function was available in Server 2012 R2 in its first iteration, but it is not often actually used. Thus, for most folks, this is going to be brand new. This new certificate rebinding feature, when enabled, causes IIS to automatically recognize a new certificate installation and automatically rebind the appropriate website to use the new copy of the certificate instead of the expiring one. Let's look at the interface so that you know how to turn this option on and off. We will also take a little look under the hood so that you can understand how this functionality works.

Getting ready

This work will be accomplished on our Windows Server 2019 web server. We have IIS installed and have an HTTPS website running with an SSL certificate already bound to the site.

How to do it...

Follow these steps to enable Certificate Rebinding on your IIS web server:

1. Open **Internet Information Services (IIS) Manager**.
2. In the left-hand window, click on the name of your web server.
3. Double-click on the **Server Certificates** applet.
4. In the right-hand window, click on the **Enable Automatic Rebind of Renewed Certificate** link:

Figure 5.30 – The Enable Automatic Rebind of Renewed Certificate link

That's it! IIS has now been configured so that it will recognize the installation of a renewed certificate and will rebind your website automatically to make use of the new certificate. Now, let's take a little look at how this process actually works.

5. Use either the Command Prompt or the **Start** screen to launch `Taskschd.msc`. This is the **Windows Task Scheduler**.

6. In the left-hand pane, navigate to **Task Scheduler Library | Microsoft | Windows | CertificateServicesClient**:

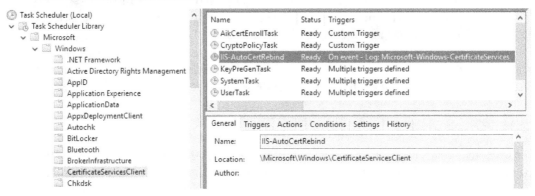

Figure 5.31 – The IISAutoCertRebind scheduled task

7. You can see a scheduled task listed here that is called **IIS-AutoCertRebind**. This is the magic of Certificate Rebind. When a certificate gets added or renewed on your Server 2019 system, an event is logged. When this event is logged, this scheduled task picks it up and uses the information that it has from IIS about the certificates in order to rebind the websites onto the new certificates.

8. If you head back into IIS and click on **Action** for **Disable Automatic Rebind of Renewed Certificate**, you will notice that our scheduled task disappears from the list.

There is no PowerShell equivalent for this command, but you can export the scheduled task from a server that has certificate rebinding enabled and import it into other IIS servers.

How it works...

Certificate rebinding is a simple action to enable inside IIS, but it can make all the difference as to whether you have a good or bad day at the office. When enabled, this feature builds a scheduled task inside Windows that triggers the commands to bind our IIS website to its new certificate. This task is triggered by an event that is logged in Windows when our new certificate is installed or renewed. With certificate rebinding enabled and the configuration of your certificate distribution set to happen automatically through Autoenrollment, you can now have a truly automated certificate renewal system inside your network!

Hosting multiple websites on your IIS server

Spinning up a web server, implementing the IIS role, and hosting a website are great first steps. Depending on the size and importance of your website, you may even require multiple web servers running that will serve up exact copies of the same website. You would then have a load balancer configured to send traffic between the multiple web servers. On the other hand, it's just as likely that your website will actually be an underutilization of your server's resources, rather than an overutilization, and so you have now created a new web server hosting a single website and it's really not being taxed at all. Is there a way that we can make use of that extra hardware that is currently sitting idle? Perhaps you have additional websites or web services that need to be turned on, for which you were planning to spin up multiple servers. The good news is that IIS can host many different websites at the same time. We can take that underutilized server and create additional websites on it so that you can serve up multiple web pages from the same server.

There are a couple of different ways that we can host multiple websites on the same IIS server at the same time: by using multiple ports, IP addresses, or hostname headers. Let's take a minute and test the first two of these in this recipe. We will look at hostname headers in the next recipe.

Getting ready

We are going to use IIS on our WEB01 server in order to host multiple websites. We will also need access to DNS in order to create names for these websites.

How to do it...

Follow these steps to host multiple websites on the same IIS server:

1. First, we need to create some sites that will be served up by IIS. Inside my `C:\ inetpub` folder, I am simply creating four new folders. Inside each folder will be a simple `Default.htm` file that contains some text. This way, I can serve up these different web pages on different sites inside IIS, and later browse to them individually to prove that IIS is serving up all of the different web pages:

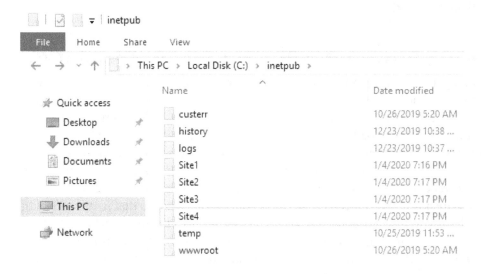

Figure 5.32 – Creating new sites in the inetpub directory

2. Now, open **Internet Information Services (IIS) Manager** and browse to the **Sites** folder. Right-click on **Sites** and choose **Add Website...** four different times to walk through the process of creating your four new websites. For each site, make sure to choose the appropriate folder on the hard drive for serving up the correct page.

3. At this point in time, we only have one IP address on our web server. So, in order to allow IIS to host multiple websites on this single IP address, we are going to take the approach of having each website run on its own port number. When you configure the **Add Website** screen, identify a unique port number under the **Binding** session for each site. This will permit all four websites to run at the same time using the same IP address, because each site will be running on a unique port number:

Figure 5.33 – Creating the new website with a different port number

4. Now, you can see that all four of our websites have started, and each is running on its own port number:

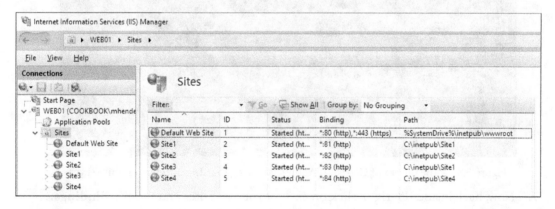

Figure 5.34 – The four new sites we just created

5. Client computers in the network can now browse the following links and successfully see the four different web pages being served up by our IIS server:

    a. `http://web01.ad.cookbook.packt.com:81`

    b. `http://web01.ad.cookbook.packt.com:82`

    c. `http://web01.ad.cookbook.packt.com:83`

    d. `http://web01.ad.cookbook.packt.com:84`

6. Requiring the users to type in a specific port number when they want to access websites isn't something they are going to appreciate. Sometimes, this is OK (such as when you have an API service that is coded into another program and thus not used by humans), but most of the time, it's not. So, let's try hosting these four different websites on our WEB01 server in a different fashion. Instead of using different port numbers, we are now going to take the approach of hosting each website on its own unique IP address. In order to start this process, open the NIC properties of the WEB01 server and add three additional IP addresses that we can use specifically for hosting these websites:

```
Administrator: Windows PowerShell

PS C:\Users\mhenderson> Get-NetIPAddress | Format-Table

ifIndex IPAddress                                    PrefixLength
------- ---------                                    ------------
17      fe80::30c0:90f5:1477:7701%17                           64
1       ::1                                                   128
17      172.16.97.24                                           24
17      172.16.97.23                                           24
17      172.16.97.22                                           24
17      172.16.97.21                                           24
1       127.0.0.1                                               8
```

Figure 5.35 – The output of Get-NetIPAddress showing four IP addresses on this server

7. Now, back inside IIS, right-click on each of your websites and modify **Bindings...** so that each website is, once again, using the default port 80, but is also running on its own unique IP address:

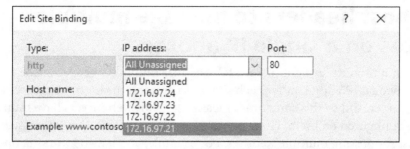

Figure 5.36 – Edit Site Binding now has four IP addresses and the port set to 80

8. Once the four websites are running on their own IP addresses, you can create DNS host records so that each site has a unique DNS name on the network as well. Simply point these four new DNS names to the corresponding IP address where the site is running. With that, your client computers can now access the websites via individual hostnames on the network:

- `http://site1.ad.cookbook.packt.com`

- `http://site2.ad.cookbook.packt.com`

- `http://site3.ad.cookbook.packt.com`

- `http://site4.ad.cookbook.packt.com`

This can be seen in the following screenshot:

Name	Type	Data
site1	Host (A)	172.16.97.21
site2	Host (A)	172.16.97.22
site3	Host (A)	172.16.97.23
site4	Host (A)	172.16.97.24

Figure 5.37 – The four new records just created in DNS

How it works...

Whether you decide to host multiple websites on a single web server by splitting up access at the port level or the IP address level, it is important to know that you can push the limits of your web server a little bit by hosting multiple things at the same time. IIS is more than capable of handling this division of resources. As long as your hardware is keeping up with the task, you can continue to grow vertically in this way and save the number of servers you have, rather than having to grow out horizontally by installing server after server after server as you begin to need additional web resources.

Using host headers to manage multiple websites on a single IP address

As we just saw, it is pretty straightforward to configure multiple websites inside IIS by assigning individual IP addresses for each site. It is common to run more than one site on a single web server, and so this sometimes means that your web servers have numerous IP addresses configured on them. However, there is really no need to use that many IP addresses just for hosting multiple websites. For example, you may be working on a web server that is internet-facing and there is a restriction on the amount of available public IP addresses that can be used. Or maybe each IP address allocation means coordinating with your network team, which might take days to navigate. We want to host multiple websites on a single IP address, but you don't want to force your users into having to type in specific port numbers in order to gain access to the right website.

This is where host headers come into play. Host headers can be configured on your websites so that the site responds to a request coming from the client. These header requests allow the web server to distinguish between traffic for different websites, directing users to the appropriate site inside IIS. Let's take the four sites we just made in the previous recipe and convert them so that they all use the same IP address.

Getting ready

We will complete this recipe from inside IIS on our Server 2019 web server. We will also utilize a client computer to test connectivity to the websites once we have finished setting them up.

How to do it...

To create two websites that share the same IP address and split traffic by using host headers, follow these steps:

1. If you haven't completed the previous recipe, go back and do *steps 1* through *4*. We will be reusing those websites here.

2. Open **Internet Information Services (IIS) Manager** from the **Tools** menu of Server Manager.

3. In the left-hand window, expand the name of your web server. You should see the four sites (Site1, Site2, Site3, and Site4) from the previous recipe.

4. Right-click on Site1 and choose **Edit Bindings…**. Then, click the **Edit** button to edit the current site binding.

5.   Here's the part that is new territory. Set **IP Address** to **All Unassigned** and **Port** to
      80 (if they aren't already). Then, in the **Host name** field, enter the DNS name that
      requests for this website will be coming in with. So, whatever DNS name your users
      are going to type into their browser is the name that you'll need to enter here. We
      are going to use `mysite1.ad.cookbook.packt.com`:

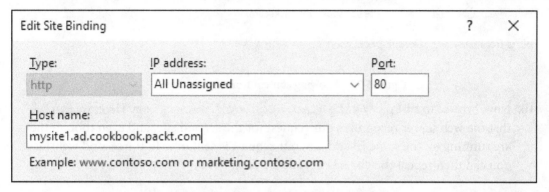

Figure 5.38 – Setting the host name header

6.   Click **OK**. With that, you have the first website up and running on the web server.

7.   Now, walk through the same process we completed here for `site2`, `site3`, and
      `site4`. We're going to specify the same **All Unassigned** IP address and port 80
      since our example hostname is going to be `site2.ad.cookbook.packt.com`
      instead of `site1`.

8.   We now have four websites, all running on the same IP address and port on
      the same web server. Let's do a test to find out whether IIS is smart enough to
      distinguish between the sites when we try to browse these websites from our
      client computer.

> **Tip**
> Remember to create DNS records for these websites! You will need host records
> created for `site1` through `site4`, and they all need to be pointed at the IP
> address of the web server. You could use a CNAME record to point them to the
> name of the web server to save when you're updating lots of records if the IP
> address of the server ever changes.

9. On a client computer, browse to `http://site1.ad.cookbook.packt.com`. You should see the text from the `Default.htm` file that we put into the `Site1` folder on the web server:

This is from site1.ad.cookbook.packt.com

Figure 5.39 – Showing content from our first site

10. Now, browse to `http://site2.ad.cookbook.packt.com`. Here, we can see that the web server recognizes our request for the second site, and even though they are running on the same IP address, our request is sent over to the second website. You can then repeat this for `site3` and `site4`:

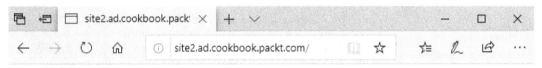

This is from site2.ad.cookbook.packt.com

Figure 5.40 – Showing content from our second site

How it works...

When we set up websites inside IIS to utilize different host headers, this gives us the ability to publish multiple sites on the same IP address and port numbers. This can be very useful in cases where IP addresses are limited or where you don't want to configure multiple addresses on the web server. IIS can listen on the same IP and port for web requests coming into different hostnames and forward those requests on to the appropriate website based on the host header name that was requested by the client computer. It is important to note that requests for these sites *must* be accessed by their domain name to work properly; you cannot type the IP address of the website into the browser and expect it to work since we are now sharing that IP address between two or more different sites.

6

Remote Access

With Windows Server 2019, Microsoft brings a whole new way of looking at remote access. Companies have historically relied on third-party tools to connect remote users to the network, such as traditional and SSL VPNs provided by appliances from large networking vendors. I'm here to tell you those days are gone. Those of us running Microsoft-centric shops can now rely on Microsoft technologies to connect our remote workforce. Better yet is that these technologies are included with the Server 2019 operating system and have functionality that is much improved over anything that a traditional VPN can provide.

A regular VPN does still have a place in the remote access space, and the great news is that you can also provide one with Server 2019. This chapter contains some recipes on setting up VPNs, but our primary focus for this chapter will be **DirectAccess (DA)**. DA is kind of like an *automatic VPN*. There is nothing the user needs to do in order to be connected to work. Whenever they are on the internet, they are connected automatically to the corporate network. DA is an amazing way to have your Windows 8 and Windows 10 domain-joined systems connected back to the network for data access and for managing those traveling machines. DA has been around since 2008, but the first version came with some steep infrastructure requirements and was not widely used. Server 2019 brings a whole new set of advantages and makes implementation much easier than in the past. I still find many server and networking admins who have never heard of DirectAccess, so, let's spend some time together exploring some of the common tasks associated with it.

There are two flavors of remote access available in Windows Server 2019. The most common way to implement the Remote Access role is to provide DirectAccess for your Windows 8 and 10 domain-joined client computers and use a VPN for the rest. These DA machines are typically your company-owned corporate assets. One of the primary reasons why DirectAccess is usually only for company assets is that the client machines must be joined to your domain because the DA configuration settings are brought down to the client through a GPO. I doubt you want home and personal computers joining your domain.

A VPN is therefore used for down-level clients such as OSX or non-domain-joined Windows clients and for home and personal devices that want to access the network. Since this is a traditional VPN listener with all regular protocols available such as L2TP and SSTP, it can also connect devices such as smartphones and tablets to your network.

There is a third function available within the Server 2019 Remote Access role called the **Web Application Proxy (WAP)**. This function is not used for connecting remote computers fully to the network, unlike DirectAccess and VPN; rather, WAP is used for publishing internal web resources out to the internet. For example, if you are running Exchange and SharePoint Server inside your network and want to publish access to these web-based resources to the internet for external users to connect to, WAP would be a mechanism that could publish access to these resources. The term for publishing to the internet like this is a **reverse proxy**, and WAP can act as such. It can also behave as an ADFS proxy.

For further information on the WAP role, please visit `http://technet.microsoft.com/en-us/library/dn584107.aspx`.

In this chapter, we will cover the following recipes:

- DirectAccess planning questions and answers
- Configuring DirectAccess, VPN, or a combination of the two
- Pre-staging Group Policy Objects to be used by DirectAccess
- Enhancing the security of DirectAccess by requiring certificate authentication
- Building your Network Location Server on its own system
- Enabling Network Load Balancing on your DirectAccess servers
- Adding a VPN to your existing DirectAccess server
- Replacing your expiring IP-HTTPS certificate
- Reporting on DirectAccess and VPN connections

DirectAccess planning questions and answers

One of the most confusing parts about setting up DirectAccess is that there are many ways to do it. Some are good ideas, while others are not. Before we get rolling with the recipes in this chapter, first, we are going to cover a series of questions and answers to help guide you toward a successful DA deployment. One of the first questions that always presents itself when setting up DirectAccess is, "How do I assign IP addresses to my DA server?" This is quite a loaded question because the answer depends on how you plan to implement DA, which features you plan to utilize, and even on how secure you believe your DA server to be. Let me ask you some questions, pose potential answers to those questions, and discuss the effects of making each decision:

1. **Which client operating systems can connect using DirectAccess?**

    Windows 8 Enterprise, Windows 8.1 Enterprise, and Windows 10 Enterprise or Education. You'll notice that the Professional SKU is missing from this list. This is because Windows 8 and Windows 10 Pro *do not* contain the DirectAccess connectivity components. Yes, this does mean that Surface Pro tablets cannot utilize DirectAccess out of the box. However, I have seen many companies install Windows 10 Enterprise on their Surface tablets, effectively turning them into *Surface Enterprises*. This works well and does indeed enable them to be DA clients.

    > **Tip**
    > Windows 7 was also a supported DirectAccess client, but as of January 2020, Windows 7 is out of support and should be avoided where possible in Enterprise environments.

2. **Do I need one or two NICs on my DirectAccess server?**

    Technically, you could set up a DirectAccess server with either option. In practice, however, it really is designed for dual-NIC implementation. Single NIC DirectAccess works okay sometimes to establish a proof-of-concept to test out the technology, but I have seen too many problems with single NIC implementations in the field to ever recommend it for production use. Stick with two network cards, one facing the internal network and one facing the internet.

3. **Do my DirectAccess servers have to be joined to the domain?**

    Yes.

4. **Does DirectAccess have site-to-site failover capabilities?**

Yes, although Windows 7 clients cannot use it. This functionality is called multisite DirectAccess. Multiple DA servers that are spread out geographically can be joined in a multisite array. Windows 8 and 10 client computers keep track of each individual entry point and can swing between them as needed or at user preference. Windows 7 clients do not have this capability and will always connect through their primary site.

5. **What are these things called 6to4, Teredo, and IP-HTTPS that I have seen in the Microsoft documentation?**

6to4, **Teredo**, and **IP-HTTPS** are all IPv6 transition tunneling protocols. All DirectAccess packets that are moving across the internet between a DA client and DA server are IPv6 packets. If your internal network is IPv4, then when those packets reach the DirectAccess server, they get turned into IPv4 packets by some special components called DNS64 and NAT64. While these functions handle the translation of packets from IPv6 into IPv4 when necessary inside the corporate network, the key point here is that all DirectAccess packets that are traveling over the internet part of the connection are always IPv6. Since the majority of the internet is still IPv4, this means that we must tunnel those IPv6 packets inside something to get them across the internet. That is the job of 6to4, Teredo, and IP-HTTPS. 6to4 encapsulates IPv6 packets in IPv4 headers and shuttles them around the internet using protocol 41. Teredo similarly encapsulates IPv6 packets inside IPv4 headers, but then uses UDP port 3544 to transport them. IP-HTTPS encapsulates IPv6 inside IPv4 and then inside HTTP encrypted with TLS, essentially creating an HTTPS stream across the internet. This, like any HTTPS traffic, utilizes TCP port 443. The DirectAccess traffic traveling inside either kind of tunnel is always encrypted since DirectAccess itself is protected by IPsec.

6. **Do I want to enable my clients to connect using Teredo?**

Most of the time, the answer here is yes. Probably the biggest factor that weighs on this decision is whether you are still running Windows 7 clients. When Teredo is enabled in an environment, this gives the client computers an opportunity to connect using Teredo, rather than all clients connecting over the IP-HTTPS protocol. IP-HTTPS is sort of the catch-all for connections, but Teredo will be preferred by clients if it is available. In Windows 8 and 10, there are enhancements that bring IP-HTTPS performance almost on par with Teredo, so environments that have been fully upgraded to Windows 8 and higher will receive fewer benefits from the extra work that goes into making sure Teredo works.

7. **Can I place my DirectAccess server behind a NAT?**

Yes, though there is a downside. Teredo cannot work if the DirectAccess server is sitting behind a NAT. For Teredo to be available, the DA server must have an external NIC with two *consecutive public IP addresses* – true public addresses. If you place your DA server behind any kind of NAT (including 1:1 NAT or proxy ARP), Teredo will not be available and all clients will connect using the IP-HTTPS protocol.

8. **How many IP addresses do I need on a standalone DirectAccess server?**

I am going to leave single NIC implementation out of this answer since I don't recommend it anyway. For scenarios where you are sitting the external NIC behind a NAT or, for any other reason, are limiting your DA to IP-HTTPS only, then we need one external address and one internal address. The external address can be a true public address or a private NATed DMZ address. This is the same with the internal address; it could be a true internal IP or a DMZ IP. Make sure both NICs are not plugged into the same DMZ, however. For a better installation scenario that allows Teredo connections to be possible, you would need two consecutive public IP addresses on the external NIC and a single internal IP on the internal NIC. This internal IP could be either a true internal or DMZ, but the public IPs really must be public for Teredo to work.

9. **Do I need an internal PKI?**

Maybe. If you are completely Windows 8 and above, then, technically, you do not need an internal PKI, but you really should use it anyway. Using an internal PKI, which can be a single simple Windows CA server (see *Chapter 4, Working with Certificates,* for more details), greatly increases the security of your DirectAccess infrastructure. You'll find out during this chapter just how easy it is to implement certificates as part of the tunnel building authentication process, making your connections stronger and more secure.

Configuring DirectAccess, a VPN, or a combination of the two

Now that we have some general ideas about how we want to implement our remote access technologies, where do we begin? Most services that you want to run on a Windows Server begin with a role installation, but the implementation of remote access begins before that. Let's walk through the process of taking a new server and turning it into a Microsoft Remote Access server.

Getting ready

All our work will be accomplished on a new Windows Server 2019 instance. We will be taking the two-NIC approach to networking, and so we have two NICs installed on this server. The internal NIC is plugged into the corporate network, while the external NIC is plugged into the internet for the sake of simplicity. The external NIC could just as well be plugged into a DMZ.

How to do it...

Follow these steps to turn your new server into a Remote Access server:

1. Assign IP addresses to your server. Since this is a multi-homed system with both internal and external networks connected, make sure you follow the steps in the *Multi-homing your Windows Server 2019* recipe in *Chapter 3, Networking*. Remember, the most important part is making sure that the Default Gateway goes on the external NIC only.

2. Join the new server to your domain.

3. Install an SSL certificate onto your DirectAccess server, which you plan to use for the IP-HTTPS listener. This is typically a certificate purchased from a public CA.

4. If you're planning to use client certificates for authentication, make sure to pull down a copy of the certificate from your internal CA to your DirectAccess server.

> **Tip**
> You want to make sure certificates are in place before you start the configuration of DirectAccess. This way, the wizards will be able to automatically pull in information about those certificates in the first run. If you don't, DA will set itself up to use self-signed certificates, which are a security no-no.

5. Use Server Manager to install the **Remote Access** role. You should only do this after completing the previous steps.

6. If you plan to load balance multiple DirectAccess servers together later, make sure to also install the feature called **Network Load Balancing**.

7. After selecting your role and feature, you will be asked which Remote Access role services you want to install. For our purposes of getting the remote workforce connected back into the corporate network, we want to choose **DirectAccess and VPN (RAS)**:

Select the role services to install for Remote Access

Role services

- [x] DirectAccess and VPN (RAS)
- [ ] Routing
- [ ] Web Application Proxy

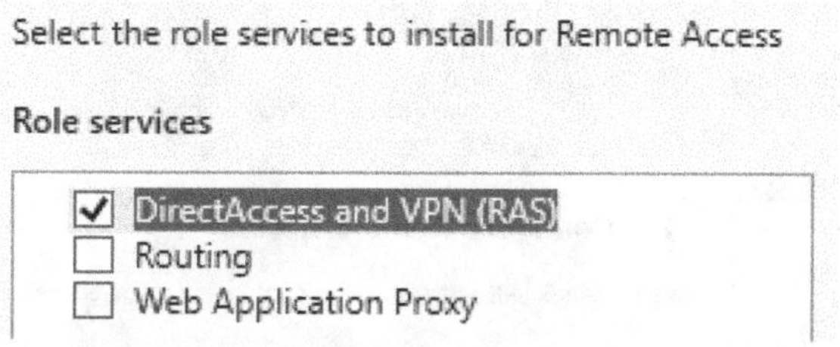

Figure 6.1 – Adding the DirectAccess and VPN (RAS) role to your Windows server

8. Now that the role has been successfully installed, you will see a yellow exclamation mark notification near the top of Server Manager, indicating that you have some **Post-deployment Configuration** that needs to be done.

> **Important**
> Do *not* click on **Open the Getting Started Wizard**!

Unfortunately, Server Manager leads you to believe that launching the **Getting Started Wizard (GSW)** is the logical next step. However, using the GSW as the mechanism for configuring your DirectAccess settings is kind of like roasting a marshmallow with a pair of tweezers. In order to ensure you have the full range of options available to you as you configure your remote access settings and that you don't get burned later, make sure to launch the configuration this way:

1. Click on the **Tools** menu from inside Server Manager and launch the **Remote Access Management** Console.

2. In the left window, navigate to **Configuration | DirectAccess and VPN**.

3. Click on the second link, the one that says **Run the Remote Access Setup Wizard**. Please note that, once again, the top option is to run that pesky Getting Started Wizard. Don't do it! I'll explain why in the *How it works...* section of this recipe:

Figure 6.2 – Showing where the Run the Remote Access Setup Wizard item is located

4. Now, you have a choice that you will have to decide on yourself. Are you configuring only DirectAccess, only VPN, or a combination of the two? Simply click on the option that you want to deploy. Following your choice, you will see a series of steps (*Steps 1* through 4) that need to be accomplished. This series of mini wizards will guide you through the remainder of the DirectAccess and VPN particulars. This recipe isn't large enough to cover every specific option included in those wizards, but at least you now know the correct way to bring a DA/VPN server into operation.

There's really only one part of this recipe that can be achieved by PowerShell, and it's the same as we've seen multiple times in this book. You can use the Add-WindowsFeature cmdlet to add the DirectAccess and VPN roles to your server. The configuration wizards (*Step 10* onward) stay the same.

How it works...

The remote access technologies included in Server 2019 have great functionality, but their initial configuration can be confusing. Following the procedure listed in this recipe will set you on the right path to be successful in your deployment and prevent you from running into issues down the road. The reasons that I absolutely recommend you stay away from using the shortcut deployment method provided by the Getting Started Wizard are twofold:

- The Getting Started Wizard skips a lot of options as it sets up DirectAccess, so you don't really have any understanding of how it works after finishing. You may have DA up and running but have no idea how it's authenticating or working under the hood. This holds so much potential for problems later, should anything suddenly stop working.

- GSW employs a number of bad security practices in order to save time and effort in the setup process. For example, using the GSW usually means that your DirectAccess server will be authenticating users without client certificates, which is not a best practice. Also, it will co-host something called the NLS website on itself, which is also not a best practice. Those who utilize the Getting Started Wizard to configure DirectAccess will find that their GPO, which contains the client connectivity settings, will be security-filtered to the Domain Computers group. Even though it also contains a WMI filter that is supposed to limit that policy application to only mobile hardware such as laptops, this is a terribly scary thing to see inside GPO filtering settings. You probably don't want all your laptops to immediately start getting DA connectivity settings, but that is exactly what the GSW does for you. Perhaps worst, the GSW will create and make use of self-signed SSL certificates to validate its web traffic – even the traffic coming in from the internet! This is a terrible practice and is the number one reason that should convince you that clicking on the Getting Started Wizard is not in your best interests.

Pre-staging Group Policy Objects to be used by DirectAccess

One of the great things about DirectAccess is that all the connectivity settings the client computers need in order to connect are contained within a **Group Policy Object (GPO)**. This means that you can turn new client computers into DirectAccess-connected clients without ever touching that system. Once configured properly, all you need to do is add the new computer account to an Active Directory security group and, during the next automatic Group Policy refresh cycle (usually within 90 minutes), that new laptop will be connecting via DirectAccess whenever you're outside the corporate network.

You can certainly choose not to pre-stage anything with GPOs and DirectAccess will still work. When you get to the end of the DA configuration wizard, it will inform you that two new GPOs are about to be created inside Active Directory. One GPO is used to contain the DirectAccess server settings, while the other GPO is used to contain the DirectAccess client settings. If you allow the wizard to handle the generation of these GPOs, it will create them, link them, filter them, and populate them with settings automatically. Half of the time, I see folks do it this way and they are forever happy with letting the wizard manage those GPOs now and in the future.

The other half of the time, it is desired that we maintain a little more personal control over the GPOs. If you are setting up a new DA environment but your credentials don't have permission to create GPOs, the wizard is not going to be able to create them either. In this case, you will need to work with someone on your Active Directory team to get them created. Another reason to manage GPOs manually is to have better control over the placement of these policies. When you let the DA wizard create these GPOs, it will link them to the top level of your domain. It also sets Security Filtering on those GPOs so they are not going to be applied to everything in your domain, but when you open the **Group Policy Management** console, you will always see those DA policies listed right up there at the top level of the domain. Sometimes, this is simply not desirable. So, for this reason as well, you may want to choose to create and manage the GPOs by hand so that you can secure their placement and links where you specifically want them to be located.

Getting ready

While the DirectAccess wizards themselves are run from the DA server, we do not do all this work on the DA server. The Group Policy settings that we will be configuring will be done within Active Directory, and we will be doing the work from a Windows 10 computer with the Active Directory RSAT tools installed.

How to do it...

To pre-stage GPOs for use with DirectAccess, follow these steps:

1. On your machine, launch the **Group Policy Management** console.

2. Navigate to **Forest | Domains | Your Domain Name**. There should be a listing here called **Group Policy Objects**. Right-click on that and choose **New**.

3. Name your new GPO something like `DirectAccess Server Settings`.

4. Click on the new **DirectAccess Server Settings** GPO; it should automatically open on the **Scope** tab. We need to adjust the **Security Filtering** section so that this GPO only applies to our DirectAccess server. This is a critical step for each GPO to ensure the settings that are going to be placed here do not get applied to the wrong computers:

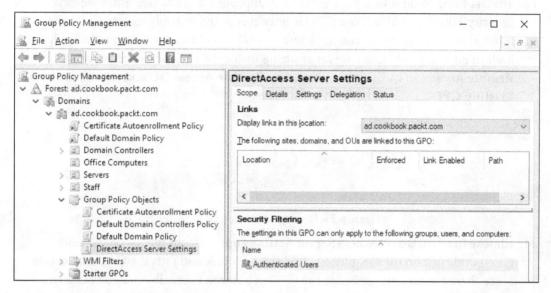

Figure 6.3 – The Group Policy Management console showing the DirectAccess Server Settings GPO

5. Remove **Authenticated Users** that are prepopulated in that list. The list should now be empty.

6. Click the **Add...** button and search for the computer account of your DirectAccess server. Mine is called RA01. By default, this window will only search user accounts, so you will need to adjust **Object Types** so that it includes **Computers** before it will allow you to add your server to this filtering list.

7. Your **Security Filtering** list should now look like this:

Figure 6.4 – The Security Filtering list has been replaced with our RA server

8. Now, click on the **Details** tab of your GPO.

9. Change **GPO Status** to **User configuration settings disabled**. We're doing this because our GPO is only going to contain computer-level settings, nothing at the user level.

10. The last thing to do is link your GPO to an appropriate container. Since we have Security Filtering enabled, our GPO is only ever going to apply its settings to the RA01 server, but without creating a link, the GPO will not even attempt to apply itself to anything. My RA01 server is sitting inside the OU located at **Servers\ Remote Access**, so I will right-click on my **Remote Access** OU and choose **Link an Existing GPO…**:

Figure 6.5 – Linking an existing GPO

11. Choose the new **DirectAccess Server Settings** option from the list of available GPOs and click on the **OK** button. This creates a link and puts the GPO into action. Since there are no settings inside the GPO yet, it won't actually make any changes on the server. The DA configuration wizards take care of populating the GPO with the settings that are needed.

12. Now, we simply need to rinse and repeat *Steps* 2 through *11* to create another GPO, something like **DirectAccess Client Settings**. You want to set up the client settings GPO in the same way. Make sure that it is filtering to only the Active Directory Security Group that you created to contain your DirectAccess client computers. Also, make sure to link it to an appropriate container that will include those computer accounts. So, your client's GPO may look something like this:

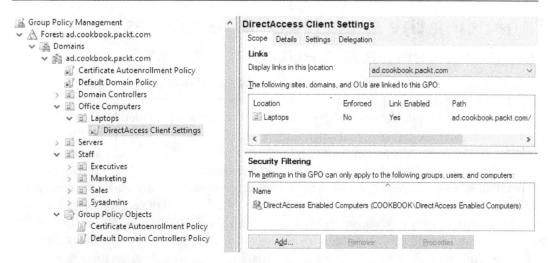

Figure 6.6 – The Client Settings GPO. Yours might be linked to more than one location.

Later in this book (in *Chapter 10, Group Policy,*) we will go through Group Policies in more detail, which will include PowerShell examples.

How it works...

Creating GPOs in Active Directory is a simple enough task, but it is critical that you configure the **Links** and **Security Filtering** settings correctly. If you do not take care to ensure that these DirectAccess connection settings are only going to apply to the machines that actually need the settings, you could create a world of trouble with internal servers getting remote access connection settings and causing them issues with connecting while inside the network.

The key factors here are to make sure your DirectAccess Server Settings GPO applies to only the DA server or servers in your environment, and that the DirectAccess Client Settings GPO applies to only the DA client computers that you plan to enable in your network. The best practice here is to specify this GPO to only apply to a specific Active Directory security group so that you have full control over which computer accounts are in that group. I have seen some folks do this based only on the OU links and include whole OUs in the filtering for the "client's" GPO (foregoing the use of an AD group at all), but doing it this way makes it quite a bit more difficult to add or remove machines from the access list in the future.

See also...

- *Chapter 10, Group Policy*

Enhancing the security of DirectAccess by requiring certificate authentication

When a DirectAccess client computer builds its IPsec tunnels back to the corporate network, it can require a certificate as part of that authentication process. In earlier versions of DirectAccess, the one in Server 2008 R2 and the one provided by **Unified Access Gateway (UAG)**, these certificates were required in order to make DirectAccess work. Setting up these certificates really isn't a big deal at all. If there is a CA server in your network, you are already prepared to issue the necessary certificates at no cost. Unfortunately, though, there must have been enough complaints being sent to Microsoft in order for them to make these certificates recommended instead of required. Due to this, they created a new mechanism in Windows 8 and Server 2012 called **Kerberos proxy**. This can be used to authenticate the tunnels instead. This allows the DirectAccess tunnels to build without a computer certificate, making that authentication process easier to set up initially, but less secure overall.

I'm here to *strongly* recommend that you still utilize certificates in your installs! They are not difficult to set up and using them makes your tunnel authentication stronger. Furthermore, many of you may not have a choice and will still be required to install these certificates. Only simple DirectAccess scenarios that are all Windows 8 or higher on the client side can get away with the shortcut method of foregoing certificates. Anybody who still wants to connect Windows 7 via DirectAccess will need to use certificates as part of their implementation. In addition to Windows 7 access, anyone who intends to use the advanced features of DirectAccess, such as load balancing, multisite, or two-factor authentication, will also need to utilize these certificates. With any of these scenarios, certificates become a requirement again, not a recommendation.

In my experience, almost everyone benefits from being DirectAccess-connected, and it's always a good idea to make your DA environment redundant by having load balanced servers. This further emphasizes the point that you should just set up certificate authentication right out of the gate, whether or not you need it initially. You might decide to make a change later that would require certificates, and it would be easier to have them installed from the get-go than trying to incorporate them later into a running DA environment.

Getting ready

In order to distribute certificates, you will need a CA server running in your network. Once these certificates have been distributed to the appropriate places, the rest of our work will be accomplished from our Server 2019 DirectAccess server.

How to do it...

Follow these steps to make use of certificates as part of the DirectAccess tunnel authentication process:

1. The first thing that you need to do is distribute certificates to your DA servers and all DA client computers. The easiest way to do this is by building a new template on the CA server that is duplicated from the in-built Computer template. Whenever I create a custom template for use with DirectAccess, I try to make sure that it meets the following criteria:

   a. The **Subject Name** of the certificate should match the **Common Name** of the computer (which is also the FQDN of the computer).

   b. The **Subject Alternative Name (SAN)** of the certificate should match the **DNS Name** of the computer (which is also the FQDN of the computer).

   c. The certificate should serve the **Intended Purposes** of both **Client Authentication** and **Server Authentication**.

2. For the actual distribution of these certificates, I'm going to direct you to review a couple of other recipes in this book. You can issue these certificates manually using **Microsoft Management Console (MMC)**, as described in the *Using MMC to request a new certificate* recipe in *Chapter 4, Working with Certificates*. Otherwise, you can lessen your hands-on administrative duties by enabling Autoenrollment, which was discussed in the *Configuring Autoenrollment to issue certificates to all domain-joined systems* recipe in *Chapter 4, Working with Certificates*.

3. Now that we have distributed certificates to our DirectAccess clients and servers, log into your primary DirectAccess server and open up the **Remote Access Management** Console.

4. Click on **Configuration** in the top-left corner. You should now see steps 1 through 4 listed.

5. Click **Edit...** listed under step 2.

6. Now, you can either click **Next** twice or click on the word **Authentication** to jump directly to the authentication screen.

7. Check the box that says **Use computer certificates**.

8. Now, we must specify the Certification Authority server that issued our client certificates. If you used an intermediary CA to issue your certificates, make sure to check the appropriate checkbox. Otherwise, most of the time, certificates are issued from a root CA, and in this case, you would simply click on the **Browse...** button and look for your CA in the list:

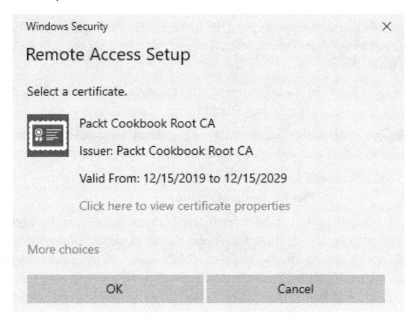

Figure 6.7 – Selecting the certificate authority to use

> **Tip**
> This screen is sometimes confusing because people expect to have to choose the certificate itself from the list. This is not the case. What you are actually choosing from this list is the CA server that issued the certificates.

9. Make any other appropriate selections on the **Authentication** screen. For example, if you still have Windows 7 computers that you want to connect via DirectAccess, select the checkbox for **Enable Windows 7 client computers to connect via DirectAccess**. I do not, so I will be leaving that unchecked:

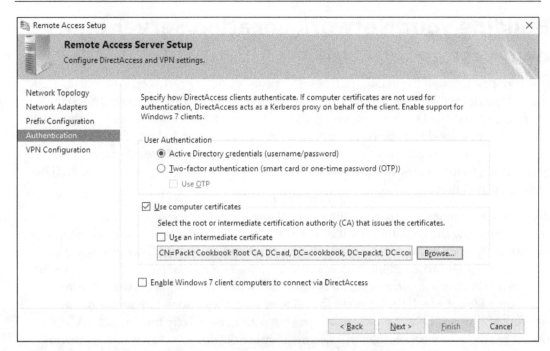

Figure 6.8 – Enabling computer certificates in the RA configuration setup

Don't forget that, once you're finished on the Remote Access setup screens, you need to click the **Finish…** button at the bottom of the screen.

How it works…

Requiring certificates as part of your DirectAccess tunnel authentication process is a good idea in any environment. It makes the solution more secure and enables advanced functionality. This is the primary driver for some companies simply because they still have Windows 7 clients to connect via DirectAccess. However, I suggest that anyone using DirectAccess in any capacity make use of these certs. They are simple to deploy, easy to configure, and give you some extra peace of mind since you know that only computers with a certificate issued directly to them from your own internal CA server are going to be able to connect through your DirectAccess entry point.

Building your Network Location Server on its own system

If you zipped through the default settings when configuring DirectAccess, or worse, used the Getting Started Wizard, chances are that your **Network Location Server (NLS)** is running right on the DirectAccess server itself. This is not the recommended method for using NLS; it really should be running on a separate web server. In fact, if you want to do something more advanced later, such as setting up load balanced DirectAccess servers, you're going to have to move NLS onto a different server anyway, so you might as well do it right the first time.

NLS is a very simple requirement, but a critical one. It is just a website; it doesn't matter what content the site contains, and it only has to run inside your network. Nothing has to be externally available. In fact, nothing *should* be externally available, because you only want this site to be accessed internally. This NLS website is a large part of the mechanism by which DirectAccess client computers figure out when they are inside the office and when they are outside. If they can see the NLS website, they know they are inside the network and will disable DirectAccess name resolution, effectively turning off DA. If they do not see the NLS website, they will assume they are outside the corporate network and enable DirectAccess name resolution.

There are two *gotchas* with setting up an NLS website:

- The first is that it **must** be HTTPS, so it needs a valid SSL certificate. Since this website is only running inside the network and being accessed from domain-joined computers, this SSL certificate can easily be one that has been issued from your internal CA server. So, there's no cost associated here.

- The second catch that I have encountered a number of times is that, for some reason, the default IIS splash screen page doesn't make for a very good NLS website. If you set up a standard IIS web server and use the default site as NLS, sometimes, it works to validate the connections, while other times, it doesn't. Given that, I always set up a specific site that I've created myself, just to be on the safe side.

So, let's work together to follow the exact process I always take when setting up NLS websites in a new DirectAccess environment.

Getting ready

Our NLS website will be hosted on an IIS server that runs Server 2019. Most of what we'll do will be accomplished from this web server, but we will also be creating a DNS record and will utilize Windows 10 with the RSAT tools for that task.

How to do it...

Let's work together to set up our new Network Location Server website:

1. First, decide on an internal DNS name to use for this website and set it up in the DNS of your domain. I am going to use `nls.ad.cookbook.packt.com` and will create a regular host (A) record in our internal DNS that points `nls.ad.cookbook.packt.com` to the IP address of my web server.

2. Now, log into that web server so that we can create some simple content for this new website. Create a new folder called `C:\inetpub\nls\`.

3. Inside your new folder, create a new `Default.htm` file.

4. Edit this file and throw some simple text in there. I usually say something like `This is the NLS website used by DirectAccess. Please do not delete or modify me!`:

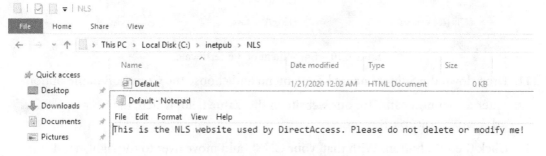

Figure 6.9 – The contents of our default.htm file for our new NLS website

5. Remember, this needs to be an HTTPS website, so before we try setting up the actual website, we should acquire the SSL certificate that we need to use with this site. Since this certificate is coming from my internal CA server, I'm going to open up MMC on my web server to accomplish this task.

6. Once MMC is opened, snap in the **Certificates** module. Make sure to choose **Computer account** and then **Local computer** when it prompts you for which certificate store you want to open.

7. Navigate to **Certificates (Local Computer) | Personal | Certificates**.

8. Right-click on this **Certificates** folder and choose **All Tasks | Request New Certificate....**

9. Click **Next** twice; you should see your list of certificate templates that are available on your internal CA server. If you do not see one that looks appropriate for requesting a website certificate, you may need to check over the settings on your CA server to make sure the correct templates have been configured for issuance.

10. My template is called **Custom Web Server**. Since this is a web server certificate, there is some additional information that I need to provide in my request in order to successfully issue a certificate. So, for this, go ahead and click on the link that says **More information is required to enroll for this certificate. Click here to configure settings**:

Figure 6.10 – Enrollment of the certificate

11. Drop down the **Subject name | Type** menu and choose the **Common name** option.

12. Enter a common name for our website in the **Value** field, which, in my case, is `nls.ad.cookbook.packt.com`.

13. Click the **Add** button. With that, your CN should move over to the right-hand side of the screen, like this:

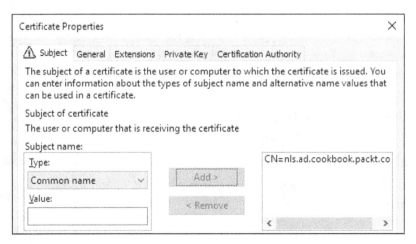

Figure 6.11 – Customizing our certificate request for the IIS site

Click on **OK** and then click on the **Enroll** button. You should now have an SSL certificate sitting in your certificates store that can be used to authenticate traffic moving to our `nls.ad.cookbook.packt.com` name:

1. Open **Internet Information Services (IIS) Manager** and browse to the **Sites** folder. Go ahead and remove the default website that IIS had automatically set up so that we can create our own NLS website without any fear of conflict.

2. Click on the **Add Website…** button.

3. Populate the required information, as shown in the following screenshot. Make sure to choose your own IP address and SSL certificate from the lists:

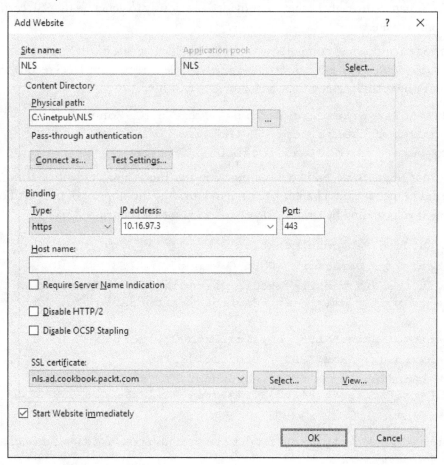

Figure 6.12 – The example IIS configuration for our NLS website

4. Click the **OK** button. Congratulations! You now have an NLS website running successfully in your network! You should be able to open up a browser on a client computer sitting inside the network and successfully browse to `https://nls.ad.cookbook.packt.com`.

If you've been following this book from the beginning, then you may have noticed that the process we followed here is almost identical to one from our *Chapter 5, Internet Information Services*. This is good news – it means that we can do almost all of this in PowerShell. The only part we cannot do easily in PowerShell is generate our SSL certificates. Let's take a look:

1. Follow *Steps 6* through *13* that we provided previously to generate the SSL certificate for our website.

2. On your Windows 10 computer with RSAT installed, create our DNS records. Using the `Add-DNSServerResourceRecordA` cmdlet. create your DNS record. For our example, this is going to be as follows:

    ```
    Add-DnsServerResourceRecordA -Name nls -ZoneName
    ad.cookbook.packt.com -IPv4Address 172.16.97.3
    -ComputerName dc01.ad.cookbook.packt.com
    ```

3. On your IIS machine, build out our new website. This is almost identical to what we did in the previous chapter. We need to know the thumbprint of our certificate (which you can find by running `dir Cert:\LocalMachine\My\`):

    ```
    Import-Module WebAdministration
    New-Item -Type Directory -Path C:\InetPub\NLS
    "This is the NLS website used by DirectAccess. Please do not
    delete or modify me!" | Set-Content C:\inetpub\NLS\default.
    htm
    New-Website -Name "NLS" -PhysicalPath C:\inetpub\NLS\
    New-WebBinding -Name "NLS" -Protocol HTTPS
    (Get-WebBinding -Name "NLS" -Protocol HTTPS).
    AddSslCertificate("57B42F29BCF499964407E42F23ADC587D3892E47",
    "my")
    ```

For a more in-depth look at what each of these commands does, take a look at *Chapter 5, Internet Information Services*.

How it works...

In this recipe, we configured a basic Network Location Server website for use with our DirectAccess environment. This site will do exactly what we need it to when our DA client computers try to validate whether they are inside or outside the corporate network. While this recipe meets our requirements for NLS and, in fact, puts us into the good practice of installing with NLS being hosted on its own web server, there is yet another step you could take to make it even better. Currently, this web server is a single point of failure for NLS. If this web server goes down or has a problem, we will have DirectAccess client computers inside the office thinking they are outside, and they will have some major name resolution problems until we sort out the NLS problem. Given that, it is a great idea to make NLS redundant. You could cluster servers together using **Microsoft Network Load Balancing (NLB)**, or even use a hardware load balancer if you have one available in your network. This way, you can run the same NLS website on multiple web servers and know that your clients will still work properly in the event of a web server failure.

Enabling Network Load Balancing on your DirectAccess servers

DirectAccess is designed so that you always get a single server environment up and running first before you start tinkering with arrays or load balancing. This way, you can validate that all of the environmental factors are in place and working and that you can successfully build DA tunnels from your client computers before introducing any further complexity into the design. Once established, however, it is a common next step to look into turning up another new server and creating some redundancy for your new remote access solution.

While joining two similar servers together to share the load is commonly called clustering, and sometimes I hear admins refer to it as such in the DirectAccess world, load balancing DA servers together actually has nothing to do with Windows clustering. When you install both the remote access role and the Network Load Balancing feature on your remote access servers, you have already equipped them with all the parts and pieces they need in order to communicate with each other and run an Active/Active sharing configuration. The operating system will make use of Windows NLB to shuttle traffic to the appropriate destinations, but everything inside NLB gets configured from the Remote Access Management Console. This gives you a nice visual console that can be used to administer and manage those NLB settings, right alongside your other remote access settings.

Once DirectAccess has been established and is running on a single server, there really are just a couple of quick wizards to run through to configure this NLB. However, the verbiage in these options can be quite confusing, especially if you're not overly familiar with the way that DirectAccess transmits packets. So, let's take some time to walk through creating an array from our existing DA server and adding a second node to that array.

Getting ready

We are going to use our existing RA01 server, which is already running DirectAccess. This, and our new server, RA02, are both running Windows Server 2019. They both have the Remote Access role and the Network Load Balancing feature installed. Both are joined to our domain and have their required certificates (SSL and IPsec) installed for use with DirectAccess. The same SSL certificate has been installed on both servers; since they are going to be sharing the load and all the requests to both systems will be coming in from the same public DNS name, they are able to share that certificate.

If your DirectAccess servers are virtual machines, there is one very important prerequisite: you must go into your VM's NIC settings and enable MAC address spoofing. In VMware ESXi/vSphere, this is called **Enable spoofing of MAC addresses**. On Hyper-V, this is called **Enable MAC address spoofing**. Without this feature enabled for each of your NICs, your network traffic will stop working altogether when you create a load balanced array.

How to do it...

For the purposes of this recipe, we are going to assume that RA01 has been configured for use with Teredo, meaning that it has two public IP addresses assigned on the external NIC. We are using this as an example because it is the most complex configuration to walk through when setting up NLB. The same procedure applies for a single IP on the external NIC; it would simply mean that you are only configuring one **Virtual IP (VIP)** instead of two. Let's get started:

1. First, we need to have a clear understanding of which IP addresses are going to be used where. This is critical information to possess and understand before we try to start any kind of configuration. The current RA01 IP addresses are as follows:

    a. **External IPs:** 192.0.2.10 and 192.0.2.11

    b. **Internal IP:** 172.16.97.7

2. These three IP addresses that are currently running on RA01 are going to turn into our **Virtual IPs (VIPs)**. These are the IP addresses that are going to be shared between both DirectAccess servers. Since we are changing the roles of these IPs, this means that we need to dedicate new **Dedicated IPs (DIPs)**, both internally and externally, to both RA01 and RA02.

3. These new IP address assignments are as follows:

   a. External VIPs (shared): 203.0.113.10 and 203.0.113.11

   b. Internal VIP (shared): 172.16.97.17

   c. RA01 External DIP: 203.0.113.12

   d. RA01 Internal DIP: 172.16.97.18

   e. RA02 External DIP: 203.0.113.13

   f. RA02 Internal DIP: 172.16.97.19

4. So, to summarize, when using Teredo (dual public IPs) and creating a two-node DirectAccess server load balanced array, you will need a total of four public IP addresses and three internal IP addresses.

5. On RA01, we are going to leave the VIPs in place for now. The DirectAccess wizards will change them for us later.

6. On the new RA02 server, set its final DIP addresses on the NICs. So, in our example, the external NIC gets 203.0.113.13 and the internal NIC gets 172.16.97.9.

7. There are only four steps to take on a DirectAccess array node server such as RA02, or any additional DA server that you want to add to the array in the future:

   a. Assign IP addresses

   b. Join it to the domain

   c. Install the certificates

   d. Add the Remote Access role and Network Load Balancing feature

8. The remainder of its configuration can be accomplished from the Remote Access Management Console on RA1.

9. On RA01, your primary DirectAccess server, open **Remote Access Management Console**.

10. In the left window, navigate to **Configuration | DirectAccess and VPN**.

11. Now, over in the right-hand **Tasks** pane, down at the bottom, choose **Enable Load Balancing**:

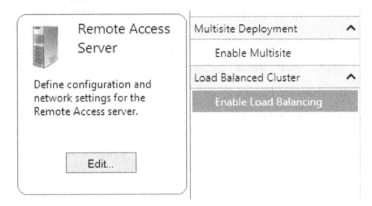

Figure 6.13 – The location of the Enable Load Balancing button

12. You may be presented with some configuration issues if your existing configuration is not suitable. If you have any errors, resolve them until there are none left, and then click **Next**.

13. Choose **Use Windows Network Load Balancing (NLB)**. You can see there is also an option for using an external load balancer, if you have one available to you. I find that the majority of customers utilize the built-in NLB, even when hardware load balancers are available.

14. The next screen is **External Dedicated IP Addresses**. This is where things start to get confusing and mistakes are often made. If you read the text on this screen, it is telling you that the current IP addresses being assigned to the NICs are now going to be used as VIPs. You do not need to specify anything about the VIPs on this screen. Instead, what we are doing on this screen and the next is specifying what *new* DIPs are now going to be assigned to the physical NICs on this server. First, since this is the external screen, we specify our new public IP, which will be used by RA01:

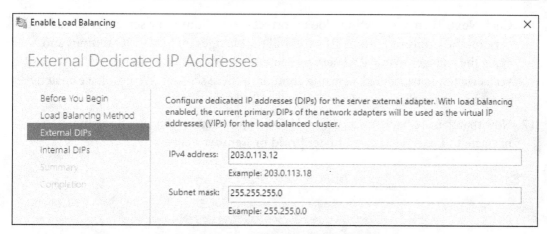

Figure 6.14 – Configuring the dedicated external IP address just for RA01

15. On the following screen, do the same thing but this time for the internal NIC. The current IP address of 172.16.97.7 is going to be converted into a shared VIP, so we need to specify the new internal DIP that is going to be assigned to RA1's internal NIC:

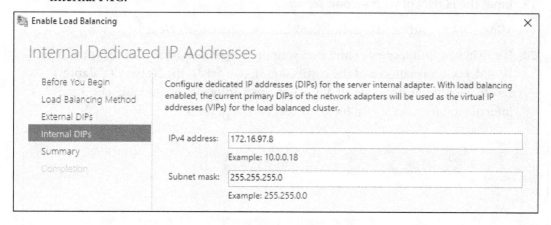

Figure 6.15 – Configuring the dedicated internal IP address just for RA01

> **Tip!**
> Now, you can see why having a definitive list of IP addresses before starting this wizard is important!

16. Click **Next**. Then, if everything looks correct on the **Summary** screen, go ahead and click on the **Commit** button. This will roll the changes into the GPO settings and apply the changes to our RA1 server. Remember that nothing has been done to RA2 yet as we haven't specified anything about it in these screens. We now have an active array, but so far, there is only one member: RA1.

17. Now that you are back inside the main **Configuration** screen, go ahead and navigate **to Load Balanced Cluster | Add or Remove Servers**:

Figure 6.16 – The Add or Remove Servers link

18. Click on the **Add Server…** button.

19. Input the FQDN of your second server.

    Mine is RA02.ad.cookbook.packt.com. Then, click **Next**.

20. If you have appropriately configured your second remote access server with correct IP address information and the certificates that it needs, the **Network Adapters** screen should self-populate all of the necessary information. Double-check this information to make sure it looks correct and click **Next**:

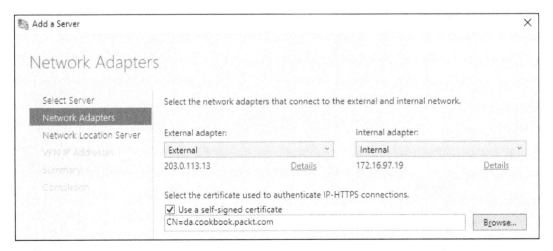

Figure 6.17 – The details for the second server have been set correctly

21. If you are using a VPN static pool, you will be asked to configure the IP address pool for your new server. It must not overlap with an existing server.

22. If the **Summary** page looks correct, click on the **Add** button.

23. Click **Close**. Then, back on the **Add or Remove Servers** screen, you should now see both of your remote access servers in the list. Go ahead and click on the **Commit** button to finalize the addition of this second node:

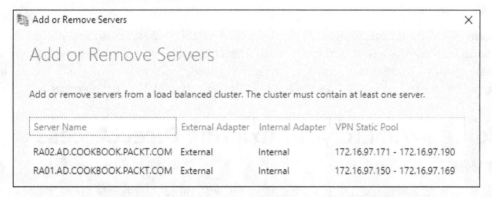

Figure 6.18 – The Add or Remove Servers screen showing two configured DA nodes

Following the addition of the second node, I always go back into the NIC properties of both NICs on both servers and make sure that all the expected IP addresses were added correctly. Sometimes, I find that the wizard is unable to successfully populate all of the VIPs and DIPs, and that I have to add them manually afterward. Each NIC now has a specific DIP, as listed at the beginning of this recipe. In addition to those DIPs, the external NIC on each server should also list both external VIPs, and the internal NIC on each server should list the internal VIP. The TCP/IPv4 properties of the NICs sure look to be overly populated with IP addresses, but this is all normal and "fine" for a successfully load balanced DirectAccess array.

How it works...

The ability to load balance DA servers together right out of the box with Windows Server 2019 is an incredibly nice feature. Redundancy is key for any good solution and configuring this array for an Active/Active failover situation is a no-brainer. While the wizards for enabling NLB are centralized right alongside all the other DirectAccess settings, they can certainly be confusing when you run through them for the first time. As with any system whose job is to shuttle network traffic around, planning correctly for IP addressing and routing is key to the success of your DirectAccess NLB deployment. Hopefully, this recipe has helped clear up questions surrounding this commonly requested task on our remote access servers.

Following the creation of your array, you will notice that navigating some of the screens inside the Remote Access Management Console has changed slightly. When you access screens such as **Configuration** to make changes, **Operations Status** to check on the status of your servers, or **Remote Client Status** to see what clients are connected, you will now notice that the nodes are listed separately. You can now click on the individual node name to see information on those screens that is specific to one particular server in the array, or you can click on **Load Balanced Cluster** in order to see information that is shared among all of the array members.

One other important note: Now that we have a load balanced array up and running, it is easy to add a third node to this array as well! Your DirectAccess array can grow as your company grows – to up to eight node servers, if required. Simply add additional servers to this array by navigating to the **Load Balanced Cluster | Add or Remove Servers** task.

Adding a VPN to your existing DirectAccess server

It is fairly common when starting work with the new Remote Access role for administrators to choose the **Deploy DirectAccess only** option. Maybe you initially thought this box was only going to be used for DA, or that all your client connections would be handled by only the DA role. While this is true for some organizations, it is common to get some benefit from having both DirectAccess and a VPN configured on your remote access entry point. Maybe you have some mobile phones or personal tablets that you want connected to the corporate network. Or perhaps you want your home computers or Macs running OSX to connect remotely. These are scenarios that are outside the scope of DirectAccess and require some other form of VPN connectivity.

Making significant changes on a production server can be intimidating, and you want to make sure that you select the right options. Also, IP addressing remote access servers isn't always a cakewalk, and so it would be natural to assume that turning a DirectAccess server into a DirectAccess plus VPN server would involve some additional IP addressing. You would actually be wrong about that last one. A VPN can share the public IP address already configured and running for your DA clients, so, thankfully, when you decide to add a VPN to your server, you don't have to reconfigure the NICs in any way. Since we don't have to make networking changes first, let's jump right into taking our production DA server and adding the VPN role to it.

Getting ready

For this recipe, we are working from our new DirectAccess server, which is a Windows Server 2019 server that has the Remote Access role installed.

How to do it...

To add VPN functionality to your existing 2019 DirectAccess server, follow these steps:

1. Open **Remote Access Management Console** from the **Tools** menu inside Server Manager.

2. In the left window, navigate to **Configuration | DirectAccess and VPN**. This is the screen where you can see the four setup steps listed in the middle.

3. Now, over on the right, you will see a section of buttons related to **VPN**. Go ahead and click on **Enable VPN**:

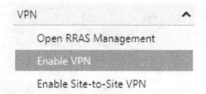

Figure 6.19 – Enabling VPN configuration on our Direct Access Server

4. You will receive a pop-up message asking you to make sure you intend to configure VPN settings on this server. Go ahead and click **OK**. This will cause your remote access server to spin through some processes, reaching out to the GPOs and reconfiguring the necessary settings so that they include VPN connectivity.

5. A VPN is now enabled on our server, but we have yet to configure IP addressing that will be handed out to the client computers. Once you are back at the main **Configuration** screen, click the **Edit...** button listed under step 2.

6. There is now a fourth screen available inside this mini wizard called **VPN Configuration**. Go ahead and click on that.

7. If you want VPN clients to pull IP addresses from an internal DHCP server, leave the radio button set to **Assign addresses automatically**. If you would rather specify a particular range of IP addresses that should be handed out to client computers, choose **Assign addresses from a static address pool** and specify the range of addresses in the given fields:

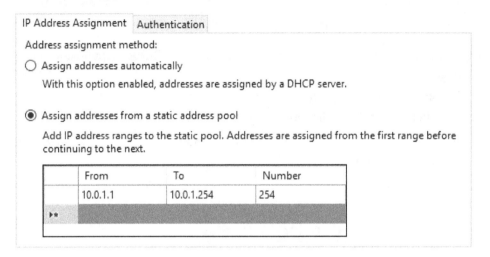

Figure 6.20 – Configuring the IP address assignment for our VPN clients

When you specify a static range like this, your remote access server will start handing out these addresses to the client computers that connect using a VPN. However, these client computers will most likely not be able to connect to any internal resources without a little additional networking consideration. When you create a static address pool for assigning IP addresses to VPN clients, there are two rules you need to keep in mind:

- The pool of addresses to be handed out to clients should come from a subnet that does not exist in the remote access server's internal routing table. For example, my network is 172.16.97.x and I am going to assign VPN client licenses from 10.0.1.x.

- You need to set the default route for this other subnet so that it points back to the internal IP address of the remote access server. If you don't do this, traffic from the VPN clients might make its way into the 10.0.1.x subnet, but responses from that subnet aren't going to know how to get back to the VPN client computers. By setting a default route on the 10.0.1.x subnet to point back to the internal NIC of the remote access server, you can fix this.

How it works...

The act of enabling a VPN on a DirectAccess server is a single action, but without a couple of extra configuration steps, that VPN enablement isn't going to do much for you. With this recipe, you should now have the information you need to enable and configure a VPN on your remote access server and get those machines connected that do not meet the requirements to be DirectAccess-connected. In the field, I find that most companies try to get all the computers they can connected via DirectAccess, because it is a much easier technology to deal with on the client side and is better for managing domain-joined systems. When faced with the need to connect computers that aren't Windows 7, 8, or 10, or are not domain-joined, it is nice to know that traditional VPN connectivity options exist right in our Server 2019 operating system.

Replacing your expiring IP-HTTPS certificate

DirectAccess has the ability to utilize certificates in a couple of different ways. Depending on how you configure DA, there are different places that certificates may or may not be used, but one common variable in all DirectAccess implementations is **IP-HTTPS**. This is a transition technology that is always enabled on a DA server, and it requires an SSL certificate to work properly. IP-HTTPS traffic comes in from the internet, and so I always recommend that the SSL certificate used for the IP-HTTPS listener should be one purchased from a public CA entity.

As with any SSL certificate, they are only valid for a certain time period. Typically, these certificates are purchased on a 1- or 2-year basis. This means that, eventually, you will have to renew that certificate and figure out how to make DirectAccess recognize and utilize the new one. IP-HTTPS makes use of a web listener inside IIS, and so it is a natural assumption that when you need to change your certificate, you do so inside IIS. This is an incorrect assumption. What's worse is that you can actually dig into the site inside IIS, change the certificate binding, and cause it to work for a while. This is not the correct place to change the certificate! If you simply change the binding inside IIS, your change will eventually be reversed, and it will go back to using the old certificate. Unfortunately, I get calls quite regularly from customers who do this and then have all sorts of users unable to connect remotely because the DA server has reverted to using the old, now expired, certificate.

Let's work through this recipe together to configure our DirectAccess so that it utilizes a new certificate that was recently purchased and installed on our server.

Getting ready

We have DirectAccess up and running on our Windows Server 2019 Remote Access server. Our SSL certificate that we use for IP-HTTPS is about to expire and we have renewed it with our CA. The new copy of the certificate has already been downloaded and installed on the server itself, so now, we just need to figure out where it needs to be adjusted for DirectAccess to start using it.

How to do it...

To adjust the DirectAccess configuration so that it starts using a new certificate for the IP-HTTPS listener, follow these steps:

1. Open **Remote Access Management Console** on your DirectAccess server.

2. In the left window, browse to **Configuration | DirectAccess and VPN**.

3. Under **Step 2** of the configuration, click on **Edit...**:

Figure 6.21 – Editing our DA configuration

4. Click **Next**.

5. You will now see the currently assigned certificate for IP-HTTPS. This is the certificate that is about to expire. Go ahead and click on the **Browse...** button:

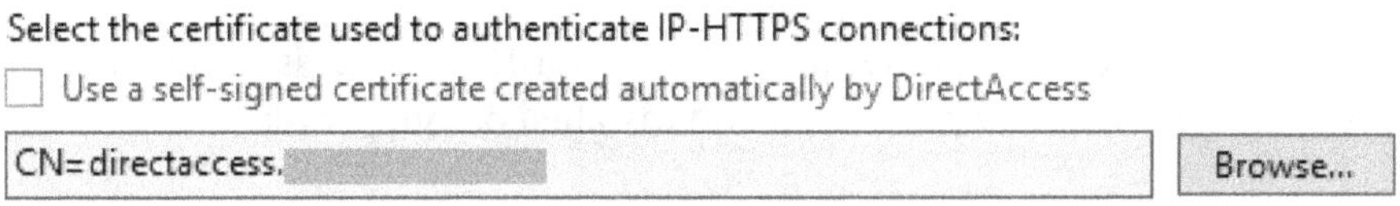

Select the certificate used to authenticate IP-HTTPS connections:

☐ Use a self-signed certificate created automatically by DirectAccess

CN=directaccess.⬛⬛⬛⬛⬛⬛⬛⬛⬛⬛   Browse...

Figure 6.22 – Selecting a new certificate to be bound to our IP-HTTPS endpoint

6. Now, simply choose the new certificate with the new expiration date from the newly opened list of available certificates.

7. Click **Next** a couple more times to complete the **Step 2** wizard.

> **Important**
>
> Keep in mind that the IP-HTTPS certificate is a per-node setting. If you have an array of multiple DirectAccess servers, you make all changes from the primary server's console, but you must install the certificate on each server and then make the certificate change on each node separately within the configuration.

8. At this point, nothing has actually been changed with the live configuration. To make this change active, you need to press the **Finish...** button, which is near the bottom of the **Remote Access Management Console**:

 Some configuration changes have not been applied. Click Finish to apply the changes.

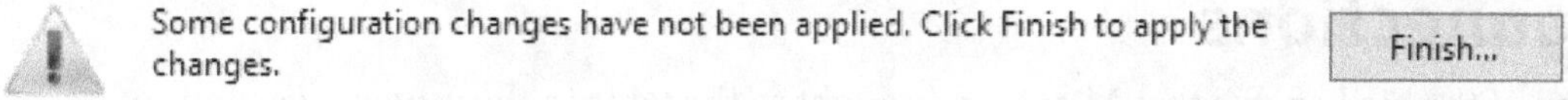

Figure 6.23 – Configuration change warning

9. If everything in the review looks good, click on **Apply**. This will push your changes into action. The new certificate is now in place and working to validate those IP-HTTPS connections.

How it works...

Replacing the SSL certificate that is used by IP-HTTPS is a regular and necessary task for any DirectAccess server administrator, but one that only comes around maybe once per year. This generally means that, by the time your certificate expiration date rolls around, you have probably forgotten where this setting is in the configuration. I hope this recipe can be a quick reference to alleviate that worry.

I always check the certificate from outside the network after making the change to ensure the new certificate is really the one that is now live on the system. If you take a computer outside of your network on the internet, try browsing to a dummy site from your public DNS record on your DirectAccess server. For example, if the public DNS record that you are using on your server is `directaccess.example.com`, try browsing to `https://directaccess.example.com/test`. You can expect to get a 404 error because the page we are requesting doesn't actually exist, but when you get this 404 error, you should have the ability to view which certificate is being used to validate your web traffic. View the certificate's details and make sure that it is your new certificate with the newest validity dates. Furthermore, if you encounter any kind of certificate warning message when you try to browse to this test website, this probably indicates that there is some kind of problem with the certificate, so you may need to investigate it further.

Reporting on DirectAccess and VPN connections

One of the big benefits that Microsoft brought to the table in these newer versions of the remote access role is reporting. In the past, it was difficult to tell who was connected and even harder to find out what they were doing or when they had been connected previously. Historical reporting on remote sessions was kind of absent. All that changes in the newer editions since we now have a nice interface to show us who is connecting, how often they are connecting, and even some information on what things they are doing while they are connected. Here, we'll look into those interfaces and explore some of the information that can be consumed. We will also make sure you know how to turn on historical reporting, as it is not enabled by default.

Getting ready

We will complete this recipe from our Windows Server 2019 Remote Access server, which is servicing both DirectAccess and VPN clients.

How to do it...

Follow these steps to get familiar with the remote access reporting options available in Server 2019:

1. Open the **Remote Access Management Console** from the **Tools** menu inside Server Manager.

2. In the left window, browse to **Remote Client Status**. Here, you will see a list of all the currently connected devices and users. This shows both DirectAccess connections and VPN connections.

3. If you click on a connection, you will see some additional data displayed below it. You can easily find out whether the user is connected using DirectAccess or a VPN, as well as some more specific information about their connection:

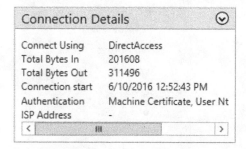

Figure 6.24 – Connection details showing an existing DirectAccess client connection

4. Look over toward the left a little, where it says **Access Details**. Here, you can see what internal resources have been accessed by the user and computer:

Protocol	Port	IP Address
6	80	192.168.250.45
6	445	192.168.250.18
17	389	192.168.250.2

Figure 6.25 – Viewing the resources accessed by the DA client

5. Once your environment is large enough that this screen becomes filled with connections, the **Search** box at the top comes in very handy. You simply type in any information you want to search for, and the results in the window will filter down to your search criteria.

6. If you would like to display more data on the screen, you can right-click on any of the existing column names and select additional columns to show or hide:

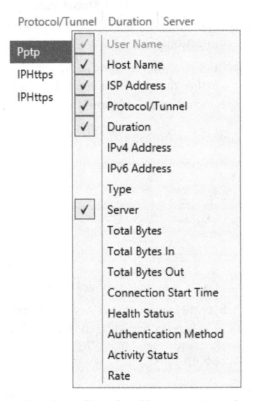

Figure 6.26 – Showing the column filters for adding/removing columns from the display

7. All this information is great! But what if we want to look back and view this data historically? Maybe you want to view connections from the past day or week. Maybe you need to come up with a report on how many connections happened over the past month. In the left window, click on **Reporting** to get started with that.

8. Since reporting is not enabled by default, we don't have any data here yet. Instead, you will see a message indicating that you need to configure accounting. Go ahead and click on this link:

Figure 6.27 – The Configure Accounting link

9. Now, you will see options for **Use RADIUS accounting**, **Use inbox accounting**, or both. RADIUS accounting implies that you have a RADIUS server set up and ready to accept this kind of data. I don't see many customers using this option. Instead, most select **Use inbox accounting**, which writes all the data right to **Windows Internal Database (WID)** on the DirectAccess server itself:

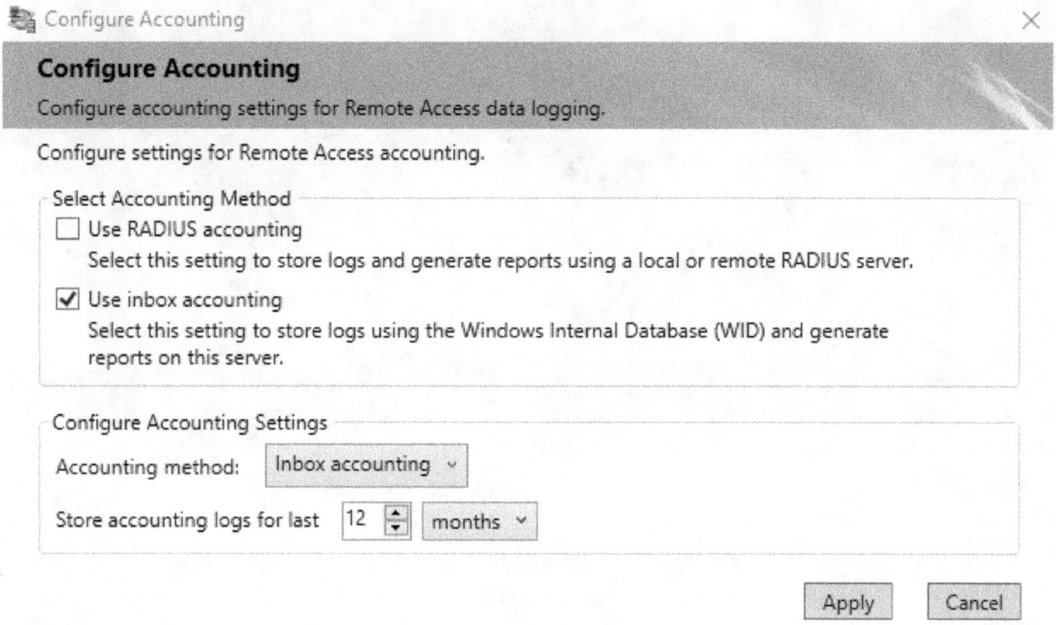

Figure 6.28 – Enabling inbox accounting

10. Once you have made your selection, click **Apply**. You will see that the **Reporting** screen now looks a lot more like the **Remote Client Status** screen, except that inside **Reporting**, you have additional options where you can select date ranges and pull historical information.

How it works...

Reporting user connection data is critical to most remote access systems. The inclusion of this data, particularly for historical connections, is a great feature addition that I am sure every remote access administrator is going to make use of. With a simple configuration change, we set up our Windows Remote Access server to keep track of these DirectAccess and VPN connections so that we can run and save reports on that data in the future.

7
Remote Desktop Services

Remote Desktop Services (**RDS**) is an outstanding way to provide users with access to applications and data, without those applications and data needing to reside on their local workstations. Formerly known as Terminal Services, this technology enables companies to retain control of all data and apps on centralized Remote Desktop servers, which users connect to from their workstations in order to access these items. There are two primary means of providing this information to users. The first is through a remote session, where users log into a **Remote Desktop Session Host** (**RDSH**) server and end up landing inside a session hosted on the server. This session looks and feels like a regular desktop computer to the user, as they have a full desktop and Start button and can launch any application available to them within that session. They are also able to save documents inside their session, keeping everything centralized. This is the most common flavor of RDS that I see used in the field and is where we will focus the majority of our administrative tasks that we'll discuss in this chapter.

A second way to provide data to users via RDS is **RemoteApp**. This is a neat function that is able to provide only the application itself remotely to the user's computer, rather than a full desktop session. This is a nice way to further restrict the access that is being provided to the user and simplifies the steps the user must take in order to access those resources.

An RDS environment has the potential to contain many servers, enough to fill its own book. Given that, we'll work together to get a simple RDS environment online that you can start testing with, and provide you with knowledge of some common administrative tasks that will be useful in an environment like this.

In this chapter, we'll cover the following recipes:

- Building a single server RDS environment
- Adding an additional RDSH server to your RDS environment
- Installing applications on an RDSH server
- Disabling the redirection of local resources
- Shadowing another session in RDS
- Installing a printer driver to use with redirection
- Removing an RD Session Host server from use for maintenance
- Publishing WordPad with RemoteApp
- Adding support for OpenGL and OpenCL applications

Basics of an RDS environment

I would like to take a minute and describe the different parts that could potentially make up your RDS environment. We won't be covering the installation or use of all components that might be involved with a full RDS deployment, but you should at least be aware of the components and their intended functions:

- **Remote Desktop Protocol (RDP)**: This is the name of the protocol given to Remote Access. In the same way you use HTTP to access websites, you use RDP to access remote desktops.

- **RDSH**: This is the most common type of RDS server as it is the one hosting the programs and sessions that users connect to. Depending on the size of your environment, there may be many of these servers running concurrently. In the past, this was called a Windows Terminal Server. If you see the phrase *Terminal Server* in use, this is what they're referring it.

- **Remote Desktop Connection Broker**: This is like the load balancer for RDS servers. It distributes users evenly across RDSH servers and helps users reconnect to existing sessions rather than create fresh ones.

- **Remote Desktop Licensing**: This is responsible for managing the licenses that are required for RDS use in a network.

- **Remote Desktop Gateway**: This is a gateway device that can bring remote users out on the internet into an RDS environment. For example, a user at home could utilize the connection provided by an RD Gateway in order to access work information.

- **Remote Desktop Web Access**: This enables users to access desktops and applications by using the local **Start** menu on their Windows 7, 8, or 10 computers. Users can also utilize this to access applications via a web browser.

- **Remote Desktop Virtualization Host**: This is a role that integrates with Hyper-V in order to provide virtual desktop sessions to users. The difference here is that resources given to those users are spun up from Hyper-V, rather than shared resources such as an RDSH.

Many of these roles can be placed together on a single server, which is what we will be doing in our recipes to bring a simple RDS environment online. As your deployment grows and you continue to add users and servers, it is generally a good idea to make these roles decentralized and redundant when possible.

Building a single server RDS environment

If you aren't coming into an environment where RDS is already up and running, it will be helpful to understand where the roles come from and how they are put into place. In this recipe, we are going to combine a number of Remote Desktop roles on a single server so that we can take a look at that installation process. When we are finished, we should have an RDS server that will allow users to connect and utilize a Remote Desktop session.

Getting ready

We will be using a Windows Server 2019 machine to install the RDS roles. This server is already joined to our domain. In our example, our server is called RDS01. You can run these steps from either the RDS server itself or a Windows 10 machines with the RSAT tools installed.

How to do it...

The following steps will direct you through installing the roles necessary for starting your first simple RDS server:

1. Open Server Manager and click on the **Add roles and features** link.

2. Click **Next**, which will bring you to the **Select installation type** screen. This is where we differ from normal as far as role installations go. For most roles, we tend to blow right through this screen without a second thought. For RDS, though, we need to make a change on this screen.

3. Choose the option for **Remote Desktop Services installation** and click **Next**:

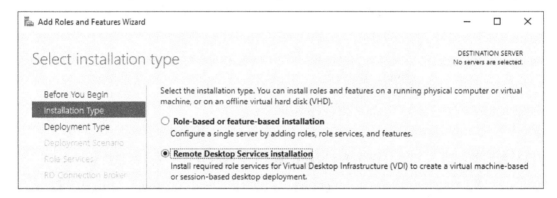

Figure 7.1 – Selecting the Remote Desktop Services installation option

4. Leave the default setting as **Standard deployment** and click **Next**. On this screen, we can choose the **Quick Start** option since we are intending to only configure a single server at this time. I am choosing not to take this shortcut because we want to take a good look at the different services that are going to be installed and want to leave our installation open to having multiple RDS servers down the road.

5. With this RDS server, we are planning to provide access to traditional desktop sessions, not integration with Hyper-V. So, on the **Select deployment scenario** screen, choose **Session-based desktop deployment**:

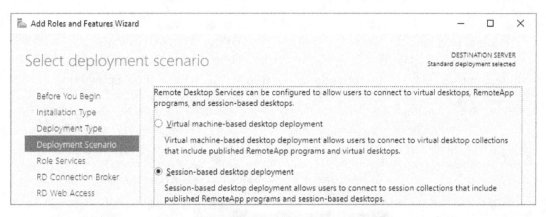

Figure 7.2 – Session-based desktop deployment

6. We will now see a summary of the role services required for our installation. Based on the options we have chosen, you should see **RD Connection Broker, RD Web Access,** and **RD Session Host** in this list. The next few screens will be used to define which servers are going to be used for these roles.

7. Since we are installing everything on a single server, for now, we only have one option in the **Server Pool** list, and we can simply move it over to the right column. Go ahead and click the arrow to do this on the **RD Connection Broker** page:

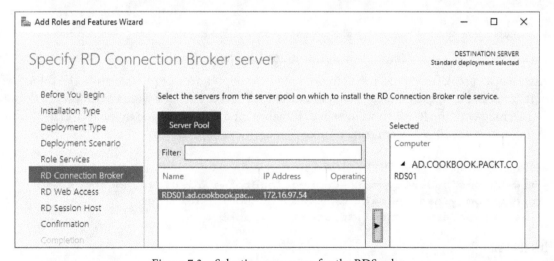

Figure 7.3 – Selecting our server for the RDS roles

8. Now, do the same thing on the next two screens. In our example, we are using the server named RDS01, so I am going to use it as both the RD Web Access server as well as the RD Session Host server.

9. Now, you should be on the **Confirm selections** screen, which gives you a summary of the actions about to be performed. For us, all three RDS services are being installed on the RDS01 server. We must now check the box that says **Restart the destination server automatically if required** and then press the **Deploy** button:

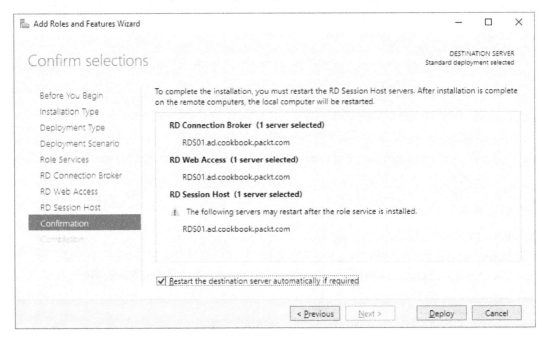

Figure 7.4 – RDS installation confirmation screen

After a brief break from PowerShell in the previous chapter, we're right back into the thick of it. You can run these cmdlets from either the RDS server itself, or with a Windows 10 machine with the RSAT tools installed. It makes little difference due to the fact that Windows Server 2019 has amazing remote management capabilities:

```
Import-Module RemoteDesktop
New-RDSessionDeployment -ConnectionBroker rds01.ad.cookbook.
packt.com -SessionHost rds01.ad.cookbook.packt.com
-WebAccessServer rds01.ad.cookbook.packt.com
```

It's that simple.

How it works...

We can follow this recipe to get our first simple RDS environment up and running. Our server will now allow users to connect and access virtual sessions that are hosted right on this RDS01 server. To log in, users can either launch the Remote Desktop Connection tool on their client computer and type in the RDS01 name of our server or open a web browser and head over to `https://rds01/rdweb`. Either way, they will land inside a desktop session that looks and feels pretty similar to a Windows 10 desktop. Inside this desktop provided by the RDS server, the user can launch applications and save documents, having everything run and stored right on the server itself rather than their local desktop computers. From this simple, single server RDS implementation, we can build and grow out to provide additional RDS roles on more servers, or for the purposes of handling additional user loads:

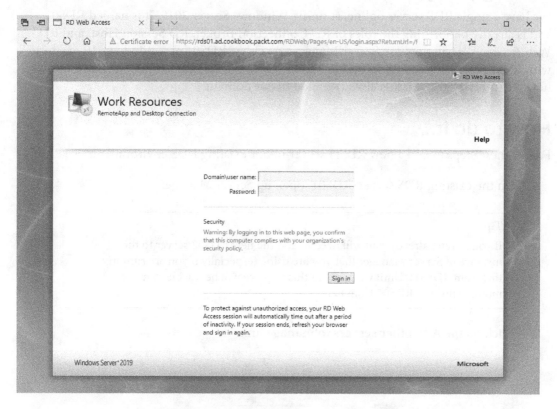

Figure 7.5 – The Remote Desktop Web Access portal running on rds01

Adding an additional RDSH server to your RDS environment

Most RDS implementations start out with a single server or at least a single RDSH. Once you have the roles established for successful connectivity here, it is a natural next step to add additional RDSH servers to accommodate more users. Or perhaps you want to segregate different types of users (and their applications) onto different RDSH servers. Whatever your reasoning, chances are that, at some point, you will want to add additional servers to your RDS environment. Let's add a second server to ours so that you can see how this process works.

Getting ready

We have a single RDS server online, running Windows Server 2019. It is named RDS01 and is already performing the roles of RD Connection Broker, RD Session Host, and RD Web Access. We will now use Server Manager on either RDS01 or a Windows 10 machine with RSAT installed to add a second RDSH server to our infrastructure. The name of our new server is RDS02, and it is already joined to our domain.

How to do it...

Follow these steps to add a new RDSH server to our existing RDS environment:

1. On the existing RDS server, RDS01, open up Server Manager.

> **Tip**
> If you haven't already, you will need to add the new RDS02 server to the instance of Server Manager that you are using (especially if you are running this from RDS01). Until we perform this step, we will be unable to make modifications to RDS02 from here.

2. Click on the **Add other servers to manage** link:

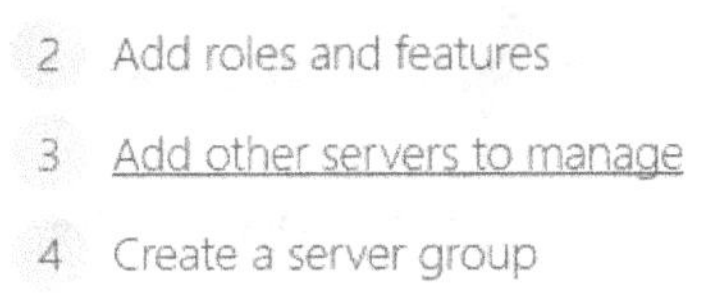

Figure 7.6 – The Add other servers to manage link

3. Type in the name of the new server that you intend to turn into an RDSH. For our example, the server name is RDS02. Then, click the right-hand arrow to add this server to the **Selected** list and click on **OK**.

4. Now, back on the main page of Server Manager, go ahead and click on the listing for **Remote Desktop Services** in the left window. This will bring us into the management interface for RDS. Take a look at **DEPLOYMENT OVERVIEW**, which is a self-generated diagram of what your current RDS deployment looks like. Since we are only testing with our current servers and not accessing them from outside the network, we will see plus symbols next to **RD Gateway** and **RD Licensing**. This simply means we have not configured these roles yet and that we could click on those pluses and follow the prompts if we wished to. We have no requirement for these services at the moment, so we will ignore this for now:

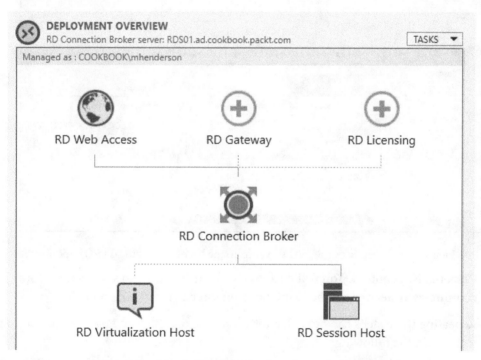

Figure 7.7 – A basic RDSH deployment layout being shown

5. To add a new RDSH server, head over to the top-right of this window and click on the link that says **Add RD Session Host servers**:

Figure 7.8 – The Add RD Session Host servers link

6. Since we added it to Server Manager earlier in this recipe, we should now be able to see the new server in this list, available to be selected. Select the new RDS02 server and click the arrow to move it into the **Selected** column. Then, click **Add**:

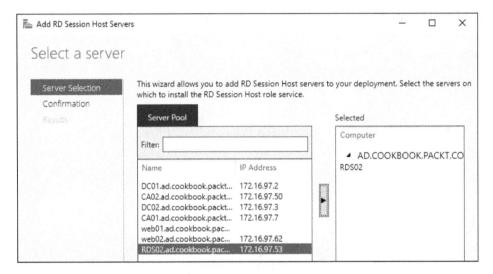

Figure 7.9 – Selecting our RDS02 server from the list of servers to add to the pool

7. Click the **Next** button. You will need to check the box that says **Restart remote computers as needed** on the **Confirmation** screen. Then, click on **Add**.

Repeating these steps can be with another simple one-liner in PowerShell. You can simply run the following:

```
Add-RDServer -Role RDS-RD-SERVER -Server rds02.ad.cookbook.
packt.com -ConnectionBroker rds01.ad.cookbook.packt.com
```

-   `Add-RDServer` is the cmdlet you use to add a server to a Remote Desktop pool.

-   `-Role RDS-RD-SERVER` indicates that we want this server to be a normal Remote Desktop server (not a licensing server or a connection broker). See the MSDN documentation for `Add-RDServer` for all the possible options for this flag.

- `-Server rds02.ad.cookbook.packt.com` is the FQDN of the server we want to add to the pool.

- `-ConnectionBroker rds01.ad.cookbook.packt.com` is the FQDN of the server running the Connection Broker role. In the previous recipe, we installed this role on our rds01 server.

How it works...

In this recipe, we used the Remote Desktop Services management console to take a new server that we had running and turned it into a **Remote Desktop Session Host (RDSH)** server. This RDSH is now part of our RDS infrastructure and can be managed right from this centralized management platform. In an RDS environment, this is typically the way that new roles are added to servers that are being brought into the environment. Using the centralized management console to perform many tasks in RDS makes a lot of sense because it is easy to see the big picture of your RDS infrastructure as you make changes or updates.

See also...

- The `Add-RDServer` cmdlet documentation: `https://docs.microsoft.com/en-us/powershell/module/remotedesktop/add-rdserver?view=win10-ps`

Installing applications on an RDSH server

As soon as you take a Windows server and turn it into a RDSH server to be used within an RDS environment, the way that applications work on that server changes significantly. Whenever programs and apps are installed on that RDSH, it needs to be put into a special **Install Mode**. Placing the server into Install Mode prior to launching the program installer is important to make sure that applications are going to be installed in a way that will allow multiple users to run them simultaneously. Remember, our RDSH servers will be hosting multiple user sessions – probably dozens of them.

Using Install Mode is so important to applications working properly on an RDSH that you really should not install any programs on the server before you turn it into an RDSH. Once that role has been established, then apps can be safely installed, as long as you are using Install Mode. Programs installed prior to converting that server into an RDSH may not work properly, and you might have to uninstall and reinstall them. There are a couple of different ways that Install Mode can be invoked during a program's installation; we'll take a look at both of them.

Getting ready

We need to install a program on our RDSH server. This box is running Windows Server 2019 and is already part of our RDS environment. We will also need, of course, the application installer files that we intend to launch.

How to do it...

One way to properly install programs on an RDSH is by using the Control Panel

1. Click on the **Start** button and type **Control Panel**. This will open the old-fashioned Control Panel. Note that this functionality is not found in the new Windows settings interface.

2. Click on **Programs**.

3. Click the button that says **Install Application on Remote Desktop...**:

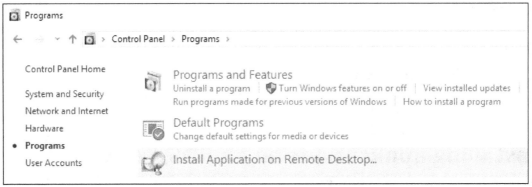

Figure 7.10 – Location of the Install Application on Remote Desktop... button

4. Click **Next**. Now, you will be able to specify the location of your installer file for the application:

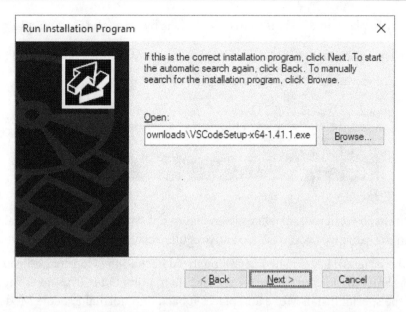

Figure 7.11 – Choosing the installer location for the program we want to install

5. Click **Next**, and your program will install. When finished, make sure you click the **Finish** button on the Install Mode mini wizard screen so that the RDSH is placed back into Execute Mode and is ready for normal operation:

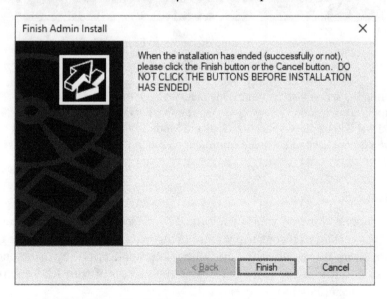

Figure 7.12 – The Finish button in the installation wizard

The second way to place an RDSH into Install Mode is by using the Command Prompt:

1. Right-click on the **Start** button and choose to open **Windows PowerShell (Admin)**.

2. Type change user /install and press *Enter*:

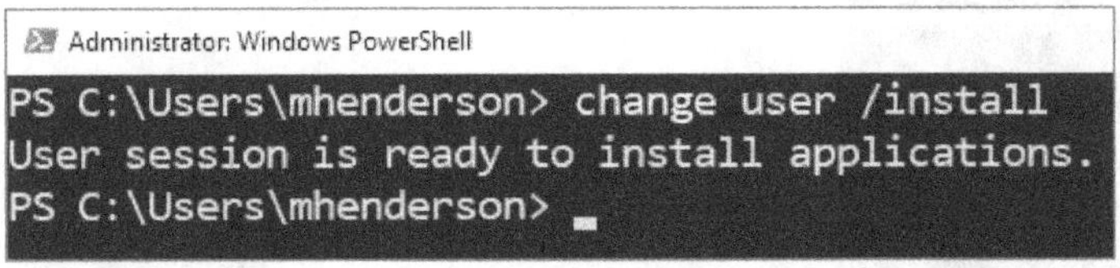

```
Administrator: Windows PowerShell
PS C:\Users\mhenderson> change user /install
User session is ready to install applications.
PS C:\Users\mhenderson> _
```

Figure 7.13 – Running the change user /install command in PowerShell

3. Now, find your program installer file and launch it. Walk through the installation steps in the same way you would on any regular server or computer.

4. Once the program has finished installing, head back to the Command Prompt window and type in **change user /execute**. Then, press *Enter*. This takes the RDSH out of the special Install Mode and places it back into normal Execute Mode:

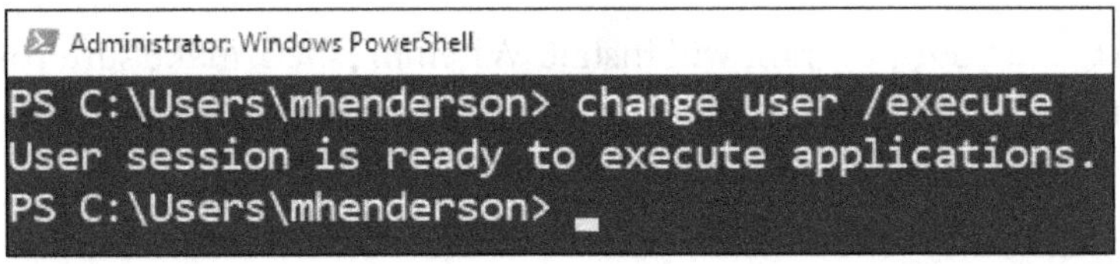

```
Administrator: Windows PowerShell
PS C:\Users\mhenderson> change user /execute
User session is ready to execute applications.
PS C:\Users\mhenderson> _
```

Figure 7.14 – Returning the server to Execute Mode

> **Tip**
> Restarting the server also automatically places it back into Execute Mode. If your application installer asks you to restart as part of the installation process, your RDSH will be placed back into Execute Mode when it boots, and in that case, you do not have to enter the command manually.

How it works...

When installing applications on an RDSH, it must be placed into a special Install Mode. Doing this remaps certain parts of the program being installed so that it can be run and utilized by many users at the same time. Installing your applications by using one of the methods discussed in this recipe will be critical to the success of your RDS environment being able to provide applications to users.

Also, keep in mind that it is recommended you have no users logged into an RDSH during the time of installation. When you are building fresh servers, this is easy as you don't typically allow anyone to connect until everything is installed and configured. But if you need to install new programs or updates for existing programs onto a production RDSH, you will want to take steps to ensure that users are not logged into the server before you place it into Install Mode and launch those executables. If you are running a farm of RDS servers and want to remove just one or some of them for maintenance or the installation of an application, make sure to check out the *Removing an RD Session Host server from use for maintenance* recipe.

I mentioned placing the RDSH into Install Mode even when just installing updates to existing applications. This is important. However, you do not need to place a server into Install Mode in order to install regular Windows operating system updates. These will install correctly, even when the server is in normal Execute Mode.

Disabling the redirection of local resources

One of the neat things about users connecting to virtual sessions within an RDS environment, especially when connecting remotely, is local resource redirection. This feature enables users to have access to things that are local to where they are sitting, from inside their virtual session, such as the clipboard, so that copy and paste functions will work between the local computer and RDS session and drive redirection so that you can save documents back and forth between the local hard drive and the RDS session. One of the most common uses of resource redirection is printers so that users can print from inside their RDS session, which is sitting on a server in the corporate network, directly to a printer on the local network where they are connected. An example could be someone needing to print a work document on a home printer.

This redirection technology can be very helpful but is often not desirable from a security and policies standpoint. Many organizations have a written security policy, which dictates that corporate data must remain within the corporate network and cannot move outside. Most often, I see this in medical environments, where strict standards are in place to make sure data stays private and secure. This means that data cannot be copied and pasted to the local computer, documents cannot be saved outside the RDS session, and that printing documents is also often not allowed.

While it may be disappointing that you cannot use these functions if your security policy dictates it, thankfully, disabling redirection is an easy thing to accomplish. Follow along to learn where these settings reside.

Getting ready

We need to logged into our Server 2019 RDSH server, or a Windows 10 machine with RSAT installed. Our RDS server is hosting some sensitive information and we want to make sure that users cannot save documents to their local computers, cannot print documents to local printers, and cannot copy/paste within the clipboard in order to move data from the RDS session to their local computers.

How to do it...

Follow along to disable these redirection features on our RDSH collection:

1. Open **Server Manager** and click on **Remote Desktop Services** to open the management of your RDS environment. Then, click on **Collections**.

2. If you do not currently have existing collections, click **Tasks** and then **Create Session Collection**. Follow the wizard to create a basic collection that contains our two RDS servers.

3. Now, click on the name of your collection. For our example, this one is called **My RDSH servers**.

4. Near the top of the screen, look for the section called **Properties**. Drop down the **Tasks** box and click on **Edit Properties**:

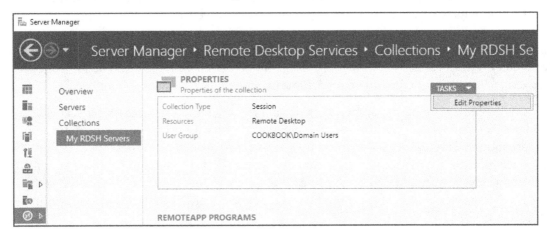

Figure 7.15 – Location of the Edit Properties button

5. Click on **Client Settings**.

6. Here, you will see a list of items that are currently capable of being redirected. Go ahead and deselect each of the redirections that you want to disable. For our example, we are unchecking **Drives**, **Clipboard**, and **Allow client printer redirection**:

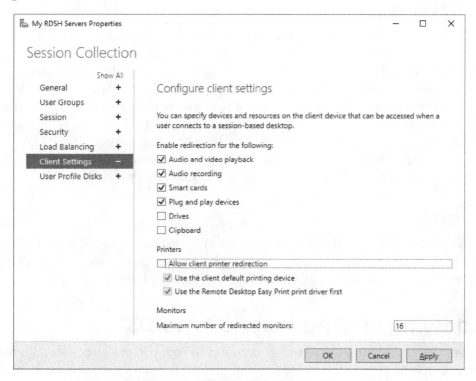

Figure 7.16 – Unchecking client settings in the collection properties

7. Click **OK**. Now, those redirected resources will no longer be available to client computers connecting to this RDSH collection.

    You can also achieve this using the New-RDSessionCollection and Set-RDSessionCollectionConfiguration PowerShell cmdlets:

```
New-RDSessionCollection -CollectionName "My RDSH
Servers" -SessionHost @("rds01.ad.cookbook.packt.com",
"rds02.ad.cookbook.packt.com") -ConnectionBroker rds01.
ad.cookbook.packt.com
```

```
Set-RDSessionCollectionConfiguration -CollectionName
"My RDSH Servers" -ClientDeviceRedirectionOptions
AudioRecording,AudioVideoPlayBack,SmartCard,
`PlugAndPlayDevice -ConnectionBroker rds01.ad.cookbook.
packt.com -Verbose -ClientPrinterRedirected:$false
```

In this case, when we call `Set-RDSessionCollectionConfiguration`, we only need to list the options we want enabled. Any options that are excluded will be disabled.

How it works...

Providing users with the capability of moving data back and forth between their local computers and RDS sessions sounds like a great feature but sometimes needs to be disabled. With some simple checkboxes, we can disable these capabilities wholesale so that you can adhere to security policies and make sure sensitive data remains protected. Once you are familiar with the location of these settings, the enablement or disablement of them is intuitive and easy to accomplish. What is even better is that these settings can be changed at any time; it doesn't have to be a decision that you make while the RDS environment is being built. If you make the decision to turn some of these options on or off down the road, you can make these changes at any time to a production RDS.

See also...

- The MSDN documentation for `Set-RDSessionCollectionConfiguration`: https://docs.microsoft.com/en-us/powershell/module/ remotedesktop/new-rdsessioncollection?view=win10-ps

Shadowing another session in RDS

Let's say you receive a phone call from a remote user in your company; they are currently sitting in a hotel and are having trouble figuring out how to open an application. This application isn't installed on their local computer; they are an RDS user, and they connect to a virtual session on an RDSH server in your network whenever they need to access this app. You think about asking for their password as that way, you could just log into the RDSH as them and take care of the problem. But alas, asking for a password is a serious breach of company security policy. Instead, perhaps you can use online meeting software to share the screen of their laptop and try to walk them through fixing the problem. But that would mean walking them through the installation of that meeting software and hoping you could explain how to use it over the phone.

Looking for a better solution? Use the *Shadowing* feature of RDS. If you log into the RDSH server where the user is already logged in, you can simply shadow their session in order to see what they are seeing. You can then work together to resolve the issue. You'll be able to take control and fix the problem, and maybe they can even take some notes and learn how to do it themselves next time to save making a phone call.

This recipe is included here, in particular, because RDS Shadowing was always available in older versions of Terminal Server, but was then removed from Server 2012 RDS. Well, good news! It was brought back by popular demand in Server 2012 R2 and remains here to stay in Windows Server 2019!

Getting ready

Our remote user is logged into a virtual session on our RDSH server, which is called RDS01. This is a Server 2019 machine that is part of our RDS infrastructure.

How to do it...

Let's help this remote user by shadowing their RD session:

1. First, we need to log into the same RDSH server that the user is logged into. On your computer, open **Remote Desktop Connection** and input the server name in order to connect.

2. Now that you are logged into the RDSH, right-click on the **Taskbar** and open **Task Manager**:

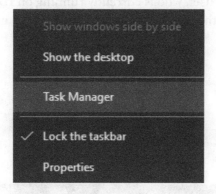

Figure 7.17 – Opening Task Manager

3. Click on **More details** in order to see more information about the server.

4. Navigate to the **Users** tab.

5. Right-click on one of the column headings and choose to show the **ID** column:

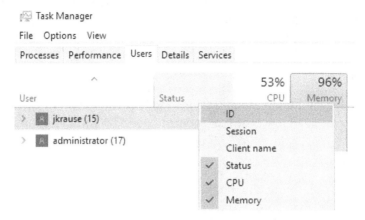

Figure 7.18 – Adding a column to the task manager

6. Leave Task Manager open so that you can see the username that you want to connect to and their ID number.

7. Now, open a Command Prompt and type in **mstsc /shadow:<id> /control**. So, for our particular **jkrause** user, who is currently running on ID 3, as you can see inside Task Manager, we use the **mstsc /shadow:3 /control** command:

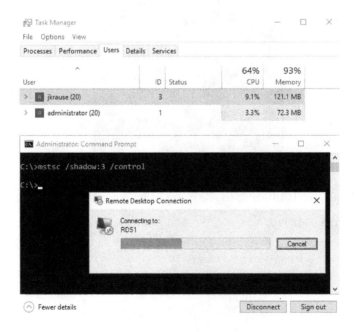

Figure 7.19 – Connecting to the session to shadow

8. This command will launch a shadowing session to the RD session of the ID number that you used, so make sure to use the correct ID for the user you want to shadow. Since we used the **/control** switch, you should also have the capability of using your own mouse and keyboard inside the user's session.

> Tip
>
> The mstsc command is short for Microsoft Terminal Services Client, so-called due to its original version for Windows NT 4, which was released in 1996!

How it works...

While shadowing in Server 2019 isn't quite as easy as it used to be in earlier versions of Terminal Server, it's great to know that this capability has returned after a noticeable absence in Server 2012. RDS Shadowing is a great tool to use for troubleshooting or collaboration as it enables you to share the screen of other personnel and assist with your own keyboard and mouse control when necessary. Having two sets of eyes on the same RD session can be invaluable in many situations; go try it out today!

Installing a printer driver to use with redirection

When a user connects to an RD session, if the client and server are configured properly, that connection will attempt to set up printer redirection between the RD session and the local computer. Specifically, what happens is that every printer that is installed on the local computer will be configured as a separate printer inside the user's RD session. This is a feature that enables users to be able to print to their local printers, even if the information they are accessing and printing is located halfway around the world.

When the RD connection builds these virtual printers, it attempts to use real printer drivers for them. For example, if the printer is an HP LaserJet 4100 and the RDSH server has the HP LaserJet 4100 driver installed, then when that printer gets set up inside the user session, it will utilize that existing, official driver. If the user logs into an RDSH with a printer whose driver does not exist on the RDSH server, however, by default, that printer will not be installed. There is a setting in the same configuration page where we enable or disable printer redirection on the RDSH server collection that can partially help with this. If you select the option on that screen for **Use the Remote Desktop Easy Print print driver first,** when the real driver doesn't exist for a particular printer, it will use a generic driver that may or may not actually work with the printer. This can certainly help bridge the gap when it comes to missing printer drivers but doesn't always solve the problem.

The best way to make sure your users are going to be able to print properly is to install the real driver on the RDSH. So, what's the point of this recipe? Who doesn't know how to install a printer driver, right? I'm writing this because most printer driver software packages are now full-blown applications, and we don't need a quarter of what comes with them. Driver install packages consume much more space than necessary for use with RDS, and we have to take into consideration that we are installing actual applications, which could potentially show up inside user sessions and cause confusion. So, what is the answer? Extract the simple driver files from those driver packages and use just the files themselves in order to install the driver on Windows. Let's do one together so you can see what I'm talking about.

Getting ready

We will be installing this printer driver on our RDSH server running Windows Server 2019. For our example, we will be using a Brother MFC-J625DW printer since this is the one, I installed for a customer just recently. Brother is usually good with providing a simple, small driver download that contains only the files we need for the driver itself.

How to do it...

Let's work together to download and install this printer driver on our RDSH so that it can be used for printer redirection:

1. First, download the driver files onto your RDSH server. Make sure to choose the driver for the server's operating system, not the client. So, when possible, I am going to choose Windows Server 2019. You can see in the following list that Windows Server 2019 is not an option available to me with this particular model of printer, and that is okay. In the event that the actual operating system driver is not available, you can often use one from a recent version of Windows and make it work. I will attempt to download the Windows 10 64-bit driver and see if it will install on my Windows Server 2019. Alternatively, I could probably get the Windows Server 2012 R2 64-bit or Windows Server 2016 64-bit driver to install as well:

Figure 7.20 – The Brother website's download page and selecting the Windows 10 (64-bit) software

2. We can see that there are a few different options available for downloading the driver. The first that is presented is the full software package, but that is 134 MB. Remember, as we mentioned earlier, the full software package is totally unnecessary on an RDS server. We only need the driver. A little further down the page, there is an option for **Add Printer Wizard Driver**. This is exactly what we need, and what do you know – it's only 23 MB!

 Drivers

Title	Description	Release Date (Version)	Size
Printer Driver & Scanner Driver for Local Connection	This download only includes the printer and scanner (WIA and/or TWAIN) drivers. ...more	11/28/2012 (D1)	23.04 MB
Add Printer Wizard Driver	This download only includes the printer drivers and is for users who are familiar with ...more	11/28/2012 (1.11)	23.04 MB

Figure 7.21 – Only downloading the precise part of the driver we need

> **Tip**
> With most driver downloads, you will also have to double-click on it once it's been downloaded in order to extract the files.

3.   Right-click on the **Start** button and choose **Settings**.

4.   Navigate to **Devices | Printers and Scanners**.

5.   Click the link on the right-hand side of the screen for **Print server properties**, which is located under **Related settings**:

Figure 7.22 – The Print server properties link, located on the right-hand side of this screen

6.   Browse to the **Drivers** tab. This displays a list of currently installed printer drivers on this server. Then, click the **Add...** button. If this button is disabled, click the **Change Driver Settings** button to enable it.

7.   Click **Next** twice. We can leave the **Processor Selection** screen marked as only **x64** since Windows Server 2019 only comes in 64-bit.

8.   Now, click on **Have Disk...** and browse to the location of the driver files that you downloaded. You are looking for an **INF** file that typically sits in the root of that driver folder. Sometimes, you will have to poke around a little until you find it, but the file is always an **INF** file:

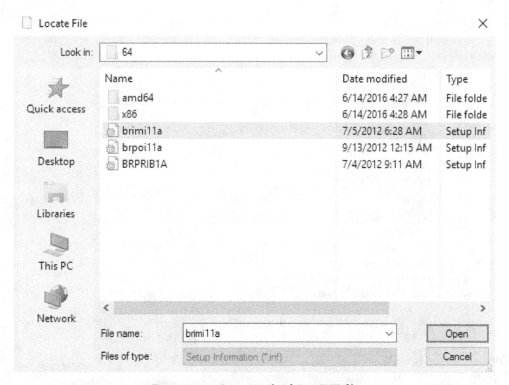

Figure 7.23 – Locating the driver INF file

9. Once you have selected the **INF** file, the **Add Printer Driver Wizard** window will now display a list of the drivers that are contained within that **INF** file. Choose the specific printer driver that you want to install and click **Next**:

Figure 7.24 – Showing the list of device drivers being installed

10. Click **Finish** and the driver will install. You should now see it in the list of printer drivers that are installed on this server:

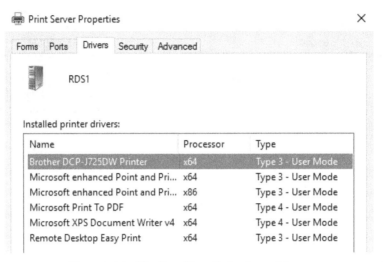

Figure 7.25 – The list of installed printer drivers

How it works...

Installing printer drivers on RDSH servers is a common administrative task in environments where printer redirection is allowed. We walked through one of the nice, simple installers that was easy to extract and contained only the actual driver files that we needed. These kinds of driver downloads are perfect for our purposes here.

As you experience more and more of these driver installations, you will start to learn which manufacturers provide simple driver packages for this purpose and which ones do not. Ultimately, though, the software always contains the simple driver files; sometimes, it's just a matter of launching the huge installer program so that it places the files somewhere in a temporary location on the hard drive.

What I normally do in these situations is launch the installer and walk it through whatever steps are necessary in order to see that it is unpacking/extracting files. Once it has done that, you don't have to run any more of the wizard to install the software applications because you know that the driver files you need are sitting on the hard drive of the server somewhere – we just need to find them. Using a utility such as FileMon can help identify file locations that have been recently modified and is a pretty quick way to track down those driver files that are usually hidden away in a temp folder. Once you find the files, you can copy and paste them into a more permanent folder for driver installation purposes, cancel out of the install wizard, and walk through the steps in this recipe to install that driver manually instead.

Removing an RD Session Host server from use for maintenance

Occasionally, you will have to perform some maintenance on your RDSH servers. Whether this is for installing updates, installing new applications, or taking them down for some physical maintenance, it will happen sooner or later. If you have multiple RDSH servers in a collection and simply take one offline, user loads will eventually sort themselves out as the RD broker will send new connections to the RDSH servers that are still online. However, you will have caused frustration and headaches for any users who were logged in when you shut it down. It is much more user-friendly to flag an RDSH to make it unable to accept new user connections and let the existing ones dissolve naturally over a period of time. This is like a *drain stop* in the Network Load Balancer world.

Let's look at the setting included in RDS that allows us to flag an RDSH as unusable and force the broker to keep new connections from coming through to it. We'll also reverse that change to make sure it starts accepting user connections again after our maintenance is complete.

Getting ready

We have an RDS environment configured with two RDSH servers. These are called RDS01 and RDS02, and we are required to do some maintenance on RDS02. Our work will be accomplished from inside the Remote Desktop management console of RTDS01 or a Windows 10 computer equipped with RSAT.

How to do it...

To stop new user connections from flowing to RDS02, follow these steps:

1. Open **Server Manager** and click on **Remote Desktop Services** in the left window.

2. Navigate to **Collections | My RDSH Servers**. This is the name of the collection in my environment; you will need to click on whatever the name of your collection is.

3. Scroll down to the bottom, where you can see the **Host Servers** section. You will see a list of RDSH servers that are part of your collection.

4. Right-click on the RDSH server that we need to perform some maintenance on. In our case, it is **RDS02**.

5. Click on **Do not allow new connections**:

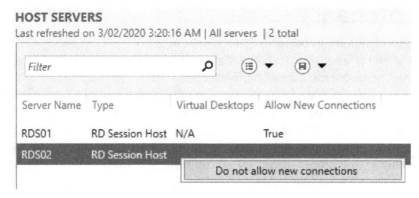

Figure 7.26 – Disabling new connections to an RDS host

6. This will cause any new connections to be sent over to RDS01 or whatever other RDSH servers you have in your collection. Then, once your maintenance is complete and you are ready to reintroduce RDS02 back into the collection, simply right-click on its name here again and, this time, choose **Allow new connections**:

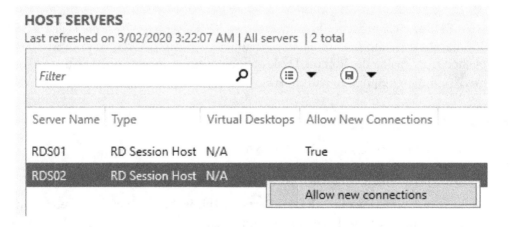

Figure 7.27 – Enabling new connections to an RDS host

The PowerShell cmdlet for achieving the same is `Set-RDSessionHost`:

```
Set-RDSessionHost -SessionHost "rds02.ad.cookbook.packt.com"
-NewConnectionAllowed No -ConnectionBroker "rds01.ad.cookbook.
packt.com"
```

```
Set-RDSessionHost -SessionHost "rds02.ad.cookbook.packt.com"
-NewConnectionAllowed Yes -ConnectionBroker "rds01.ad.cookbook.
packt.com"
```

These two one-liners are an example of both disabling and enabling new connections to a given RDS host.

How it works...

This simple option can be a very helpful utility when you're considering performing maintenance within your RDS infrastructure. Remember, disallowing new connections to a particular RDSH does not mean that it is immediately available for maintenance as existing users will still be logged into it. We have only set it so that no new connections will flow there. You can give it some planned time to naturally drop the remaining connections that do exist on the server before performing your maintenance.

Publishing WordPad with RemoteApp

Most of the recipes in this chapter are focused on full desktop sessions provided by RDSH servers because this is the most common scenario that I find RDS being used for in the field. One additional piece I would like to take a quick look into is RemoteApp publishing. This is the ability to publish individual applications out to remote users from an RDSH server, rather than a full desktop session. It provides a seamless window for the application, allowing RemoteApp to look and feel like any other program on the user's computer. Let's set up a sample application and test using it from a client computer. For the sake of simplicity in demonstrating this capability, we will use WordPad as our application to publish and launch.

Getting ready

To publish WordPad as a RemoteApp, we will use Server Manager from any of our RDS machines or use a Windows 10 machine with RSAT installed. We will also use a client computer in order to test accessing this application once we have finished publishing it.

How to do it...

To publish WordPad as a RemoteApp, follow these steps:

1. On RDS01, launch **Server Manager** and click on **Remote Desktop Services** from the left window.

2. Browse to the collection of RDSH servers where you want to publish this new application. For our example, I am browsing to **Collections | My RDSH Servers**.

3. Near the middle of this window, you will see a section called **REMOTEAPP PROGRAMS**. Click on the link in the middle of this window that says **Publish RemoteApp programs**:

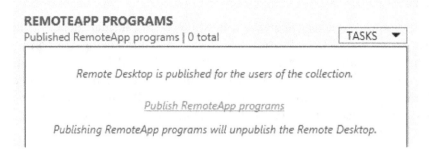

Figure 7.28 – The Publish RemoteApp programs link location

4. The wizard will now poll the server for a list of available applications. Look through the list until you see **WordPad**; it will probably be at the bottom. Choose it and click **Next**:

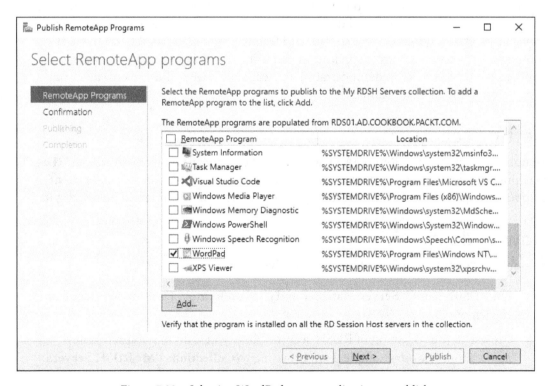

Figure 7.29 – Selecting WordPad as our application to publish

5. On the **Confirmation** screen, click **Publish**.

6. Now that we have published the WordPad application, log into a client computer so that we can test accessing it.

7. On the client computer, open up a web browser and navigate to **https://RDS01/RDweb**:

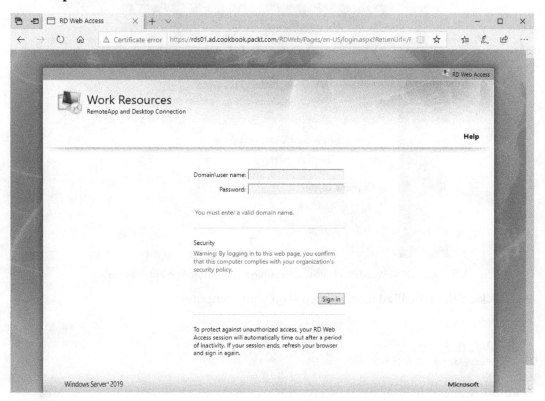

Figure 7.30 – The Remote Desktop Web App login screen

8. Input your credentials. Now, you should see our published resources that are available in the RDS environment. As expected, WordPad is now visible here:

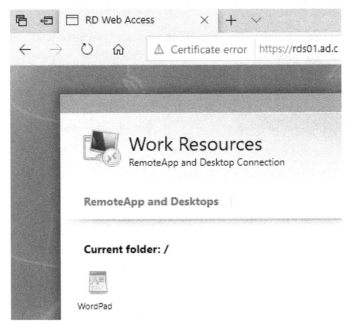

Figure 7.31 – WordPad is now accessible as a RemoteApp application

9. Click on the **WordPad** icon to open it on your computer:

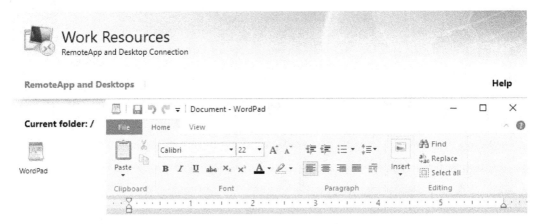

Figure 7.32 – WordPad is being run as a remote application off our RDS servers

How it works...

If you do not have a need for users to receive access to a full desktop when they log into the RDS environment, you have the option of publishing individual applications instead. This can be useful for restricting the resources that employees have access to, or perhaps for someone such as a vendor or a temporary assignment that only needs access to certain programs and data. While this was a very simple demonstration of using the WordPad program baked into Windows, you can use this same process with other applications you have installed on your RDSH servers.

> **Important!**
> Make sure you install the applications on all the RDSH servers in your collection.

Adding support for OpenGL and OpenCL applications

Modern operating systems such as Windows Server 2019 are built to solve modern problems. A lot of modern problems these days are solved with the use of OpenCL computations. OpenCL is hardware-accelerated computing, most usually found on dedicated graphics cards. That's right – the same kind of graphics cards you might put in a gaming PC. There are also dedicated server-grade compute cards that deliver the same computation performance but are packaged in a way that makes them easier to sell to data centers. However, I have seen (and built) data center servers that contain consumer-grade graphics cards. Sometimes, multiple cards in the single server.

There is also OpenGL, which allows for graphics-heavy computations, such as CAD, 3D rendering, or even high-resolution video streaming. Most cards that support one will support the other.

The good news for Remote Desktop users is that we can now allow people to use these compute-intensive applications remotely. If your server is equipped with a suitable graphics card, we can tell RDS that it can use that capability for Remote Desktop sessions.

Getting ready

We need to have our RDS servers joined to the domain and placed under a domain OU. We're going to use tools either installed on a Windows 10 machine with RSAT installed or a domain controller. You can run this recipe for any RDS server, but it will only be useful if you have an RDS server with a GPU installed.

How to do it...

On our Windows 10 computer with RSAT, or a domain controller, follow these steps:

1. Open the **Group Policy Management** screen by clicking **Start** and then typing *Group policy management*. It should show up as a search result.

2. Locate the OU where you have placed your RDS servers. In my example, it can be found under `Servers\RDS`. Right-click the OU and choose **Create a GPO in this domain, and Link it here…**:

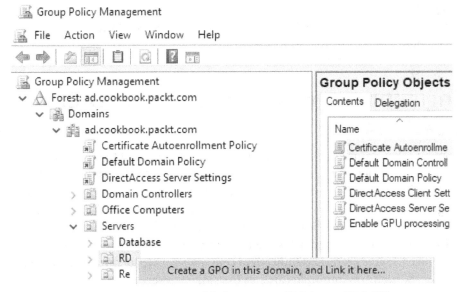

Figure 7.33 – Creating and linking a new GPO in our RDS OU

3. Name your GPO something appropriate, such as *Enable GPU processing*, and click **OK**.

4. Right-click your new GPU and choose **Edit…**.

5. On the left-hand side, navigate to **Computer Configuration | Policies | Windows Administrative Templates | Windows Components | Remote Desktop Services | Remote Desktop Session Host | Remote Session Environment**.

6. Under settings on the right-hand side, locate **Use hardware graphics adapters for all Remote Desktop Services sessions**. Right-click this and choose **Edit**.

7.   Change the option to **Enabled** and click **OK**:

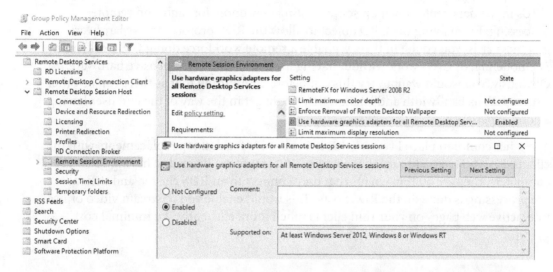

Figure 7.34 – Showing the location of the GPO option and setting it to Enabled

8.   You can validate that the setting has been applied by executing gpresult /R on an RDS server and looking for *Applied Group Policy Objects* and seeing if our new GPO is listed. It typically shows up within an hour, or after a restart:

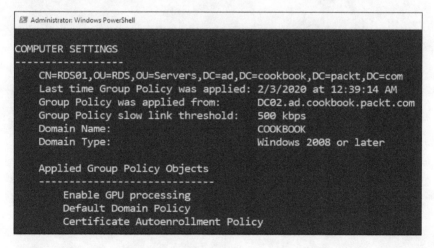

Figure 7.35 – Showing that the Enable GPU processing GPO has been applied

How it works...

GPUs in the data center open up some exciting new doors for high-end remote processing. By enabling the GPO object to allow the RDP protocol to use hardware graphics cards, you could, in theory, enable a remote workforce doing GIS work, light 3D modeling, or CAD work without having to send them very expensive hardware. Obviously, you would want to try this out before committing to it as there can be other issues, such as bandwidth and latency, that might get in the way of the end user having a good experience.

The other common place I've seen this being used is for desktop replacements with thin clients. Say you have a library that contains 30 computers. Instead of having 30 actual computers, they are 30 thin clients that only connect to an RDS cluster, and then all the processing is done on the RDS hosts. This would enable you to stream video or use interactive web pages on your thin clients much more efficiently at a minimal cost.

8
Monitoring and Backup

Monitoring and backing up servers are usually mundane tasks that are easily overlooked or forgotten. When everything is running smoothly, you may not even think about whether your servers have backed up properly, maybe for weeks at a time. Except in the largest of companies, there usually aren't dedicated backup admins or performance monitoring gurus. In IT, we all wear many different hats and they don't always fit on top of each other. The key phrase here is *when everything is running smoothly*. Unfortunately, this state of bliss cannot continue indefinitely. Hardware fails, malware and crypto lockers happen, and files are accidentally deleted. Suddenly, those dull chores of due diligence, such as monitoring the health of your servers and making sure you have solid backups, jump from backburner to mission-critical on the importance scale.

There are many third-party tools available for performing functions such as data backups and performance monitoring, and because these tools exist, it is easy to automatically assume that they will do a better job than anything that comes with the operating system. Given that, we often categorize backups and monitoring into areas where we will have to spend extra money. I'm not trying to argue that every add-on tool for these functions is unnecessary, because they do certainly benefit the right kinds of company. But anyone willing to dig into Server 2019 and discover what it can accomplish on its own accord, without extra add-ons, I think will find that it meets the needs of many businesses.

The good news is that performing monitoring and backups have never been easier than they are in Windows Server 2019. In this chapter, we'll explore some of the tools that exist to make these areas of your infrastructure efficient and automatic by completing the following recipes:

- Using Server Manager as a quick monitoring tool
- Using the Task Manager to its full potential
- Configuring a full system backup using Windows Server Backup
- Recovering data from a Windows backup file
- Using IP Address Management to keep track of your used IP addresses
- Checking for viruses and adding ransomware protection

Using Server Manager as a quick monitoring tool

Sometimes, change is difficult for old-school IT guys. You know, the ones who prefer keyboards over mice and command lines over graphical interfaces. Starting in Server 2012, Server Manager changed a lot. I found at that time that many admins automatically disliked it, even before they started using it. It looks *cloudy* and full of links to click on rather than applications. It's certainly more of a web app interface than the Server Manager we are used to. And the Windows Admin Center that we touched on in earlier chapters of this book – that's a literal web page!

Let's use this recipe to point out some of the important data that exists in Server Manager and discover for ourselves that Microsoft may actually have a valid point in causing it to open automatically every time that you log into a server. No, it's not just there to annoy you.

Getting ready

All we need is Windows Server 2019 or a Windows 10 machine with RSAT installed. The servers we are looking at are domain joined with a few roles installed so that we can get a better feel for the layout of data on a production system.

How to do it...

Follow these steps to discover some of the functions that Server Manager can perform:

1. Open up **Server Manager**. If you are logging onto a server rather than using RSAT, it will probably open automatically. Otherwise, click on the **Server Manager** button inside your Start menu.

2. If this is a Windows 10 machine with RSAT installed, you may need to add some servers to Server Manager to get any useful information. If so, click **Manage** and then **Add Servers**. Then, follow the on-screen instructions to add some servers to your Server Manager:

Figure 8.1 – The location of the Add Servers menu item in Server Manager

3. Normally, at the top of Server Manager is a section entitled **Welcome to Server Manager**. In the lower-right corner of that section is a button that says **Hide**. Go ahead and click on that button to hide this section of the screen.

4. Now, look at the information on your screen. The normally green bars listed under each service that the servers have added to Server Manager are your first indication as to whether everything is running smoothly. Almost everything is green on mine, which means almost everything is OK, but there are some problems with my services:

Figure 8.2 – Server Manager showing the health of various functions within our servers

5. Let's take a closer look at the issues my servers have. Let's take a look at the box that's highlighted in red:

Figure 8.3 – There are six errors with my services and one error with my manageability

6. If I click on the **Services** button, where it is indicating that I have six notifications, I can see the details of what is going on. Right here, I can right-click on the warning message and choose **Start Services** as a repair method:

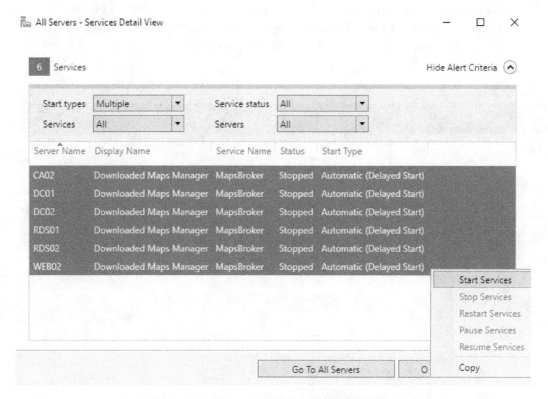

Figure 8.4 – A list of services that should be running but aren't

> **Tip**
>
> Why does Windows Server 2019 have a Downloaded Maps Manager? I don't know. However, it breaks on almost every single Windows Server installation I have ever seen. You *can* choose to ignore this specific error if you wish, but for the sake of having a nice green dashboard, you may prefer to fix it. Or, you can disable the service entirely since it's a map downloader, which makes no sense.

7. If you are looking at a role-specific error, there will be a button near the bottom of this screen to take you to that service's management page. For example, if you were looking at an AD DS error, there would be a button saying **Go To AD DS**. Upon clicking that button, you will see that it brings us to the same screen as if we had clicked on **AD DS** in the left window pane in Server Manager. On this screen, we can see even more information about our AD DS role and any trouble that it may be having:

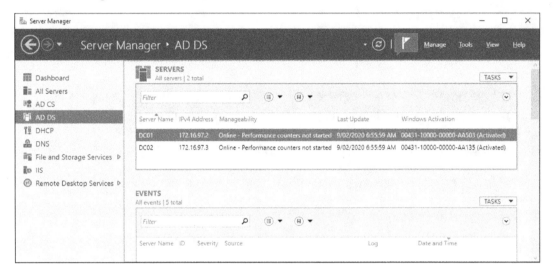

Figure 8.5 – The AD DS screen inside Server Manager

> **Tip**
> For any role that you have installed on your server, there is a quick link to that role's section of Server Manager in the left window pane. Click on each role to view the events and information specific to that role.

8. Scroll down near the bottom of this page to view a list of events that are happening on this server, without having to open a separate Event Viewer window:

EVENTS
All events | 5 total   TASKS ▼

Filter   🔍   (≣) ▼   (▣) ▼   ⌄

Server Name	ID	Severity	Source	Log	Date and Time
DC01	2089	Warning	Microsoft-Windows-ActiveDirectory_DomainService	Directory Service	8/02/2020 11:27:30 PM
DC01	2089	Warning	Microsoft-Windows-ActiveDirectory_DomainService	Directory Service	8/02/2020 11:27:30 PM
DC01	2089	Warning	Microsoft-Windows-ActiveDirectory_DomainService	Directory Service	8/02/2020 11:27:30 PM
DC01	2089	Warning	Microsoft-Windows-ActiveDirectory_DomainService	Directory Service	8/02/2020 11:27:30 PM
DC01	2089	Warning	Microsoft-Windows-ActiveDirectory_DomainService	Directory Service	8/02/2020 11:27:30 PM

Figure 8.6 – A list of recent events that can be opened from within Server Manager

9. If you are logged onto a Windows Server 2019 box directly (and not using Windows
    10 with RSAT), many of the items on the **Local Server** screen are links to open
    additional configuration windows. For example, where it tells us that **the IE
    Enhanced Security Configuration** is currently **On**, if we click on the word **On
    (Recommended)**, we get the properties page for configuring the IE Enhanced
    Security Configuration settings on this server:

Figure 8.7 – Modifying a system setting from within Server Manager

How it works...

Server Manager is full of opportunities that allow you to quickly find information that will help you monitor your servers. This recipe is just a sample of the data that you can pull into Server Manager, so I suggest that you continue navigating around in there to make it look and feel the best that it can for your environment. Another extremely helpful option here is to use Windows 10 with RSAT and add multiple servers into Server Manager for monitoring purposes. If you use the **Manage** menu near the top and the **Add Servers** function in that menu, you can add additional systems into your Server Manager window pane. Doing this causes Server Manager to pull information not only about the local server that you are logged into, but also about these remote servers, all into one pane of glass. This way, you can use Server Manager on one server in order to monitor and maintain your entire server infrastructure, if you choose to do so.

Using the new Task Manager to its full potential

We have all used *Ctrl + Alt + Delete* to open Task Manager and attempt to close problematic applications. With the Task Manager provided by Windows Server 2019, we can do much more right from that same interface. Let's work through this recipe to explore some of the new things that can be done to take full advantage of this tool.

Getting ready

We are logged into a Windows Server 2019 server. This is the only system required for our recipe.

How to do it...

Follow these steps to learn a little more about Task Manager:

1. Right-click on the taskbar and choose to open **Task Manager**. This is an alternate way to get into the utility, other than using the *Ctrl + Alt + Delete* key combination. I prefer using the taskbar and right-clicking because, when using the keyboard, it is easy to open the wrong Task Manager when you are using a virtualization console or RDP to administer remote servers.

    > **Tip**
    > If you are using Remote Desktop, the shortcut is *Ctrl + Alt + End*, not *Delete*.

2. You are now looking at the simple version of Task Manager, where you can choose an application and click **End task** in order to forcibly close that application. To dig a little deeper, click on the **More details** link near the bottom:

Figure 8.8 – The basic Task Manager view

Now this is more like it! We can see all the open applications at a quick glance, including how many resources each one is consuming. This makes it easy to identify applications that might be stuck and consuming large amounts of CPU or memory. It also lists **Background processes** separately, which can be hugely helpful for finding malware or rogue processes. In this case, it's consuming 1.4 TB of RAM.

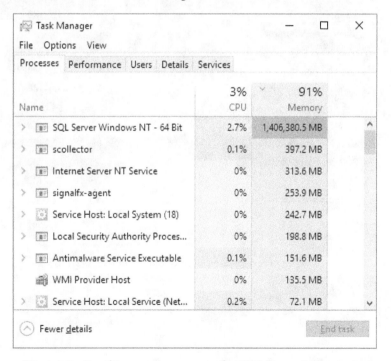

Figure 8.9 – For this server, we can see that SQL Server is consuming the majority of the system memory.

3. The **Details** and **Services** tabs are fairly self-explanatory. **Details** will show even more information about the individual processes that are running and consuming resources on your server. The **Services** tab shows a list of services installed on your server and their current statuses.

4. Click on the **Users** tab and then click the arrow listed under your username to see the expanded view. Listed under each username are the applications that those users have open. This sorted list of running programs is especially nice when logged into a server hosting many user connections at once, such as a Remote Desktop Session Host:

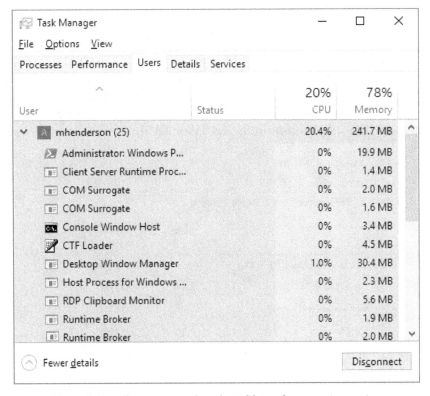

Figure 8.10 – The processes the selected logged on user is running

5. Now, browse over to the **Performance** tab. You will find that this screen looks much nicer than in previous versions. You can click between the different performance counters on the left to see the different details. If you right-click on the graph itself, you will notice there are some additional options. You can click on **Graph summary view** in order to change the Task Manager window into a smaller, graph-only mode that you can leave running in the corner of the screen. You can also choose to copy the screen, which can be helpful for grabbing a quick copy of this data and sending it on for troubleshooting or monitoring purposes:

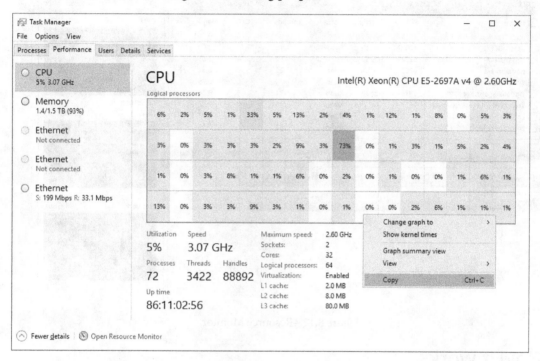

Figure 8.11 – Right-clicking on the Task Manager graph and choosing Copy

Tip

Once you go past a certain number of cores, the Task Manager no longer shows individual graphs and instead just displays a percentage number, as shown in the preceding screenshot.

6. At the bottom of your Task Manager screen, click on **Open Resource Monitor**. This runs the new Resource Monitor, which is an even more extensive tool for monitoring hardware resources and utilization. This is very helpful for monitoring hardware in real-time:

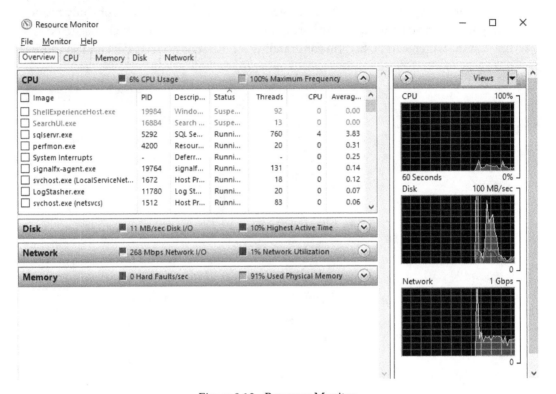

Figure 8.12 –Resource Monitor

How it works...

The Task Manager provided with Server 2019 contains many additional pieces of information that are helpful for monitoring system performance in real-time. As you start to administer your new Server 2019 machines, make sure you spend some time in this interface so that you are familiar with the new layout when you need to access information quickly.

Configuring a full system backup using Windows Server Backup

Maintaining a good backup solution is critical to administering a corporate server environment in today's IT world. There are limitless potential options for designing your particular backup plan, all the way from file copy backups to redundant servers sitting in hot standby mode.

While many third-party tools and technologies allow you to back up all your servers simultaneously while retaining multiple previous versions of each, those tools are not always on the table because of cost and implementation complexity. Let's take a few minutes to familiarize ourselves with the built-in backup solution that Microsoft provides free of charge, right in the Server 2019 operating system.

Getting ready

We are logged into our Server 2019 web server. We will be using the built-in Windows Server Backup tool in order to create a full image of this server.

How to do it...

Follow these steps to back up your Server 2019 using the built-in Windows Server Backup tool:

1. Open **Server Manager** and click **Add roles and features**. Go through this wizard, following the steps in order to install the **Windows Server Backup** feature. Remember that this is a feature, not a role, so look for it on the second screen. If you are adding the feature via `Install-WindowsFeature`, its name is `Windows-Server-Backup`

2. Launch **Windows Server Backup** from your **Start** menu or from the **Tools** menu inside Server Manager:

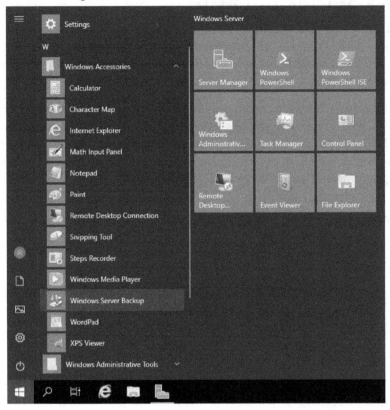

Figure 8.13 – Windows Server Backup in the Start menu

3. In the left window pane, choose **Local Backup**.

4. Then, toward the right of your screen, click on the **Backup Schedule...** action and click on **Next**.

5. On the **Select Backup Configuration** screen, I am going to choose **Full server**. If you have only specific items you would like to back up, you can use the **Custom** option for that purpose:

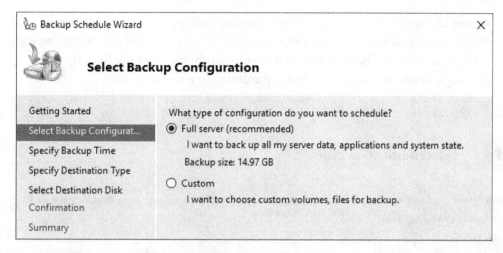

Figure 8.14 – Selecting the full server backup

6. Specify the schedule for how often you would like these backups to run. I'm going to have mine run every morning at **2:00 AM**. This is the local time *on the server*, so keep that in mind if your servers are set to a time zone such as UTC and you are not in UTC:

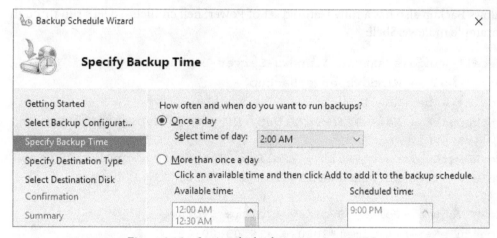

Figure 8.15 – Setting the backup time to 2:00 AM

7. As you can see in the text, the best way to store backups is to have a dedicated hard disk plugged into your server. In this example, we will be using this, but if you do not have a dedicated backup hard drive, you can choose to either back up to an existing volume (for example, a blank partition) or a network share:

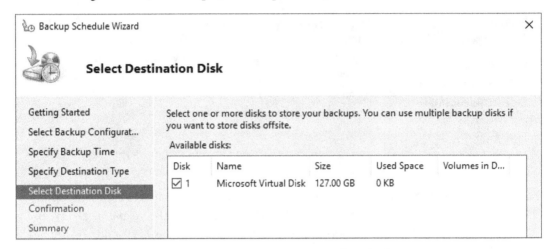

Figure 8.16 – Selecting which disk to send our backups to

Windows Backup also has a fully featured set of PowerShell cmdlets, so let's run through this example in PowerShell:

```
Install-WindowsFeature Windows-Server-Backup
Import-Module WindowsServerBackup
$Policy = New-WBPolicy
$BackupDisk = New-WBBackupTarget -Disk (Get-WBDisk)[1] -Label
"FullBackup"
Add-WBBackupTarget -Policy $Policy -Target $BackupDisk
$Volume = Get-WBVolume -AllVolumes | Where {$_.Mountpath -eq
"C:"}
Add-WBVolume -Policy $Policy -Volume $Volume
$Schedule = [DateTime]"2020-02-16 02:00:00"
Set-WBSchedule -Policy $Policy -Schedule $Schedule
Set-WBPolicy -Policy $Policy
```

This is a bit different to some of the PowerShell that we've seen before, so let's walk through some of the differences. The key difference is that instead of our PowerShell cmdlets affecting Windows Backup directly, we build a new object (`$Policy`) that represents what we want the backup policy to look like. Then, we make that policy active as follows:

1. `Install-WindowsFeature`: This only needs to be done once per server and does what it sounds like – it installs the Windows Backup feature.

2. `$Policy = New-WBPolicy`: This creates the policy object that we're going to change with further cmdlets so that it looks like the backup we want to run.

3. `$BackupDisk = New-WBBackupTarget -Disk (Get-WBDisk)[1] -Label "FullBackup"`: This creates an object to represent the second disk on our system (the index of `[1]` is the second disk as they start counting at `[0]`).

4. `Add-WBBackupTarget -Policy $Policy -Target $BackupDisk`: This assigns our backup disk as the disk we set in *Step 3*.

5. `$Volume = Get-WBVolume -AllVolumes | Where {$_.Mountpath -eq "C:"}`: This creates an object that represents our C: as that's the only disk we're going to be backing up in this system.

6. `Add-WBVolume -Policy $Policy -Volume $Volume`: This adds our disk from *Step 5* to our new backup policy.

7. `$Schedule = [DateTime]"2020-02-16 02:00:00"`: This creates a date object to represent when we want the backup to start. The date portion should be the date the backups are to start (either day or tomorrow's date, most likely) and the time the backups are to run. It is best to write the date in YYYY-MM-DD format so that there is no confusion between month and day.

8. `Set-WBSchedule -Policy $Policy -Schedule $Schedule`: As in the previous steps, this sets the schedule from *Step 7* in our backup policy.

9. `Set-WBPolicy -Policy $Policy`: This sets the backup policy we just created to active. It will start at whatever date and time we set in *Step 7*.

> **Remember**
> Taking backups is only half the solution. A backup that hasn't been tested is almost as risky as not having a backup at all as you don't know if your backups are working! We will look at how to restore a backup in the next recipe.

How it works...

In this recipe, we installed the Windows Server Backup feature into our server and walked through the wizard in order to schedule daily full backups. We also looked at the PowerShell equivalent of the same steps. This is a straightforward process, but the storage location of your backup files can take a little bit of consideration. A dedicated hard disk is the best solution for storing backups; that way, if your drive goes down, you will have all the backup files on another physical disk. And then, of course, if you configure an option for replicating that data to another physical site, or rotating drives on a schedule, that will protect your data even better in the event of a site failure or catastrophe. Storing these on a separate volume on the same disk is also an option, but then you are in a situation where that physical disk is a single point of failure for both your live operating system and the backup files. The third option is storing backup files on the network. This is something that I expect a lot of admins will choose, but you have to keep in mind that when making this configuration, you will only be able to have one backup file stored in that network location at a time from your server, as they will be overwritten with each new backup process.

There is a second action available from inside the backup console that we didn't touch on. In order to accomplish ad hoc backups, or backups that you intend to create manually on an as-needed basis, you can launch an action called **Backup Once…**. Use this to create a manual backup copy at any time.

Recovering data from a Windows backup file

Creating a backup or even a backup schedule is easy enough, but what is the process for restoring information from one of those backup files that we have sitting around? This is where the rubber really meets the road, as they say. Let's run through the process of restoring some data from a backup file that was taken yesterday. Perhaps some data was corrupted or accidentally deleted. Whatever the reason for our recovery needs, we will work together to restore some data from a backup file and get comfortable with that interface.

Getting ready

We are still working on our Server 2019 web server. This server was previously configured for Windows Server Backup, so it already has that feature installed. Yesterday, we created a full backup of our server, and today, we need to recover some of the data from that backup file.

How to do it...

Follow these steps in order to restore the server using the Windows Server Backup utility:

1. Open the Windows Server Backup management interface. You can launch this from either the **Start** menu or from the **Tools** menu of Server Manager.

2. Choose **Local Backup** from the left window pane.

3. Near the right-hand side of your screen, click on the **Recover...** action:

Figure 8.17 – The Recover... link on the right-hand side of the screen

4. Since our backup file is stored right here on one of the server's volumes, we will choose **This server** and click **Next**.

5. Now, you will see a calendar with bold dates indicating which days have valid backup files that you can restore back to. We are selecting the backup that ran yesterday and clicking **Next**:

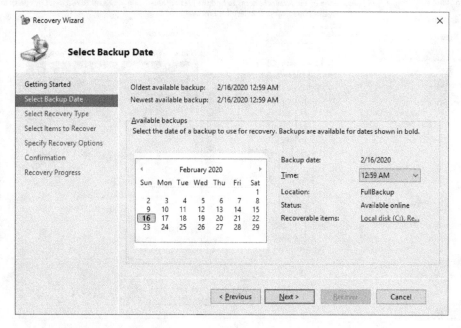

Figure 8.18 – Selecting which point-in-time backup we want to restore

6. Now, on the **Select Recovery Type** screen, we are going to choose **Files and folders** and click **Next**.

> **Tip**
> You will notice a grayed-out option here for Hyper-V. If you use Windows Server Backup on a Hyper-V server, you have the option to back up and restore individual virtual machines on that host. This is a great feature enhancement and a good reason to start using Windows Server Backup on your Hyper-V servers.

7. Now, we are on the **Select Items to Recover** screen. Simply choose the files and folders that you want to restore from yesterday's backup. In this example, we're going to pretend that someone has requested an IIS log file that had been deleted from the server (this is a very real request that has happened to me many times). Let's restore that log file for them:

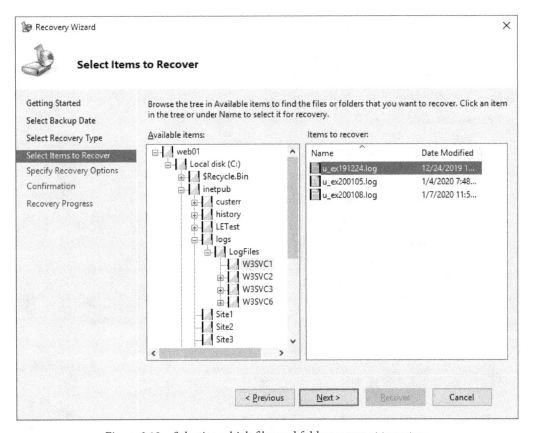

Figure 8.19 – Selecting which files and folders we want to restore

8. Set the option to recover files to **Original location** and click **Overwrite the existing versions with the recovered versions**. This will ensure that the files from yesterday's backup get placed on top of the files that still exist on our server today.

9. On the **Confirmation** screen, you will see a summary of the items that are going to be recovered. If everything looks good, click on the **Recover** button.

How it works...

This recovery recipe is a good baseline for getting familiar with the options that are available to you for restoring from Windows backup files. Here, we restored some simple files that had been deleted from our web server. In the event of a more serious system failure, where you might need to take a full disk backup and recover the whole thing onto a new server, that process is slightly more complicated. To accomplish a full system recovery of that magnitude, you would boot the server into your Windows setup disk and choose to run the Windows Recovery Environment. Through this tool, you can make use of your Windows backup file and restore the server.

Using IP Address Management to keep track of your used IP addresses

The **IP Address Management (IPAM)** tool is a little-known utility built into Windows Server 2019. IPAM is a way that you can centrally monitor and manage some of the common infrastructure roles spread out around your network. Specifically, for this recipe, we will be taking a look at IP addressing by using IPAM. Particularly in environments where there may be many different DHCP servers hosting different scopes spread out around your network, IPAM can be extremely useful for pulling all that information into one management interface. This saves a lot of time and effort as opposed to launching the DHCP Manager console on each of your DHCP environments separately and trying to monitor them individually.

Getting ready

We have a domain network running that consists of all Server 2019 servers. Included in our network is a domain controller that is also serving as a DHCP server. We are adding a new server to this mix called IPAM01. This new server will be our IPAM management server since the IPAM feature should *not* co-exist with either the AD DS role or with the DHCP role.

How to do it...

Let's take a look at our IP address utilization with the IPAM feature:

1. While logged into the new server that you intend to use for IPAM, install the **IP Address Management (IPAM) Server** role. If you are using PowerShell, the command will just be `Install-WindowsFeature IPAM -IncludeManagementTools`.

2. Once the feature has been installed, you should see a new listing for IPAM in the left window pane of Server Manager. Go ahead and click there.

3. You will see that step 1 is already accomplished; the IPAM console is successfully connected to the local server. Go ahead and click on step 2 in order to provision the IPAM server:

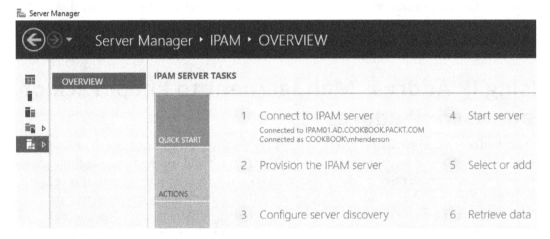

Figure 8.20 – The IPAM screen in Server Manager

4. Click **Next**, after reading the information listed on that screen. As you can see, the best way to set up the interaction between the IPAM server and the infrastructure servers is to utilize Group Policy. We will define the settings for that in an upcoming screen in this wizard.

5. You should now be on the **Configure database** screen. We will leave the default option selected to utilize **Windows Internal Database (WID)**. The second option, for SQL servers, is for much more advanced installations where you would want to integrate the IPAM database into other tools.

6. Now, we get to select our provisioning method, which is where we are going to tell IPAM to use Group Policy in order to distribute the settings that it needs in order to manage and grab data from our infrastructure servers. Define a GPO prefix that is specific to this IPAM server:

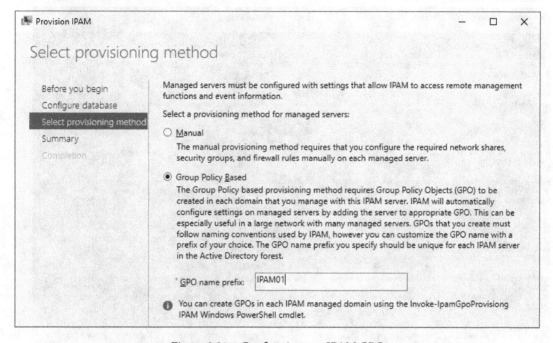

Figure 8.21 – Configuring our IPAM GPO

7. Before we complete this wizard, we need to take a special action in order to provision these GPOs so that the wizard can make use of them. To do this, we are going to use a PowerShell cmdlet. Open up PowerShell with administrative rights. Make sure you are logged into the server as a domain admin before running this cmdlet.

8. Type the `Invoke-IpamGpoProvisioning` command into PowerShell.

9. It will ask you to key in the name of your domain, as well as the GpoPrefixName. This is the same prefix that you just typed into the IPAM Wizard, so make sure you enter it exactly the same:

Figure 8.22 – Running Invoke-IpamGpoProvisioning from PowerShell

10. Now that our GPOs have been created, head back over to the IPAM wizard and click the **Apply** button to finish it.

11. Now, back at the IPAM section of Server Manager, click on step 3 – **Configure server discovery**.

12. Use the **Add** button in order to query your domain for infrastructure services that can be monitored by IPAM. Select the roles you would like to pull data from (I am going to leave all three checked) and click the **OK** button:

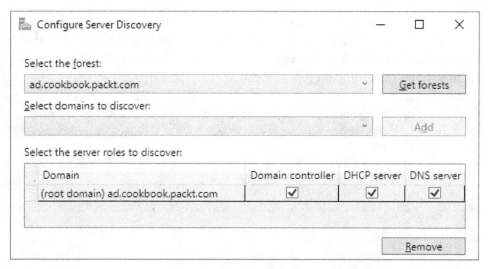

Figure 8.23 – Adding domains to server discovery

13. Click on step 4 – **Start server discovery**. Wait for discovery to complete. This may take a long time for large networks.

14. Click on step 5 – **Select or add servers to manage and verify IPAM access**.

15. Right-click on the server that you want to collect data from and choose **Edit Server…**:

Figure 8.24 – Editing a domain controller for IPAM discovery

16. Change the server's **Manageability status** field to **Managed**.

17. Now, head back to the main IPAM window in Server Manager and click on step 6 – **Retrieve data from managed servers**.

> **Tip**
> You may have to wait for a little while to allow Group Policy to do its job in rolling out the settings.

18. Once data collection completes, you can browse around inside the IPAM management console and view data about your DNS and DHCP infrastructure. For example, click on **IP Address Range Groups** to see a list of the DHCP scopes that are present on the DHCP servers that you are currently managing:

Figure 8.25 – Showing the usage of a DHCP range

How it works...

The **IP Address Management** (**IPAM**) tool takes a little bit of work to configure initially but can be very beneficial later. Once configured to pull in data from your Domain Controllers, DNS servers, and DHCP servers, IPAM can be your one-stop-shop for monitoring and managing data related to these infrastructure roles. This is particularly helpful where you have many servers providing these roles, such as the case of multiple DHCP servers that each contain different scope definitions. In the past, you would have had to log into each DHCP server or at least do remote management of them via Server Manager or some other tool, but ultimately, you would still be viewing and managing the DHCP scopes individually. With IPAM, it brings all this information into one place so that you can make decisions and configuration changes within your network while looking at the overall bigger picture.

Checking for viruses and adding ransomware protection

Monitoring and scanning for viruses or ransomware on a Windows Server historically isn't a task that would have shown up in a book about the operating system, because, in the past, this functionality was always provided by third-party software. And in the case of ransomware, by the time they hit your network, it's usually too late for any antivirus to do anything about it.

Starting with Windows 8, we got something called Windows Defender built into the Windows desktop operating system; this provided some semblance of free, built-in antivirus protection. Well, I'm excited to say that Windows Defender has continually improved over the past few years and is now called Windows Security, includes not just antivirus but also ransomware protection, and is available to us inside the Microsoft Server operating system!

Installing third-party antivirus programs on servers has always been dangerous territory because they love to consume memory and cause random reboots. I've dealt with many different kinds of issues with antivirus programs on Windows Servers. Thankfully, all this functionality is now is baked right into the operating system, so we should never have to worry about those kinds of problems. Let's take a look at some of the options, which now come standard as part of the Windows Server 2019 operating system.

Getting ready

Any Windows Server 2019 will do for this task as Windows Security exists on them by default. Today, I happen to be using my WEB01 web server, and I want to make sure that my antivirus is turned on and protecting this system. We'll also protect our IIS web folders from ransomware.

How to do it...

Follow these steps to look into the Windows Defender settings on your server:

1. From the **Start** menu, navigate to **Windows Security**. It should just be in the root of the **Start** menu:

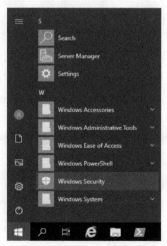

Figure 8.26 – The Windows Security Start menu item

2. This is very similar to Windows Security that ships with Windows 10, albeit with different options. If you click the **Virus & threat protection** icon, you will be shown the details about the most recent antivirus scan. From there, you can start a new scan or view files that have been quarantined already:

Figure 8.27 – The Windows Security Virus & threat protection screen

3. Windows Server 2019 also has an excellent first line of defense against ransomware and crypto lockers. It's one thing to have a backup to restore from, but wouldn't it be good if you had two lines of protection? Scroll down through the **Virus & threat protection** screen until you find **Ransomware protection**.

4. Click the **Manage ransomware protection** link:

Figure 8.28 – The Manage ransomware protection link

5. Under **Controlled folder access**, switch this to **On**.

6. Click **Add a protected folder** and navigate to a folder to protect. In our example, we're going to protect our **C:\inetpub** directory for IIS:

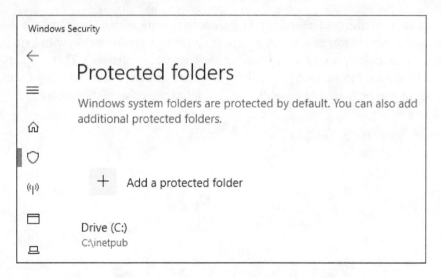

Figure 8.29 – Adding our IIS directory to ransomware protection

328 Monitoring and Backup

7. For now, that's all you need to do to protect that folder. However, you might have legitimate applications that need to modify the data in those folders. If you find your applications are being blocked, you can click the **Allow an app through Controlled folder access** link on the **Ransomware protection** page.

8. Click **Add an allowed app**, then choose **Recently blocked apps**.

9. If your application was blocked by Windows Security, it will show up and you can permit it.

How it works...

I believe that having the Windows security functionality built into the Windows Server 2019 operating system is going to be a game-changer. The process of installing third-party antivirus software onto your servers is one of those things that always make admins cringe. You never really know whether it's going to play well with the server you have built. Now, I'm sure that many of you are not going to automatically trust Windows as an enterprise-ready and capable antivirus solution, but I believe that too will change over time. If it wasn't doing a good job, wouldn't Microsoft have thrown it away at this point, rather than continuing to improve it and now trusting it enough to exist inside a server operating system?

It is easy to disable Windows Defender if you want to continue using an antivirus that you have to pay extra money for, or a server where the antivirus is interfering with existing functionality (particularly on systems running very, very old software). That is your prerogative. However, I think that particularly for small and medium businesses, this new inclusion is going to be incredibly useful from a safety and security standpoint.

9
System Insights

We just spent part of the previous chapter looking at some of the built-in tools of Windows Server 2019 for monitoring the performance of your systems. But what if you want to do forecasting of your future performance needs? Forecasting your future needs is critical in any growing environment. You really want to know that your servers are going to run out of CPU or network bandwidth *before* they run out, not after! I've seen companies that have created their own very complicated forecasting systems only to see most of the system abandoned for a simple spreadsheet and some educated guesses.

System Insights might be able to remove that guesswork for you and replace that spreadsheet in your own organization. Now, wouldn't that make budgeting your next financial year's server purchases easier to justify to your chief financial officer?

This chapter is going to show you a feature that is brand new to Windows Server 2019 – System Insights. Over the next pages, we're going to cover the following topics:

- Installing System Insights
- Windows Server System Insights capabilities
- Managing System Insights
- Managing Windows Server System Insights from PowerShell
- Aggregating prediction outcomes

Installing System Insights

Before System Insights can be used, it needs to be installed. System Insights is an extension of the Windows Admin Center and can be configured by either the Admin Center web UI or via PowerShell. In this recipe, we will look at both ways of installing the extension.

Getting ready

To install System Insights, you will need a working copy of the Windows Admin Center version 1909 or higher, and a Windows Server 2019 server you wish to monitor. We will be performing this recipe from the computer where Windows Admin Center was installed.

You can find the installation instructions for Windows Admin Center back in *Chapter 1, Learning the interface,* by reading the *Managing your servers through the Windows Admin Center* recipe.

> **Important**
>
> System Insights was added to Windows Server 2019 in version 1903 (also called the May 2019 update). At the time of writing this book, the Windows Server 2019 evaluations that Microsoft offers free of charge are older than this and require several rounds of Windows Updates to be upgraded to a version that contains System Insights.

How to do it...

First, we need to verify that System Insights is activated on Windows Admin Center. System Insights comes by default with Windows Admin Center 1909 or higher. You can verify that it is installed by following these simple steps:

1. Click your Start menu and open **Windows Admin Center**.

2. Click on the gear icon on the upper-right-hand corner to open the **Settings** screen.

3. Under **Gateway** in the left-hand navigation, choose **Extensions**. Once on the **Extensions** screen, choose the **Installed extensions** tab.

4. Look at the list to see if System Insights is installed:

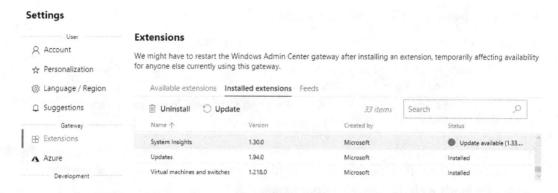

Figure 9.1 – The System Insights extension in the Windows Admin Center

5. If the extension is not installed, click **Available extensions**, locate **System Insights**, and click **Install**.

6. Back on the server list, click on the server you want to enable Insights for. In my case, this is CA01. Once you are connected to that server, choose **System Insights** in the left-hand navigation.

7. Click the **Install** button. System Insights will then begin installing on that server:

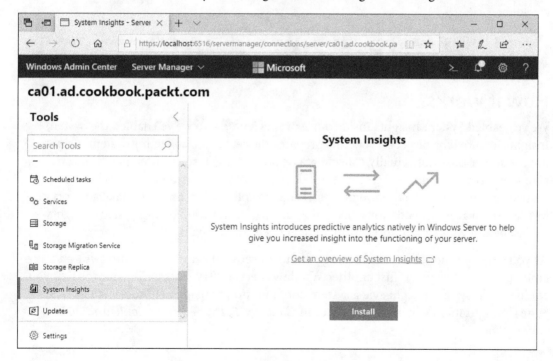

Figure 9.2 – A server that does not have System Insights enabled

8. And, as usual, let's look at how we would do this recipe with PowerShell.

9. To verify that the System Insights extension is installed, we would run the following:

```
Import-Module "$env:ProgramFiles\Windows Admin Center\
PowerShell\Modules\ExtensionTools"
```
```
Get-Extension | ? { $_.Id -eq "msft.sme.system-insights"
} | Select Id, Version, Status
```

10. There is probably going to be more than one version of the extension listed. If any of them say **Installed**, then you're good to go! If your extension is out of date, you can update it with the following command:

```
Update-Extension -ExtensionId msft.sme.system-insights
```

11. OK. Now that we have verified that our Windows Admin Center has System Insights enabled, we can go ahead and install the System Insights component on the server that we want to monitor.

To install System Insights via PowerShell, on your machine that has Windows Admin Center installed, simply run the following command in an Administrator PowerShell console:

```
Install-WindowsFeature System-Insights -IncludeManagementTools
-ComputerName CA01
```

How it works...

We've enabled System Insights inside our Admin Center, and we've enabled the System Insights feature on a target server. This prepares the server for collecting system insights, but the server does not actually collect data or present any results immediately. It can take weeks (or even months) to get useful data out of System Insights. This is because System Insights has to have enough historical data collected in order to make any sort of forecasting or recommendations. So, make sure you're not configuring System Insights a week before your system forecasting budget needs to be finalized!

As you may have noticed with our usage of the PowerShell `Install-WindowsFeature` cmdlet, System Insights is just another Windows Server 2019 feature. This means that you could enable System Insights via a system configuration management tool such as Desired State Configuration, which we will cover in *Chapter 15, Desired State Configuration and Automation.*

See also

- *Chapter 1, Learning the Interface* – the *Managing your servers through the Windows Admin Center* recipe

Windows Server System Insights capabilities

System Insights has several items it can forecast on. The common ones are things such as CPU and disk usage, but Microsoft are adding new features to System Insights on a regular basis. In this recipe, we're going to look at the some of the actual forecasting that System Insights can do.

Getting ready

We need a Windows server that has had System Insights enabled for long enough that it's collected some data and presented some forecasts. In this example, we have had System Insights running for around 3 months on our CA01 server.

How to do it...

We're going to complete this in Windows Admin Center. Follow these steps:

1. Open **Windows Admin Center** from the Start menu.

2. Locate the computer you want to look at the insights for and click on its name to connect to it.

3. In the left-hand navigation, find the **System Insights** menu item and click on it:

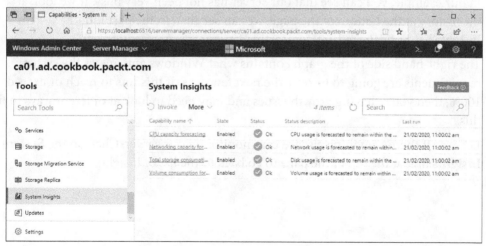

Figure 9.3 – The default System Insights view for a server

4. You will be presented with a list of insights that this server has been collecting. In our example, we have CPU, networking, storage, and volume forecasts. Let's look at **CPU capacity forecasting** by clicking on its link.

5. Here, you will be presented with some basic details about the data that the server has been collecting, along with 1 months' worth of historical notes about the data that was collected:

Figure 9.4 – The System Insights forecasting overview

6. In our example, you can see that our server has not been very busy. If we look at the history at the bottom of the page, we can see that, in the past month, System Insights has not detected any forecasting issues.

7. The right-hand side of the graph contains what Windows anticipates the system requirements are going to be over the next few days. If this was to reach or exceed 100%, then you're having growth issues and may need to look at different ways to fix this.

8. Let's see if there's anything else we can monitor on our server. Click on the **System Insights** link at the top of the page to go back to the list of insights.

9. Click **Add or remove capabilities**. In my version, this is labeled as **(Preview)**, but by the time you read this, it may be a fully supported feature:

Figure 9.5 – The Add or remove capabilities button

10. My System Insights tells me that I can also monitor physical disk anomalies. This would be very useful for a bare-metal server with local storage. Click on **Install** for any additional things you wish to collect insights for:

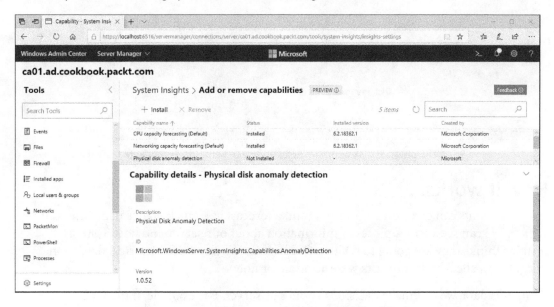

Figure 9.6 – Adding an optional Insights capability

11. Back on the System Insights page, we can see our newly added capability. It won't gather any data for a while, but once it gets a baseline of how your system behaves normally, it will be able to tell you if anything is abnormal:

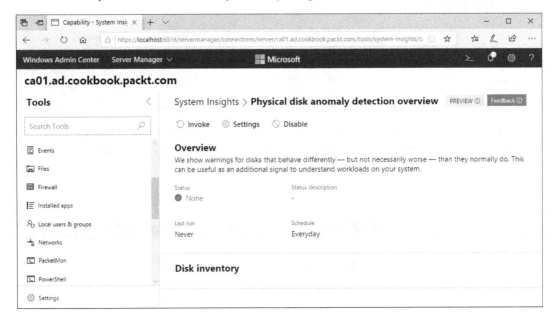

Figure 9.7 – The physical disk anomaly detection page before it has collected any data

How it works...

System Insights can give you an overview and a forecast at a quick glance using the Admin Center. We can see various pieces of information about our server and how System Insights thinks they are going to scale in forecasting. We also have historical data so that Insights can check if its forecasts were accurate or not.

Using this data, we can make decisions about our server. For example, if the CPU predictions do not match reality, perhaps you have a runaway process that needs to be investigated. If your storage is filling up at a steady rate, System Insights can tell you when it will be full before it gets full.

Managing System Insights

The defaults that come with System Insights might be fine for some predictions, but you may be looking for predictions with a higher degree of granularity. Alternatively, you may wish to run the predictions more often, or in some cases ignore certain days from your predictions.

Maybe you have some actions you want to complete when a certain prediction status happens; for example, spinning up additional web servers if System Insights predicts an overload. Well, with System Insights, we can also do these things.

Getting ready

We need to have a server being managed by System Insights – that's it.

How to do it...

1. Locate the server you wish to manage in **Windows Admin Center** and click on its link.

2. In the left-hand navigation, find **System Insights**.

3. Click on an insight you want to manage. In this example, we're going to look at **Networking capacity forecasting**.

4. Click the **Settings** button at the top of the Insights page:

Figure 9.8 – The settings button in System Insights

5.   From here, there are two screens we can look at: **Schedule** and **Actions**. We're going to look at **Schedule** first:

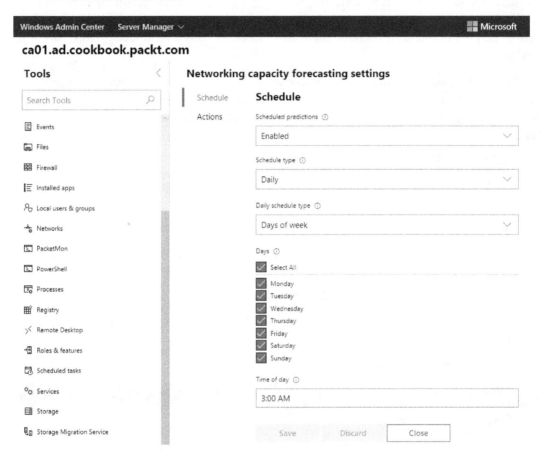

Figure 9.9 – Schedule settings for an insight

6. From here, we can adjust many parts of our schedule:

    a. **Schedule predictions:** Setting this to **Disabled** turns off any predictions for this insight.

    b. **Schedule type:** By default, this is **Daily**. If you need more granularity for your data collection, you can change this to **Hourly** or **Minute**. This will greatly increase the amount of data being collected by Insights.

    c. **Daily schedule type:** If you are running on a **Daily** schedule, here, you can choose whether you want the data collection to run on specific days of the week (**Days of the week**), or a pattern of days (**Interval**; for example, every second day, or every fifth day).

    d. **Days:** If you are running a **Days of the week** schedule, you can choose which specific days you want to schedule them to run on. You may wish to exclude days for various reasons, such as when very heavy batch jobs run where their impact is not relevant to your capacity planning.

    e. **Prediction interval (days):** If you are running an **Interval** schedule type, here is where you enter the interval you want running. For example, entering 3 would run the schedule every third day.

    f. **Time of day:** If you are running a **Daily** schedule type, this is the time of the day the schedule should run on. Generally, you would want this to be out of business hours.

    g. **Prediction Interval (hours/minutes):** If you are running an **Hourly** or **Minutes** schedule, enter the schedule here. For example, for ours, if you entered the number 6, the schedule would run every 6 hours.

7. Now, let's look at the **Actions** screen. Click on **Actions** on the left-hand side of the settings screen.

8. You should see a series of actions such as **Ok, Warning**, **Critical**, **Error**, and **None**.
    Here, you can specify a PowerShell script to be executed when a specific event
    occurs. For example, if a **Critical** error occurs, you may have a PowerShell script
    that spins up additional web servers. Or maybe it sends an alert to a monitoring
    system to raise an alert about the insight. This is very useful as a lot of monitoring
    systems on the market do not know about System Insights or how to monitor them
    natively. This way, you can integrate System Insights into your existing monitoring
    solutions:

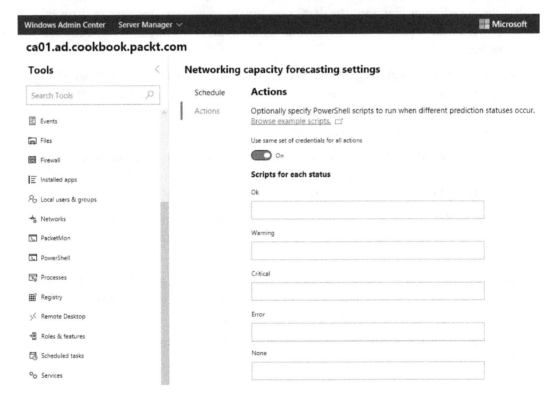

Figure 9.10 – Setting scripts for different insights statuses

How it works...

Individual system insights can be configured in different ways. I have found that the
standard **Daily** schedule works fine for most scenarios, but of course, everyone's situation
is different! You might find that a different setting works better for you.

The most interesting feature here, though, is the **Actions** screen. Using this, you can integrate System Insights into existing monitoring systems by sending them data via PowerShell. Most monitoring systems have the ability to have data pushed to them from external sources, so with a bit of programming, you should be able to get Insights into your monitoring so that everyone can see it.

Managing Windows Server System Insights from PowerShell

We've seen a lot of what we can do with System Insights from the Windows Admin Center. Now, we'll look at some of the things we can script with it via PowerShell. This is important, because scripting System Insights via PowerShell will allow you to take advantage of some of the more advanced System Insights features.

Getting started

You'll need a Windows Server with System Insights installed. You can either run PowerShell directly on that box, or you can use a PowerShell remote session from a Windows 10 computer. In our case, we will be using CA01.

How to do it...

1. Open PowerShell on your server with System Insights installed. If you are accessing this from a remote computer, this would be `Enter-PSSession CA01`.

2. Let's take a quick look at the System Insights PowerShell module before going any further. If you run `Get-Module SystemInsights`, you should see some details about our module:

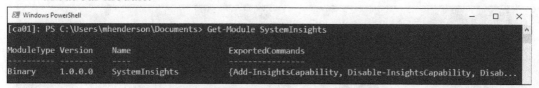

Figure 9.11 – The System Insights PowerShell module

3. The `ExportedCommands` property looks interesting. Let's look at that in more detail by running `Get-Command -Module SystemInsights`. You should have a list that looks like this:

```
Add-InsightsCapability
Disable-InsightsCapability
```

```
Disable-InsightsCapabilitySchedule
Enable-InsightsCapability
Enable-InsightsCapabilitySchedule
Get-InsightsCapability
Get-InsightsCapabilityAction
Get-InsightsCapabilityResult
Get-InsightsCapabilitySchedule
Invoke-InsightsCapability
Remove-InsightsCapability
Remove-InsightsCapabilityAction
Set-InsightsCapabilityAction
Set-InsightsCapabilitySchedule
Update-InsightsCapability
```

4. A lot of these cmdlets are named like the things we were doing in the previous recipe. Let's look at some of them now. We haven't imported the System Insights module yet, so let's do that with `Import-Module SystemInsights`.

5. Run the `Get-InsightsCapability` command. This should give you the same list of Insights as we saw in the previous recipe. For the rest of this recipe, we're going to be focusing on getting as much detail out of our `Volume consumption forecasting` insight as possible.

6. Let's take a look at the history we have for our volume consumption forecasting capability. To do this, you would run `Get-InsightsCapabilityResult -Name "Volume consumption forecasting" -History`:

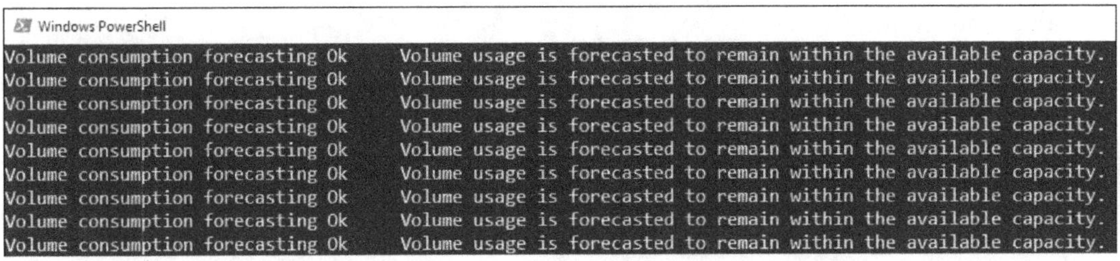

Figure 9.12 – Looking at the history for one of our Insights capabilities

7. We can dig into these by going a step further. What if we wanted to see what actual data System Insights was using to determine its result? If you run `(Get-InsightsCapabilityResult -Name "Volume consumption forecasting" -History) | Select-Object Status, LastRun, Output`, take a look at the `Output` column. You will see a reference to a JSON document.

8. Let's take a look at that JSON a bit further. We're going to run a more complicated command now, which is going to show how the PowerShell pipeline can be used to its full advantage:

```
$Insight = Get-Content (Get-InsightsCapabilityResult
-Name "Volume consumption forecasting" -History | Sort-
Object LastRun -Descending | Select-Object -First
1).Output | ConvertFrom-Json
```

   a. `$Insight` = means that the output from this command is going to be saved as `$Insight`. This will make it easier to refer to later.

   b. `Get-Content` is an instruction to PowerShell to load the contents of a file. We'll tell it which file to load in the next set of instructions.

   c. The brackets (or braces, if you prefer) around the next few commands tells PowerShell to execute this functionality as if it was its own command.

   d. `Get-InsightsCapabilityResult` does the same thing it does in the previous steps of this recipe – it selects all the results from the System Insights runs.

   e. `Sort-Object` sorts all our results by their `LastRun` date, with the most recent at the top.

   f. `Select-Object` tells PowerShell to just use the first item in the list and to ignore the rest.

   g. `.Output` is the property that contains the path to the JSON file. This is the output of the result of the command we put in brackets.

   h. `ConvertFrom-JSON` converts the JSON file that we just read with `Get-Content` into a PowerShell object that we can query.

9. If the previous command ran successfully, you should have no output from PowerShell. Run $Insight and see what comes back. If it ran correctly, you should see something like this:

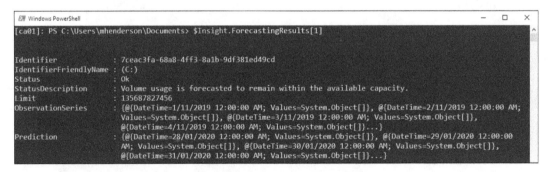

Figure 9.13 – PowerShell reading the contents of an Insights result file

10. Let's look at ForecastingResults in more detail. Run $Insight. ForecastingResults.

11. In our example, I can see that Insights has done forecasting on multiple volumes, but the one I'm most interested in is C:. In my example, that's the second insight. Because indexes start counting at zero, to get the second index, we use the reference of [1], so we will run $Insight.ForecastingResults[1]:

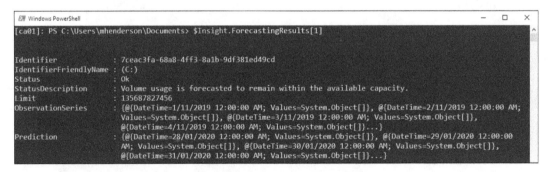

Figure 9.14 – The forecasting results for C:

12. Now, we have two interesting properties here: ObservationSeries and Prediction. ObservationSeries is going to show us the data that System Insights has observed during its data collection, while Prediction is going to tell us what it thinks the future holds for these metrics. Let's look at Prediction by running $Insight.ForecastingResults[1].Prediction.

13. This gives us a bunch of future data points of what System Insights believes your system is going to look like in the future. You could continue to use the PowerShell pipeline to send this data somewhere else, such as a processing application, a dashboard, or even convert it into an Excel spreadsheet for further analysis.

How it works...

In this recipe, we started to delve much deeper into the flexibility and power that PowerShell brings to system management. We spent a lot of time looking at one specific part of System Insights – fetching as much data about a specific insight as we could.

However, there were a lot of cmdlets that we didn't really go over here. In your own time, you can explore these cmdlets and see what sort of functionality you can unlock with them.

Looking at the kinds of data we were able to extract from System Insights via PowerShell that we were unable to access via Windows Admin Center, you may be able to imagine a world where all these details insights predictions are sent to third-party monitoring systems. Wouldn't it be nice to know that a given server is likely to run out of disk space, or CPU capacity, a month before it happens?

Aggregate prediction outcomes

So far, we've looked at a lot of insights about individual servers. But what if we need to look at groups of servers as a whole?

For example, you might have a rack of 24 servers, each with a 10 Gbps connection and a top-of-rack network switch that can aggregate a total of 40 Gbps of bandwidth. That means that your total rack network activity could be 240 Gbps, but you must squeeze it all down a 40 Gbps connection. Wouldn't it be good to know when your rack is predicted to approach its 40 Gbps limit?

Alternatively, you may have a cluster of storage servers. You're not too concerned with each individual server's disk usage, but you are interested in the cluster as a whole. You want to know when the total space on all your servers is predicted to pass through a threshold so that you can add more storage or purge old files.

We can use the lessons we've learned in the previous recipes (and previous chapters!) to start looking at insights from a group of servers.

Getting started

You will need multiple Windows servers that have been collecting insights for a period of time. You will also need a Windows 10 machine to run PowerShell commands from. In this example, we are collecting metrics from `core01` and `core02`. In our example, these are storage servers.

How to do it...

In our example, we're going to aggregate insights about disk usage from two storage servers: `core01` and `core02`. However, the possible ways to do this are varied! You may wish to use a different insight or groupings of servers. Let's take a look:

1. On your Windows 10 machine, open PowerShell.

2. We're going to create a small array to reference the names of the servers we want to query. In our case, we'll run `$Servers = @("core01","core02")`.

3. Optionally, we can validate that our connection to the servers is working. By executing `Invoke-Command -ComputerName $Servers -ScriptBlock { Get-Host }`, we can validate that our PowerShell remoting is working. You should return objects that represent each server (in my case, two). If you have any errors here, now is the time to fix them before continuing:

Figure 9.15 – Testing PowerShell remoting

4. In the previous recipe, we saw how we can use PowerShell to get the complete prediction data from Insights. We're going to do that again, but this time, we're going to run it remotely and feed the results back to our Windows 10 computer. This will allow us to run the same command against multiple servers. Let's take that script and store it in a variable so that we can use it:

```
$InsightsScript = {Get-Content
(Get-InsightsCapabilityResult -Name "Total storage
consumption forecasting" -History | Sort-Object
LastRun -Descending | Select-Object -First 1).Output |
ConvertFrom-Json}
```

5. Now, let's collect our prediction data from our two hosts. This is going to look like this:

```
$InsightsData = Invoke-Command -ComputerName $Servers
-ScriptBlock $InsightsScript
```

Note that this command could take a while to run, depending on how many servers you are running it against, as well as the latency between your Windows 10 machine and the servers.

6. If we look at $InsightsData now, we should see that two lots of Insights predictions have been returned to us:

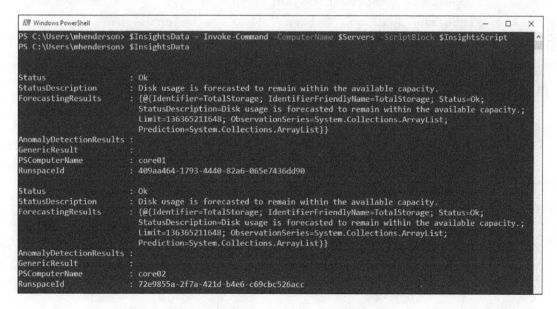

Figure 9.16 – Our two sets of Insights data

7. Let's say we want to see the next 3 days' worth of aggregate prediction data. Let's start by recording the date range we want to query, and then filter our data down to that. Finally, we will group our data into specific days:

```
$GroupedData = $InsightsData.ForecastingResults.Prediction
| Where-Object { $_.DateTime -ge $StartDate -and
$_.DateTime -le $EndDate } | Group-Object DateTime.
```

8. If you look at $GroupedData, you will probably have some output that looks like this:

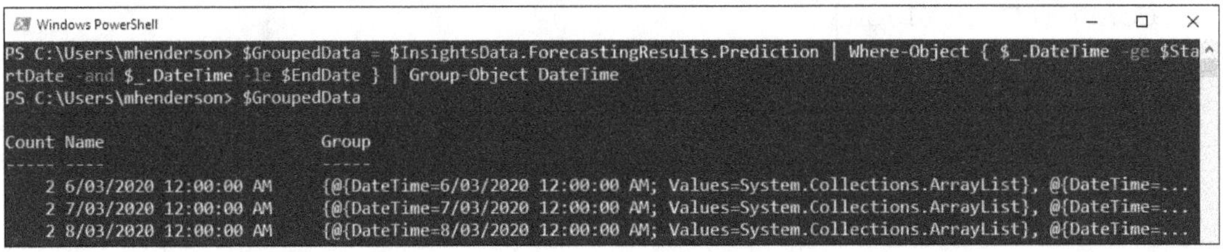

```
Windows PowerShell                                                                      —   □   ×
PS C:\Users\mhenderson> $GroupedData = $InsightsData.ForecastingResults.Prediction | Where-Object { $_.DateTime -ge $Sta
rtDate -and $_.DateTime -le $EndDate } | Group-Object DateTime
PS C:\Users\mhenderson> $GroupedData

Count Name                           Group
----- ----                           -----
    2 6/03/2020 12:00:00 AM          {@{DateTime=6/03/2020 12:00:00 AM; Values=System.Collections.ArrayList}, @{DateTime=...
    2 7/03/2020 12:00:00 AM          {@{DateTime=7/03/2020 12:00:00 AM; Values=System.Collections.ArrayList}, @{DateTime=...
    2 8/03/2020 12:00:00 AM          {@{DateTime=8/03/2020 12:00:00 AM; Values=System.Collections.ArrayList}, @{DateTime=...
```

Figure 9.17 – Grouping our forecasting results by date

9. Now that we have a filtered view of the data we're working on, let's actually aggregate something. That's what we're here for, after all! This script is a bit more complicated, so I'm going to break it up into multiple lines:

```
$GroupedData | ForEach-Object {
  $Totals = $_.Group.Values | Measure-Object -Sum
  Write-Host "$($_.Name) $($Totals.Sum/1Gb)Gb"
}
```

This results in the following output:

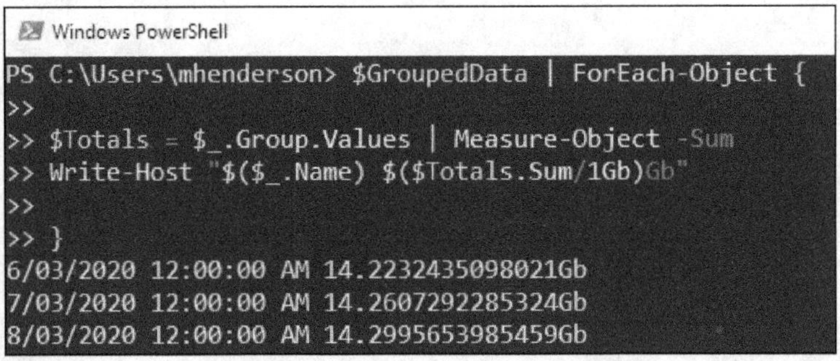

```
Windows PowerShell
PS C:\Users\mhenderson> $GroupedData | ForEach-Object {
>>
>> $Totals = $_.Group.Values | Measure-Object -Sum
>> Write-Host "$($_.Name) $($Totals.Sum/1Gb)Gb"
>>
>> }
6/03/2020 12:00:00 AM 14.2232435098021Gb
7/03/2020 12:00:00 AM 14.2607292285324Gb
8/03/2020 12:00:00 AM 14.2995653985459Gb
```

Figure 9.18 – Showing the amount of remaining space predicted

10. As you can see, Insights is predicting that I'm going to have around 14 GB of data remaining over the next 3 days. Let's break down what's happening in that script block:

    `$GroupedData` puts the data we've been collating onto the PowerShell pipeline.

    `ForEach-Object` executes the following command for every item in our grouping.

    `$Totals = $_.Group.Values | Measure-Object -Sum` looks at all the values in this group and sums them all together. `$_` represents the current item on the pipeline, which will be a single grouping.

    `Write-Host "$($_.Name) $($Totals.Sum/1Gb)Gb"` takes the date of our group (which is in the name field) and the sum of the totaling we did in the previous step. Dividing the objects by `1Gb` converts the numbers from bytes (which is what Insights provides) into gigabytes. The final `Gb` is just to make the number look nice when it's displayed.

11. And there you have it – our aggregated data. This is just one example of many possible things we could do. As we mentioned previously, we could be collecting data on all the servers in a given rack, a storage cluster, a database server, or a collection of DirectAccess servers.

12. Now, that was a lot of individual lines of code. What would it look like if we put them all together?

```
$Servers = @("core01","core02")
$InsightsScript = {Get-Content (Get-InsightsCapabilityResult
-Name "Total storage consumption forecasting" -History | Sort-
Object LastRun -Descending | Select-Object -First 1).Output |
ConvertFrom-Json}
$InsightsData = Invoke-Command -ComputerName $Servers
-ScriptBlock $InsightsScript
$GroupedData = $InsightsData.ForecastingResults.Prediction |
Where-Object { $_.DateTime -ge $StartDate -and $_.DateTime -le
$EndDate } | Group-Object DateTime
$GroupedData | ForEach-Object {
  $Totals = $_.Group.Values | Measure-Object -Sum
  Write-Host "$($_.Name) $($Totals.Sum/1Gb)Gb"
}
```

> **Tip**
> This script uses a lot of longhand PowerShell to make it easier to understand what's going on. You could simplify it by using `%` instead of `ForEach-Object` and `?` instead of `Where-Object`. There is other PowerShell shorthand you could use as well.

13. With a small amount of work, you could turn this code snippet into a PowerShell script that you could call with parameters to make collecting this data easier. You could also plug this into your monitoring system if it supports collecting data from external scripts.

How it works...

PowerShell and Insights together are a very powerful combination. What we saw in this recipe was just one possible outcome of their combination. Using PowerShell remoting, we collected Insights data from multiple hosts, and then aggregated it into a single number, breaking it down by date.

Instead of looking at prediction data, you may also choose to look at historical data. You could just as easily aggregate on historical trends. You could aggregate on any Insight offered. For example, you might want to keep track of historical trends of network bandwidth usage on your VPN servers, as well as keep an eye on bandwidth predictions for the future.

Insights, PowerShell aggregation, and a monitoring system with dashboards can create a very powerful capacity planning tool.

10
Group Policy

In this book, we have already discussed a few recipes that call for the modification of **Group Policy Objects** (**GPOs**), but we have not taken the time to discuss why Group Policy is important in the first place. To those who have worked within Active Directory for a while, Group Policy may be familiar territory. I still find, though, that many IT folks working in the server administrator role are not overly familiar with Group Policy and how it can benefit them. Particularly in smaller companies, this incredibly powerful feature of Windows tends to be overlooked. It is easy to think of Active Directory as the storage container for your user and computer accounts because those are the core necessary tasks that it accomplishes. But as soon as you install the Domain Services role to configure your first domain controller, you have automatically included Group Policy capabilities in that domain.

Group Policy is a centralized administration tool for your domain-joined systems. To summarize its capabilities, you can create policies in Active Directory, assign those policies to particular users or computers, and, within those policies, change any number of settings or configurations that are within the Windows operating system. The item inside Active Directory that contains these settings is called a **GPO**, so we will be focusing on the creation and manipulation of these in order to make some centralized management decisions that will affect large numbers of computers in our environment. GPOs can be utilized for user accounts, client computer settings, or for putting configurations onto your servers. Any domain-joined system can be manipulated by a GPO, and typically settings put into place by GPOs cannot be overridden by users, making them a very integral part of security for companies familiar with making use of Group Policy regularly.

We will place several different configuration settings inside the GPOs that we create throughout this chapter, but we will not come close to covering even a fraction of the available settings that could be manipulated. For full coverage of the Group Policy settings that are available, please check out the following link: `http://www.microsoft.com/en-us/download/details.aspx?id=25250`.

Unlike the other chapters in this book, there isn't going to be an abundance of PowerShell. The simple fact is that Group Policy management is really only manageable via the GUI tools.

Let's walk through some recipes together to make sure you are able to interact with Group Policy comfortably and begin to explore its underlying capabilities:

- Creating and assigning a new GPO
- Mapping network drives with Group Policy
- Redirecting the **Documents** folder to a network share
- Creating a VPN connection with Group Policy
- Creating a printer connection with Group Policy
- Using Group Policy to enforce an internet proxy server
- Viewing the settings currently enabled inside a GPO
- Viewing the GPOs currently assigned to a computer
- Backing up and restoring GPOs
- Working with WMI filters to assign GPOs
- Plugging in ADMX and ADML templates

Creating and assigning a new Group Policy Object

In order to start using Group Policy, we first need to create a Group Policy Object. Most commonly referred to as a GPO, this object contains the settings that we want to deploy. It also contains the information necessary for domain-joined systems to know which machines and users get these settings and which ones do not. It is critical that you plan GPO assignment carefully. It is easy to create a policy that applies to every domain-joined system in your entire network but depending on what settings you configure in that policy, this can be detrimental to your servers. Often, I find that admins who are only somewhat familiar with Group Policy are making use of a built-in GPO called Default Domain Policy. This, by default, applies to everything in your network. Sometimes, this is what you want to accomplish, but most of the time, it is not!

We are going to use this section to detail the process of creating a new GPO and use some assignment sections called **Links** and **Security Filters**, which will give us complete control over which systems receive these systems and, more importantly, which do not.

Getting ready

This recipe will be accomplished from a Windows 10 computer with RSAT installed, connected to a Windows Server 2019 domain. Alternatively, you can complete this from the domain controller itself if need be.

How to do it...

Follow these steps to create and assign a new GPO:

1. Open **Server Manager**, click on the **Tools** menu, and choose to open the **Group Policy Management Console**.

2. Expand your domain name and click on the folder called **GPOs**. This shows you a list of your current GPOs.

3. Right-click on the **GPOs** folder and click on **New**.

4. Insert a name for your new GPO. I am going to call mine `Map Network Drives`. We will end up using this GPO in the next recipe, *Mapping network drives with Group Policy*:

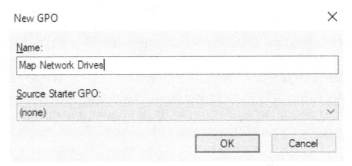

Figure 10.1 – Naming our new Group Policy Object

5. Click **OK** and then expand your **Group Policy Objects** folder if it isn't already. You should see the new GPO in this list. Go ahead and click on the new GPO in order to see its settings.

6. We want this new GPO to apply only to a specific group of users that we have established. This assignment of the GPO is handled at the lowest level by the **Security Filtering** section, which you can see in the following screenshot. You can see that, by default, **Authenticated Users** is in the list. This means that if we created a link between this GPO and an **Organizational Unit (OU)** in the domain, the policy settings would immediately start applying to any user account:

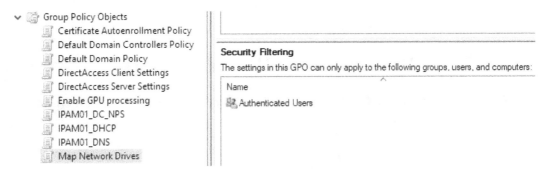

Figure 10.2 – The security filtering options for our new Group Policy Object

7. Since we want to make absolutely sure that only specific user accounts get these drive mappings, we are going to modify the **Security Filtering** section and list only the user group that we have created to house these user accounts. Under the **Security Filtering** section, click on the **Remove** button in order to remove **Authenticated Users** from this list. It should now be empty.

8. Now, click on the **Add...** button, which is also listed under the **Security Filtering** section.

9. Type in the name of your group that you want to filter this GPO for. My group is called **Sales Group**. Click **OK**.

10. Now, this GPO will only apply to users we place into the group called **Sales Group**, but at this point in time, the GPO isn't going to apply to anywhere because we have not established any links. The following screenshot shows the top section of your **Scope** tab, which is currently blank:

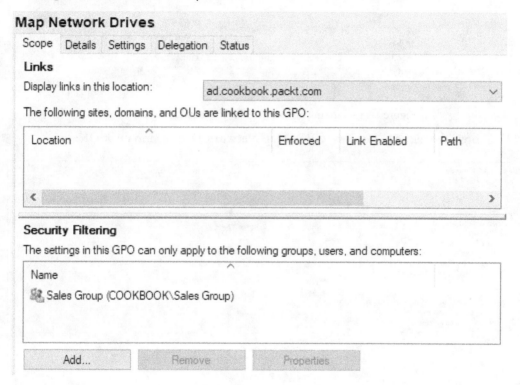

Figure 10.3 – Filtering our GPO to just Sales Group

11. We need to link this GPO to some place in our domain structure. This is essentially telling it *apply this policy from here down* in our OU structure. By creating a link with no security filtering, the GPO will apply to everything under that link. However, since we do have security filtering enabled and specified down to a particular group, the security filtering will be the final authority in saying that these GPO settings will only apply to members of our sales group. For this example policy, I want it to apply to the OU called **Laptops**, under **Office Computers**.

12. Right-click on the OU called **Laptops** and then click on the option for **Link an Existing GPO...**:

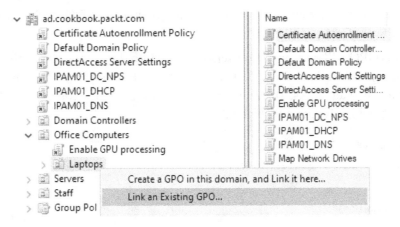

Figure 10.4 – Linking an existing GPO to our Laptops OU

13. Choose the name of our new GPO, **Map Network Drives**, and click **OK**:

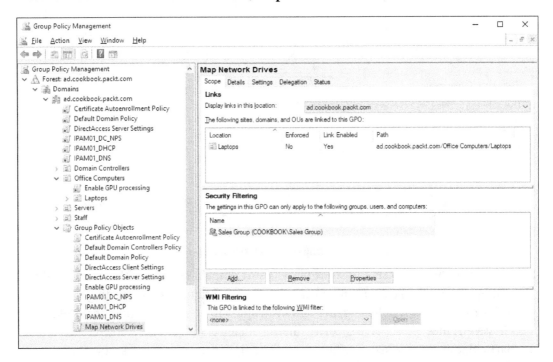

Figure 10.5 – Our newly configured Group Policy Object linked and filtered

Our new GPO is now linked to **Laptops**. So, at this level, any system that's placed inside that OU would get these settings – that is, if we hadn't paired it down a step further with the **Security Filtering** section. Since we populated this with only the name of our specific sales group, this means that this new drive mapping policy will only apply to those users that are added to this group.

How it works...

In our example recipe, we created a new Group Policy Object and took the necessary steps in order to restrict this GPO to the computers and users that we deemed necessary inside our domain. Each network is different, and you may find yourself relying only on **Links** to keep GPOs sorted according to your needs, or you may need to enforce some combination of both **Links** and **Security Filtering**. In any case, whichever works best for you, make sure that you are confident in configuring these fields so that you know, beyond a shadow of a doubt, where your GPO is being applied.

You may have noticed that, in this recipe, we didn't actually configure any settings inside the GPO, so at this point, it still isn't doing anything to those in the sales group. Continue reading to navigate the actual settings portion of Group Policy.

Mapping network drives with Group Policy

Almost everyone uses mapped drives of some flavor in their networks. Creating drive mappings manually as part of a new user startup process is cumbersome and unnecessary. It is also work that will probably need to be duplicated as users move from one computer to another in the future. If we utilize Group Policy to centralize the creation of these drive mappings, we can ensure that the same users get the same drive mappings wherever they log into the network. Planned correctly, you can enable these mappings so that they appear on any domain-joined system across the network by the user simply logging into the computer like they always do. This is a good, simple first task to accomplish within Group Policy to get our feet wet and to learn something that could turn out to be useful in your organization.

Getting ready

This recipe will be accomplished from a Windows 10 computer with RSAT installed, connected to a Windows Server 2019 domain. We will assume that you have already created a new GPO for this task that has been configured for **Links** and **Security Filtering**.

How to do it...

To create a drive mapping in Group Policy, follow these steps:

1. Open the **Group Policy Management** console from the **Tools** menu of Server Manager.

2. Expand the name of your domain and then expand the **Group Policy Objects** folder. There, we will see our new GPO called **Map Network Drives**.

3. Right-click on the **Map Network Drives** GPO and click on **Edit...**:

Figure 10.6 – Editing our existing GPO

4. Navigate to **User Configuration | Preferences | Windows Settings | Drive Maps**.

5. Right-click on **Drive Maps** and choose **New | Mapped Drive**:

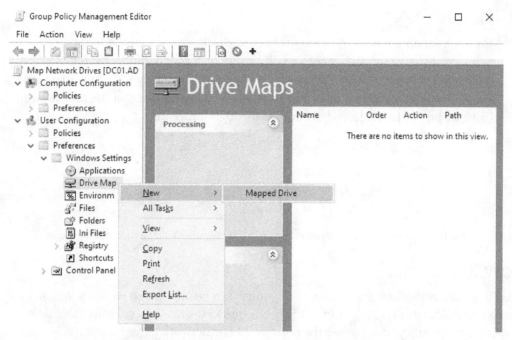

Figure 10.7 – Creating a new Mapped Drive configuration

6. Set **Location** as the destination URL of the drive mapping and use the **Label as** field if you want a more descriptive name to be visible to users.

7. Choose a drive letter to be used for this new mapping from the drop-down menu listed on this screen:

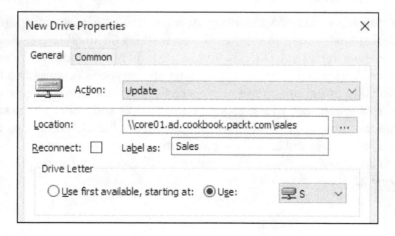

Figure 10.8 – The mapped drive settings

8. Click **OK**.

9. We are assuming you have already created the links and security filtering appropriate to where you want this GPO to apply. If so, you may now log into a computer on your domain as a user account that this policy will apply to. Once logged into the computer, open File Explorer; you should see that the new network drive was mapped automatically during the login process:

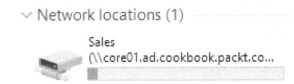

Figure 10.9 – Our mapped network drive created by our GPO after a user has logged in

How it works...

There are a few different ways that drive mappings can be automated within a Windows environment, and this recipe outlines one of the quickest ways to accomplish this task. By using Group Policy to automate the creation of our network drive mappings, we can centralize the administration of this task and remove the drive mapping's creation load from our helpdesk processes.

Redirecting the Documents folder to a network share

Users are accustomed to saving documents, pictures, and more in their Documents folder, because that is what they do at home. When working on an office computer at their workplace, the natural tendency is to save in the local Documents folder as well. This is often not a desired behavior because backing up everyone's Documents folders individually would be an administrative nightmare. So, a common resolution to this problem is to provide everyone with mapped network drives and train users to save documents into these mapped drives. This is good in theory, but difficult to execute in practice. As long as users still have the capability to save documents in their local Documents folder, there is a good chance that they will save at least some things in there without realizing it.

This recipe is a quick Group Policy change that can be made so that the Documents folders on your domain-joined computers get redirected to a network share. This way, if users do save a document in Documents, that file gets written over to the file server where you have directed them.

Getting ready

We will set up our new GPO using a Windows 10 computer with RSAT installed, connected to a Server 2019 domain.

How to do it...

To redirect the Documents folders via Group Policy, follow these steps:

1. Launch the **Group Policy Management** console from the **Tools** menu of Server Manager.

2. Right-click on the name of your domain and choose **Create a GPO in this domain, and Link it here…**:

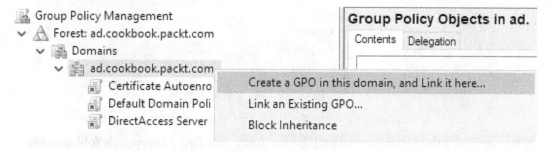

Figure 10.10 – Creating and linking a new GPO in a single step

3. Input something in the **Name** field for your new GPO. I am going to call mine **Redirect My Documents**. Then, click **OK**.

4. Browse to the **Group Policy Objects** folder that is listed under your domain name.

5. Right-click on the name of our new redirection GPO and click **Edit…**.

6. Navigate to **User Configuration | Policies | Windows Settings | Folder Redirection | Documents**.

7. Right-click on **Documents** and go into **Properties**:

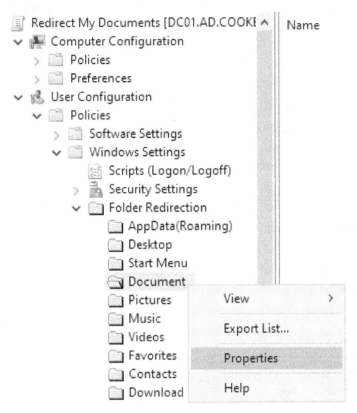

Figure 10.11 – Locating the Properties menu for Documents folder redirection

8. Drop down the **Setting** menu and choose **Basic - Redirect everyone's folder to the same location**.

9. Type in the **Root Path** field where you want everyone's Documents folder to be directed to. I am going to use a share that I have created on our file server. Mine will look like this: \\core01.ad.cookbook.packt.com\users\:

Figure 10.12 – Configuring the document redirection properties

10. Click **OK**. You may receive a warning message about folder redirection not working with Windows 2000. Assuming you don't have any Windows 2000 or Windows XP machines still on the network, you can ignore this message and click **OK**.

11. Your setting should be put immediately into place within the GPO. Now, go ahead and log into a test client machine and open the Documents folder.

12. Create a new text document inside the local Documents folder. We are just creating something here in local Documents so that we can see where it is actually being stored.

13. Now, log into your file server and check inside the Users directory that we specified. We now have a folder in there with my username, and inside that folder is a Documents folder that contains the new text document that I just created and stored inside the local Documents folder on my client computer!

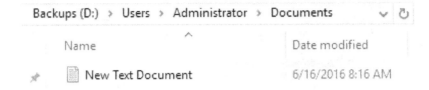

Figure 10.13 – Windows Explorer showing the new file

How it works...

Redirecting everyone's Documents to be automatically stored on a centralized file server is an easy change with Group Policy. You could even combine this configuration with another that maps a network drive, then simply specify the drive letter under your **Document Redirection** settings rather than typing out a network path that could potentially change in the future. However you decide to configure it in your environment, I guarantee that using this setting will result in more centralized administration of your data and fewer lost files for your users.

Creating a VPN connection with Group Policy

If you have administered or helped support a VPN connectivity solution in the past, you are probably familiar with setting up VPN connection profiles on client computers. In an environment where VPN is utilized as the remote access solution, what I commonly observe is that the VPN profile creation process is usually a manual step that needs to be taken by human hands, following the user's first login to the computer. This is inefficient and easily forgotten. With tools that exist in Windows Server 2019, you can automate the creation of these VPN connections on client computers. Let's use Group Policy to create these profiles for us during user login.

Getting ready

We will use a Windows 10 computer with RSAT installed to configure our new Group Policy Object. Once finished, we will also use Windows 10 to make sure that our VPN profile was successfully created. For this recipe, we are going to assume that you've created the GPO and set up links and filtered them according to your needs before getting started with the actual configuration of this GPO.

How to do it...

Follow these steps to configure a GPO that will automatically create a VPN connection profile on your remote client computers:

1. Inside the **Group Policy Management** console, right-click on your new GPO that will be used for this task and click on **Edit...**.

2. Navigate to **User Configuration | Preferences | Control Panel Settings**.

3. Right-click on **Network Options** and choose **New | VPN Connection**:

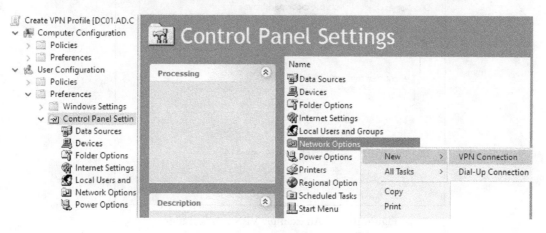

Figure 10.14 – Creating a new VPN connection in our Group Policy Object

4. Input something in the **Connection name** field for this new VPN connection; this name will be displayed on client computers. If you are connecting to an IP address, enter that here. Otherwise, tick the box for **Use DNS name** and then enter the DNS name for the VPN endpoint. Depending on the needs for your particular VPN connection, you may also have to visit the additional tabs available on this screen to finish your specific configurations. Then, click **OK**:

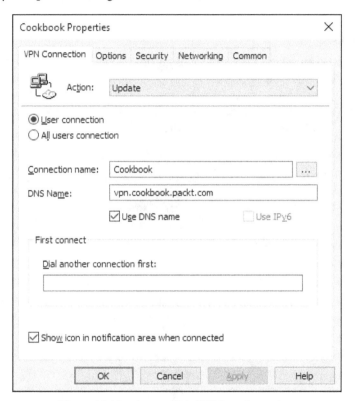

Figure 10.15 – An example VPN configuration

5. Now, log into your client computer and click on the **Network** icon in the system tray, the same place where you would click in order to connect to a wireless network. Here, you can see that, during our login to this computer, a new VPN connection called **Cookbook** was added and is now available to click on.

How it works...

In this recipe, we used Group Policy to automate the creation of a new VPN connection for our remote laptops. Using a GPO for something like this saves time and effort since you are no longer setting up these connections by hand during a new PC build. You can also use this function to update settings on an existing VPN connection in the future, if you need to change IP addresses or something like that. As you are starting to see throughout these recipes, there are all kinds of different things that Group Policy can be used to accomplish.

Creating a printer connection with Group Policy

Let's say you just installed a new network printer in the office. You have installed it on a few computers to make sure it works properly, but now you are staring down the rows and rows of computers that would like to print to this printer occasionally. The prospect of logging into every computer in order to launch and walk through the printer creation wizard isn't sounding like the way you would like to spend your Friday night. Let's see whether we can, once again, make use of Group Policy to save the day. We will utilize a new GPO that will be configured to automatically install this new printer on the client desktops.

Getting ready

We are assuming you have already created the new GPO and have linked it accordingly so that only computers that need this new printer are going to receive these GPO settings. We are going to use the Group Policy Management console on our Windows 10 computer that has RSAT installed.

How to do it...

To configure your new GPO for a new printer creation, follow these steps:

1. Open the **Group Policy Management** console from the **Tools** menu of Server Manager.

2. Right-click on the new GPO that is going to be used for printer creation and click **Edit…**. You can also create a new GPO for this if required.

3. Navigate to **User Configuration | Preferences | Control Panel Settings**.

4. Right-click on **Printers** and choose **New | TCP/IP Printer**:

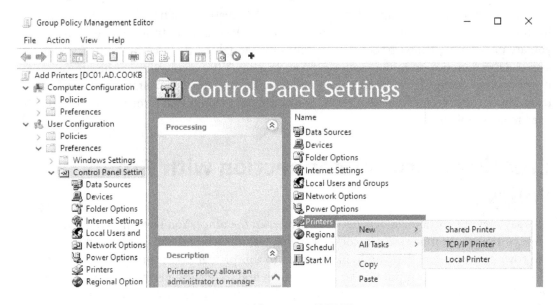

Figure 10.16 – Adding a new TCP/IP printer

5. Input the information that is necessary for the printer connection. Since we chose to set up a new TCP/IP printer, we need to input something in the **IP Address** and **Local Name** fields for users to be able to see this new printer in their list. I am also going to choose **Set this printer as the default printer...only if a local printer is not present**. **Printer path** is used when installing the printer to fetch a driver from. Our printer provides its own driver, so we're just entering the same IP address here. If your printer does not, you will have to install and share the printer somewhere (perhaps a server) where Windows clients can fetch their drivers from:

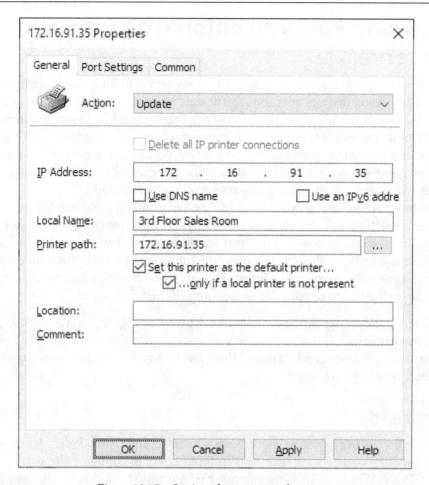

Figure 10.17 – Settings for our example printer

6. Click **OK**. Now, this printer will be distributed to those users you filtered the GPO to.

How it works...

Using Group Policy to automate regular IT tasks makes a lot of sense for all kinds of technologies. In this recipe, we built a simple printer connection so that we didn't have to do it by hand on our dozens of computers that needed to be able to print here.

Using Group Policy to enforce an internet proxy server

Many networks of significant size use a forward proxy server to filter their internet traffic. This is essentially a box that sits near the edge of the corporate network; whenever client computers in the network try to access the internet, their requests are sent out through this server. Doing this enables companies to monitor internet use, restrict browsing permissions, and keep many forms of malware at bay. When implementing a proxy server, one of the big questions is always, "How do we enforce the use of this proxy?". Some solutions do a default route through the proxy server so that all traffic flows outbound that way at a network level. More often, though, it is desirable for the proxy server settings to be configured at the browser level because it is probably unnecessary for all traffic to flow through this proxy; only the browser's web traffic should do so. In these cases, you could certainly open the Internet Explorer options on everyone's computers and enter the proxy server information, but that is a huge task to undertake, and it gives users the ability to remove those settings if they choose to.

By using Group Policy to set the Internet Explorer proxy configuration, this task will be automated and hands-off. This also ensures that users are not able to manipulate these fields in the future, and you can be assured that your web traffic is flowing through the proxy server as you have defined it.

Getting ready

Our GPO has already been created. Here, we will be using the Group Policy Management console on our Windows 10 computer with an RSAT client to configure the settings within the GPO. A Windows 10 client computer is also sitting, waiting for use, as we will want to test this GPO after we've finished the configuration.

How to do it...

Follow these steps to set everyone's internet proxy settings via Group Policy:

1. Open the **Group Policy Management** console from the **Tools** menu of Server Manager.

2. Find the new GPO that you have created for this task, right-click on it, and choose **Edit...**.

3. Navigate to **User Configuration | Preferences | Control Panel Settings | Internet Settings**.

4. Right-click on **Internet Settings** and choose **New | Internet Explorer 10**:

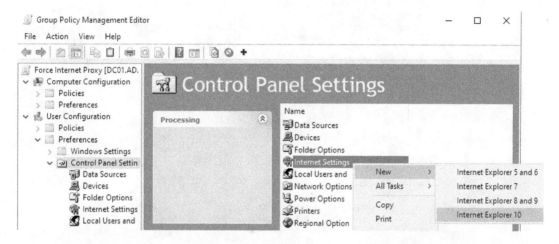

Figure 10.18 – Creating a new Internet Explorer 10 GPO setting

> **Tip**
> You may have to create multiple policies here if you are using multiple versions of Internet Explorer on your workstations.

5. You will see a dialog box that looks just like the regular internet options available in Internet Explorer. You have the ability to change many things here, but for our purposes, we are heading over to the **Connections** tab.

6. Click on the **LAN settings** button.

7. Check the box for **Proxy server**. Then, input the **Address** and **Port** fields for your particular proxy server:

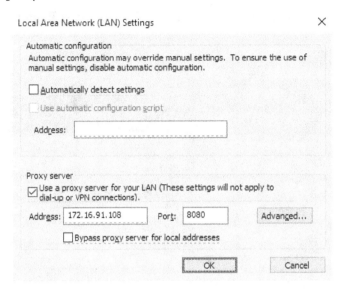

Figure 10.19 – Configuring Internet Explorer proxy options

8. Click **OK**. Now, your setting will be put into place.

9. Now, log into the client computer and see whether this proxy server information was successfully implemented. Launch Internet Explorer and open **Internet options**.

10. Browse to the **Connections** tab and click on the **LAN settings** button to ensure your proxy server settings have been properly plugged in. Also, notice that they are now grayed out, showing you that they have been configured by Group Policy and cannot be manipulated manually.

How it works...

Using Group Policy to assign internet proxy server settings to all of your client computers with one simple GPO creation is another example of the power behind Group Policy. The possibilities for the centralized administration of your domain-joined machines are almost endless; you just need to do a little digging and find the right place inside the GPOs for changing your settings. Maybe you don't have a proxy server in your network and don't need this recipe. However, I still encourage you to take the steps listed here and apply them to some piece of technology that you do utilize. I guarantee anyone working in IT will find some setting inside Group Policy that will benefit them! Go out and find some that will help save you time and money.

Viewing the settings currently enabled inside a GPO

So far, we have been creating GPOs and putting settings into them, so we are well aware of what is happening with each of our policies. Often, though, you enter a new environment that contains a lot of existing policies, and you may need to figure out what is happening in those policies. I have had many cases where I've installed a new server, joined it to the domain, and it broke. It doesn't necessarily nose dive, but some component won't work properly or I can't flow network traffic to it for some reason. Something like that can be hard to track down. Since the issue seemed to happen during the domain-join process, I suspected that some kind of policy from an existing GPO had been applied to my new server and was having a negative effect on it. Let's take a look inside Group Policy and at the easiest way to display the settings that are contained within each GPO.

Getting ready

For this recipe, we only need access to the Group Policy Management console, which I am going to run from my Windows 10 computer with RSAT installed.

How to do it...

To quickly view the settings contained within a GPO, follow these steps:

1. In the domain controller, open up Server Manager and launch the **Group Policy Management** console from inside the **Tools** menu.

2. Expand the name of your domain, then expand the **GPOs** folder. This displays all of the GPOs currently configured in your domain.

3. Click on one of the GPOs so that you see the **Links** and **Security Filtering** sections in the right window pane.

4. Now, click on the **Settings** tab near the top.

5. Once you have the **Settings** tab open, click on the **show all** link near the top-right. This will display all the settings that are currently configured inside that GPO:

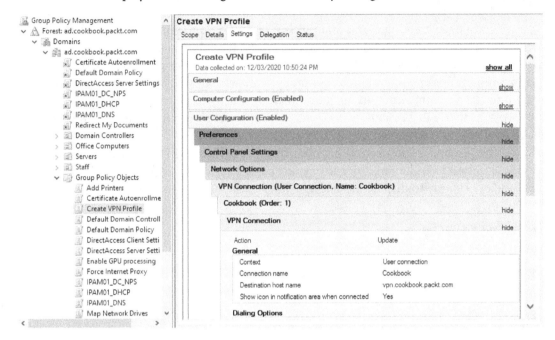

Figure 10.20 – The settings in our Create VPN Profile GPO

How it works...

In this very simple recipe, we used the Group Policy Management console in order to view the currently configured settings inside our GPOs. This can be very useful for checking over existing settings and for comparing them against what is actually being configured on the client computers. Taking a look through this information can also help you spot potential problems, such as duplicate settings spread across multiple GPOs.

See also

Viewing the settings included in a GPO can be helpful during troubleshooting, but there are many other tools that can also be used in order to troubleshoot Group Policy. Here are a couple of links to help you understand the recommended procedures for troubleshooting Group Policy:

- http://technet.microsoft.com/en-us/library/jj134223.aspx
- http://technet.microsoft.com/en-us/library/cc749336%28v=ws.10%29.aspx

Viewing the GPOs currently assigned to a computer

Once you start using Group Policy to distribute settings to many client computers, it will quickly become important to be able to view the settings and policies that have or have not been applied to specific computers. Thankfully, there is a command built right into the Windows operating system that can be used to display this information. There are a number of different switches that can be used with this command, so let's explore some of the most common ones that I see used by server administrators.

Getting ready

We have a number of GPOs in our domain now; some are applied at the top level of the domain, while some are only applied to specific OUs. We are going to run some commands on our Windows 10 client in order to find out which GPOs have been applied to it and which have not.

How to do it...

Let's use the `gpresult` command to gather some information on the policies that have been applied to our server:

1. Log into the computer, or whatever server computer you want to see these results on, and open up an administrative prompt.

2. Type `gpresult /r` and press *Enter*. This displays all of the resultant data on which policies have been applied and have not been applied to our system. You can scroll through this information to get the data that you need:

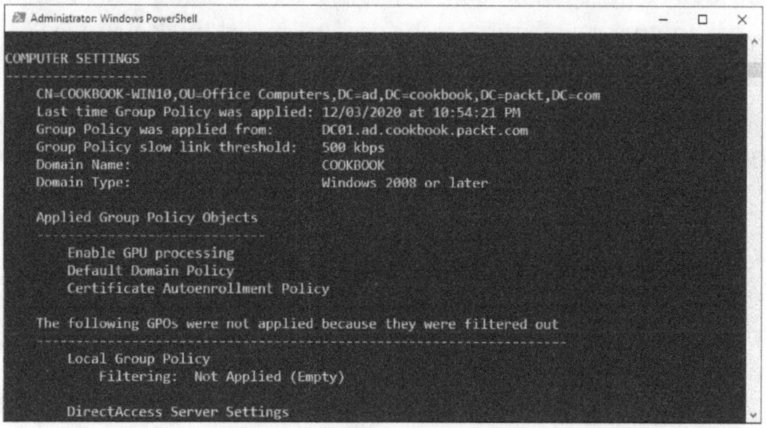

Figure 10.21 – Part of the gpresult output of our test machine

3. Now, let's clean that data up a little bit. For instance, the general output we just received had information about both computer policies and user policies. Now, we want to display only policies that have been applied at the user level. Go ahead and use the `gpresult /r /scope:user` command:

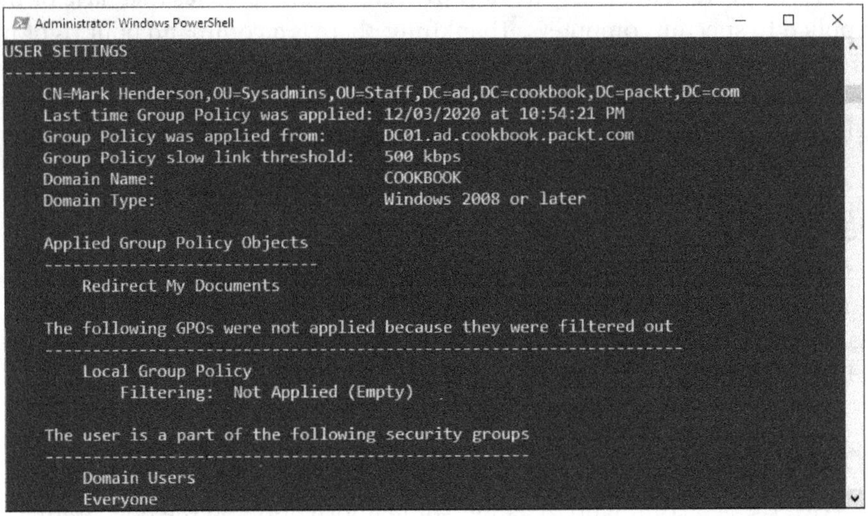

Figure 10.22 – Just viewing the user GPOs that have been applied

> **Tip**
> You can use either the `/SCOPE:USER` switch or the `/SCOPE:COMPUTER` switch in order to view the user or computer policies that have been applied to the system.

4. And if you aren't a huge fan of looking at this data via Command Prompt, never fear! There is another switch that can be used to export this data in HTML format. Try using the `gpresult /h c:\gpresult.html` command.

5. After running the preceding command, browse to your `C:` drive; you should have a file sitting there called `gpresult.html`. Go ahead and open that file to see your `gpresult` data in a web browser with a nicer look and feel:

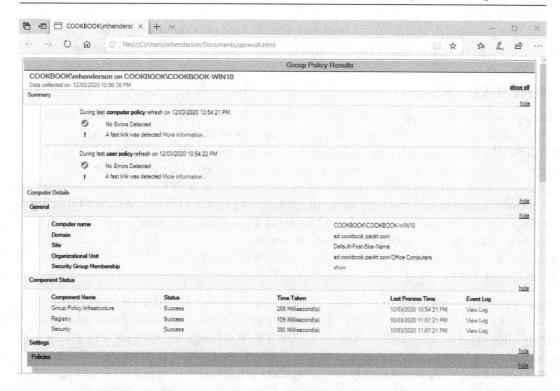

Figure 10.23 – The results of gpresult in HTML format

6. There is another often overlooked command that can be used to show exactly which GPO settings have been applied to your computer. This is called **Resultant Set of Policy (RSOP)**. Go ahead and run the `rsop` command. It may take a few moments to generate the report, but then you should have a screen that looks familiar to you already but showing all the GPO settings that have been applied:

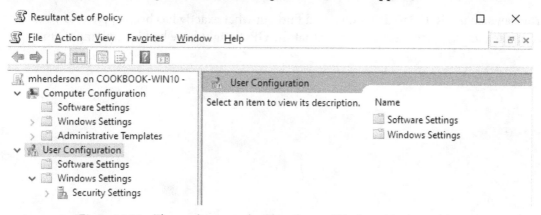

Figure 10.24 – The resultant set of policies for our Windows 10 test machine

7. You can also view any GPO errors by right-clicking on either **Computer Configuration** or **User Configuration**, then going to the **Error Information** tab.

How it works...

The gpresult command can be used in a variety of ways to display information about which GPOs and settings have been applied to your client computer or server. This can be especially useful when trying to determine what policies are being applied, and maybe even more helpful when you're trying to figure out why a particular policy hasn't been applied. If a policy is denied because of rights or permissions, you will see it in this output. This likely indicates that you have something to adjust in your **Links** or **Security Filtering** settings in order to get the policy applied successfully to your machine. However, if you decide to make use of the data for yourself, make sure to play around with the gpresult command and get familiar with its results if you intend to administer your environment using Group Policy.

There's one additional note to mention about another command that is very commonly used in the field. Windows domain-joined machines only process Group Policy settings every once in a while; by default, they will refresh their settings and look for new policy changes every 90 minutes. If you are creating or changing policies and notice that they have not been applied to your endpoint computers yet, you could hang out for a couple of hours and wait for those changes to be applied. If you want to speed up that process a little, you can log into the endpoint client computer, server, or whatever it is that should receive the settings, and use the gpupdate /force command. This will force that computer to revisit Group Policy and apply any settings that have been configured for it. When we make changes in the field and don't want to spend a lot of time waiting around for replication to happen naturally, we often use gpupdate /force numerous times as we make changes and progress through testing.

You can also use RSOP to drill down and find out what exactly has been applied to your computer, as well as to view any errors that the GPO might have had in applying them.

Backing up and restoring GPOs

As with any piece of data in your organization, it is a good idea to keep backups of your GPOs. Keeping these backups separately from a full domain controller or full Active Directory backup can be advantageous, as it enables a quicker restore of individual GPOs in the event of an accidental deletion. Or perhaps you've updated a GPO, but the change you made is now causing problems and you want to roll that policy back to make sure it is configured the way that it was yesterday. Whatever your reason for backing up and restoring GPOs, let's take a look at a couple of ways to accomplish each task. We will use the Group Policy Management console to perform these functions, and we will also figure out how to do the same backups and restores via PowerShell.

Getting ready

We are going to perform these tasks from a Windows 10 computer with an RST client in our environment. We will utilize both the Group Policy Management console and the PowerShell command line.

How to do it...

There is a GPO in our domain called Map Network Drives. First, we will use the Group Policy Management console to back up and restore this GPO:

1. From the **Tools** menu of Server Manager, open up the **Group Policy Management** console.

2. Navigate to **Forest | Domains | Your Domain Name | GPOs**.

3. If you want to back up a single GPO, simply right-click on the specific GPO and choose **Back Up…**. Otherwise, it is probably more useful for us to back up the whole set of GPOs. To accomplish that, right-click on the **GPOs** folder and then choose **Back Up All…**:

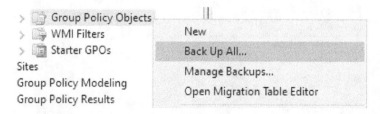

Figure 10.25 – Backing up our Group Policy Objects

4. Specify a location where you want the backups to be saved, as well as a description for the backup that's been set. Then, click **Back Up**:

Figure 10.26 – The location and description of our GPO backup

5. Once the backup process is complete, you should see the status of how many GPOs were successfully backed up:

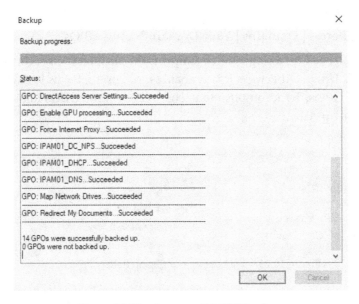

Figure 10.27 – A successful GPO backup

Now, let's try accomplishing the same full GPO backup, but this time using PowerShell:

1. Open an administrative PowerShell prompt.

2. Use the following command:

```
Import-Module GroupPolicy
Backup-GPO -Path 'C:\GPO Backups\' -All
```

This will result in the following output:

Figure 10.28 – Our GPO backup being run from PowerShell

Now that we have two full backup sets of the GPOs, let's try to restore the GPO called Map Network Drives:

1. Navigate back inside the **Group Policy Management** console and find the **GPOs** folder. This is the same location that we used to back up a minute ago.

2. Right-click on the **Map Network Drives** GPO and choose **Restore from Backup…**:

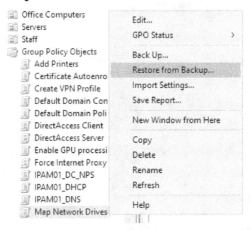

Figure 10.29 – Restoring an individual GPO

3. Click **Next** and specify the folder where your backup files are stored. Then, click **Next** again.

4. As long as a backup copy of the **Map Network Drives** GPO exists in that folder, you will see it in the wizard. Select that GPO and click **Next**:

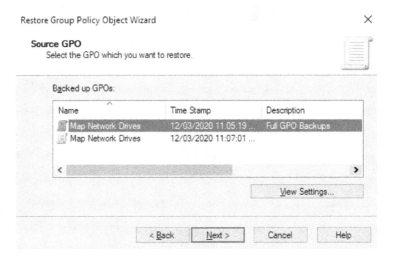

Figure 10.30 – Choosing which version of our GPO to restore

5. Click **Finish** and the GPO will be restored to its previous state.

Now, we will restore the same Map Network Drives GPO but using PowerShell, as follows:

1. Head back to your administrative PowerShell prompt.

2. Use the following command to restore the previous version of this GPO from the backup we created earlier:

```
Restore-GPO -Name "Map Network Drives" -Path
C:\GPO_Backups_PowerShell
```

This results in the following output:

Figure 10.31 – Restoring our GPO via PowerShell

> **Tip**
> Rather than typing out the name of the GPO in this command, you could specify the GUID of the policy. This number is generally a lot longer than the name, however, and so I tend to see admins preferring to utilize the name of the policy. For example, the GUID of our Map Network Drives GPO is `77eed750-de8e-44e9-9649-96cab2f2abdc`.

How it works...

Backing up and restoring GPOs is going to be a regular task for anybody administering Active Directory and Group Policy. In this recipe, we walked through each process, using a couple of different tools for each procedure. The Group Policy Management console is nice because it is graphically interfaced, and it is easy to look at the options available to you. PowerShell is often preferred, however, because it can be automated (think scheduled backups). It also facilitates remote execution of these commands from another machine inside the network.

See also

Here are some links if you want more extensive information about the PowerShell cmdlets we used in this recipe:

- `https://docs.microsoft.com/en-us/powershell/module/grouppolicy/backup-gpo?view=win10-ps`

- `https://docs.microsoft.com/en-us/powershell/module/grouppolicy/restore-gpo?view=win10-ps`

Working with WMI filters to assign GPOs

Previously in this chapter, we looked at how we can use OUs and security groups to filter our GPOs. This is useful in a lot of situations. If you have a neatly organized Active Directory environment, everything should be filed away into an appropriate group or OU. But what if you *don't* have a neatly organized OU, or if you want to filter your GPOs on something other than OU?

For example, you might have a GPO you only want applied to laptops, but your OUs are not organized and just dumps all laptops and desktops together into a single OU. Or perhaps you want to apply a GPO only to virtual machines, but there's no way to tell from Active Directory whether a machine is a virtual machine or not. Another common case is that you have a lot of computers in a single OU, but you only want to apply a GPO to machines that match a certain name.

The good news is that we can do this by using something called WMI filters. **WMI** stands for **Windows Management Instrumentation** and is a way of querying almost anything you need to know about a Windows computer, including its name, its manufacturer, its BIOS revision, how many hard drives it has, and when Windows was first installed. You name it, you can probably figure it out via WMI.

In this recipe, we're going to look at how we can use WMI to filter our GPOs even further.

Getting ready

We're going to be using Windows 10 with RSAT installed to modify our Group Policy. We're going to modify an existing GPO to stop it from being applied to any laptops.

How to do it...

1. From the **Tools** menu of Server Manager, open the **Group Policy Management** console.

2. Navigate to **Forest | Domains | Your Domain Name | WMI Filters**. If you've been following this book from beginning to end, you might already have some filters in there. We're going to ignore any existing filters for now and pretend that we're doing this from scratch.

3. Right-click on **WMI Filters** and choose **New**:

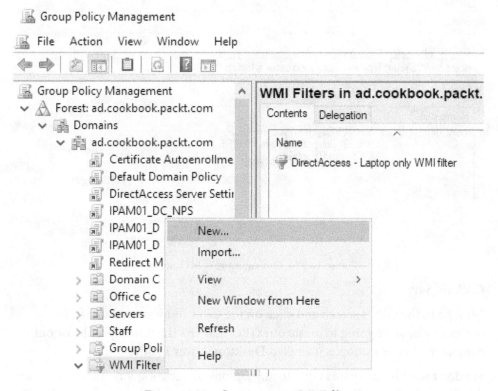

Figure 10.32 – Creating a new WMI filter

4. We now have our **New WMI Filter** screen. Give your filter a name. I strongly recommend providing it with a description as well so that you can remember why this filter was created in the first place. We will name it Exclude Laptops.

5. Under the **Queries** section, click the **Add** button.

6. You will now have a screen that's asking for a namespace and a query. We're going to leave the namespace as the default; that is, root\CIMv2.

7. Under **Queries**, enter Select PCSystemType from Win32_ComputerSystem WHERE (PCSystemType!=2) and click **OK**. We will go into more detail about what this actually means later on:

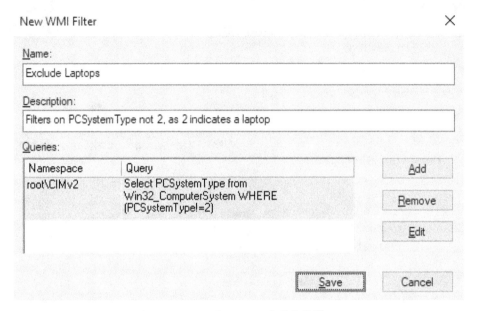

Figure 10.33 – Our example WMI filter

8. Click on **Save**.

9. Now, go to the **GPOs** screen and click on the GPO you want to modify. In our example, we're going to locate our GPO that sets the power profile for our computers. In our example, it's called **Desktop Power Profile**.

10. We don't want to apply this GPO to any laptops in our company. This is because this is our power profile for desktops. At the bottom of the **Scope** screen, there is a dropdown for **WMI Filtering**. Select the new WMI filter we just created from within that list.

11. You will be asked whether you want to change the WMI filter. Click **Yes**. Your GPO will now no longer apply to laptops:

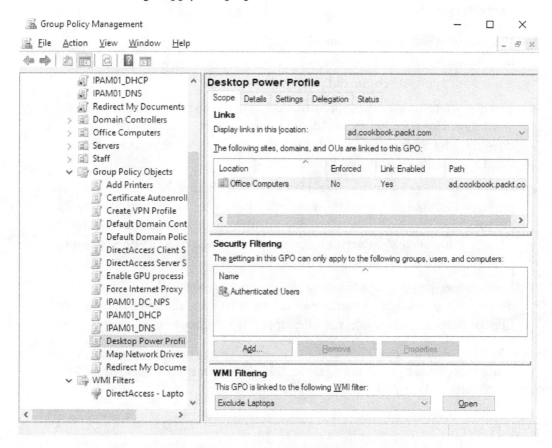

Figure 10.34 – A GPO with a WMI filter applied

Now, let's just take a step back and look more at what went on in *step 7*. We entered our WMI filter, but it might not have made much sense to you what we did here:

```
Select PCSystemType from Win32_ComputerSystem WHERE
(PCSystemType!=2)
```

This is a WMI query. It also looks like a SQL query – and that's not by mistake. WMI is a database that Windows keeps and contains information about your computer. Let's look at this query in more detail:

1. Open a PowerShell console as an administrator.

2. Execute the `Get-WmiObject -Query "Select * from Win32_ComputerSystem"` command.

3. This query returns some basic information from the `Win32_ComputerSystem` WMI class. However, PowerShell doesn't show us the full story by default, so let's expand it a bit more using `Get-WmiObject -Query "Select * from Win32_ComputerSystem" | Format-List *`.

4. Now, we have a lot more information to look at, including the `PCSystemType` property. But what does everything mean? What are we looking at? Thankfully, Microsoft has very extensive online documentation for WMI classes. The link for `Win32_ComputerSystem` is https://docs.microsoft.com/en-us/ windows/win32/cimwin32prov/win32-computersystem.

5. Every property in the class has some documentation attached to it. The documentation for `PCSystemType` indicates that a code of 2 is a mobile computer (for our purposes, a laptop), 1 is a desktop, 3 is a workstation, and so on.

So, our WMI query is looking at the `Win32_ComptuerSystem` class and looking to see whether `PCSystemType` is not equal to 2. If that statement is true, then the WMI filter is successful and the policy applies.

How it works...

WMI filters are a very powerful thing. We've only just scratched the surface in this recipe. There are thousands of pieces of information that are gathered by WMI. You could have one GPO only apply to Dell computers, and a different one for HP. And this can be done without having to worry about having your Active Directory OUs completely organized and neat – although this should not be an excuse to not keep them neat and tidy.

However, you do need to be a bit careful with WMI filters. If they are overused or poorly designed queries, they can put a load on your clients. These filters are queried every time the GPOs are applied, which is frequently. You don't want your computers bogging down every 90 minutes because of heavy WMI queries being run for GPO filters.

Have a look around and experiment with WMI PowerShell cmdlets and see what else you can discover about your computer. How would you write a WMI query that would be applied to every computer whose name began with WEB?

See also

- The MSDN documentation for Win32 classes in WMI: `https://docs.microsoft.com/en-us/windows/win32/cimwin32prov/win32-provider`

- PowerShell WMI cmdlets: `https://docs.microsoft.com/en-us/powershell/module/microsoft.powershell.core/about/about_wmi_cmdlets?view=powershell-5.1`

Plugging in ADMX and ADML templates

Someday, you may find yourself in a position where you are following a setup guide or some article that instructs you to configure certain options inside a GPO. However, when you go and look for those options, they do not exist. How is that possible, if the documentation clearly shows the options existing inside Group Policy? This is the magic of ADMX and ADML files. Many configurations and settings exist inside Group Policy right out of the box, but some technologies build on additional settings or fields inside GPOs that do not exist by default. When this happens, those technologies will include files that can be placed on your domain controller. These files are then imported automatically by Group Policy, and the settings will then appear in the normal GPO editing tools. The trickiest part about doing this is figuring out where the ADMX and ADML files need to reside in order for them to be seen and imported by Group Policy. Let's figure it out together.

Getting ready

I run across this problem regularly when setting up DirectAccess. There is a special tool that you can install on your Windows desktop computers that tells you some information about the DirectAccess connection, but this tool needs to be configured by a GPO. The problem is that the settings for the tool don't exist inside Group Policy by default. So, Microsoft includes, in the tool's download files, an ADMX file and an ADML file, both of which need to be plugged into Group Policy. We have downloaded this tool, called the DirectAccess Connectivity Assistant, and I have the ADMX and ADML files now sitting on the hard drive of my domain controller. The work we need to accomplish will be done right from this Windows 10 computer with RSAT installed that we've been using to configure all our GPOs up until this point.

How to do it...

In order to pull settings from ADMX and ADML files into Group Policy, follow these steps:

1. Copy the **ADMX** file into `C:\Windows\PolicyDefinitions` on your domain controller. In my case, the filename is `DirectAccess Connectivity Assistant GP.ADMX`.

2. Copy the **ADML** file into `C:\Windows\PolicyDefinitions\en-US` on your domain controller. In my case, the filename is `DirectAccess Connectivity Assistant GP.adml`:

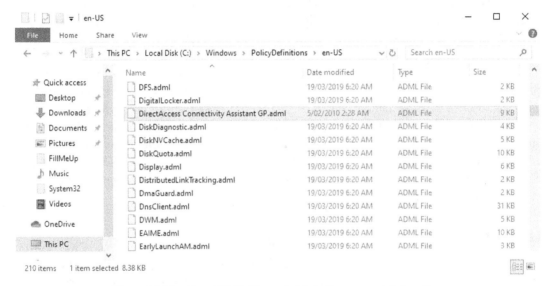

Figure 10.35 – Our ADML file copied into its appropriate location

3. Now, open the **Group Policy Management** console.

4. Edit the GPO that you want to use with these new settings. Here, you can see that we have some brand-new settings available to us inside here that did not exist 5 minutes ago! These new settings show up inside **Computer Configuration | Policies | Administrative Templates**:

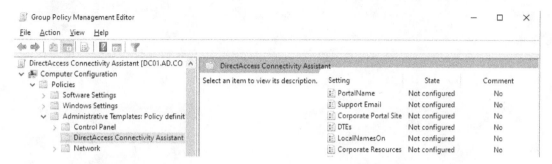

Figure 10.36 – Group Policy Management Editor now showing our new options

How it works...

You can import new settings and configuration options into Group Policy by taking ADMX and ADML files and putting them into the proper folders on your domain controller server. What we walked through in this recipe is an example of how to accomplish this task on a computer, but what happens if your GPOs are managed by many computers and domain controllers? Do you have to copy the files onto each server? No, that is not the proper way to go about it. In an environment where you have multiple domain controllers, the ADMX and ADML files need to go inside something called the Active Directory Central Store. Instead of copying the ADMX and ADML files into their locations on the C drive, open up File Explorer and browse to \\<DOMAIN_NAME>\ SYSVOL\<DOMAIN_NAME>\Policies\PolicyDefinitions. This Central Store location will replicate to all your domain controllers. Simply place the files here instead of on the local hard disk, and your new settings will then be available within the Group Policy console from any of your domain controllers.

11
File Services and Data Control

On any given day, roughly 500 million tweets are sent, 95 million photos are shared on Instagram, 294 billion emails are sent, and 3.5 billion Google searches are run. These numbers are incredible and as all that data comes and goes, it is easy in this day and age to think of this information as being stored in *the cloud*, a magic box in the sky. All that data is sitting somewhere, though – on hard drives, installed inside servers, sitting inside data centers. All this talk about cloud services has really morphed companies into talking about private clouds, and when you break it down, what they are really talking about is different ways to provide a centralized group of information to users that may be accessing it from various places. There are numerous technologies baked into Server 2019 that can assist with centralizing and securing your data, and this chapter will take us through some of the most common.

File storage needs exist for any organization of any size. Whether we are talking about simple document storage for your team of users to utilize or something such as block storage that's accessed over a network by a high-performance computing environment, you are going to have servers in your network that are responsible for storing data safely and securely.

The File Services role has grown significantly over the years as our storage needs have changed and evolved. Many of us can no longer satisfy the data needs for our environments with simple file shares and physical disks. Let's use this chapter to explore some of the more interesting ways that data can be managed in a Windows Server 2019 environment:

- Enabling Distributed File System and creating a Namespace
- Configuring Distributed File System Replication
- Creating an iSCSI target on your server
- Configuring an iSCSI initiator connection
- Configuring Storage Spaces
- Turning on Data Deduplication
- Setting up Windows Server 2019 work folders
- Configuring a Scale-Out File Server

Enabling Distributed File System and creating a Namespace

Distributed File System (**DFS**) is a technology included with Windows Server 2019 that enables multiple file servers to share a single Namespace, enabling end users to access files and folders from a single network name. DFS has been around as a standard Windows component since Windows 2000 – it's not a new technology. However, early versions had a lot of accessibility and replication issues. As of Server 2019, though, DFS is a very solid technology. It allows those accessing files to not have to worry about which server they are currently in contact with; they simply utilize the Namespace of the DFS environment and let the servers do all the grunt work in making sure that all the files and folders are available to the users, no matter where those files happen to be physically sitting. Another way to think of it is as a collection of network shares, all stuck together under the same umbrella that is the **DFS Namespace**. Users access folders and files via the Namespace, and have access to everything in one place. It helps to think of DFS Namespaces sort of like CNAME records in DNS. They essentially allow us to virtualize the file resources.

Let's work together to get a basic DFS environment up and running with a single Namespace created so that we can test browsing to it without having to specify the name of our file server. We will also be taking steps during this recipe to prep our DFS server for replication, synchronizing files between two file servers.

The actual configuration of replication will be accomplished in our next recipe, but when we build out the FILE01 server, we are prepping it for that role as well.

Getting ready

We are working inside a domain environment, and the actual work we'll be doing in this recipe will be accomplished from our new file server. This is called FILE01 and is running Windows Server 2019. It has been joined to the domain, but nothing else has been configured.

How to do it...

Follow these steps to configure this new file server for DFS:

1. Log into FILE01 and launch Server Manager. Click on the **Add roles and features** link.

2. Click **Next** a few times until you reach the **Select server roles** screen.

3. Navigate to **File and Storage Services | File and iSCSI Services**.

4. Check the box for **DFS Namespaces**. When prompted to install additional required features, click **Add Features**.

5. Also, check the box for **DFSR**. You should now have **File Server**, **DFS Namespaces**, and **DFSR** checked on your **Roles** screen:

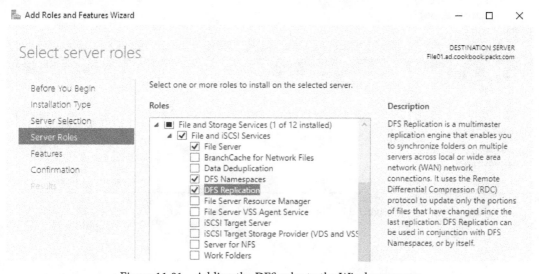

Figure 11.01 – Adding the DFS roles to the Windows server

6. Click **Next, Next,** and then **Install**. This will place the necessary roles onto FILE01.

7. Now, open Server Manager's **Tools** menu and launch **DFS Management**:

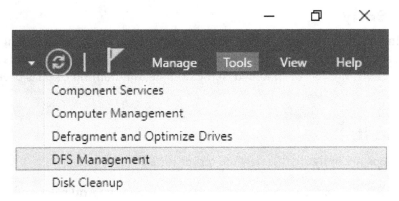

Figure 11.02 – Loading the DFS Management tool

8. First, we are going to create a Namespace that will be published on our domain. Right-click on **Namespaces** and choose **New Namespace…**.

9. Enter the name of the server that is going to be your **Namespace server**. We are going to use the primary file server, FILE01:

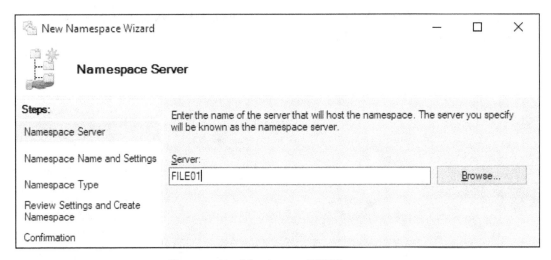

Figure 11.03 – Naming our DFS Namespace

10. On the next screen, **Namespace Name and Settings**, input a name for this new Namespace. My first share is going to be for IT purposes, so I'm calling mine IT. Then, click on the **Edit Settings...** button.

11. The wizard is going to create a new share for my Namespace storage location. If you would like this share to be created in a particular place on the hard drive, specify it here. I am also going to choose the option for **Administrators have full access; other users have read and write permissions** so that users without administrative rights can still save into this Namespace:

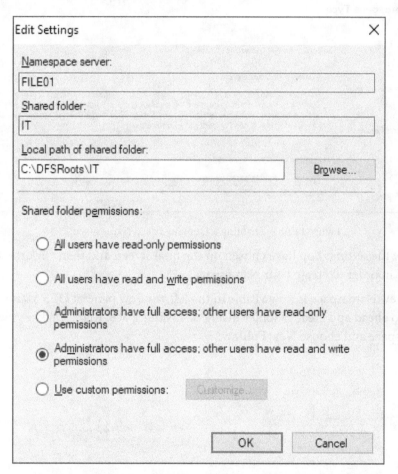

Figure 11.04 – Setting our DFS share settings

12. Click **OK**, then click **Next**.

13. Typically, you want to choose the default options on the **Namespace Type** screen. It should be pre-selected as **Domain-based Namespace**, which is great, together with **Enable Windows Server 2008 mode**. Here, you can also see a preview of the final Namespace name listed for your review. Just go ahead and click **Next** on this screen:

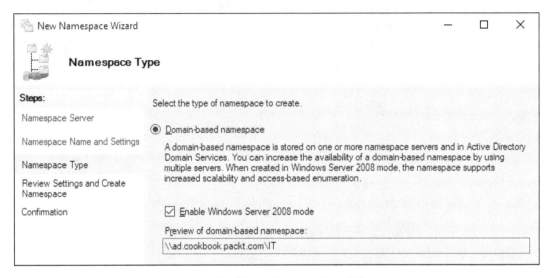

Figure 11.05 – Enabling a Domain-based Namespace

14. Review the settings you have chosen on the final screen and then click the **Create** button in order to create your Namespace.

15. Your new Namespace is now visible in the left window pane of **DFS Management**. Let's go ahead and create a folder inside this Namespace. Right-click on the new Namespace and choose **New Folder...**:

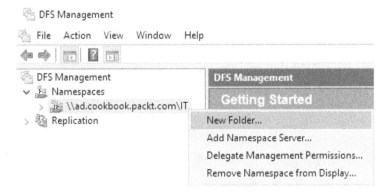

Figure 11.06 – Creating a new folder in our DFS Namespace

16. Input a name for your new folder in the **Name** field; this is the name that will be displayed inside the DFS Namespace when users access it. Then, click the **Add...** button to specify a share that this new folder is going to link to. In this example, I am specifying a folder that happens to be sitting here on FILE01, but you could even specify a network share that is on another server:

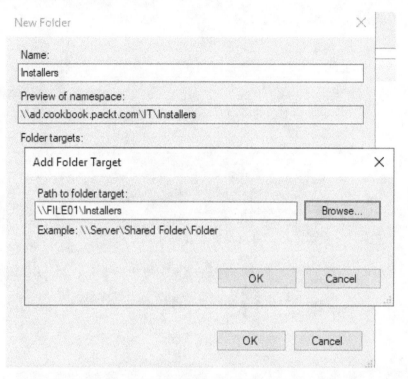

Figure 11.07 – Adding a file share to our Namespace

17. When you click **OK**, if the share that you entered doesn't already exist, you will be asked whether or not you want the wizard to create it for you. You likely want to choose **Yes** so that it creates the new shares for you.

18. After choosing **Yes** in order to create the new shared folder, there is another screen that allows you to specify permissions on this new folder. Go ahead and choose the permission setting that is appropriate for the kind of information you are planning to place in this folder. You must also specify the physical location of this share on the hard drive:

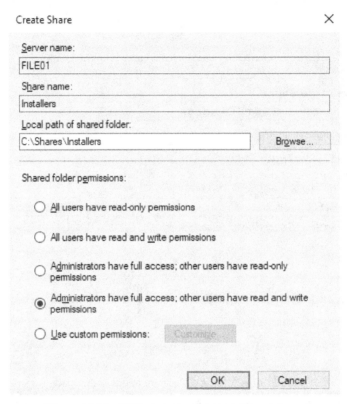

Figure 11.08 – DFS can create our new shares for us

19. Now that we have a DFS Namespace created and a folder within that Namespace, let's test this out! Log into a client computer and try browsing to \\ad.cookbook.packt.com (or use its NetBIOS name; that is, \\cookbook\it):

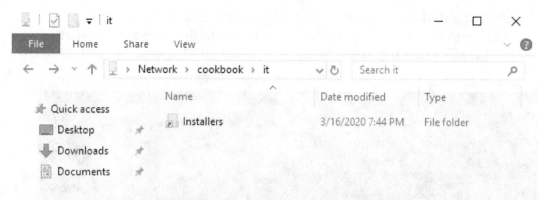

Figure 11.09 – The Installers share in our DFS Namespace

Now, let's look at how we can achieve the same thing via PowerShell:

1. Open PowerShell as an administrator on our `FILE01` server.

2. `Install-WindowsFeature -Name FS-DFS-Namespace,FS-DFS-Replication -IncludeManagementTools` will install our DFS roles.

3. `Import-Module dfsn` will import our DFS module so that we can start to use its cmdlets. You might have to restart your PowerShell session after installing the Windows features to get PowerShell to recognize the cmdlets.

4. `New-DfsnRoot -TargetPath "\\file01\IT" -Type DomainV2 -Path "\\cookbook\IT"` will create our empty DFS Namespace.

5. PowerShell cmdlets do not have the GUI advantage of being able to create our folders all in one step, so first, we have to create our folder to share using `New-Item -ItemType Directory -Path C:\Shares\Installers`.

6. `New-SmbShare -Path C:\Shares\Installers\ -Name Installers` will share our **Installs** folder.

7. `New-DfsnFolder -Path "\\cookbook\IT\Installers"` `-TargetPath "\\file01\Installers"` is the final command we need to use in order to add our new Installers share to our DFS Namespace:

Figure 11.10 – Creating our DFS Namespace via PowerShell

How it works...

In this recipe, we took a new file server and turned it into our first DFS box. The new Namespace that we created now contains a folder where users are able to store documents and is published on the domain so that these files and folders can be accessed via the DFS Namespace name, rather than needing to know the name of our specific file server. DFS is a great tool for centralizing data and creating ease-of-use for employees in your company when they need to access their data. It is also a great tool for redundancy via replication. We'll discuss that in more depth in just a minute.

Configuring Distributed File System Replication

Distributed File System Replication (DFSR) is a piece of DFS that enables automatic file replication between multiple servers. In the first recipe of this chapter, we added the roles and created a DFS Namespace so that we have access to the files and folders that are sitting within our DFS environment. So far, though, this is all sitting on a single file server. Follow along to enable the *R* part of DFSR, replication. We will set up DFSR between the two file servers in our environment, FILE01 and FILE02, and test it to make sure that data is being synchronized between the two.

Getting ready

We already have a DFS server online, FILE01. It is hosting a DFS Namespace with a folder inside. A new file server, FILE02, is online and joined to the domain. This recipe expects that you have already installed the necessary roles for using this server with DFS. The procedure for installing these roles was outlined in our previous recipe, *Enabling Distributed File System and creating a Namespace*. Add the roles to the new FILE02, exactly the same way that you did for FILE01, and then continue with this recipe to configure the replication.

How to do it...

To set up DFSR between the two file servers in our environment, follow these steps:

1. On FILE01, our primary file server, launch Server Manager and then open the **DFS Management** console from inside the **Tools** menu.

2. In the left window pane, right-click on **Replication** and choose **New Replication Group...**:

Figure 11.11 – Creating a new replication group

3. Choose **Multipurpose replication group** and click **Next**.

4. Enter a name for your new replication group. I will be calling mine `FileServers`. Then, click **Next**.

5. On the **Replication Group Members** screen, click the **Add...** button and choose both file servers you want to be part of this group:

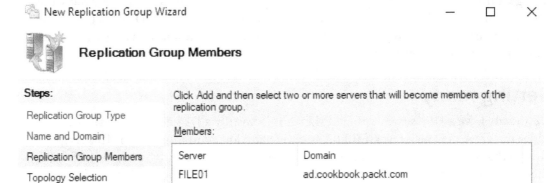

Figure 11.12 – Adding our two file services to our DFSR group

6. Leave the topology set to **Full mesh** and click **Next**.

7. Use the **Bandwidth** screen to throttle the connection if you need to; otherwise, just click **Next** again.

8. Choose **Primary member** from the list. For our example, it is **FILE01**. If you are starting a fresh empty replication group, this isn't particularly important. However, if you have an existing share that you have been using for a while, make sure you select the right server here. If there are any conflicts during replication, the files from this server will win the conflict:

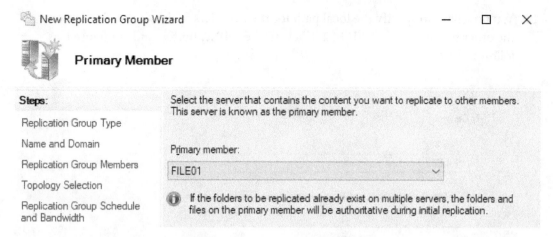

Figure 11.13 – Choosing our primary member for the replication group

9. Now, on the **Folders to Replicate** screen, use the **Add...** button in order to add all the folders that you want to replicate. For our example, I'm going to replicate the new `Installers` folder, which we configured inside our DFS Namespace:

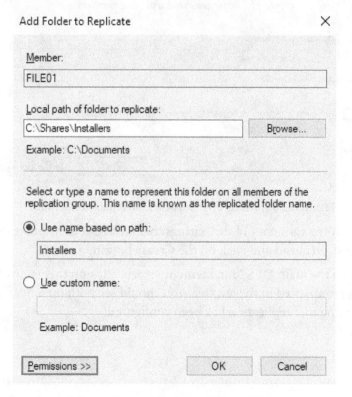

Figure 11.14 – Our source folder settings

10. You now have to specify the local path for the Installers folder so that it exists on the other member server, FILE02. Click on the **Edit…** button and configure it as follows:

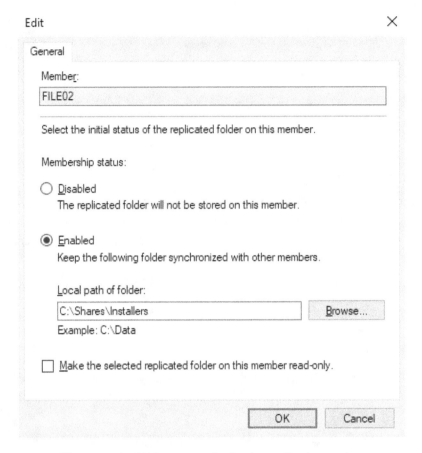

Figure 11.15 – Setting up our destination replication settings

11. Take a look at the summary of the settings that are about to be put into place and, once satisfied, go ahead and click on the **Create** button.

12. Now, back on the main **DFS Management** screen, click on the name of your new replication group listed in the left tree. You should see both member servers listed here, indicating that replication has been configured!

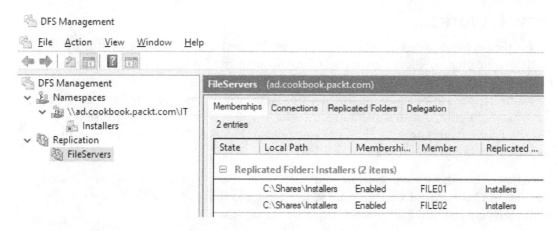

Figure 11.16 – Our configured DFSR

> **Important!**
> It can take up to 90 minutes for all members of the DFSR group to discover
> they have been added to the group and start replicating. It may take hours or
> even days for the replication to catch up if you have a lot of data, slow links, or
> have throttled the replication bandwidth.

13. Now, let's test this out. From a client computer, open up File Explorer and navigate
    to `\\mydomain\it\installers`.

14. Create a few test files in this folder.

15. Give it a little bit of time for replication to happen, then check inside the `C:\
    Installers` folder on each file server. You should see that there are copies of your
    new files now located on both servers' hard drives!

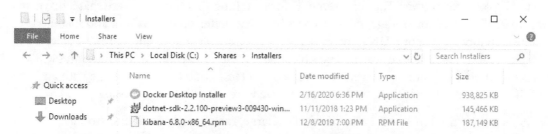

Figure 11.17 – Our replicated files showing up on both file servers

How it works...

In this recipe, we took our DFS environment and expanded its capabilities a little by adding replication. DFSR is a great tool to use for distributing files around to your branch offices, all while keeping the user experience and drive mappings similar, no matter where everyone happens to be accessing the files from. Historically speaking, Microsoft's DFS has a bad reputation due to some issues in older Windows Server operating systems. Those days are gone, and if you haven't tried out this technology in your own environment yet, you've got no reason to wait!

Note that although we have replicated our directories, our FILE02 copy of the replicated data has not been shared via DFS yet. I've left it as an exercise for you to share your replicated data and add it as another target for the existing DFS folder.

Creating an iSCSI target on your server

iSCSI is another way to share storage across a network. The term iSCSI itself has more to do with the actual protocol level and the way that the data is transported across the LAN or WAN, but what it looks like to a consumer of iSCSI is that a machine has a drive letter for a disk, but that *disk* is not physically connected to the server. For example, you might log into a server and see an M drive. This drive looks just like a local volume, but it is actually a network connection to storage that might be sitting on the other side of the data center. Sounds like a mapped network drive, right? Yes, but it works on a lower level. iSCSI virtual disks, as they are called, work with the server as if they are local disks. This gives servers the ability to interface with this data at a system level and does not require a user context in order to work, like mapped network drives do. This is commonly referred to as **block storage**.

One good example that I worked with was a database application that a customer was installing on a new server. The requirements for installing this software were that a drive was to be dedicated for storage, it had to be a full drive letter on the system, and it could not be a mapped drive or a UNC mapping. We were not able to add another hard drive to the physical server, and that wasn't desirable anyway. We utilized iSCSI to create an iSCSI target on their main storage server, and then connected to that block of storage with an iSCSI initiator on the application server where we were installing the software.

iSCSI is mostly used in storage area networks – large, rack-based server and storage installations with 10, 40, or 100 Gbps networking – but that doesn't mean it can't be used elsewhere. We have the option in Server 2019 to create our own iSCSI targets right on the server, so let's work on creating one of these targets together.

Getting ready

We have a Windows Server 2019 running, which we are going to prep to be our iSCSI target server. You can either log onto the Server directly or use Windows 10 with RSAT installed. In this example, we will be using Windows 10 with RSAT.

How to do it...

To create an iSCSI target on your server, go through the following steps:

1. Open **Server Manager**. If you are using Windows 10 with RSAT, make sure your storage server has been added to the console. Then, click on the **Add roles and features** link.

2. Click **Next** until you come to the **Select server roles** screen.

3. Navigate to **File and Storage Services | File and iSCSI Services** and check the box next to **iSCSI Target Server**:

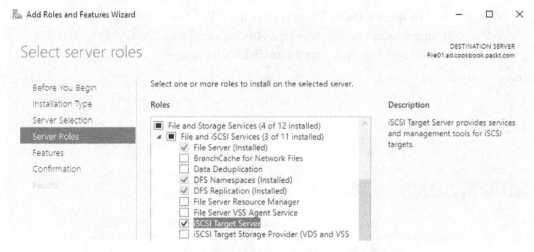

Figure 11.18 – Installing the iSCSI Target Server role

4. Click **Next**, **Next**, then **Install** to finish putting this new role into place.

5. In the left pane of Server Manager, click on **File and Storage Services**. Then, click on **iSCSI**.

6. From the **Tasks** menu located in the far-right corner, click on **New iSCSI Virtual Disk...**.

7. Ensure that you have the correct server selected and then choose a location for this iSCSI target to reside. I only have one disk in my server, so I am going to utilize my C: volume for this storage:

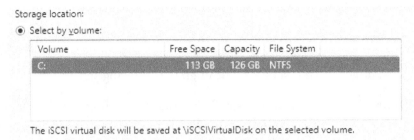

The iSCSI virtual disk will be saved at \iSCSIVirtualDisk on the selected volume.

Figure 11.19 – Selecting a disk to store our iSCSi volumes

8. On the next screen, specify a name for your iSCSI virtual disk. You can see that it is going to create and utilize a VHDX file for this storage. Nice – this means we can use the native Windows VHDX functionality later if needed.

9. Now, we need to specify **iSCSI Virtual Disk Size**. Read over the text on this screen so that you understand the different types of disks and sizing available to you. For our recipe, we are setting up a **Fixed size** disk with a size of 10 GB:

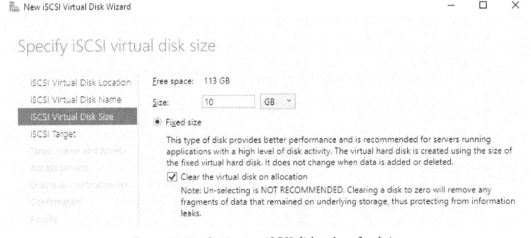

Figure 11.20 – Setting our iSCSI disk to be a fixed size

Tip

If you choose an expanding disk, be aware that is possible to allocate more disk space than you actually have on the server. This will cause issues if you run out of disk space later on. However, this is ideal if you plan on expanding the amount of storage for the server in the future.

10. Since this is our first iSCSI target on this server, the **New iSCSI target** option should be selected for you. Click **Next**.

11. Create a name for the iSCSI target. This is the name that you will use on the iSCSI initiator server later in order to connect to the storage. I am calling mine `Database1`.

12. Now, on the **Access Servers** screen, click the **Add...** button in order to specify which initiators will connect to this target later. We are going to connect to this storage from a server called FILE01, so I am adding that server to the list here:

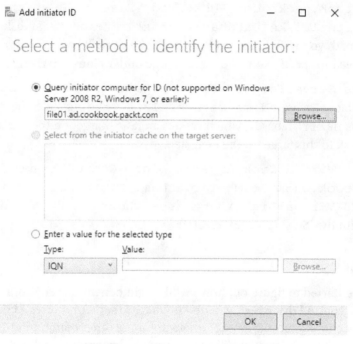

Figure 11.21 – Creating a new iSCSI initiator

13. When you add a server to this list and click **OK**, you will notice that it is specified on the **Access Servers** screen with an **iSCSI Qualified Name (IQN)** value that you did not specify. This is a unique identifier for the server to the iSCSI environment and is a normal behavior. Go ahead and click **Next**.

14. If you would like to utilize CHAP or reverse CHAP in order to authenticate connections between the initiator and target, you can use the next screen to specify usernames and passwords for those authentications. For the purposes of testing this out quickly and in a simple manner, we are not setting up anything on this page and are only clicking **Next**.

15. Review the settings and click the **Create** button to finish setting up your iSCSI target. This server is now running as a target and is waiting for a connection to it from our iSCSI initiator server.

To repeat these steps in PowerShell, do the following:

1. Open a PowerShell prompt as an administrator.

2. Use `Import-Module iscsitarget` so that we can use our iSCSI cmdlets.

3. `New-IscsiVirtualDisk -ComputerName file01.ad.cookbook.packt.com -UseFixed -Size 10GB -Path "C:\iSCSIVirtualDisks\Databases.vhdx"` creates our iSCSI disk. You can enter any path you wish here; just keep note of it as we'll have to reference it later. You will need to specify your file server name under **ComputerName**.

4. `New-IscsiServerTarget -ComputerName file01.ad.cookbook.packt.com -TargetName Database1` will create our iSCSI Server Target with the name of Database1, which creates an iSCSI target on the file server. We will link our disk to this target in the next step.

5. `Add-IscsiVirtualDiskTargetMapping -ComputerName file01.ad.cookbook.packt.com -TargetName Database1 -DevicePath "C:\iSCSIVirtualDisks\Databases.vhdx"` links the iSCSI disk we created with the iSCSI target we created.

How it works...

In this recipe, we started to figure out how iSCSI might benefit our environment. In addition to the scenario I discussed, where our database server requires a constant drive letter connection to remote storage, there are some other common utilizations for iSCSI connections. You could use iSCSI connections in order to consolidate storage. For example, you could take multiple servers that have locally attached storage and map them to iSCSI storage blocks. You could then move the physical storage to your iSCSI target for all the application servers involved. They would still access the same data, and the applications running on those servers wouldn't know any different, but the physical storage would now be consolidated into a centralized area for safekeeping and better data management.

iSCSI is also an interesting use case for diskless booting. You could equip diskless computers with NICs that are iSCSI-ready, and those computers could boot over the network, over iSCSI, to virtual disks sitting on the iSCSI target.

See also

- The iSCSI PowerShell cmdlet reference: `https://docs.microsoft.com/en-us/powershell/module/iscsitarget/?view=win10-ps`

Configuring an iSCSI initiator connection

Turning on your first iSCSI target is great, but so far, you aren't using that storage for anything. Let's take it a step further and connect a server to that storage so that it can start to be used. The device connecting to an iSCSI target is called an **iSCSI initiator**. We are going to take a file server in our environment and configure it so that it connects over the network using iSCSI to our target server. When finished, we will have a new hard disk *attached* to our server, even though it is really just block storage from the iSCSI target that is being accessed via the network.

Getting ready

We have already configured one Windows Server 2019 as an iSCSI target (`FILE01`) and are now configuring a second 2019 machine (`FILE02`) as our iSCSI initiator that will be connecting to the target.

How to do it...

Follow along to create the iSCSI initiator connection on our FILE02 server:

1. Launch **Server Manager**. Open the **Tools** menu and choose **iSCSI Initiator**.

2. If you have never tried using iSCSI on this machine before, you will receive a message that the Microsoft iSCSI service is not running. To start the service and make sure it continues to start on subsequent boots, click **Yes**:

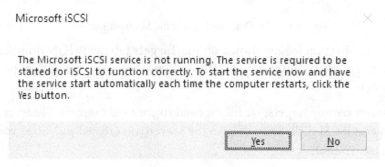

Figure 11.22 – The iSCSI service prompt

3. Currently, there is nothing listed in the **Targets** tab, which opens by default. Move over to the **Discovery** tab and click on the **Discover Portal...** button.

4. Type in the name of the server where you have an iSCSI target running and click **OK**. Now, move back over to the **Targets** tab of the **iSCSI Initiator Properties** screen:

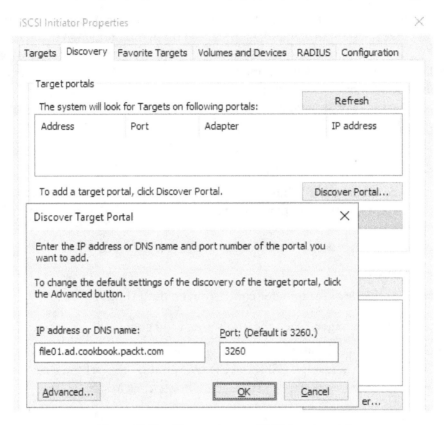

Figure 11.23 – Discovering our iSCSI target portal

5. The iSCSI connection is now shown on the **Targets** tab by its IQN number. If you can see a target, then skip to *step 14*. If you do not see any targets, then proceed with the next step.

6. If you do not see any targets, we might need to configure our iSCSI server to permit access to that iSCSI disk. Swap over to the server you created the iSCSI volume on (in our case, FILE01).

7. Launch **Server Manager**. Open up the **File and Storage Services** window and go to the **iSCSI** window.

8. You should see the iSCSI target we created in our previous recipe. Right-click the target and choose **Properties**:

Figure 11.24 – Setting the properties for our iSCSI target

9. Click on **Initiators**, then **Add…**.

10. Under **Query initiator computer for ID**, enter the full name of the server you want to give access to and click OK:

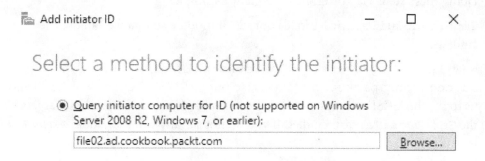

Figure 11.25 – Letting Windows figure out the IQN for our connecting machine

11. You should now have your second server's IQN listed under **Initiator IDs**. Click OK.

12. Switch back to the server we're connecting from (in my case, FILE02).

13. Click the **Refresh** button on your **Discovered Targets**. You should now see your iSCSI disk so that you can connect to it.

14. Currently, the status is set to **Inactive**. Select this connection and click on the **Connect** button:

Figure 11.26 – Confirming our iSCSI connection

15. Click **OK** to finish connecting to this iSCSI target. Make sure to leave the checkbox enabled for **Add this connection to the list of Favorite Targets** so that the connection is persistent and reconnects following server reboots.

Doing these steps via PowerShell is equally as simple:

1. `Import-Moduile iscsi` loads our iSCSI module so that we can use the cmdlets.

2. `New-IscsiTargetPortal -TargetPortalAddress file01.ad.cookbook.packt.com` connects to our file01 iSCSI target, which will allow us to see the iSCSI volumes that have been exposed. You can view these targets with the `Get-IscsiTarget` cmdlet. If you do not see any volumes, look at *steps 6–12* in this recipe.

3. `Get-IscsiTarget | Connect-IscsiTarget -IsPersistent:$true` will connect us to every iSCSI volume that the target has exposed to us. This should just be the volumes we need because in *steps 6–12*, we only exposed the volume we needed. Be careful with this exact command if you have additional volumes – you might need to filter the `Get-IscsiTarget` command in order to only return the volumes you need to connect to.

How it works...

We have now connected our iSCSI initiator to our iSCSI target, and if you open any of the normal hard disk management tools such as Disk Management on your initiator server, you will see the new *disk* listed and available! You can then manipulate this storage like you would any other physical storage, including turning it into a permanent drive letter available to the operating system.

It is important to note that an iSCSI initiator is often used without a Windows Server 2019 iSCSI target server being at the other end of the connection. One of the great things about iSCSI is that it doesn't care about what kind of storage you are connecting to, as long as that storage supports being accessed via iSCSI. There are many SAN technologies that you can acquire, or may already have running in your environment, which you can tap into by using the iSCSI initiator on your Windows server. This gives you the ability to consume storage from the non-Windows SAN device on your Windows application and file servers.

Configuring Storage Spaces

Storage Spaces is an incredibly cool technology that isn't marketed very much; it just does its job and does it well. How many times have you caught yourself stuck between a rock and a hard place because you are running out of room on a single hard drive on one of your servers? I have plenty of times, especially working with technologies like RDS, which may contain a lot of user data all stored on the system drive. In most current server hardware, it is easy to add multiple hard drives, but not always easy to decide how to partition and volume those drives so that you don't run out of space on C: while having 200 GB of free space on D:.

These kinds of situations are where Storage Spaces can save a lot of time and headaches. What if you didn't have to worry about what size hard disks you were running as your primary drive, secondary drive, and so on? What if you could lump them all together and utilize the storage out of one big bucket, or pool, as you will? This is exactly what we can accomplish with Storage Spaces in Windows Server 2019. You combine multiple physical hard disks into a storage pool, and then, within that pool, you can create one or many volumes to consume that storage space. The multiple disks combine storage to behave as one large drive, with options for RAID-style redundancy built into the storage pool configuration. Let's work together to combine a few hard drives and create a new single volume to be used by the operating system.

Getting ready

We are going to configure Storage Spaces on our FILE02 server, which is running Windows Server 2019. Our FILE02 server has multiple disks attached, not all of them the same size. We can perform these actions from either our server itself, or from a Windows 10 machine with RSAT installed.

How to do it...

To enable Storage Spaces on your server, use the following steps:

1. Make sure you have hard drives connected that you intend to utilize for your storage pool. On our FILE02 server, I have added three new drives, all of various sizes. We also have our iSCSI disks from the previous recipe!

2. Launch **Server Manager** and click **File and Storage Services** from the left window pane.

3. First, click on **Disks** and make sure that we can see the new drives that we are going to combine to make a storage pool:

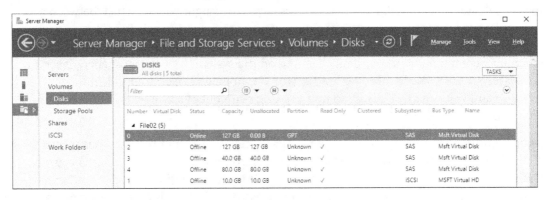

Figure 11.27 – Our server is showing all the disks we expect

4. Now that we have confirmed our disks our visible within Windows, go ahead and click on **Storage Pools**.

5. Open the **Tasks** menu and choose **New Storage Pool…**:

Figure 11.28 – New storage pool

6. Enter something in **Storage Pool Name** and click **Next**.

7. Select the physical disks that you want to be included in this pool. I am going to add all three unused drives on my system. I'm not going to use the iSCSI disk:

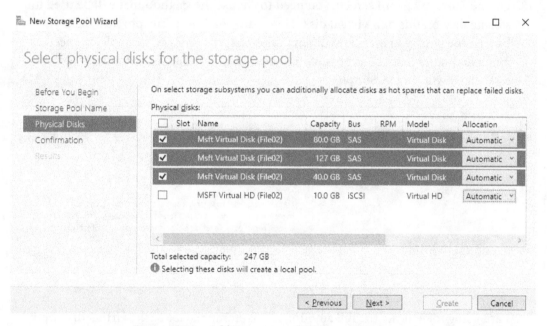

Figure 11.29 – Adding our new disks to our storage pool

8. Click **Next**, then click **Create**. Once you've finished building, you will be taken back to the **Storage Pools** section of Server Manager, where you can now see the new pool listed. The disks are now grouped together in a pool but are not yet usable by the operating system.

9.   Click on the name of your new storage pool in order to select it.

10. Now, down in the **Virtual Disks** section, drop down the **Tasks** menu and choose **New Virtual Disk…**.

11. Select the storage pool from which you want to create a volume and give it a virtual disk name. If you are mixing SSDs and regular HDDs, you can enable tiering if you wish by ticking **Create storage tiers on this virtual disk**.

12. On the **Enclosure Awareness** screen, you can tick the box to enable **Enclosure awareness**, if it is supported. This won't work on virtual machines, but for physical servers that might have multiple disk arrays (for example, a server that has additional disk shelves attached), this will ensure that Windows lays the data out so that if an entire disk shelf fails, you will keep as much data as possible.

13. On the **Storage Layout** screen, you need to choose the method that will be used for storing data on this new virtual disk. Depending on how many physical disks you have in the pool, you may have different options here. For our example, we need as much data storage space as possible and are not worried about redundancy across disks. So, I will choose **Simple**:

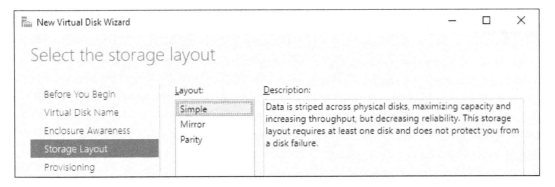

Figure 11.30 – Choosing the Simple layout

14. I am going to dedicate the full amount of this storage space to the virtual disk right away, so I will leave the **Provisioning** screen selected for fixed provisioning.

15. On the **Size** screen, it will indicate how much free space exists in the pool. Simply size your new virtual disk to a number that is equal to or below that number. I am going to consume the full space of the pool, so I can either enter 117 GB as indicated or choose the radio button for maximum size:

Figure 11.31 – Setting our virtual disk to the maximum size

16. Finish up the wizard and your new virtual disk will be created! When you finish this virtual disk creation wizard, you will be automatically placed inside **New Volume Wizard**. Walk through these steps or utilize a regular tool such as disk management in order to create your new volume, format it, and assign it a new driver letter. Then, you can start using the new volume as you would use any regular volume inside Windows:

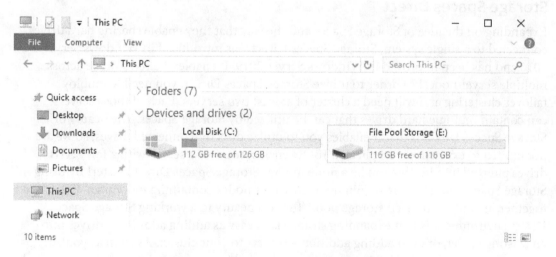

Figure 11.32 – Our storage pool shows up like normal Windows storage

How it works...

By combining these three small hard drives into one storage pool, we can build a single volume that is larger than any one of the hard drives on their own. Storage Spaces can be used like this, or in a myriad of other ways, to create multiple pools and volumes at will, simply by bundling together groups of physical drives on the system.

Hard disk space utilization is something that we have traditionally planned very hard for. What size drives to get? Do they need to match? How large does each of my volumes need to be? Should I use RAID? Should I use dedicated hardware for that RAID? Storage Spaces is a way to bring many of those questions together, package them up, and throw them in the trash can.

Storage Spaces is also present on Windows 10 Professional, so you can use this same recipe on your local computer if you wanted!

See also

There's a lot to discuss in this section as we take a brief look at Storage Spaces Direct and Storage Replica.

Storage Spaces Direct

Expanding on the idea of Storage Spaces and the way that they enable sharing hard drives connected to a single system, Storage Spaces Direct was introduced in Windows Server 2016 and has been improved in Windows Server 2019. It enables shared storage across multiple server nodes! In order to utilize Storage Spaces Direct, you need to employ failover clustering and will need a cluster of at least two servers. Each of those servers can contain multiple hard drives that can be utilized by Storage Spaces. The beauty of Storage Spaces Direct is that it enables you to utilize directly-connected drives, so we are not limited to expensive, complicated JBOD enclosures. Got a server with a few SATA drives plugged into it? This can be a node in your Storage Spaces Direct cluster! By using Storage Spaces Direct, you can join up to 16 server nodes containing more than 400 drives together in your centralized storage pool! The real beauty to a working Storage Spaces Direct environment is that expanding storage is as easy as adding additional drives into an existing server, or even adding additional servers to your cluster. As soon as you add new capacity at either the drive or server node level, the storage pool that you have created with Storage Spaces Direct will automatically start expanding to include this new storage.

A primary goal for Storage Spaces Direct is to create a very resilient atmosphere for running Hyper-V virtual machines. By utilizing technologies such as SMB3 and the ReFS filesystem, you can configure Hyper-V to store its virtual machines on top of Storage Spaces Direct to ensure that you always have at least three copies of your data resident and available within the cluster.

The actual configuration of Storage Spaces Direct is not overly complicated, but it does involve more complexity than my simple test lab and the short pages of a cookbook recipe are able to contain. You will interface with Storage Spaces Direct via PowerShell and Failover Cluster Manager, though for the best results, those of you running SCCM will have the easiest time setting up and managing this new technology as it is specifically integrated into System Center. Even though we aren't setting it up in this recipe, if this is a topic that falls into your area of influence, make sure to continue reading at the following link:

- `https://docs.microsoft.com/en-us/windows-server/storage/storage-spaces/storage-spaces-direct-overview`

Storage Replica

Another storage technology in Windows Server 2019 is Storage Replica. Contrary to Storage Spaces Direct, which is all about sharing storage between nodes, Storage Replica's job is to make sure that data is replicated quickly and securely between servers or clusters of servers. Storage Replica touts the ability to offer synchronous replication across multiple sites, with zero data loss. Another neat feature of Storage Replica is that you can swing workloads from one site to another prior to a disaster event, such as a severe storm warning in the city where your primary data center is located, when you want to swing connections to a backup data center before the storm hits.

There are three scenarios where Storage Replica can be utilized. First, if you are stretching a cluster across multiple physical sites, you can utilize Storage Replica to keep your cluster synchronized. Second, you can employ Cluster-to-Cluster replication to keep data up to date between two separate clusters that need to replicate together. Third, and perhaps the most important one to the SMB customer, is the Server-to-Server mode of Storage Replica. This enables synchronous and asynchronous replication between two servers, not necessarily in any kind of cluster scenario.

Given the robust capabilities of Storage Replica, there is a good chance that it may someday replace DFSR as the server administrator's tool of choice for replicating data between servers. One requirement that is important to point out, which does not apply to DFSR, is that we need some pretty low latency between data centers in order to utilize Storage Replica. As I write this, the current recommendation is under 5 ms between the sites. As with any brand-new technology, some time will have to pass before large production environments will choose to move over to Storage Replica for handling all of their sensitive and critical data, but I encourage you to look over this additional information and start making use of it now:

- `https://docs.microsoft.com/en-us/windows-server/storage/storage-replica/storage-replica-overview?redirectedfrom=MSDN`

Turning on data deduplication

Deduplication is something that we, as people, do naturally. Every once in a while, you clean out the refrigerator, right? And if there are seven half-empty bottles of ketchup, you probably deduplicate that and throw some away. Or your closet. If you dig around and find thirty blue shirts, chances are that you can part with a few to save some space. These things make common sense, and so does deduplication when talking about the data that is stored on our servers.

Starting with Windows Server 2012, data deduplication became possible at the filesystem level. When enabled, Windows runs scheduled optimization jobs that search for duplicate files and data and consolidates them. If you have two copies of the same file, stored in two different locations, all that is doing is consuming extra hard disk space. Data deduplication removes the secondary copy and utilizes the primary whenever that file is called for from either location on the disk.

In Server 2019, we have the ability to extend this deduplication into Hyper-V, specifically for VDI-type deployments. This is huge! Think about all of the different VDI systems that are going to be spun up by that system. With so many similar systems running under the same drive context, there is the potential to have thousands of duplicated files, all duplicated numerous times. In this recipe, we are going to walk through the steps to enable data deduplication on a server so that you can start trying this out in your own environments.

Getting ready

We will be enabling data deduplication on a single server for this recipe, running Windows Server 2019, of course.

How to do it...

To enable data deduplication on our server, follow these steps:

1. Open **Server Manager** and click on the **Add roles and features** link.

2. Click **Next** until you get to the **Select server roles** screen.

3. Expand **File and Storage Services | File and iSCSI Services** and check the box next to **Data Deduplication**:

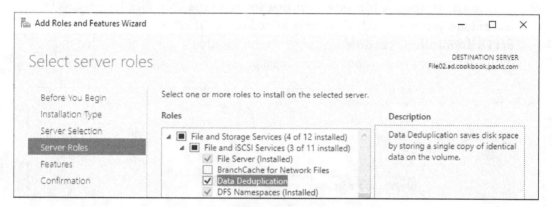

Figure 11.33 – Adding the Data Deduplication role

4. Finish the wizard in order to complete the installation of the deduplication role.

5. Now. in the left pane of Server Manager, click on **File and Storage Services**.

6. Click on **Volumes**.

7. Right-click on a data volume and choose **Configure Data Deduplication…**:

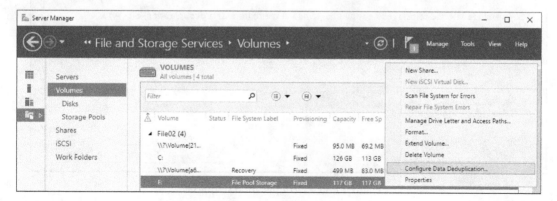

Figure 11.34 – Configuring Data Deduplication

8. Click on the **Data deduplication** drop-down box and specify whether you are intending to run deduplication on a **General-purpose file server**, **Virtual Desktop Infrastructure (VDI) server**, or **Virtualized Backup Server**. If you test out selecting one or the other, you will notice that the default list of file extensions to exclude from deduplication changes automatically. These are the file types that Microsoft has determined need to be excluded from deduplication for it to run effectively. For our purposes, we're going to use **General-purpose file server**.

9. If there are any specific files or folders that you want the deduplication process to leave alone, you can specify them here as exclusions. There is also a button named **Set Deduplication Schedule...** where you can specify the times of day that the optimization jobs run to consolidate the data:

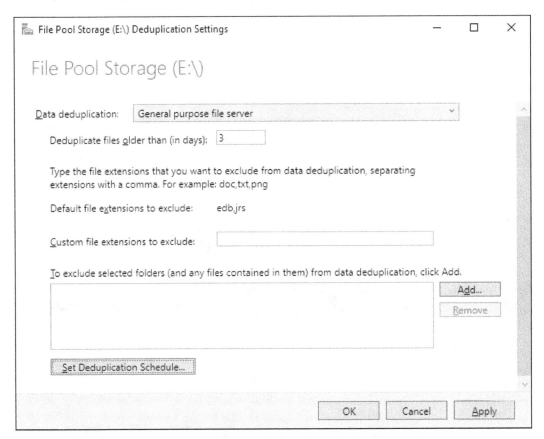

Figure 11.35 – Deduplication settings

Repeating this process via PowerShell is also very straightforward:

1. `Install-WindowsFeature FS-Data-Deduplication` adds the Windows feature if it isn't already installed.

2. `Import-Module deduplication` makes the deduplication cmdlets available to us in our session.

3. `Enable-DedupVolume -Volume E: -UsageType Default` enables deduplication on our E drive. Easy! You can change the option for `UsageType` to `Backup` or `HyperV` for other profiles.

How it works...

Data deduplication is very easy to enable but can be a powerful tool for saving disk space on your file servers. I have seen numbers that are very high on deduplication – up to 50 percent for general file shares and over 80 percent for VHD libraries! In Windows Server 2019, we have support for larger volumes and files, so the data savings are even greater. We support volumes up to 64 TB in size and individual files up to 1 TB in size. Try data deduplication on some of your own systems and watch your available disk space start to increase.

See also

Check out the following links for additional information on data deduplication in Windows Server 2019:

- `https://docs.microsoft.com/en-us/previous-versions/ windows/it-pro/windows-server-2012-r2-and-2012/ hh831434(v%3Dws.11)`

- `https://docs.microsoft.com/en-us/powershell/module/ deduplication/?view=win10-ps`

Setting up Windows Server 2019 work folders

Accessing data from wherever you happen to be is becoming more and more important with today's mobile workforce. Given this, it makes sense that more and more technologies are being designed to allow access to this data from more locations and more device types. This is what Work Folders in Windows Server 2019 is all about. It is a way to publish access to files and folders to the multiple device types that users may be logging into. These files are accessed via a web listener that is configured on the Work Folders file server, which enables this data to be accessed from inside or outside the corporate network, from both domain-joined and non-domain-joined systems.

Configuring a full-fledged Work Folders environment with all its moving parts and components is far too much data to be contained in a single recipe. Instead, we will focus on the steps that need to be taken on the file server itself in order to make it ready for hosting Work Folders. Make sure to check out the link provided at the end of this section in order to continue gaining knowledge on this subject. Once you get started with Work Folders and realize the benefits that it can provide, I have no doubt that you will also be tapping into Group Policy in order to roll some of these settings around, and working with a reverse proxy solution such as **Web Application Proxy** (**WAP**) in order to further enhance the capabilities that Work Folders can bring to the table.

Getting ready

We will complete this recipe on a Windows Server 2019 server, which we will use as a file server. Specifically, I am using the FILE02 server. To fully configure Work Folders, you will also need to acquire a valid SSL certificate and access to your public DNS environment in order to create a record.

How to do it...

Follow these steps to enable Work Folders in your environment:

1. Log into your file server and launch Server Manager.

2. Choose the link for **Add roles and features**. Walk through the role installation wizard until you get to the **Select server roles** screen.

3. Navigate to **File and Storage Services | File and iSCSI Services**. Then, check the box next to **Work Folders**. When you receive a pop-up message about adding the additional IIS feature required, make sure to click on the **Add Features** button.

4. Finish the wizard in order to install the Work Folders role on this server.

5. Once the role has finished installing, head back to Server Manager and navigate to **File and Storage Services | Work Folders**.

6. Drop down the **TASKS** menu and choose **New Sync Share…**:

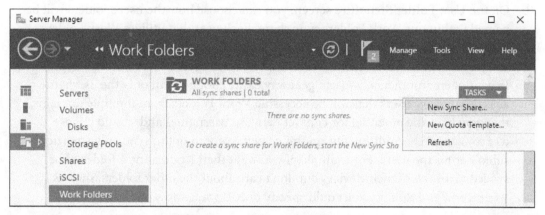

Figure 11.36 – Creating a work folder sync share

7. Choose or enter a path where you want the new Work Folders to be stored. This is the location on our file server that will be populated by folders that are named after our users. If you have already set up a folder and shared it, you will see it in the list to choose from. I have not set up any such folder yet, and so I am going to type in the location where I want the wizard to create a new folder for me:

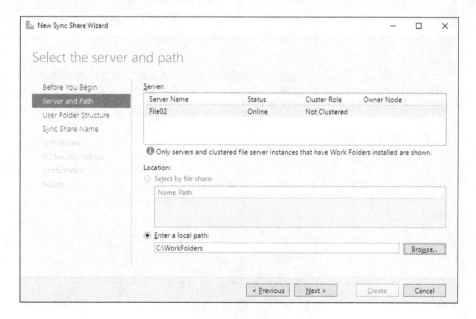

Figure 11.37 – Configuring our work folder

8. Click **Next**. If you entered the location of a folder that does not yet exist, you will be prompted with a confirmation box asking whether you want the new folder to be created. Go ahead and click **OK** on that message.

9. On the **User Folder Structure** screen, you can choose how the user's folders will be named within our Work Folders sync share. Each user that utilizes Work Folders will get their own folder set up inside our share. These individual username folders will be named via either their username alone or by their `username@domain`. In a lot of environments, you can get away easily enough with only the username alias. If you have users that will be accessing Work Folders from multiple domains, then you have the potential for conflict between usernames and should choose `alias@domain`. Additionally, on this screen, you can opt to sync only a particular subfolder for the users. For example, if you want their `Documents` folder to be synced across all of their devices but don't care about the other folders, such as `Pictures` and `Music`, you could specify only `Documents` on the line here.

10. Specify a name for **Sync Share** and click **Next** again.

11. For the **Sync Access** screen of the wizard, we need to define which users and groups have access to use this sync. I created an Active Directory Security Group called **Work Folders** and placed my users inside that group. So, on this screen, I will simply specify my **Work Folders** group:

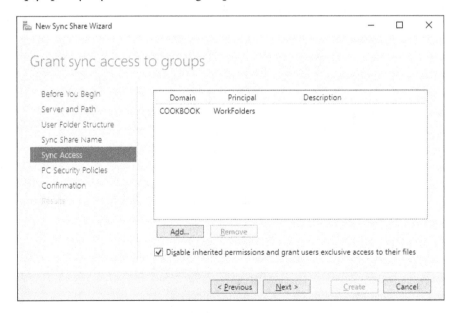

Figure 11.38 – Configuring sync access

> **Tip**
>
> Note the checkbox near the bottom of this screen. If you leave the box enabled for **Disable inherited permissions…**, then users will be granted exclusive rights to each of their folders. This means that even administrators will not have access to these folders. If you would like to change that behavior and let the normal filesystem-inherited rights persist, simply uncheck this box.

12. Click **Next, Next**, then **Create**. With that, your new WorkFolder Sync Share will be created and ready for use.

13. Client devices will connect to Work Folders on this file server via HTTPS. In order to make that happen successfully, we need to configure a DNS record that points at this file server, and an SSL certificate to be bound to the web listener on the server.

14. On your public DNS, set up the name `Work Folders.<yourdomain>` and point it at the IP address that will flow to this file server. For example, the best way to do this is to publish the web listener with a reverse proxy server of some kind; let's say that proxy server is running on the internet IP address `198.51.100.200`. You would configure a DNS record for `Work Folders.cookbook.packt.com` and point it at `198.51.100.200`, then let the reverse proxy server bring that traffic inside the network and submit it to the file server where we have Work Folders running.

15. Install an SSL certificate that contains the appropriate `Work Folders. cookbook.packt.com` name – replacing `cookbook.packt.com` with your domain name, of course – and bind it to the default website on the Work Folders server. Since the full IIS Management Console is not installed with the Work Folders role, you can utilize the IIS Management tools from another server in your network in order to bind the certificate to the default website. Alternatively, you can use the `netsh` command in order to bind the certificate to the site:

```
netsh http add sslcert ipport=<IP address>:443 certhash=<Cert thumbprint>
appid={CE66697B-3AA0-49D1-BDBD-A25C8359FD5D} certstorename=MY.
```

> **Note**
>
> Please note that the previous command should not be run exactly as shown here. There are variables in this `netsh` command that you need to adjust to your own environment. The IP address of the web server, `certhash`, and `appid` need to be adjusted to match your particulars.

16. Now, Work Folders has been configured and listening on our file server. The next step is to configure our client computers to tap into this Work Folders sync share. The process for accomplishing this is different, depending on what client devices you are connecting to, but the starting point for Windows 10 and 8.1 machines is **Control Panel | System and Security | Work Folders**.

How it works...

It is pretty easy to overlook Work Folders at first glance, thinking it is just another way to access the same data in a similar way as the folder sharing options that we have had around for years. However, looking more closely shows us that the ability to publish access to files and folders to both domain-joined systems and non-domain-joined systems, working from either the corporate network or from home, can be of enormous advantage. You could utilize Work Folders as a way to grant access to corporate data without needing to issue a company laptop. You could also grant access to file-level details without the need to incorporate some form of VPN, which may give more access to a home computer than you are comfortable with handing out. There are numerous situations where a technology such as Work Folders could increase productivity for your users and the security of the information within your IT infrastructure. One of the pain points of Work Folders in previous versions of Windows Server was that client computers were not notified of file changes for roughly 10 minutes after the changes were made. This was resolved in Windows Server 2016. As long as you are using 2016 or 2019 on the server side and Windows 10 on the clients, file changes are now reflected as soon as they are generated. Make sure to check it out!

See also

Take a look at the following link for even more detailed information on setting up Work Folders:

- `https://docs.microsoft.com/en-us/previous-versions/windows/it-pro/windows-server-2012-R2-and-2012/dn528861(v=ws.11)?redirectedfrom=MSDN`

Configuring a Scale-Out File Server

Having a huge bucket of storage is great. We've seen how we can combine multiple hard drives, replicate our data across multiple servers, and how we can present multiple different shared folders on different servers in a single, easy-to-locate structure.

But how can we combine the power of multiple servers into our storage solution? If our storage gets close to capacity in terms of CPU or RAM availability, how can we add more?

Thankfully, Windows has a solution for this too. It's called a **Scale-Out File Server**. A Scale-Out File Server has two main purposes: storing applications in a high availability, high bandwidth solution, or storing general data where the data is only accessed from a single server, but can be accessed from multiple servers if something happens to the currently active server. The application data scenario is typically used for Hyper-V virtualization roles and SQL Server roles. General file servers are typically configured in the general data scenario.

Getting started

We need a minimum of two file servers. I'm going to use FILE03 and FILE04. I can't reuse FILE01 as that's going to be providing our shared storage. FILE02 is incompatible as there are certain recipes we've done in this book that are not compatible with Scale-Out File Servers.

Scale-Out File Servers require shared storage. In our example, we're going to be using iSCSI targets from FILE01, but note that this is not suitable for live production work. In production, you would want to be using enterprise iSCSI or Fiber Channel storage, or shared local storage such as a SAS enclosure, which is connected to multiple servers.

I strongly suggest that you complete the *Creating an iSCSI target on your server* and *Configuring an iSCSI initiator* recipes before embarking on this one, as we're going to be using those two recipes again.

How to do it...

Before we can begin building our Scale-Out File Server, we need to provision some shared storage:

1. Log into FILE03, launch Server Manager, and click the **Add roles and features** link.

2. Click **Next** a few times until you reach the **Select server roles** screen.

3. Navigate to **File and Storage Services | File and iSCSI Services**.

4. Check the box for **File Server**.

5. Click **Next**. Then, on the **Features** page, check the box for **Failover Clustering and Multipath I/O**.

6. Once the roles and features have finished installing, Windows will have to restart.

7. While that server is restarting, repeat *steps 1-6* for the FILE04 server.

8. We now need to go back to the *Creating an iSCSI target on your server* recipe. You will need to follow that recipe to create the iSCSI disks we will be using for the Scale-Out File Server. You must create at least three disks that are in the same target group. Make sure you add both the Scale-Out File Servers to the list of IQNs that can access the iSCSI targets. We cannot use the iSCSI disk we created if you've already run that recipe.

9. Once that is done, log back into both of your Scale-Out File Servers and follow the recipe for *Configuring an iSCSI initiator* to create a connection on both servers. They should both connect to the same iSCSI virtual disk.

> **Note**
>
> For a production configuration, these steps are where you would configure your enterprise shared storage – whether it's iSCSI, Fiber Channel, or SAS. Other solutions might also require different MPIO configuration. You will need to confirm with your storage solutions provider.

10. Once they are connected to the same disk via iSCSI, in Server Manager, go to **Tools | MPIO**.

11. Click the tab for **Discover Multi-Paths** and tick the box for **Add support for iSCSI devices**. Then, click **Add**:

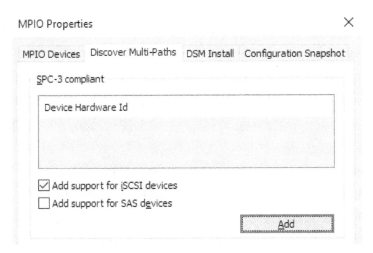

Figure 10.39 – Enabling Multi-Path I/O for iSCSI

12. Make sure this has been done on *both* Scale-Out File Servers, then restart them both.

13. Once both servers have restarted, log back into one of them (it doesn't matter which one) and load **Server Manager**.

14. Click **Tools**, then **Failover Cluster Manager**:

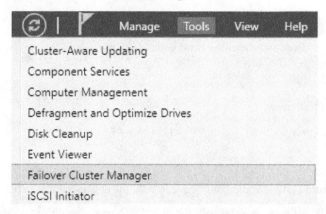

Figure 11.40 – Loading the Failover Cluster Manager

15. You will be prompted to start managing clusters through the Windows Admin Center. We're not going to be doing that for now, so feel free to close that window.

16. On the right-hand side of **Failover Cluster Manager**, click the link for **Validate Configuration**:

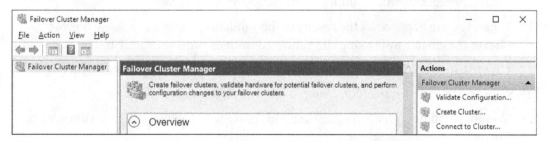

Figure 11.41 – The location of the Validate Configuration actions

17. Click next on the **Before You Begin** page.

18. One the **Select Servers or a Cluster** page, we need to add our two file servers here. I'm going to add FILE03 and FILE04:

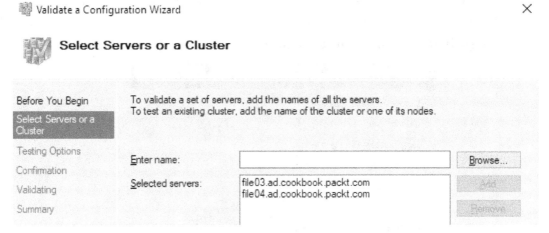

Figure 11.42 – Adding our two servers to the cluster validation list

19. Make sure **Run all tests is selected**. Then, click **Next**, then **Next** again.

20. Windows will now validate that our two servers are able to be joined together into a cluster. This may take a long time, depending on how many servers have been chosen and how many resources the servers have. Before you can continue, you will have to fix any critical issues that the validation wizard finds. If the validation wizard only finds warnings, it's up to you to decide whether they are risks worth taking. Repeat this wizard until you are happy with the results.

21. When you are happy with the results of the validation wizard, check the box for **Create the cluster now using the validated nodes…** and click **Finish**.

22. **Create Cluster Wizard** will now open. Click **Next** on the **Before You Begin** page.

23. Give your cluster a name. I'm going to call mine sofs. Click **Next** and then **Next**.

24. Windows will now create your cluster. This make take a while. When it's done, click **Finish**.

25. **Failover Cluster Manager** will now show your cluster on the left-hand side. Let's check that the iSCSI storage we configured in *steps 1* and *2* is showing up. Expand your cluster and then expand the **Storage | Pools** node.

26. Under **Actions** on the right-hand side, click **New Storage Pool**.

27. In **New Storage Pool Wizard**, click **Next** and then give your storage pool a name. I'm calling mine SOFS (which is short for Scale-Out File Server) and click **Next**.

28. Check the boxes for the disks you want to use for this Scale-Out File Server and click **Next**. You must check a minimum of three disks. You should see the three iSCSI disks we created earlier in this recipe. If you're using SAS shared storage instead of iSCSI and also using enclosure awareness, then you may have to select a specific set of disks from each enclosure.

29. Click **Create**. Your storage pool will now start being created. It may take several minutes to create the storage pool. You should now have a storage space called **Clustered Pool 1**:

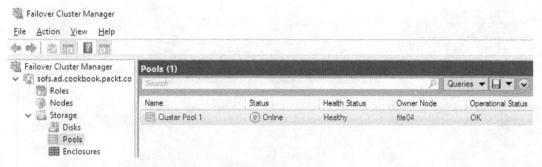

Figure 11.43 – Your clustered storage space now showing up

30. Now, we need to create a volume that we can use with our clustered storage pool. Right-click **Cluster Pool 1** and select **New Virtual Disk**.

31. Select the storage pool named SOFS and click **OK**.

    We're now in the **New Virtual Disk** wizard, which you may be familiar with from creating other storage spaces disks. Click **Next** and give our virtual disk a name.

32. Follow the rest of the wizard. I'm going to be choosing a **Mirror** layout without enclosure awareness. I'm also going to call this virtual disk's SOFS, using the maximum size.

33. When you've configured your **New Virtual Disk**, click **Create**.

34. You will now be taken to **New Volume Wizard**. You may also recognize this from previous Storage Spaces work, but this time with a slight difference. The wizard is asking you which server to provision the new volume to. Make sure your cluster is selected and click **Next:**

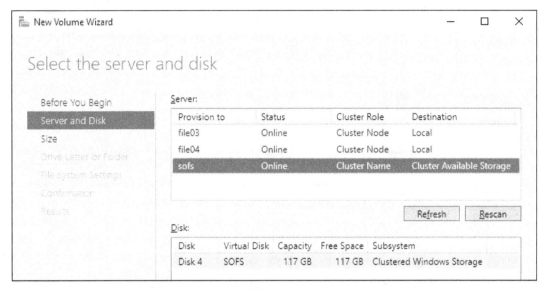

Figure 11.44 – The New Volume Wizard asking which server to provision

35. Create the size you want to create (usually the maximum) and click **Next.**

36. Continue with the rest of the wizard and click **Create** at the end.

37. Once the disk has been created, go to the **Storage | Disks** window of **Failover Cluster Manager**. Our new disk should now be showing up. Right-click the disk and choose **Add to Cluster Shared Volumes:**

Figure 11.45 – Adding our new virtual disk to Cluster Shared Volumes

38. The **Assigned To** column should now read **Cluster Shared Volume**. Once it does, navigate to the **Roles** node on the left-hand side.

39. Under **Actions** on the right-hand side, click **Configure Role…**:

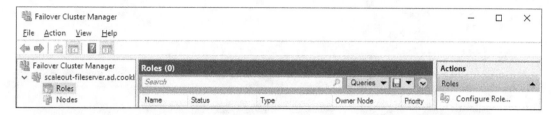

Figure 11.46 – The Configure Role… action

40. Click **Next** on the **Before You Begin** page.

41. Under **Select Role**, choose **File Server** and click **Next**:

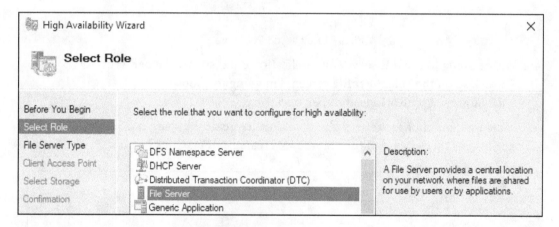

Figure 11.47 – Selecting the File Server role

42. Now, we must make our choice – are we installing a file server for general use, or for application data (see the beginning of this recipe for a discussion on what these are for)? The application data scale-out option is new in Server 2019, so we're going to choose **Scale-Out File Server for application data** and click **Next**.

43. Enter a name for our endpoint. I'm going to use sofs01. Click **Next**, then **Next**.

44. Your Scale-Out File Server will now start being created. When it's done, click **Finish**.

45. We now have our Scale-Out File Server and configured storage, but we haven't assigned any shares to it yet. In the Failover Cluster Manager, you should see your `sofs01` role. Right-click the role and choose **Add File Share**:

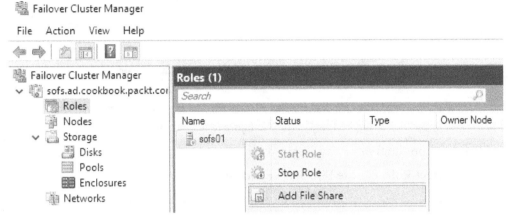

Figure 11.48 – Add File Share

46. We are going to use this server for application data (such as Hyper-V or SQL Server), so on the **Select Profile** screen, I'm going to choose **SMB Share – Applications** and then click **Next**.

47. Now, we must choose the server and volume to create the share on. Select `sofs01` as the server and the volume we created earlier. Click **Next**:

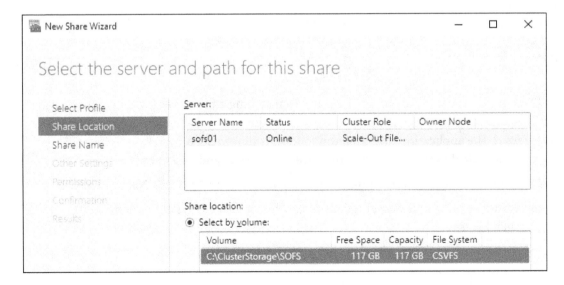

Figure 11.49 – Selecting our server and our storage

48. We now need to give our share a name. I'm going to call mine `HyperV` because in our pretend scenario, we're going to be storing Hyper-V virtual machines. Click **Next**.

49. We now have a bunch of options to choose for our share. Some may be disabled, depending on the type of storage or features that are enabled. Read through and select the options you want, then click **Next**.

50. The **Permissions** screen will now appear. If you are planning on using this for Hyper-V, pay close attention to the instructions on this page. Once you are done, click **Next**, **Create**, then **Close**.

51. Using Windows Explorer, you should now be able to browse to `\\sofs01.ad.cookbook.packt.com\HyperV` and browse your new Scale-Out File Server share!

How it works...

Scale-Out File Servers are a complicated topic. This recipe has taken us through the most basic configuration. There are numerous ways that these new file servers can be configured, and Server 2019 brings brand new configurations: the Infrastructure File Server. There is a link under the *See also* section that outlines some of the new 2019 features.

What we've seen in this recipe is only, as mentioned previously, suitable for a lab (or testing) scenario. To implement a Scale-Out File Server that is production ready, you will need proper shared storage sitting behind it. However, once you have that, you can easily scale our file servers to support dozens, or even hundreds, of other servers all utilizing its performance. When you start to reach the limits of what your current cluster can provide, you can add new nodes to your cluster to increase performance even more.

Scale-Out File Servers use the Windows Failover Clustering role. This role can be used for a variety of various high availability scenarios, not just this recipe. You might want to see what else you can do with it!

See also

- Scale-Out File Server overview: `https://docs.microsoft.com/en-us/windows-server/failover-clustering/sofs-overview`

- General Scale-Out File Server configuration instructions: `https://docs.microsoft.com/en-us/previous-versions/windows/it-pro/windows-server-2012-r2-and-2012/mt271018%28v%3dws.11%29`

- Information on the new Scale-Out File Server roles in Server 2019, including the Infrastructure role: `https://techcommunity.microsoft.com/t5/failover-clustering/scale-out-file-server-improvements-in-windows-server-2019/ba-p/372156`

12
Server Core

Anyone working with Windows servers should be familiar with **Server Core**, or at least the name. As we mentioned back in *Chapter 3, Networking*, Server Core is an alternative installation method for Windows Server 2019. It enables you to build a Windows server with significantly lower CPU, memory, and hard drive requirements. We've seen a fair bit of remote management already in this book and Server Core is how this has been possible. It is upon this shift in management mindset that many of our recipes will be focused today.

I feel that this chapter is important to include because I have the opportunity to work in new customer environments and get a feel for the way that they establish their networks and servers all the time. Do you know what I find? That everyone is running their Windows servers in the full GUI-based Desktop Experience mode. Now, there is nothing inherently wrong with that, but the fact that Server Core has been in existence since Windows Server 2008 and I rarely encounter a production server in a customer environment that is running Server Core tells me that either it doesn't work, which I know is untrue, or that people are simply scared of it because they haven't tried it out. I find the latter to be much more likely.

If you want the lower resource footprint and higher security of a semi-headless server, Server Core fits the bill. You can run almost anything on Server Core that you can run on Desktop Experience. The big difference is the way that you have to interact with that server for configuration and ongoing management. I think this is what keeps folks away from using it in production. There is always that *what if?* What if something breaks and I can't figure out how to fix it? What if I can't get into it to manage it? I hope that after walking through these recipes today, you will feel much more comfortable with managing Server Core, knowing that you can manipulate it just as extensively as you can with a full Desktop Experience version of Windows Server 2019.

Let's learn together some of the different ways in which we can take advantage of these smaller and more secure servers. This chapter will cover the following topics:

- Configuring Server Core from the console
- Switching between Server Core and Desktop Experience?
- Managing Server Core with Server Manager
- Managing Server Core using remote MMC tools
- Managing Server Core with PowerShell remoting

Building your first Server Core instance

Perhaps the most important way to increase security in your organization is to lower the security threshold, or footprint, of your servers and infrastructure. In other words, if there are any services running or ports open on your servers that aren't actually being used purposefully, you should disable or turn those particular services off. Now, hardening a Windows server by disabling services and uninstalling things isn't an easy job; you can easily turn something off that is important to the operating system and cause all kinds of problems on that server. Thankfully, there is a much safer and more secure way to harden your servers, but it requires planning from the beginning of your server build.

Server Core is a version of Windows Server 2019 that is almost a headless operating system; all of your interaction with it is either command line-driven or done remotely from other servers or systems. Server Core is an alternate installation method to the full Windows desktop version of Server 2019. It installs the necessary technical componentry to behave as a Windows server, join to your domain, and host the roles and services you need it to host, but it does all of that without a graphical desktop interface. This dramatically lowers the security vulnerability footprint and attack vectors on the server, but it does mean you have to re-wire your brain in how you interact with these servers.

Let's take a quick look at the installation process for it, and an initial glance at the interface, so you get familiar with the console you will be looking at on these new, hardened servers you are going to start using.

Getting ready

We are going to build a new instance of Windows Server 2019 but will be making sure to choose the appropriate options for installing Server Core and not the full desktop experience version of the operating system. Our new server will be a VM; it doesn't have to be actual hardware.

How to do it...

Here is a procedure that will get you started rolling out your first instance of Windows Server 2019, Server Core:

1. Create your new VM – or physical server – and insert the Windows Server 2019 installation media, just as you would if you were installing the full version of the operating system. Walk through the installation steps, the only difference being that you want to make sure to choose the default option for **Windows Server 2019 Standard**. Alternatively, you can, of course, choose the **Datacenter** installation option, but the important part here is that you do *not* choose the **(Desktop Experience)** version of the operating system, as that would give us a regular old desktop interface just like any other server. By choosing the top option, notice that it is now the default installation option; we are telling it that we want the more secure Server Core version of Windows Server 2019:

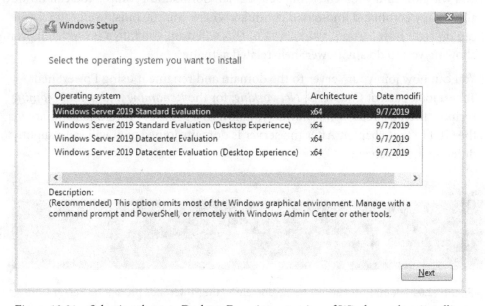

Figure 12.01 – Selecting the non-Desktop Experience version of Windows when installing

2. Finish walking through the installation wizard, and when your new server has booted, instead of being presented with the standard Windows mini-setup wizard in order to start configuring your server, you will simply be presented with the following screen:

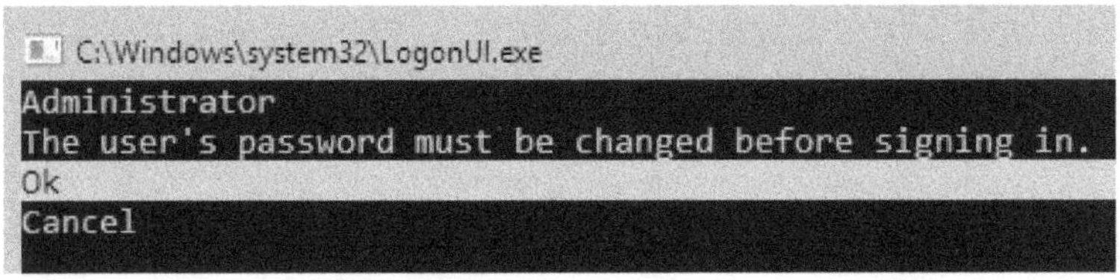

Figure 12.02 – The Server Core password change screen

3. Press *Enter* to select **Ok** and type in your new password. You can either press the *down arrow* key or the *Tab* key to move between fields. Press *Enter* when done:

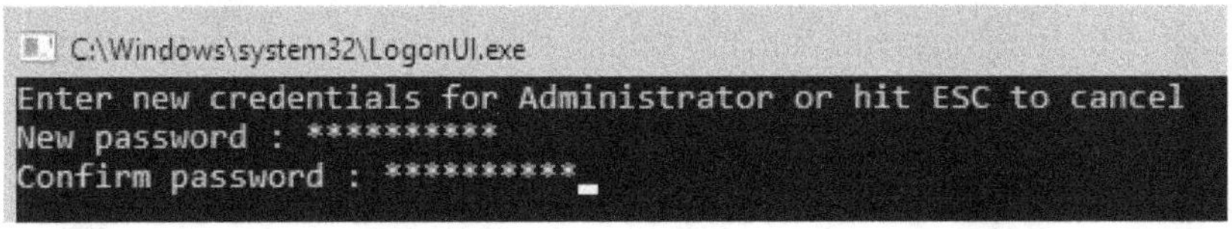

Figure 12.03 – Setting our new local administrator password

4. You will now find yourself sitting at a regular Command Prompt. You can now do almost any command line-based commands here, but the most useful thing you can do right now is run `powershell`. This will drop you into a PowerShell prompt, allowing you to do any PowerShell-related activities.

5. You can now join your server to the domain and rename it using PowerShell. Take a look back at *Chapter 3, Networking,* for the *Renaming and domain joining* recipe – there's a reason we showed you how to do this in PowerShell and not via the GUI in that chapter. After the server is domain-joined, you will see a slightly different login screen:

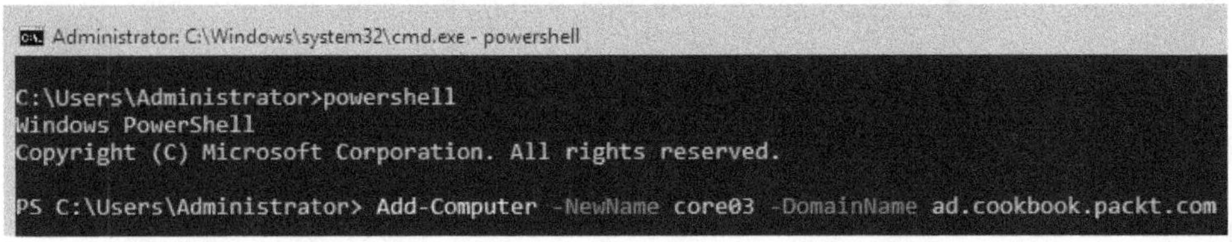

Figure 12.04 – Joining our server to the domain in the PowerShell prompt on Server Core

6. The Server Core shell is not limited to command-line interfacing. If you were to type `notepad` and press *Enter*, the Notepad application would appear, within which you can utilize your mouse as well as the keyboard:

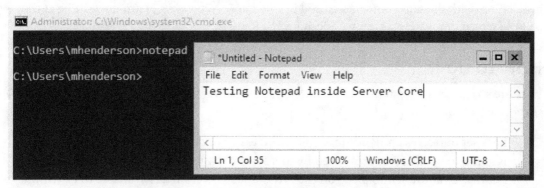

Figure 12.05 – Running Notepad from within Server Core

How it works...

It is critical that server administrators know the basics of how to get a Server Core edition of Windows up and running so they can start to use it in their day-to-day server workloads. A quick recipe in order to get the operating system up and running is a good start, but working with Server Core regularly and learning the common commands that you will need to use is essential to really get started interacting with these headless versions of the operating system.

Make sure to continue with the rest of this chapter so that you can make Server Core a reality in your infrastructure, and not just one of those things you know you should be doing but don't, simply because you are not familiar with it. Server Core can be an enormous security benefit; all you need to do is start using it!

Configuring Server Core from the console

In the previous recipe, we got Server Core installed, but we didn't do anything useful with it. In one of the screenshots, we displayed how you can flip the default Command Prompt over to PowerShell, and then run some commands, such as the `Add-Computer` cmdlet, in order to join the server to the domain. Beyond that, nothing has been configured and our server isn't performing any functions in our network yet. Let's walk through the standard items you can accomplish on any server when you bring it up for the first time in a domain network. Our hostname is already set and it's joined to our domain, but we still need to configure an IP address.

Getting ready

I have a new server and have run through the installation of Windows Server 2019. During installation, I chose the default selection for the Core version of Windows Server. Following installation, with the same process we used in *Chapter 3, Networking*, I am now sitting at the console screen of my new server, wondering what to do next.

How to do it...

Here are some steps we can take to prepare our new Server Core machine for use in the corporate network:

1. Let's set ourselves an IP address on CORE01. I have decided that 172.16.97.55 is going to be the IP address used by this system. Now we need to figure out how to put that IP address into place on the NIC. Since PowerShell is available to us within Server Core, we could spend some time digging around in these cmdlets to figure out what our NIC ID is and set the IP address using purely PowerShell (and, in fact, we will do that later on), but Server Core also has a special interface that makes this process a little bit easier.

2. From Command Prompt in the Server Core console, type sconfig. You will now be presented with a special set of tools running within the Command Prompt window that allow you to configure various aspects of the operating system:

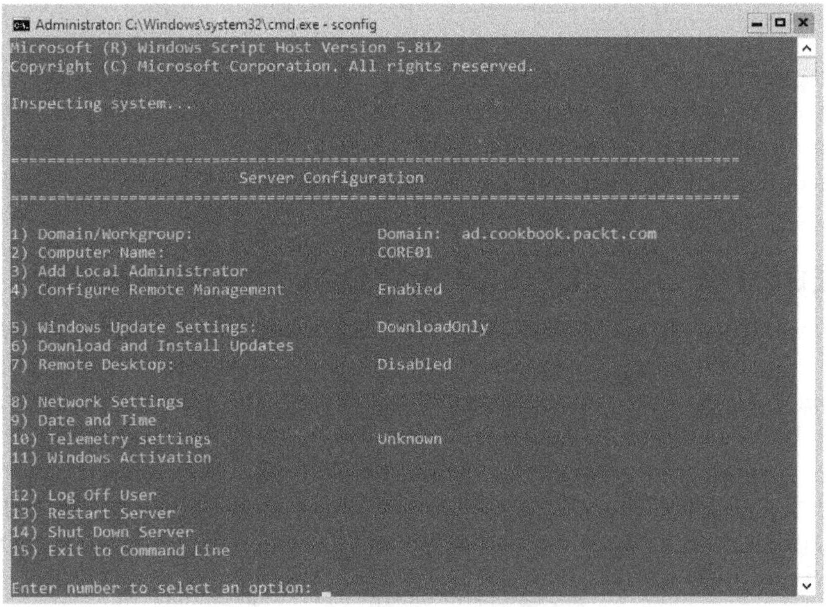

Figure 12.06 – The sconfig configuration screen

3. Take note that you can even shut down or restart your server from here. This is important to know because otherwise there is not a clearly defined way to perform these functions in Server Core. You could of course use the shutdown command, or the Restart-Computer cmdlet, which is the way I typically do it, but relying on sconfig for these kinds of administrative tasks *can* make your life a lot easier. We could have even used this to rename our server to CORE01 in the first place!

4. Press the number *8* on your keyboard, and then press *Enter*, in order to enter **Network Settings**.

5. Now type the index number of the network card that you want to manipulate. If your server, like mine, only has one NIC, then you simply press the number 1.

6. You will be presented with the current configuration of that NIC. Now choose option **1** in order to set the network adapter address:

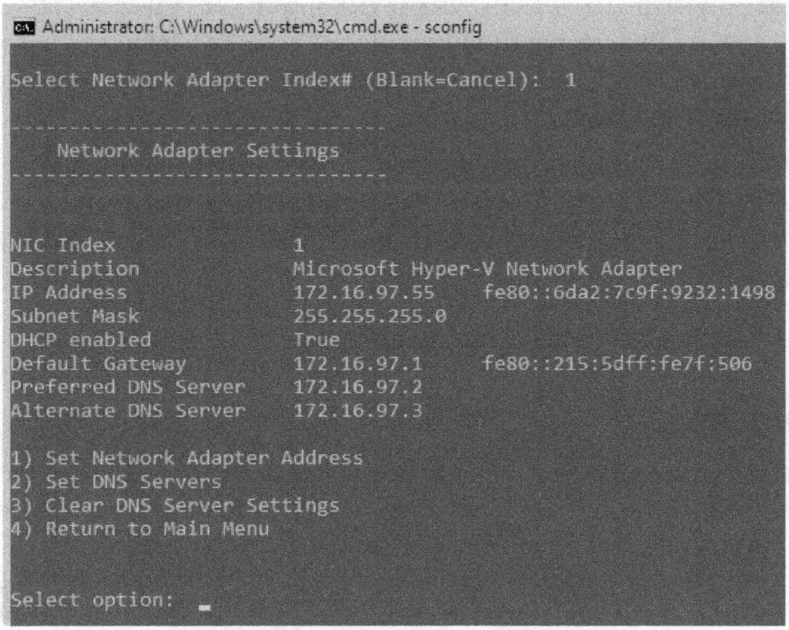

Figure 12.07 – Configuring our network adapter

7. Press *S* in order to set a **Static** IP address.

8. Type your new static IP address. I will type 172.16.97.55, and press *Enter*.

9. Continue with the steps to populate your subnet mask and your default gateway.

10. Your NIC has now been reconfigured with your new IP address! If you also need to set static DNS server addresses, go ahead and continue on with option number **2** from the prompt. Otherwise, press *4* in order to return to the main `sconfig` menu.

11. Now that we've seen how `sconfig` can be used for setting some of the basic system settings, let's see how we would have set our IP address via PowerShell instead. Type **15** to exit to the command line and press *Enter*.

12. Once back at the command line, type `powershell` and press *Enter*. You will then be taken to a PowerShell prompt.

13. Run `Get-NetAdapter`. This will show us the network adapters we have installed in our system. Note the **Name** column for the adapter you want to set. It is probably just called `Ethernet`.

14. I'm going to run `New-NetIPAddress -InterfaceAlias "Ethernet" -IPAddress 172.16.97.55 -PrefixLength 24 -DefaultGateway 172.16.97.1`. This sets the IP address of the `Ethernet` interface, and sets its subnet length to 24 (which translates to `255.255.255.0`). It also sets our default gateway to the correct value.

15. Now to set our DNS servers. Running `Set-DnsClientServerAddress -InterfaceAlias "Ethernet" -ServerAddresses @ (172.16.97.2,172.16.97.3)` sets my DNS servers to my two domain controllers.

Our servers are now ready for remote management!

How it works...

There are a variety of ways that you can interface with and manage a Server Core instance, and we will talk about some more of them in upcoming recipes. However, there are certain core –no pun intended – functions that need to be accomplished first, right from the console, before you can start thinking about doing any remote management of your new servers. The `sconfig` tool is quick to open, is very easy to use, and contains some powerful functionality for these initial configuration steps that we all must take on each of our new servers. However, it is not the only way to configure our server – we can also use PowerShell locally to set up the things we need.

Switching between Server Core and Desktop Experience?

At what point do you need to decide whether your brand new server is going to be Server Core or a full Desktop Experience version with the traditional Windows graphical interface? It would be common sense to make this decision during the operating system installation process, right? Where you choose from the installer which version of the operating system you are putting into place? You are exactly right, except that in previous versions of Windows Server, we could switch a live server back and forth between the two modes. If you had a full graphical version of a server running and wanted to change it over to Server Core to get some enhanced security benefits, you could run a command and do just that. And the same was true in reverse; if you were running Server Core and couldn't figure out how to configure something from the command interface, you could run another command that would change it over into the GUI version of the operating system. These commands were essentially just adding or removing some features within the operating system; basically, you laid down or removed the graphical shell, which was the interface for Windows Server 2012.

Does that capability still exist in Windows Server 2019? It is not very common for Microsoft to implement new capabilities in an operating system and then yank them back out again later, but you never know until you try. Let's dig up those commands that could do the switching back and forth in the past and test them out on Server 2019. You may be surprised at the results.

Getting ready

Using our `CORE01` server, which is already online, I am going to attempt to switch it from Server Core over to the Desktop Experience mode of Windows Server 2019, using some cmdlets that I know used to work in previous versions of the Windows Server operating system.

How to do it...

1. In order to test changing Server Core into a Desktop Experience version of
    Windows Server 2019, I am opening up an administrative PowerShell window
    and am going to use the following command: `Install-WindowsFeature`
    `Server-Gui-Shell, Server-Gui-Mgmt-Infra`:

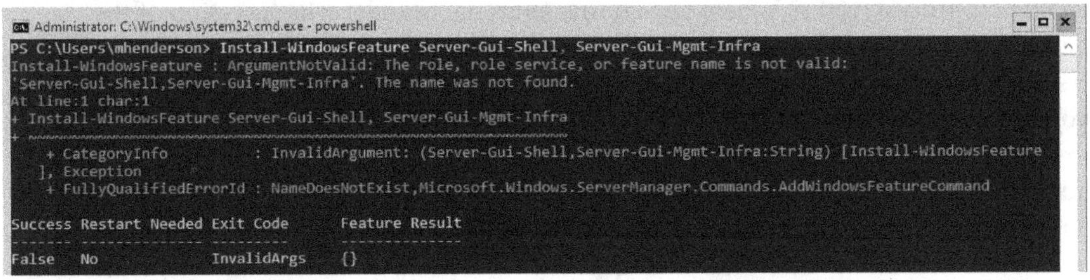

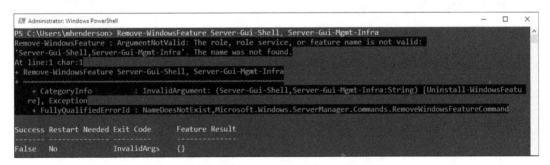

Figure 12.08 – Attempting to install the GUI shell fails

2. Uh oh, that's not a very pretty error message to see first thing in the morning. It
    appears my `Install-WindowsFeature` cmdlet is attempting to run, but it
    cannot find the role or features that I am specifying. I know that these cmdlets
    worked in Server 2012, so it's looking like they may have been removed for Server
    2019. Just to confirm, let's try the other direction. I am logging into one of my
    Windows Server 2019 Desktop Experience servers, and I am going to try changing
    it over to Server Core with the following command: `Remove-WindowsFeature`
    `Server-Gui-Shell, Server-Gui-Mgmt-Infra`:

Figure 12.09 – Attempting to remove the GUI shell fails

3. Well, unfortunately, that error message looks very similar to the one we received when we tried adding the shell to Server Core. Let's try just one more thing to make sure we have really lost this ability. In previous versions of Windows Server, you could utilize these commands; alternatively, when swinging a server from the full graphical version over to Server Core, you could actually open up the **Add/Remove Roles** function and see those features listed right on the screen. Let's walk through that wizard and check the **Features** screen to see whether or not the feature called **User Interfaces and Infrastructure** is even listed. As you can see in the following screenshot, it is no longer in our list of operating system features. It used to be listed right there, just below **TFTP Client**:

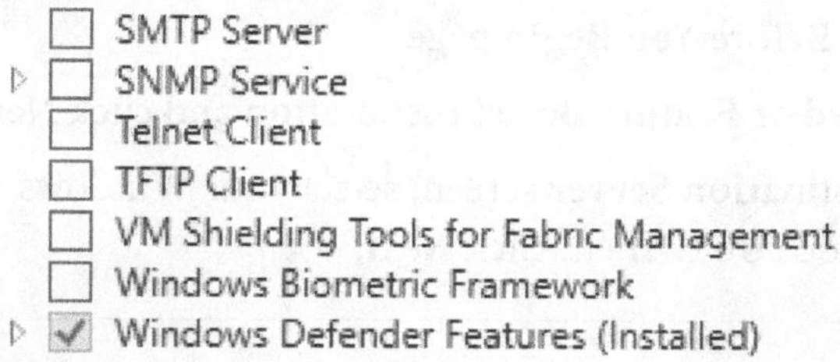

Figure12.10 – The User Interface option is not available any more

How it works...

As we have proven with this recipe, the ability to change a server between Desktop Experience and Server Core no longer exists in Windows Server 2019. While it would have been shorter and easier to simply state this fact, taking you through the example proves the point, and it also gives you the commands that you need to switch older versions of Windows Server back and forth, if that is something you were not familiar with in the past.

Limitations of Server Core

As we've seen, one of the limitations of Server Core is that you can't add the GUI component back after it's installed. So, if you're going to use Server Core (and you should), then you'll need to know that certain things do not work on Server Core.

So far in this chapter, we've mentioned a few times that Server Core can do *almost* anything that the GUI version of Windows can do. Let's take a look at some of the things that Server Core cannot do.

Getting ready

You'll need to have a fully operational Server Core machine. I'm going to be managing the server from a Windows 10 machine with RSAT installed.

How to do it...

1. On your machine with Windows 10 and RSAT, open up **Server Manager**.

2. If your server is not already listed in **Server Manager**, go to **Manage | Add Servers** and add your Server Core machine to **Server Manager**.

3. Once the server is listed, go to **Manage | Add Roles and Features**.

4. Click **Next** on the **Before You Begin** page.

5. Choose **Role-Based or Feature Based installation** and click **Next**.

6. On the **Select Destination Server** screen, select your Windows Server Core machine. Mine is core01. Then, click **Next**:

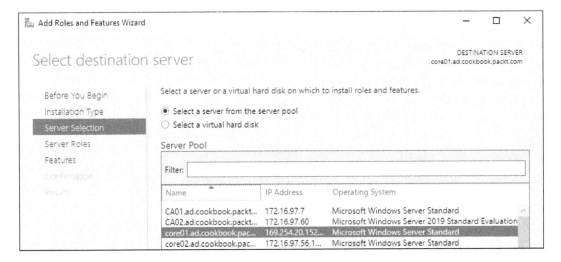

Figure 12.11 – Selecting Windows Server Core in the Add Roles and Features wizard

7. The list of roles and services you see here will be shorter than the list you're used to seeing. Certain roles are missing – **the Network Policy and Access Service** (**NPAS**), for example. This is a commonly used role if your server is going to be the authentication endpoint for Wi-Fi or networking devices.

8. Once you've seen that the list is shorter, click the **Cancel** button.

9. Open up PowerShell as administrator.

10. Run `Install-WindowsFeature NPAS -ComputerName core01`.

11. PowerShell will return an error saying that NPAS is not a valid feature name.

How it works...

As in our previous recipe, I could have just *told* you that certain services aren't going to work. But this way, we've seen for ourselves what happens when you try to add a service that is not supported on Windows Server Core.

The good news is that Server 2019 is a lot better than earlier versions of Windows at managing these expectations. In previous editions, Windows would attempt to install the incompatible service and would then give a cryptic error message.

See also

The full list of Windows roles and features that are incompatible with Server Core can be found at: `https://docs.microsoft.com/en-us/windows-server/administration/server-core/server-core-removed-roles`.

Managing Server Core with Server Manager

As we've seen, console access for configuring Server Core is pretty limited. Either we're missing something here, or Microsoft intended for us to be managing these servers differently. Cue the drumroll for remote management. Centralized administration of Windows Server operating systems is something that Microsoft really started pushing hard with the release of Server 2012, and it is increasingly important in Windows Server 2016. Tools such as Server Manager are now becoming agnostic to the local machine that they are running on. You can use Server Manager on one server to manage a different kind of server halfway across a data center, without having to make any adjustments to the way that you are handling that administration.

Several times in this book already, we've seen the option for using Server Manager right from our Windows 10 computer with RSAT installed. Clearly, the days of RDPing into every server should be diminishing. We are now technically capable of managing our servers from a single, central pane of glass. The question is this – how many server administrators are taking advantage of this functionality?

Getting ready

We have CORE01 up and running on the network. Now we are going to utilize Server Manager on a different server to manipulate these machines. I will be using Windows 10 with RSAT for this task, which has the RSAT tools installed. See the *Administering Server 2019 from a Windows 10 machine* recipe all the way back in *Chapter 1, Learning the Interface*.

How to do it...

Follow these steps to manage Server Core or Nano Server right from inside Server Manager on another of your servers in the network:

1. Open **Server Manager**, click on the **Manage** menu near the top-right corner of the screen, and choose the option that says **Add Servers**.

2. When I click the **Find Now** button, I can see a list of my domain-joined servers in the network. Since I was able to join my CORE01 server to the domain from its console, I can see it in the list. Choose CORE01 and move it over to the **Selected** side of the screen:

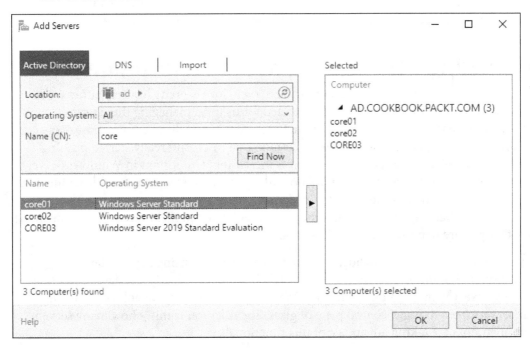

Figure 12.12 – Adding our Server Core machines to Server Manager

3. Now click **OK**, and now my Server Core servers are configurable from within my local Server Manager window. By clicking on **All Servers**, I can see them both listed, and right-clicking on the servers gives me options to do things such as opening **Computer Management** on them:

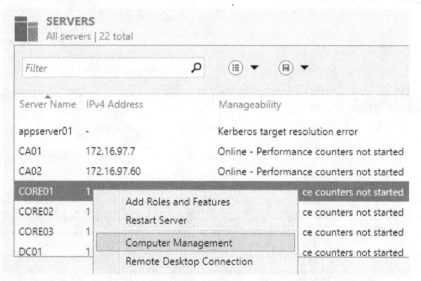

Figure 12.13 – Opening the Computer Management screen from Server Manager for a remote Server Core installation

4. In fact, let's try making a change in one of our systems right now. Now that I have added CORE01 into **Server Manager**, I will right-click on it and choose the option that you can see in the previous screenshot for **Add Roles and Features**.

5.   I am presented with the same **Add Roles and Features Wizard** that I would utilize to install a role on any other server, except that when I walk through the wizard, you can see that my default server destination for this new role or feature will be CORE01:

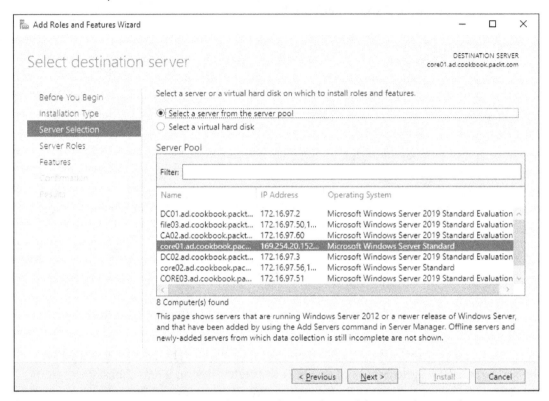

Figure 12.14 – CORE01 is the selected server for modifying via the wizard

6.   For this example, I am going to use CORE01 as a DHCP server. Therefore, I need to install the **Active Directory Domain Services** role on it. As we saw in a previous recipe, not all roles are available for installation:

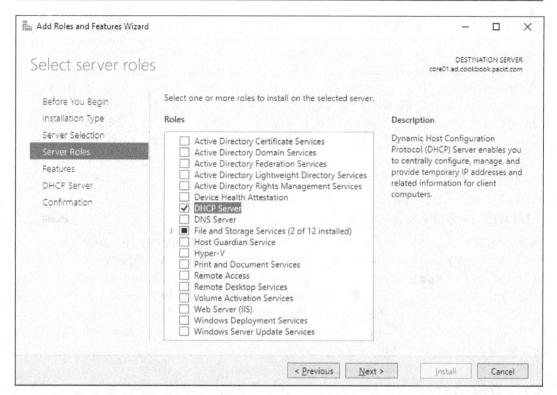

Figure 12.15 – Adding the DHCP role to our Server Core installation via Server Manager

7.   Simply run through the wizard, and then you can configure DHCP on our Server Core via Server Manager as well, or you can do it via MMC in the next recipe.

How it works...

There are certainly some useful configuration options inside Server Manager that you can use to push changes and settings to your headless servers, but they're not the only way. Continue reading through the recipes in this chapter to find some even more powerful options for tapping into your server configuration remotely. As you start navigating around Server Manager, you should also be aware that you may bump into some messages about the Windows Firewall rules needing to be adjusted on remote computers. Server Core is fairly locked down by default, so much so that even a trusted tool such as Server Manager can't always communicate with those servers to the extent that is needed. You will occasionally have to log in to the console of those Core servers in order to permit some firewall rules to be open and to allow Server Manager to do the tasks you are asking it to do. You could always push these rules out via Group Policy as well, if desired.

Managing Server Core using remote MMC tools

Another powerful way to interact with servers that you are not logged in to, or that you cannot log in to in a traditional sense, such as Nano Server and Server Core, is to make use of the MMC tools from a remote system. By launching MMC and snapping in consoles, or by running the tools straight from the **Administrative Tools** folder and then specifying which server you want to interact with, you can continue with the centralized management mentality while making changes to systems you are not actively logged in to. This feature has actually existed in Windows Server for almost 20 years, but again it's not one that is used all that often. Let's test this out together.

Getting ready

I just finished using a remote copy of Server Manager to install the DHCP role onto CORE01. Now I want to actually configure the DHCP service. Because the console of Server Core isn't going to allow me to simply log in and open the DHCP management tools, I am going to use the tools that are already installed on my Windows 10 machine with RSAT. As with most of the recipes in this chapter, you should have already done *Administering Server 2019 from a Windows 10 machine* from *Chapter 1, Learning the Interface.*

How to do it...

It is possible to remotely administer the DHCP role running on CORE01. We will cover two different ways to go about this:

1. Open the **Microsoft Management Console (MMC)**. I typically do this by invoking the **Run** prompt with *WinKey* + *R*, and then typing MMC.

2. Inside MMC, click the **File** menu and then choose **Add/Remove Snap-in**....

3. Scroll down until you find the snap-in called **DHCP**. Choose that, and click the **Add** button in order to move it over to **Selected snap-ins**.

4. If you cannot find **DHCP** in the list of snap-ins, use the *Administering Server 2019 from a Windows 10 machine* recipe from *Chapter 1, Learning the Interface* and make sure you install the DHCP RSAT tools.

5.   Press the **OK** button:

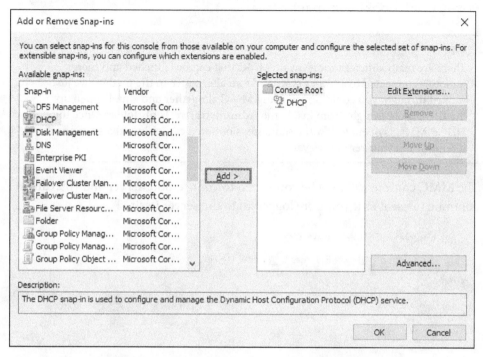

Figure 12.16 – Adding the DHCP snap-in to MMC

6.   By default, MMC opens the DHCP console pointing to our Windows 10 machine, which obviously does not have the DHCP role installed. Right-click on the **DHCP** node and choose **Add Server…**:

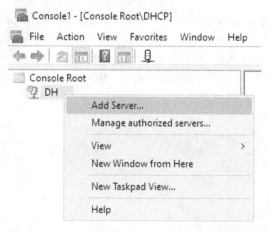

Figure 12.17 – Add Server… in the DHCP menu

7. Type the name of the server that you want to administer. I will be entering
    `core01.ad.cookbook.packt.com`.

> **Tip**
> There are many different tools inside MMC that can be launched and then
> remotely connected to another system. As an alternative to the method we just
> walked through, you could forego using MMC altogether and simply open up
> the IIS console straight from inside the **Administrative Tools** folder. Once the
> DHCP MMC is open, follow the same steps outlined earlier in order to connect
> it remotely to your remote server.

8. The MMC console will now be connected to your remote server and you can
    continue to use it as if you were logged in to the server itself:

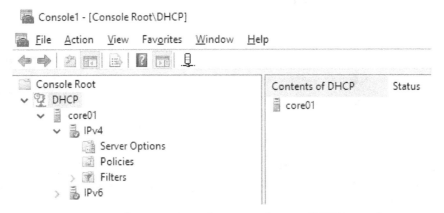

Figure 12.18 – The DHCP console connected to our CORE01 machine

9. In fact, there is one more way that mixes this recipe with the preceding recipe. Now
    that the DHCP role has been installed onto CORE01, if we go back into **Server
    Manager** and right-click on our CORE01 server, you will notice that we now have
    the option to launch **DHCP Manager** right from there:

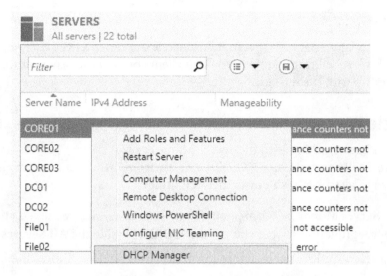

Figure 12.19 – Loading the DHCP console directly from Server Manager

How it works...

MMC contains snap-ins for most of the tools that you need to administer your servers, whether those servers are local or remote to you. I very rarely see administrators using the MMC console to its full potential. It would be quite easy to snap in all of the management tools that you need for your entire organization, connect them to the servers that are relevant for each role or task, and then have one single MMC console window that was always open on your local computer. This way, any time you need to make a change in IIS, Active Directory, DNS, Group Policy, and so on, you simply open the MMC window on your machine, without needing to log in to any servers, and make the changes.

Managing Server Core with PowerShell remoting

Now we move on to the most powerful way that we can interact with our remote and headless servers, PowerShell. If I've said it once, I've said it a thousand times – PowerShell has the capability to change anything in the operating system; it's just a matter of figuring out the right commands and cmdlets to use. By establishing a remote PowerShell connection to a server, you can manipulate any facet of that machine right from the pretty blue window that is running on your local computer. In this recipe, we will use PowerShell from our Windows 10 client computer.

Getting ready

As we continue to figure out how to remotely manage our new CORE01 server, we will now be using PowerShell from our Windows 10 client computer to see what we can and cannot accomplish with these tools.

How to do it...

Since we've just been working with the Server Manager on Windows 10, let's try to launch a remote PowerShell connection to CORE01 directly from inside Server Manager. This is a quick and easy way to establish PowerShell remoting:

1. Launch **Server Manager**. We are going to assume that you have already used the **Add Servers** function so that you can see CORE01 inside the **All Servers** screen.

2. Right-click on CORE01 and choose the option for **Windows PowerShell**:

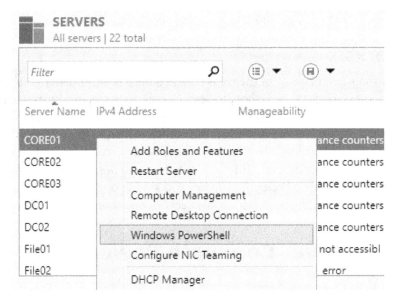

Figure 12.20 – Opening Windows PowerShell from Server Manager

3. After a couple of seconds where PowerShell is opening and creating a connection to CORE01, we are presented with a familiar blue PowerShell window. What doesn't look standard is the fact that, in front of our flashing cursor, you can see the CORE01 server name specified. This indicates that our PowerShell window is actively running against CORE01, and anything that you type into this window reflects CORE01, and not the Windows 10 machine that we are logged in to.

4. Let's prove this. As you can see in the following screenshot, I have the **System** properties open and you can see that we are currently logged in to my Windows 10 machine. However, when I enter a simple `hostname` command into my remote PowerShell window, it responds that the system hostname is CORE01:

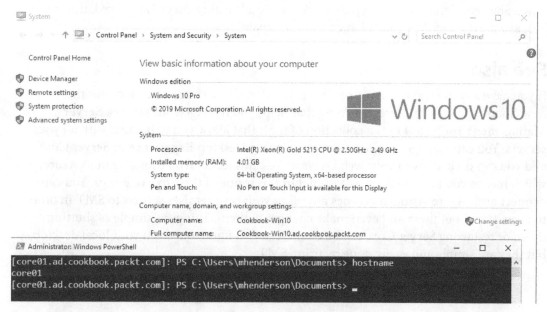

Figure 11.21 – Demonstrating remote PowerShell

5. One final step here before we move on to our other example: let's try to change something on CORE01. Earlier we installed the DHCP role onto this system, but now I have decided to use this server for a different purpose. Rather than having to launch any graphical tools or wizards, since I already have this remote PowerShell session open, I can remove the DHCP role from CORE01 with a single command:

```
Remove-WindowsFeature DHCP
```

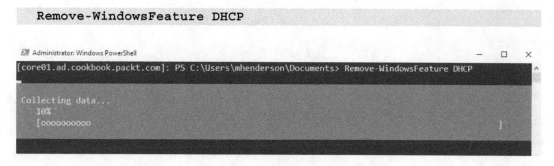

Figure12.22 – Removing the DHCP server role via PowerShell

How it works...

We have now explored a variety of ways that you can remotely connect to and manipulate your headless servers such as Server Core. PowerShell is by far the most powerful way to accomplish this, but it is also the most complicated if you are not familiar with using PowerShell cmdlets in your everyday work. While a learning curve is involved, this is the best avenue to pursue as you enhance your IT capabilities.

See also

If you have any interest in Azure, or even if you don't, make sure you check out the new cloud capability they are providing that helps you manage your servers. **Server Management Tools (SMT)** is a collection of tools that allow you to interact with all your servers. You can manage Windows servers running Desktop Experience or Server Core, and you can do it all from your web browser! Yes, this does involve logging in to Azure, which means you need an Azure account, but this is one of their free offerings. You can connect both Azure virtual machines as well as your on-premises servers to SMT in order to view data about them and even make changes to them. Things as simple as shutting down or restarting Server Core can be complicated to figure out from your local desktop, but they are simply and easily done by using SMT.

13
Working with Hyper-V

Today's server administrators eat, sleep, and breathe **Virtual Machines (VMs)**. They are flooding our computing infrastructure, quickly replacing physical servers in all facets of our technology. Thankfully, entrance into the world of virtualization is quite easy once you know which pieces of the puzzle need to work together in order to start building and hosting VMs. I have worked with many server administrators who manage the VMs themselves once they are online, but in bigger organizations, it is usually someone on the backend who is creating these VMs in the first place. This means that even someone who works with Windows servers every day might not have a lot of experience with using the Hyper-V Management Console, and this is the reason why a chapter about Hyper-V itself is important to include in this book on Windows Server 2019.

When talking about server virtualization, it is important to note the difference between a virtualization host and a VM. The host server is the big server, the (usually) physical server that provides all the resources to the smaller VMs. There are two major players in the virtualization host category. A company called VMware is popular in both personal and enterprise deployments, and, of course, there's Microsoft's own Hyper-V.

Since I live in the Microsoft world, and this is a Microsoft-centric book, we are going to focus on the virtualization capabilities provided by Microsoft Hyper-V inside the Windows Server 2019 operating system. The best part about Hyper-V is that it is available to anyone who is running the Windows Server operating system (and even Windows 10 Professional), so even if you aren't using virtualization technology in your business today, with just a few mouse clicks (or a few lines of PowerShell), you probably could be. There is even a version of Windows Server that is totally free to use as a Hyper-V host.

Virtualization is an enormous topic and there will certainly be complete books written on all the ins-and-outs of Hyper-V. This chapter will focus on the steps you will need to take in order to start using it and on the cornerstones of running a virtualized environment. We're also going to look at one of the new Server 2019 features called *nested resiliency* and how we can use it with Hyper-V. There are also other clustering options for Hyper-V you might want to research.

Windows can also do *nested virtualization*, where you can have a VM that is running inside Hyper-V and install the Hyper-V role onto that VM itself (which is, in fact, what I'm using to write this chapter)! Why in the world would you want to do that? *"To use containers,"* is the number one answer to that question, as you start to expand your DevOps capabilities by using Windows Server and Hyper-V containers to provide tiny, secure, standardized platforms for application development and expansion. We're going to look at this a lot more in *Chapter 14, Containers and Docker.*

In this chapter, we will cover the following recipes:

- Creating a Windows Server that runs Hyper-V
- Creating a Hyper-V server
- Networking your VMs
- Building your first VM
- Using the VM Settings page
- Editing virtual hard disks
- Using checkpoints as rollback points
- Using nested resiliency

Creating a Windows Server that runs Hyper-V

Before you can start building VMs to use in your environment, first, you need a virtualization host server on which Hyper-V will run. The first consideration is hardware. The hardware requirements for a server running Hyper-V depend on how many virtual servers you plan to run on top of this host platform. For example, if all you have is a quad-core desktop processor with only 8 GB of RAM, this is not going to be conducive to a successful Hyper-V environment – you will only be able turn on four or five VMs at a time, each of them with very minimal amounts of memory per VM. In my day job, I am fortunate to have both an AMD ThreadRipper desktop and a dual-Xeon desktop, each with 64 GB of RAM, that can run a lot of *small* VMs – such as what's required to write the recipes in this book.

A server-class machine with Xeon processors and 256 GB of RAM or more with solid state storage may become the criteria if you intend to run multiple dozens of servers within your virtualized environment. Or perhaps you can meet somewhere in the middle of those numbers if you are running between 1 and 10 VMs. There's not really a *right* answer here. Just make sure you have enough RAM to assign each VM the amount that it needs, plus an amount dedicated to the host operating system so that it continues to perform properly. Hard drive space is also a good consideration because you need to make sure you have enough physical storage for all those servers that you plan to spin up.

Once you have decided on the hardware, your next decision is which version of Windows Server 2019 to install on it. If you have run through the installer, you will know that you have options for Server 2019 standard and Server 2019 Datacenter. One of the most important notes I can give you regarding this topic is to be aware of what how many and what type of Windows licenses you have for virtualization. Licensing with Windows is a deep and complex issue that I'm not going to discuss in detail here – you should speak to your Microsoft licensing representative to figure out your exact needs. Look at the *Creating a Hyper-V Server* recipe for a hypervisor that doesn't require any licensing at all.

Getting ready

I have a piece of server hardware upon which I have installed Windows Server 2019. Keep in mind that each fully licensed VM you create that is running Windows Server will also require a license key; there are no freebies here with operating system licenses. You can use the Windows Server evaluation versions if you need a free, time-limited copy of Windows in order to experiment with these recipes.

How to do it...

I have already installed Windows Server 2019 on my hardware. I have two NICs on this server, because Hyper-V prefers to have one NIC dedicated to host operating system communications. The second NIC can be used as a bridge between the VMs and my physical network. Follow these steps to install the Hyper-V role:

1. Open Server Manager and click on the link for **Add roles and features**. Click **Next** until you see the **Select server roles** screen. Here, you simply choose the checkbox for **Hyper-V**.

2. Alternatively – and this can be extremely useful if your Hyper-V Server is running Server Core – the following PowerShell cmdlet can be used to install the Hyper-V role and its management features:

```
Install-WindowsFeature Hyper-V -IncludeManagementTools -Restart
```

This will result in the following output:

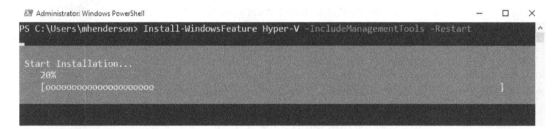

Figure 13.01 – Installing the Hyper-V role via PowerShell

3. After installing the role, you must reboot the server.

4. Once the server has finished rebooting, head into **Server Manager** and launch **Hyper-V Manager** for the first time from the **Tools** menu.

5. The following screenshot gives you a glance into **Hyper-V Manager**. This is the tool you will most often utilize to interact with the VMs that you run on this virtualization host server. As we will discuss in the upcoming recipes, there are a variety of ways that you can interact with a server running Hyper-V, and even several different ways that you can run the Hyper-V Manager console:

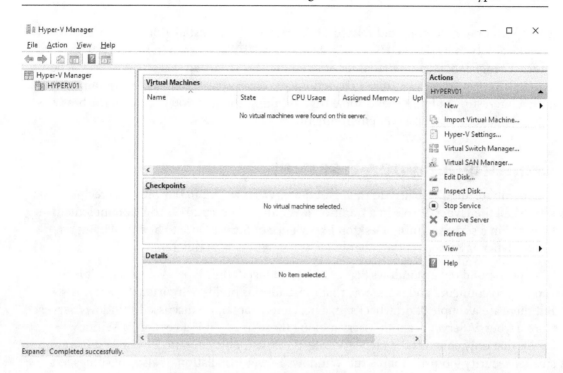

Figure 13.02 – The Hyper-V Manager

> **Tip**
> Windows 10 Professional and Enterprise also contain the Hyper-V feature.
> Installing it is a different process to what's in this book, but once it's installed,
> you can do many of the same things as Windows Server, but on your desktop.
> In fact, I have been using Hyper-V on Windows 10 to build everything
> contained in this book!

How it works...

Implementing the Hyper-V role in your new Windows Server 2019 server is the first step
toward virtualizing your infrastructure. You need to plan for hardware needs carefully,
making sure you have wiggle room in case you end up with more servers or bigger servers
than you originally planned. Now that our Hyper-V virtualization host is online, has
the role installed, and has gone through its initial configuration, it is time to really start
making use of the Hyper-V Manager console.

An important item to point out related to the Hyper-V role installation is that we now have the ability to install the Hyper-V role on a VM! This is known in the industry as *Nested Virtualization*. Your virtual servers can host other virtual servers. What is the point of that? This is primarily because of functionality in Server 2019 related to containers, but it is an interesting point to spend some time thinking about as you decide on the best way to build out your virtual server environment.

Creating a Hyper-V server

Wait a minute, didn't we just do this? Not quite. What we did in our previous recipe was install the Hyper-V role in a traditional Windows Server 2019. You can implement Hyper-V in a server running Desktop Experience or Server Core to host VMs. But an actual Hyper-V Server, on the other hand, is something a bit different.

When you build out a Windows Server 2019 and install the Hyper-V role on it, it is nice and easy to configure and is the way that most admins build their virtualization hosts. But there are a couple of drawbacks. In a previous chapter, we discussed Windows Server Core. Hyper-V Server is another server along those lines – it is a version of Windows Server that only contains the Hyper-V role. Because it only contains Hyper-V, it has a smaller security footprint than a full Windows Server installation. It also consumes less disk space.

This is the importance of Hyper-V Server. It is a completely different installer file that you can download free from Microsoft. Once implemented, this Hyper-V Server has no licensing costs associated with it. For every regular Windows Server that you host on top of your Hyper-V server, you must ensure that they are licensed appropriately, but the Hyper-V Server host machine is totally free. Given the word "free," you would think that Hyper-V Server would be prevalent inside our data centers, but it really isn't. I believe that is the result of two factors. The first is that many admins may not even know Hyper-V Server exists. Second is the fact that the interface for Hyper-V Server is more like Server Core, and it's not an entirely comforting feeling knowing that the console of your super-important, massive Hyper-V host server is only going to provide you with a Command Prompt in order to interface with it.

Let's install Hyper-V Server together so you know how to do that, and then we will look at managing VMs on this Hyper-V Server.

Getting ready

We have a new server that we are going to install Hyper-V Server 2019 on. We will also use a Windows 10 machine with RSAT installed to manage the VMs.

How to do it...

Follow these steps to implement and test your first Hyper-V server:

1. You will need to download the installer ISO from Microsoft. Open up your favorite search engine and search for `Download Windows Hyper-V Server 2019`.

2. Once downloaded, either burn the ISO file to a DVD or use an ISO-to-USB tool to create bootable media of some kind. Then, boot your new server hardware using this media.

3. As you can see, the installation wizard looks similar to that of our traditional Windows Server 2019 installer. The big difference is that the installer does not pause to ask you which version of the operating system you want to install. After specifying the installation location, it immediately starts installing Hyper-V Server 2019:

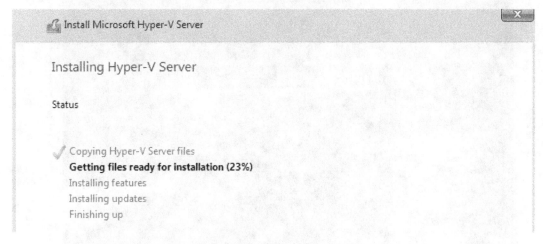

Figure 13.03 – The Hyper-V installation process

4. Following the installation, you will be presented with a window that should be familiar to anyone who has read *Chapter 12, Server Core*:

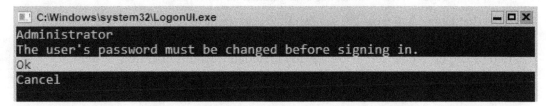

Figure 13.04 – Setting the Administrator password

5. After following the process for setting the administrator password, you are taken directly into the sconfig tool. This tool is a configuration interface for anyone working with Server Core, so if you have any experience in that area, this will all be familiar to you. As you can see, we have options available here to do things such as change the hostname, configure network settings, and join our new Hyper-V Server to the domain.

6. If you refer to the *Configuring Server Core from the console* recipe from *Chapter 12, Server Core*, you will know how to set the server name, domain, and NIC configuration for your Hyper-V server. This is the result of my server after configuration:

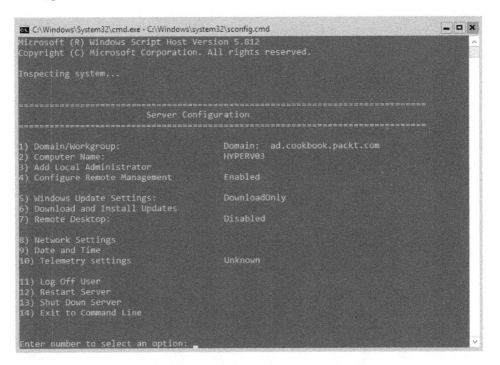

Figure 13.05 – The sconfig configuration for my Hyper-V server

7. Now that Hyper-V Server 2019 is installed and we have accomplished our typical server setup configurations, what's next? The roles and services needed for this box to be a Hyper-V host server are already included with this operating system, so all we need to do at this point is figure out how to get into the Hyper-V Manager console in order to start building VMs. For this, we are going to fall back on our Microsoft remote management mentality.

8. Log into your Windows 10 computer that has the RSAT tools installed on it. We'll use the Hyper-V Manager console from there in order to remotely manage this new Hyper-V Server. See the *Administering Server 2019 from a Windows 10 machine* recipe all the way back in *Chapter 1, Learning the Interface,* for these instructions.

9. Once inside, right-click on **Hyper-V Manager** and choose **Connect to Server...**.

10. Input the name of your new Hyper-V Server and press **OK**. In my example, I already have two other Hyper-V Servers, so my console shows a total of three servers:

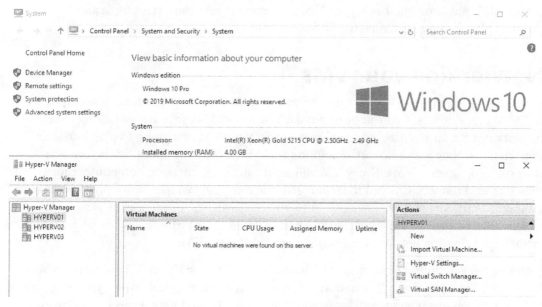

Figure 13.06 – The Hyper-V Manager running on Windows 10 connected to our Hyper-V servers

11. You can now see that we are running the Hyper-V Manager console on a Windows 10 computer but are remotely managing the Hyper-V service that is running on that new server. From here, we can build new VMs, manipulate VMs, and do anything we would otherwise normally do inside Hyper-V Manager as if it were running right on the Hyper-V server.

How it works...

Hyper-V Server is essentially a Server Core instance that is preconfigured with the Hyper-V role. The big differences between Hyper-V Server and a traditional Windows server running the Hyper-V role is the cost and the way that you interface with the server itself. By employing remote management tools from another server or directly from your workstation, you can ease the burden of learning a new interface as you start to explore whether or not Hyper-V Server is the right fit for you. For the remainder of our recipes, we will utilize Hyper-V, installed on a traditional Desktop Experience version of Windows Server 2019, but knowing that Hyper-V Server exists is very important to be able to properly plan for your virtualization infrastructure.

Networking your VMs

After getting your Hyper-V server up and running via whichever platform you choose to utilize, the next logical step will be to build a VM – right? So, why are we talking about networking? Because setting up the networks that your VMs are going to plug into is an important baseline and it is worth spending some time thinking about this before you start spinning up new VMs. Every VM will have a network interface, sometimes more than one, and those NICs need to be plugged into a switch; just like with a physical server. However, in the virtual world, we don't use physical switches, so we must tell the VMs which virtual switch to use. That means we must build these virtual switches before we can start making any network connections possible to our VMs.

Planning the right number of physical NICs to be inside your Hyper-V host server is also important. Each physical NIC can only be plugged into one physical switch, so if you plan to host VMs on this host server that need to be connected to different physical networks, you will need multiple NICs to support that scenario. Each NIC on the physical host server can be plugged into a different switch, flowing traffic to a different area of your network. We can then build virtual switches that correspond to these physical NICs so that our VMs can be plugged into any piece of the physical network that we choose.

As a simple example, think about a DirectAccess server that needs to be connected to both the internal corporate network and into a DMZ. You would need at least three NICs on that physical Hyper-V host server because one gets plugged into the internal network, one into the DMZ network, and also the host operating system on the Hyper-V Server itself prefers to have an NIC dedicated to its own communications.

Note that these do not always need to be actual NICs that are plugged into the server – if your networking utilizes **Virtual LANs (VLANs)**, then a single NIC paired with a cable might connect you to multiple networks if they've been configured correctly. You would need to coordinate with your networking team to do this.

Getting ready

We are using Windows Server 2019 running Hyper-V, which has been hosting the VMs throughout this book. This server has three NICs: one for management, one for the internal network, and one to the DMZ network.

How to do it...

Here are the steps you will need to take in order to create and manage the virtual networks on your Hyper-V Server:

1. Launch **Hyper-V Manager** from inside the **Tools** menu of Server Manager.

2. You will be presented with a list of VMs that are installed on this system. On the right-hand side of the screen, there is an **Actions** pane. Click on the link for **Virtual Switch Manager...**:

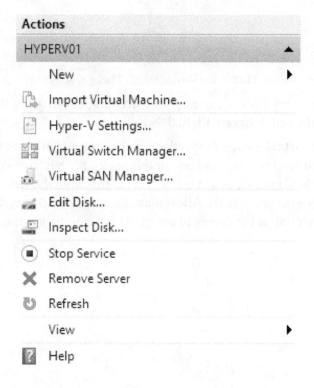

Figure 13.07 – The Actions pane in the Hyper-V Manager

3. Currently, I have no virtual switches defined, and the Virtual Switch Manager is asking me what kind of network I want to create: **External**, **Internal**, or **Private**. An *external* network links this switch to a physical network adapter. An *internal* network contains no network adapter, so hosts on that virtual network are isolated from the physical networks but can still be accessed by the Hyper-V host. A *private* network also contains no network adapter, but also isolates the VMs from the host. Only the individual VMs can talk to each other:

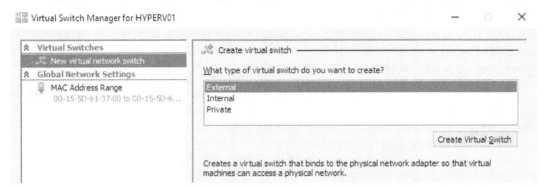

Figure 13.08 – The Virtual Switch Manager screen

4. I want to connect my VMs to my corporate network, so I'm going to choose **External** and then click **Create Virtual Switch**.

5. I now have the **Virtual Switch Properties** window shown. I'm going to name my network Packt (as this is my network for this book). My NIC that's connected to the Packt network is adapter #2, so I'm going to select that from the **External Network** list. I'm also going to uncheck the **Allow management operating system to share this network adapter** box as I am going to use my #1 NIC for management – not this one:

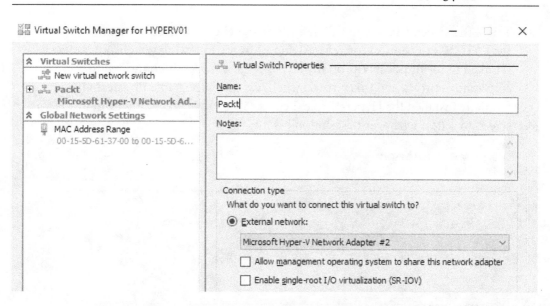

Figure 13.09 – The Virtual Switch Properties screen

6. After this is done, I'm going to click **New virtual network switch** on the left-hand side and repeat this process, this time for my DMZ network.

7. When you've done this process for all your networks, click **Apply**. The **Apply Networking Changes** screen is going to warn you to check that you have at least one network adapter that can be used for Windows management. I have left adapter #1 unconfigured, so I can safely click **Yes** on this screen:

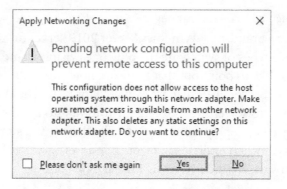

Figure 13.10 – The Apply Networking Changes screen

8.   This is the screen where you will define any switches that need to be available for the VM NICs to connect to them. As shown in the following screenshot, a switch is linked to my physical NIC on my Hyper-V host, which is connected to the corporate network, and this virtual switch was given the name **Physical NIC** when I initially installed the Hyper-V role. I can easily change that name from inside this screen to reflect whatever description I want:

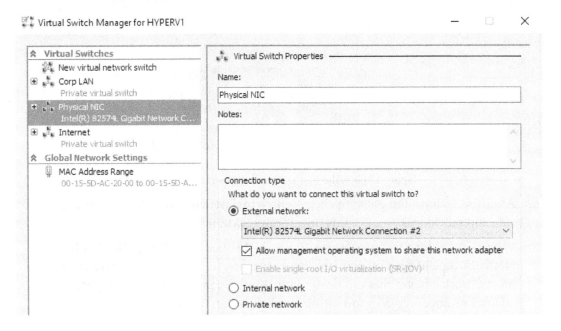

Figure 13.11 – Configuring the virtual switch properties

While I am using a brand-new Windows Server 2019 server for this recipe and the three standard types of switch are the only ones visible to me in the graphical interface, I would like to point out that there are now two additional types of Hyper-V switch in Server 2019 that are available for us to use. Why are they not visible in the previous screenshot? Because if you want to use the new switch types, you will need to deploy them via PowerShell. Here is a summary on the two additional types of switch available to us on Windows Server 2019 servers that are running the **Software Defined Networking (SDN)** stack:

- *External switch with Switch Embedded Teaming (SET)*: SET was introduced in Server 2016 and allows us to create NIC teams right in a Hyper-V switch, a feature never available in prior versions of Hyper-V. You can group between one to eight physical NICs into virtual network adapters, which will provide fault tolerance in the event of a single NIC failure. When using SET, it is important to know that all of the NIC adapters must be installed in the same physical Hyper-V host server, and that all the NICs must be identical. You can utilize the `New-VMSwitch` cmdlet combined with the `EnableEmbeddedTeaming` parameter in order to create a new SET virtual switch.

- *NAT*: Windows Server 2019 also includes a Hyper-V switch type called NAT. You would establish this type of virtual switch when you need VMs to have a shared internal network, and you would connect to the external interfaces by using a NAT'd address instead of binding them directly to an external NIC and its own physical IP addressing. NAT is also not available from the graphical console when setting up a new Hyper-V switch; you use the `New-VMSwitch` cmdlet combined with the `-SwitchType NAT` parameter to build one. This new type of switch is particularly useful for use with containers.

How it works...

From the Hyper-V Virtual Switch Manager, you can quickly create as many different virtual switches as you need to support the different kinds of VMs you are planning to create. In most testing environments, it makes the most sense to utilize internal or private switches to make sure that traffic remains segregated on the host. However, when working with production servers and VMs, you will be working mostly with external switches that are bound to physical network cards in your Hyper-V host server. This enables you to assign IP addresses to your VMs and gives them the ability to communicate with your physical network and with places like the internet. It is important to have at least some of your virtual switches configured before you start creating a lot of VMs because, as you will see in our next recipe, one of the options you can configure during the VM creation process is which virtual switch it should be connected to.

Building your first VM

If you haven't worked within Hyper-V Manager before, you are probably chomping at the bit to get your first VM created and running! There are several options that you must configure during the VM creation process. Let's take a few minutes and walk through it together so you understand what those options mean and what benefits they can bring to the table.

Getting ready

We are using a Windows Server 2019 with the Hyper-V role and management tools installed. You should have also configured your networks by following the previous recipe. You can complete this recipe from either the server itself or from a Windows 10 computer with RSAT installed.

How to do it...

Let's walk through the steps to create a brand-new VM and install an operating system on that VM:

1. Open **Hyper-V Manager** from the **Tools** menu of Server Manager, or directly from the **Administrative Tools** folder.

2. Right-click on the name of your Hyper-V Server near the top-left portion of the screen and choose **New | Virtual Machine…**:

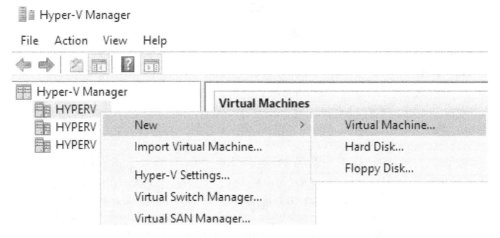

Figure 13.12 – The New | Virtual Machine… menu

3. This launches the **New Virtual Machine Wizard** window. Go ahead and click **Next** to go into the actual configuration.

4. Specify a **Name** for your new VM. This name does not have anything to do with the actual hostname of the server you are going to build; it is simply the descriptive name that will be visible inside Hyper-V Manager. Whatever name you give the VM here will also be reflected in the folder that is created to house the VM files on the hard drive of our Hyper-V host server. For example, I'm going to name mine Test Machine 01.

5. Still on the naming page, make sure to also choose a location within which Hyper-V should store this new VM. Each VM consists of some metadata-type files, as well as the virtual hard disk file, and they need to be stored somewhere. I find it is a good practice to specify something other than the default setting here. If you allow Hyper-V to bury these files inside `C:\ProgramData`, that is fine, but it can be confusing to track them down later. I typically have a dedicated drive for my VMs to reside on, and simply create a folder called `VMs`. For example, in the following screenshot, I am going to store its file inside `C:\VMs`. The wizard will then create a folder inside that location, giving me a final destination of `C:\VMs\Test Machine 01` for this VM:

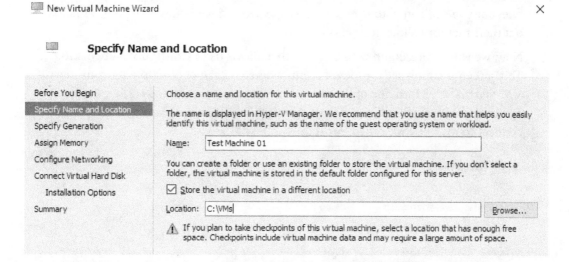

Figure 13.13 – The New Virtual Machine Wizard

6. Click **Next**. We will now be presented with an option to create our VM as a **Generation 1** or **Generation 2** VM. The only reason you would want to choose Generation 1 here is if you are going to run an old operating system that is not supported by Generation 2. Modern versions of Windows Server, Ubuntu, and most other operating systems will work just fine in Generation 2. However, operating systems such as Windows Server 2003 or other 32-bit operating systems will require Generation 1.

> **Tip**
>
> If you are running Windows Server 2003, 2008, or even 2012, the time to migrate off these operating systems has long passed. You could use the skills you're learning in this book to start that migration process!

7. Next, we have to assign an amount of RAM to the VM. It is quite common for administrators to specify a specific amount that correlates to a real amount of physical RAM, such as 1,024 MB, 2,048 MB, 4,096 MB, and so on – but there is no real reason to do this. You can type any number in here that you want. Take note of the checkbox listed on this screen as well. If you check **Use Dynamic Memory for this VM**, the VM will only consume what it actually needs in order to perform. As an example, a domain controller typically doesn't consume much RAM under normal use, even though it might have 4 GB allocated. While it seems good in theory to always have lower amounts being utilized than are assigned, when a VM needs to expand dynamic memory, you may find that you have allocated far more RAM than the server actually has. This is called oversubscribing and is normally fine, but you can run yourself into massive performance issues if all your VMs max out their memory allocations at once.

8. Now, we will be presented with a screen that allows us to **Configure Networking**. This screen is simply a drop-down menu where you can choose to plug your new VM's virtual NIC into one of the virtual switches that we created earlier. If you open that list, you should see each of them available to choose from. I am going to connect to my network called **Packt**:

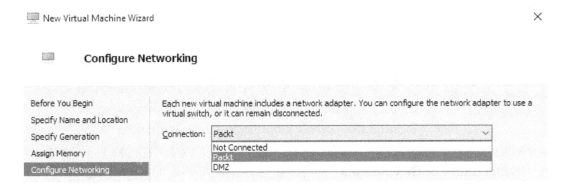

Figure 13.14 – Configuring the VM's networking

9. Now, we will find ourselves on one of the more important screens: the virtual hard disk specification. As you can see, the default location places the hard disk in a subfolder called `C:\VMs\Test Machine 01\Virtual Hard Disks\`. Most of the time, this is an appropriate location because it keeps all of the VM's files together. The most important aspect of this screen, assuming that you are asking the wizard to create a new virtual hard disk for you, is giving it a size. The default is set to 127 GB, which isn't very big compared to today's physical disk size standards. It is a fairly common misconception by new Hyper-V admins to assume that the higher you set this number, the larger the VHDX file is going to be; therefore, if you are only using 50 GB on a 300 GB drive, then you will be wasting 250 GB of your physical disk space. But this is not true! The disk will only consume as much space as is actually used. However, as with our RAM, if we over-subscribe the disk on the server, you may run into a situation where no individual VM's hard drive is full, but your server hard drive *is* full. You could always use Windows Insights (see *Chapter 9, System Insights*) to detect this ahead of time:

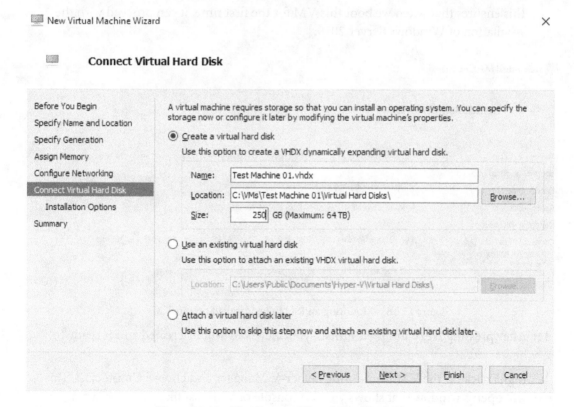

Figure 13.15 – The Connect Virtual Hard Disk screen

> **Tip**
>
> After finishing the VM creation wizard, if you seek out the actual VHDX file
> that was created, you will notice that, even though we specified 250 GB, the
> actual size of this file is only 4 MB! That will grow, of course, as we start to
> install an operating system on our new server, but it is important to know that
> the drive does not automatically consume 250 GB as soon as you create it. Note
> that it is possible to create a fixed-size virtual disk, which would consume the
> full amount of space right away, but the default option when using the wizard
> does not force that to happen.

10. After determining the size of your drive, you need to make a choice regarding how you plan to lay down an operating system on this drive. For my purposes, I will be installing Windows Server 2019 on this new VM, so here, I can point my new VM at the installation ISO file that I have placed on my Hyper-V Server's hard drive. What this does at the VM level is build a virtual DVD drive onto the VM, and then connect this ISO to it as if you were inserting an actual installation DVD. This ensures that when we boot this VM for the first time, it can proceed with the installation of Windows Server 2019:

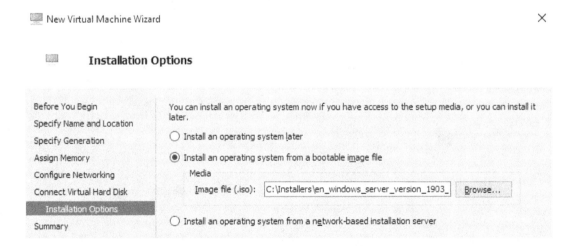

Figure 13.16 – Mounting an ISO to be installed on our VM

11. After pressing **Next** and then **Finish**, your new VM will be created and is ready to be started.

12. Right-click on the VM from inside Hyper-V Manager and choose **Connect…**. This will open a window that shows you the console of VM, just like you were sitting in front of a physical monitor plugged into a physical server.

13. From the top toolbar, click on the **Start** icon and watch as your new VM comes to life!

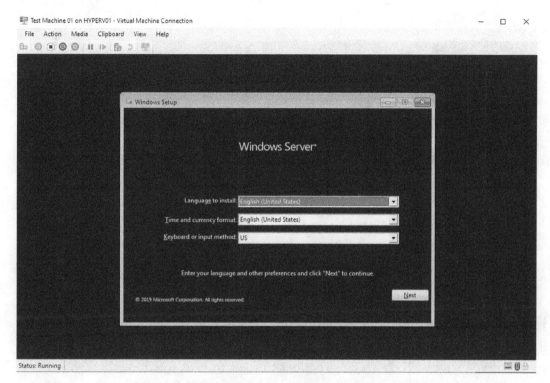

Figure 13.17 – The Virtual Machine console

14. It is also possible to spin up a new VM by using PowerShell! Take a look at the following command as an example. As you can see, the parameters specified in our command reflect the options we just walked through in the wizard.

15. I have included the -ComputerName argument here because I am running this from Windows 10 and I want to create the VM on the hyperv01 server:

```
New-VM -Name "Test Machine 02" -MemoryStartupBytes 1024Mb
-SwitchName "Packt" -NewVHDPath "C:\VMs\TestMachine02.vhdx"
-NewVHDSizeBytes 80GB -ComputerName hyperv01
```

This results in the following output:

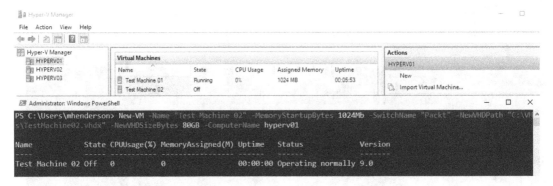

Figure 13.18 – Creating our new VM via PowerShell

16. After the command completes, your new VM is ready to go! As you can see, we did not specify which ISO to attach to the virtual DVD drive in order to boot to installation media. This, and other configuration such as the number of CPU cores, are easily accomplished from inside the VM's **Settings** window, which we will discuss further in the next recipe.

How it works...

Building VMs is one of the core tasks that you will need to accomplish regularly on your Hyper-V Servers. There are a few options to select from as you move through the configuration of your new VMs, so we wanted to take a look at them and explain some of the different options. Having the ability to create VMs from inside PowerShell can be an incredibly powerful tool – especially if you need to create multiple VMs at the same time. Think about the possibilities of automating this so that you simply launch a script and have a dozen new servers running within seconds!

Using the VM Settings page

Once you have some VMs up and running, most of the configuration that you do to these servers will be from within the operating system running inside the VM. In the case of a VM running Windows Server, you would typically interact with that operating system through either the Hyper-V Connect function, such as the one we have already looked at, or perhaps enable RDP on that new server so that you can utilize the Remote Desktop Connection client on your desktop computer to log into this new server.

However, whether you are running VMs or physical servers, there are some instances where you have to make changes or configurations to those servers that cannot be accomplished from inside the operating system; for example, if you need to exchange a hard drive, add more memory, or add a NIC and connect it to a new network. These are all valid scenarios for both physical servers and virtual servers. The difference is that you don't have a physical piece of hardware to walk up to when using VMs. So, how do you make these changes? This is where the Hyper-V Settings screens come into play.

Getting ready

We are working inside the Hyper-V Manager console of my Hyper-V host server, where I have a handful of VMs up and running. You can do this from Hyper-V Server itself, or from a Windows 10 computer using the RSAT tools remotely.

How to do it...

Follow these steps to open the core settings for one of our VMs (we will also discuss some of the more important options listed inside this interface):

1. Once inside Hyper-V Manager, right-click on a VM and look at the options available to us in this menu. We will be heading into the **Settings...** menu in just a second, but first note that right-clicking on a VM is a very quick and easy way to do things such as shutting down or powering up VMs.

   You can even use your *Ctrl* or *Shift* keys to select multiple VMs at the same time, then right-click and start up or shut down a whole batch at once:

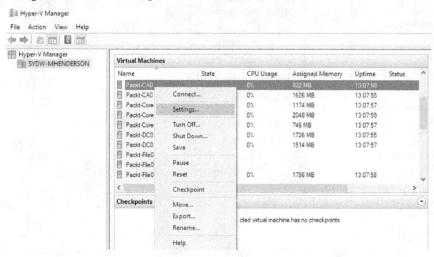

Figure 13.19 – Right-clicking a VM

2. Click on **Settings…**. Now, let's go through some of the options in this screen.

3. First, we land on the **Add Hardware** screen. This is the place where you can add components to be connected to your VM. The most common item that I have seen admins select here is **Network Adapter**. There are many reasons why a VM might need more than one NIC, and this screen is exactly the place to accomplish that. You'll notice that some of these options are grayed out; this is because some changes that you want to make to a VM require that the machine be shut down and turned off prior to making those changes. In fact, for Generation 1 VMs, you must shut them down before you can add new network cards. Fortunately, I created my VM as a Generation 2 VM, so we can add new NICs to this VM even while it is running! I will click on the **Add** button right now to test that. You will see a second **Network Adapter** show up in the list:

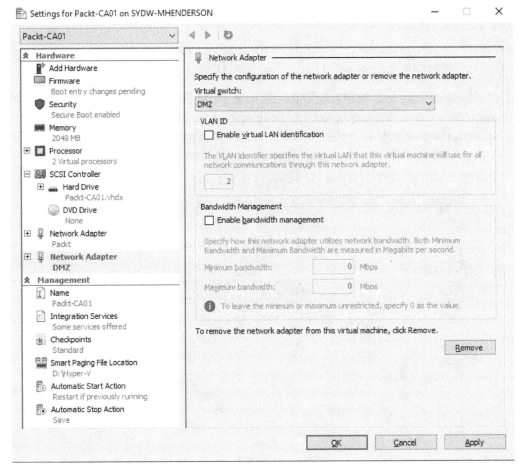

Figure 13.20 – Adding an extra NIC to our VM

4. This brings us right into another useful and commonly accessed part of the settings interface: the **Network Adapter** screen. Each virtual NIC connected to your VM is listed separately here, and by clicking on each one, you can choose which **Virtual switch** that NIC is plugged into by using the drop-down menu near the top of the screen. I have plugged one of my NICs into **Packt** and my other NIC into **DMZ**.

5. A little further down in the list, you can see the disk controller options. These settings will be different, depending on whether you are running a Generation 1 or Generation 2 VM. Gen1 VMs have IDE controllers listed in settings, but Gen2 VMs have SCSI controllers. In either case, this is the place where you can add additional hard drives to a VM, and this is also the place you visit in order to connect an ISO file to the virtual DVD drive. Over time, you will also notice here that Gen2 VMs are much easier to work with. You can add new hard drives to a system on-the-fly, while it is in the running state. With Gen1 VMs, you have no choice but to shut the system down in order to connect a new drive:

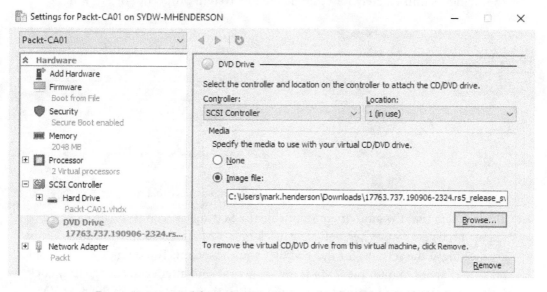

Figure 13.21 – Modifying the ISO connected to the virtual DVD drive

6. As you would expect, you can also adjust the number of **Processors** a VM has. Changing these settings requires that the VM is shut down, regardless of whether you are running either Gen1 or Gen2. Balancing the correct number of processors for a VM is an inexact science that depends on the host server's capabilities and the requirements of the VM. I would suggest having a minimum of two virtual processors for any Windows Server VM; otherwise, installing Windows Updates causes the entire VM to become unresponsive.

7. There are other options in here that are hopefully self-explanatory, but one last piece that I wanted to point out is the **Memory** category. While this isn't anything special or fancy (it's just the spot where you define the amount of RAM the system has), we are talking about it here because Windows Server 2019 can change the amount of RAM that's allocated to a VM on the fly. That means we can now change this setting and apply it while the VM is running. As shown in the following screenshot, I just moved my VM server from 2 GB to 4 GB of RAM and clicked the **Apply** button. The change is immediately reflected inside the **System** properties of my VM:

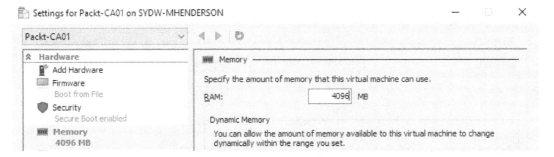

Figure 13.22 – Configuring the amount of RAM for the virtual machine

8. The last item that I want to mention inside the **Settings** screen is the drop-down menu at the very top. When you right-click on a VM and head into **Settings...**, you are looking at the settings for the VM that you clicked on. Too often, I watch people making changes to multiple VMs at the same time, but after each change they click **OK**, which closes the **Settings** window, and then they right-click on the next VM and go right back into that screen. Instead, if you simply click on this drop-down menu near the top, you can navigate between the **Settings** pages for any of the VMs running on your Hyper-V Server. If you have the need to adjust multiple VMs, this can save you some time and mouse clicks:

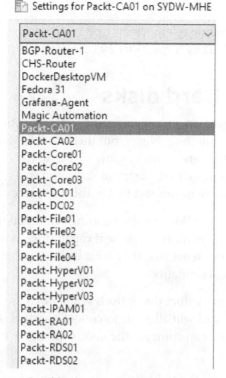

Figure 13.23 – Quickly changing VMs from the Settings screen

9. Of course, all these settings are also exposed from PowerShell. Rather than going through every single option in PowerShell here, the cmdlets you want to look at are Get-VM and Set-VM.

10. We will look at one more obscure option that you may find useful in the future. You can install Hyper-V inside Hyper-V itself, but we need to enable the feature for this first. To enable this feature (also called Nested Virtualization), we need to use Set-VMProcessor for each VM we want to enable it for:

```
Set-VMProcessor -VMName "HyperV01"
-ExposeVirtualizationExtensions:$true
```

How it works...

As you start administering your Hyper-V Servers, the settings screen for your VMs is likely the most common place that you will visit. Adjusting hardware and plugging in NICs are tasks that need to be done quickly and easily, so it is important that you become familiar with navigating this portion of Hyper-V Manager.

See also

The Hyper-V PowerShell module reference: `https://docs.microsoft.com/en-us/powershell/module/hyper-v/?view=win10-ps`

Editing virtual hard disks

When we run out of disk space on a physical hard drive, our options are limited. We can replace that drive with something bigger, but then need to worry about moving all the data over successfully. If we are running some sort of RAID or Storage Spaces, then perhaps we could add a new drive to the array of disks, but that is only possible if we have set up the correct infrastructure to support this in the first place.

Thankfully, when working with VMs that are running on virtual hard disks, we add a little bit more flexibility to our drive management capabilities. After all, these virtual hard disks are just files. So, it makes sense that they are a little bit easier to manipulate than a mechanical disk with physical limitations.

In this recipe, we are going to explore the options available to us inside the **Edit Virtual Hard Disk Wizard**. This wizard will allow us to choose a virtual hard disk, and then do one of three things with it: we can compact the disk, expand the disk, or we can convert the disk into a different type.

Getting ready

Our work will be accomplished from inside Hyper-V Manager running either on the Hyper-V server itself or remotely from a Windows 10 computer with RSAT. You do not even need a VM inside Hyper-V Manager, as the disk management functions can be performed against any VHD or VHDX file, regardless of whether they are assigned to a VM or not.

How to do it...

Here are the steps required in order to edit your virtual hard disks:

1. Inside **Hyper-V Manager**, look at the right-hand side of your screen. Inside the **Actions** pane, click on **Edit Disk...**.

2. Click **Next** and browse to the location of the VHD or VHDX file that you want to manipulate:

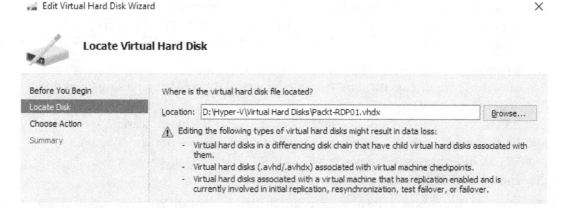

Figure 13.24 – The Edit Virtual Hard Disk Wizard

> **Important**
>
> As you can see in the warning presented on this screen, certain types of virtual disks could be negatively affected by editing. Make sure you are not trying to edit a disk in one of those three conditions.

3. Next, we need to choose the **Action** that we want to perform against this virtual disk:

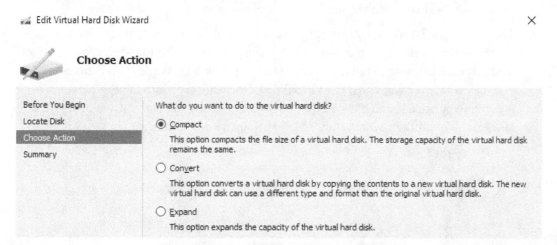

Figure 13.25 – Choosing an option for our virtual disk

4. **Compact** is pretty self-explanatory; it will reclaim free space within the disk and compact it so that it's as small as possible. There are no additional screens you need to run through on this; you simply click **Finish**.

5. **Expand** is also straightforward and is the one you will most likely use the most. Type in a new maximum size for your virtual hard disk, and the file will be expanded to accommodate the larger threshold.

6. **Convert** is the option we are going to choose in this recipe because it gives us the opportunity to discuss the different types of virtual disks. After choosing **Convert** and clicking **Next**, you will be asked whether you want this file to be a **VHD** or a **VHDX**. The only reason you would choose a VHD is when you are going to implement an operating system on the VM that doesn't support running on a VHDX disk, such as Windows Server 2008 R2 or earlier. Otherwise, you will always choose VHDX here.

7. Now, we choose what type of virtual hard disk to convert to. When you allow the VM creation wizard to set up a new disk for you, it always chooses **Dynamically expanding**. This is most often what is desired by admins, because the VHDX file will start off very small, and it will only grow as it needs to. This keeps physical disk space utilization at a minimum. However, just like with dynamically expanding RAM, it takes resources in order to adjust a hard drive size on the fly. So, if you are aiming for a VM that is super-efficient, it will be in your best interests to set that VHDX file to **Fixed size**. Doing so will cause the VHDX file to consume the entire amount of disk space as soon as the disk is created or converted, which takes a toll on the amount of physical space you have available. However, it is faster and more useful for workloads that require high disk performance.

8. The VHDX file I am currently editing was configured by the wizard, and so it is currently **Dynamically expanding**. I am going to change it to **Fixed size**, and on the next screen, I'm going to tell it where to store my new VHDX file. This is necessary because, whenever you convert a virtual disk from one type into another, Hyper-V is going to create a brand-new VHDX file and then copy the entire drive over to the new one. We can then switch that VM over to using our fixed disk:

Figure 13.26 – The output disk after conversion

9. To repeat these steps via PowerShell, you would use the `Convert-VHD` cmdlet:

```
Convert-VHD -Path 'D:\Hyper-V\Virtual Hard Disks\Packt-RDP01.
vhdx' -DestinationPath 'D:\Hyper-V\Virtual Hard Disks\Packt-
RDP01_fixed.vhdx' -VHDType Fixed
```

How it works...

Editing your virtual disks won't often be necessary if you plan carefully for disk sizes and types during the VM creation process. However, you may come into a Hyper-V environment that was established before your time with a company and are now being tasked with cleaning up and making that Hyper-V Server more efficient. Adjusting disk sizes and types can be part of that overall goal of improving the health of your Hyper-V servers.

Using checkpoints as rollback points

Backing up physical servers and restoring them to previous points in time has always been a little bit tricky in the Windows Server world. When something goes wrong with a server, in most cases, it is preferable to fix the issue rather than to simply rollback to a previous version. If you do want to make the decision to roll back an operating system on a physical server, you typically require downtime. This happens because, regardless of how you're going to restore your server, you must stop Windows from running in order to replace its files on the disk. No matter which technology you have used to take the backup, you must take the server down at least temporarily while you accomplish the restore.

Hyper-V changes everything. When working with our VMs, we can take and restore checkpoints whenever we feel the need. This capability was called Snapshots in previous versions of Hyper-V; the term checkpoints was introduced in Windows Server 2016. We can also create two kinds of checkpoints: standard or production. In this recipe, we will walk through the creation and restoration of both types of checkpoints to see what benefits each type holds.

Getting ready

All our backup and restoration work will be accomplished from within Hyper-V Manager running from on the Hyper-V server itself or remotely from a Windows 10 machine with RSAT installed.

How to do it...

We have Hyper-V Manager open and have several different VMs running here. Let's explore the capabilities of checkpoints together:

1. Decide on the VM that you want to checkpoint. I am going to use my DC01 server. Find that machine in the list, right-click on it, and choose **checkpoint**:

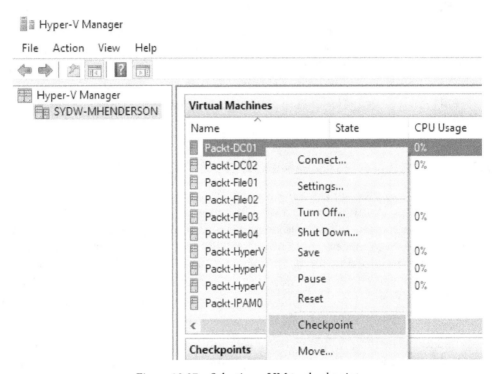

Figure 13.27 – Selecting a VM to checkpoint

2. A checkpoint is now automatically created. But what kind of checkpoint did we create? There was no warning to tell us. Well, I happen to know that we just created a **standard** checkpoint. I discovered this by running Get-VMcheckpoint -VMName "Packt-DC01" in PowerShell:

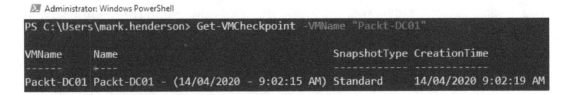

Figure 13.28 – Get-VMcheckpoint showing one snapshot

3. What if I wanted to create a **production** snapshot? And what is the difference between the two? Right-click on the VM and choose **Settings…**.

4. On the **Settings** screen, go to the **checkpoints** screen:

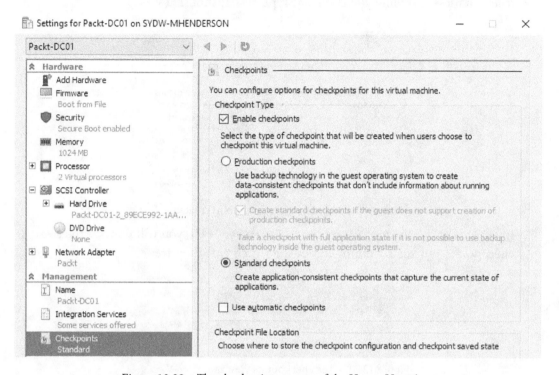

Figure 13.29 – The checkpoints screen of the Hyper-V settings

5. As you can see, this is the screen where you can choose whether you want to create **production checkpoints** or **standard checkpoints**. There is also a good description of each kind. In previous versions of Hyper-V, we could only do standard checkpoints, called Snapshots; we had no other options. standard checkpoints essentially just create a differencing disk from our VHDX file. When you restore a standard checkpoint, it replaces everything right back to the way it was running, including application-level content. production checkpoints, on the other hand, use backup software inside the guest (VM) operating system. This is similar to logging into that VM, opening up Windows Backup, and creating a backup file – except you get to do it in one click and it only takes a few seconds to accomplish. We will talk about the pros and cons of each type of checkpoint in the *How it works…* section at the end of this recipe.

6. Go ahead and change **checkpoint Type** to **production checkpoints**. Then, right-click on your VM and choose **checkpoint** again. This will create a second checkpoint for us, with this one being of the production type. This time, you will receive a message telling you about the type of snapshot that was created:

Figure 13.30 – production checkpoint created

7. If you look at the checkpoints option in the Hyper-V UI, you will now see the two checkpoints, but again nothing indicating which type they are:

Figure 13.31 – The checkpoints view in Hyper-V

8. We can run the PowerShell code again from earlier to see our checkpoint types (run `Get-VMcheckpoint -VMName "Packt-DC01"`).

9. Now, we want to try restoring these checkpoints, thus bringing our VM back to those particular moments in time. If you want to test the fact that these rollbacks are really working, you could go make some changes in the operating system at this time. Maybe create some files on the hard drive so that you can verify that, after accomplishing the rollback, those files have been removed.

10. To rollback a VM to a previous checkpoint, simply right-click on the standard checkpoint that you want to recover and choose **Apply…**:

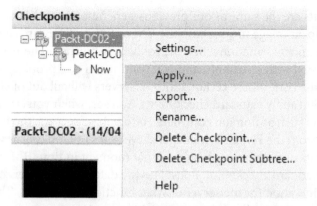

Figure 13.32 – Applying the VM snapshot

11. The VM is immediately reverted to the standard checkpoint that we created a few minutes ago. It even has all the applications still up and running on the screen, exactly as the machine was the moment I created that checkpoint image.

> **Important!**
> Make sure to read the *How it works...* section of this recipe carefully. While the standard checkpoint may seem like the better approach because of the immediate restores, it comes with some caveats that you need to be aware of!

12. Now that we have successfully restored a standard checkpoint, let's try restoring the production checkpoint that we created, which was the second one. The procedure is the same: right-click on the checkpoint and choose **Apply...**.

13. This time, however, you will notice that the VM turned itself **OFF** when we chose to restore the checkpoint.

14. Click the **Start** button to bring our VM back to life; it boots right up. But this is a fresh boot, not the immediate application-aware restore that happened with our first checkpoint rollback. The VM has now been restored back to that initial production checkpoint we took. As you have seen, the major difference with our procedure here was that we had to turn the server back on following the restore process.

How it works...

The capability in Windows Server 2019 Hyper-V to create checkpoints is a very powerful one. Previous versions of Windows Server called this feature Snapshots, and for the most part, checkpoints work in the same way. The major difference is that we now have two different types of images that we can create when we choose to checkpoint our VMs.

Standard checkpoints are the same as our previous-generation snapshots – they allow for immediate rollback to an image file, keeping the VM online and running, and remembering even application-specific information when the rollback is finished. There is one major problem that has existed with snapshots, and will continue to be a problem with standard checkpoints. This is the issue where certain kinds of servers will fall out of sync with other servers when you apply standard checkpoints. You see, when you create standard checkpoints of servers such as domain controllers or database servers, the file that is created is a simple snapshot from the Hyper-V Manager's level – it's not looking at what is going on inside the VM or its own operating system at that moment in time. This means that, when you restore a standard checkpoint, it just lays the data back down exactly how it was before, with no consideration for the server or what function it performs. This often results in **domain controllers (DCs)** falling out of sync with other DCs in your network and data being skewed after the restore. This causes big problems for companies.

Production checkpoints are the newer option. Even though they are slower to restore and your VM will shut itself down following the rollback of a production checkpoint, which results in downtime for this server, production checkpoints make use of backup and recovery tools such as Volume Shadow Copy Services inside the guest operating system. This means that those checkpoint files will be more comprehensible to the VM itself and will recover more smoothly in a production environment.

> **Important**
>
> production checkpoints are the only checkpoint type supported by DCs. However, unlike older versions of Hyper-V and Windows Server, checkpointing domain controllers is now a safe operation as long as you only ever restore to a production checkpoint.

Using nested resiliency

If you've done a quick search for the phrase nested resiliency, you may have already discovered that this is not a Hyper-V feature, but rather a Windows Storage Spaces feature. To be frank, this recipe could also have been in *Chapter 11, File Services and Data Control*. However, here we are in *Chapter 13, Working with Hyper-V*, so we are very clearly not in that chapter. So, why are we here? Well, Hyper-V has had a variety of methods of redundancy over the years. It's an issue every company that uses virtualization has to solve at one point or another – what do we do when we've outgrown a single Hyper-V Server? How do we protect against hardware failures that would take our company offline if we lost our server? The same questions can also be asked of a file server: what if we outgrow one file server? How do we protect our file server from hardware failures?

Windows Server 2019 introduces a brand-new feature called nested resiliency that can solve both of these problems. If you have exactly two Hyper-V Servers, we can use nested resiliency to create a high availability pair. Back in *Chapter 11*, *File Services and Data Control*, when we built out our Scale-Out File Server for use with Hyper-V, we needed a lot of additional hardware – storage servers that were separate from our Hyper-V Servers, high speed storage networks, and so on. With nested resiliency, both your Hyper-V Server and your storage servers are the same machines. So, if you have two Hyper-V Servers, you can solve both problems at once, without having to purchase any additional hardware.

Getting started

nested resiliency does require a fairly specific set of requirements to work:

- You must be using Windows Server 2019 Datacenter Edition from a regular release (for example, Windows Server v1903 will *not* work as this is a Semi-Annual Channel release).

- You must have installed Windows Admin Center on a Windows 10 PC. You can find instructions for this back in *Chapter 1*, *Learning the Interface.*

- You must have exactly two Hyper-V Servers.

- Your Hyper-V Servers must have at least four additional hard drives that are not configured in RAID. Your boot drives can be in RAID. It would be preferred if your storage was identical in both servers.

- You can use SSDs to speed up the storage, but we will be configuring this example using just regular hard drives.

- Nested Resiliency is a product of Windows *Storage Spaces Direct*. You will need to ensure your production hardware is compatible with Storage Spaces Direct as well.

With that all out of the way, I will be performing all this work from a Windows 10 computer that has both RSAT and the Windows Admin Center installed on it. I also have two fresh Windows Server 2019 Datacenter servers called `hyperv04` and `hyperv05` that I will be using. Make sure that any additional disks attached to your Hyper-V server are completely blank, as any data on them may be lost during this process.

How to do it...

From my Windows 10 PC with RSAT installed, do the following:

1. We're going to be doing a lot of work in PowerShell for this recipe, because that's the only place most of the configuration tools exist. So, open up a **PowerShell** prompt as an administrator.

2. First, we need to install the required Windows roles on our two Hyper-V servers. Run this command twice, changing the -ComputerName argument to suit each Hyper-V server:

```
Install-WindowsFeature -ComputerName Hyperv04 -Name "Hyper-
V", "Failover-Clustering", "Data-Center-Bridging", "RSAT-
Clustering-PowerShell", "Hyper-V-PowerShell", "FS-FileServer"
-Restart
```

3. Once both servers have restarted, you should configure your Hyper-V networking. Refer to the *Networking your VMs* recipe in this chapter for more details. Ensure that both of your Hyper-V hosts have a network that is configured as **External** and that the name of the network is identical on both hosts. In this example, I called mine Packt.

4. We now need to create a failover cluster. If you did the Scale-Out File Server in *Chapter 11, File Services and Data Control*, this may already be familiar to you. To validate that the servers are ready for clustering, run the following PowerShell command:

```
Test-Cluster -Node hyperv04,hyperv05 -Include "Storage Spaces
Direct", "Inventory", "Network", "System Configuration"
```

5. If that test passes, great. If you have any errors, you will need to fix them before continuing. If you receive any warnings, you should review these and decide whether you are willing to accept them. The Test-Cluster cmdlet should have provided you with the path to a HTML report you can look at to see more details:

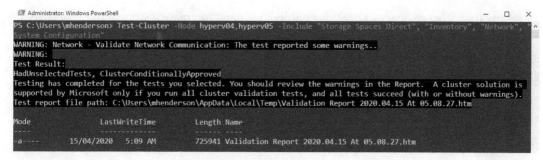

Figure 13.33 – Output of the Test-Cluster command

6. Once you are ready to create your cluster, we can do that with a simple PowerShell one-liner. I'm going to call my cluster `storage-direct`, but you are free to call yours whatever you choose:

```
New-Cluster -Name storage-direct -Node hyperv04,hyperv05
-NoStorage
```

7. Now that we've created our cluster, our commands, from this point forward, are going to reference the cluster name we just created, so it's important that you remember what it was. Otherwise, we would end up creating the storage cluster on our Windows 10 PC – not something we want to do!

8. The next thing we need to do is enable Storage Spaces Direct on our newly formed cluster. This can be done with the following command. I am assuming that all the disks in your server are completely blank and unformatted. If that is not the case, have a look at the *See also* section of this recipe for a link to some instructions on how to clear your disk configuration:

```
Enable-ClusterStorageSpacesDirect -CimSession storage-direct
```

This results in the following output:

```
Administrator: Windows PowerShell                                      –  □  ×
PS C:\Users\mhenderson> Enable-ClusterStorageSpacesDirect -CimSession storage-direct

Enable-ClusterStorageSpacesDirect -CimSession storage-direct
    0/1 completed
    [                                                                        ]
  storage-direct: Enabling cluster Storage Spaces Direct
      Waiting until physical disks are claimed
      [000000000000000                                                       ]

    15% Complete
```

Figure 13.34 – Enabling Cluster Storage Spaces Direct

9. Now that Storage Spaces Direct is enabled, we need to create a storage tier. This storage tier is where we tell Storage Spaces to create nested resiliency. There are two types of resiliency we can use: two-way mirror or mirror-accelerated parity. They sound confusing, and they can be. We're going to keep this recipe simple and choose two-way mirror, but you can read more about exactly what the differences are by looking at the links in the *See also* section of this recipe. What you need to know about this is that we're going to have four copies of all our VMs – two copies on each server in our cluster:

```
New-StorageTier -StoragePoolFriendlyName S2D* -FriendlyName
NestedMirror -ResiliencySettingName Mirror -MediaType HDD
-NumberOfDataCopies 4 -CimSession storage-direct
```

10. The command we just ran looks confusing, so let's walk through it a bit:
    a. `New-StorageTier` is the cmdlet that creates a Storage Spaces storage tier, while `-StoragePoolFriendlyName` refers to the storage pool name we want to use. When we ran `Enable-ClusterStorageSpacesDirect` earlier, it created at least one storage pool that begins with the name `S2D`. Depending on the type of storage in your server, you may have more than one storage pool. This tells the new storage tier that we want to use the storage pools whose name begins with `S2D`.

    b. `-FriendlyName` is just a name that we are going to refer to our storage tier as.

    c. `-ResiliencySettingName` allows us to specify what kind of resiliency we want to use. We're using `Mirror`.

    d. `-MediaType` allows us to specify what kind of disks we want to use. If your server was equipped with SSDs, you could also specify `SSD` instead of `HDD` here.

    e. Regarding `-NumberOfDataCopies`, we want four total copies of our data (two on each server), so this is the part that tells the storage tier that we want nested resiliency.

    f. `-CimSession` is the name of our failover cluster and it tells the `New-StorageTier` cmdlet where to create the new tier:

Figure 13.35 – The New-StorageTier cmdlet

11. Now that we have our storage tier configured for nested resiliency, we need to create a volume on that tier that we can use for storing our VMs. We do this with the following command:

```
New-Volume -StoragePoolFriendlyName S2D* -FriendlyName HyperV
-StorageTierFriendlyNames NestedMirror -StorageTierSizes 100GB
-CimSession storage-direct
```

Let's dissect that command:

a. New-Volume: This is the cmdlet that is going to create our usable volume.

b. -StoragePoolFriendlyName: This should be the same as what we used in the previous command.

c. -FriendlyName: Just a name we're going to use for our volume. You should make this something that makes sense as we'll be using it later.

d. -StorageTierFriendlyNames: The storage tier friendly name that we created in the previous command.

e. -StorageTierSizes: The size of the virtual disk we want to create.

f. -CimSession: The name of our failover cluster:

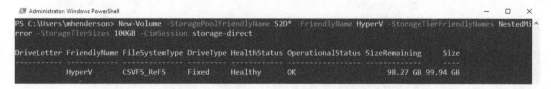

Figure 13.36 – Creating a nested volume with New-Volume

12. OK – so far, we have configured our Hyper-V networking, combined our servers into a failover cluster, deployed Storage Spaces Direct, enabled nested resiliency and created a nested volume – all from PowerShell! Now, it's time for us to switch over to **Windows Admin Center**. If you do not have it installed yet, refer to the instructions in *Chapter 1*, *Learning the Interface*, for this. Once it's installed, open the **Windows Admin Center**.

13. Once Windows Admin Center has loaded, we need to tell it that we want to manage our cluster. On the home page, click the **Add** link:

Figure 13.37 – The Windows Admin Center

14. From the type of resource, click **Add** under **Windows Server Cluster**.

15. Enter the cluster name from the previous steps. In our example, this is `storage-direct`. Leave the rest of the options as their defaults and click **Add**:

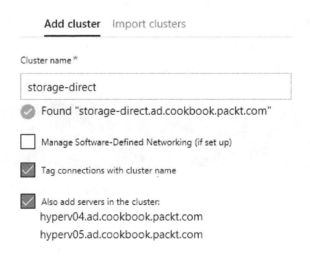

Figure 13.38 – Adding our cluster to Windows Admin Center

16. Once your cluster has been added to Windows Admin Center, click on its name in the connections list to browse to it.

17. You should now be on the Windows Admin Center Cluster Dashboard, which contains a lot of various information. We're not going to focus too much on most of it right now. Click on the **Volumes** icon under **Storage** on the left-hand side.

18. Once on the **Volumes** screen, click the **Inventory** tab at the top of the page.

19. We should now see at least two volumes, and one of them should be the HyperV volume we just created. Look at the **Resiliency** and **File System** columns in particular:

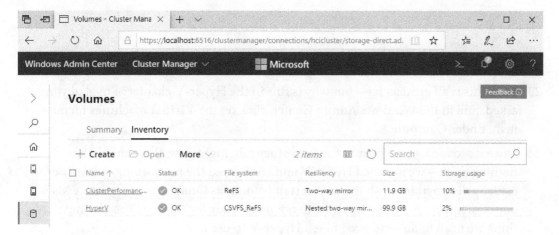

Figure 13.39 – Volume Inventory in the Windows Admin Center

20. Resiliency for our HyperV volume is listed as **Nested two-way mirror**. Perfect! That's exactly what we needed. We now know we have four copies of our data at any given moment and can survive all but the most serious of server hardware disasters.

21. **File System** may not be one you're familiar with. If you've worked with Windows before, you no doubt recognize NTFS, and if you've been around for a while you might remember the FAT filesystems. But what is CSVFS_ReFS? Well, CSV stands for *Cluster Shared Volume* and is the technology Windows failover cluster uses to make a single volume available to multiple servers. FS just stands for *File System*. ReFS stands for *Resilient File System* and was introduced in Windows Server 2012. It's not seen around much but expect to see it more and more often as you start to use these advanced filesystems. Thus, the full name for this filesystem is *Cluster Shared Volumes File System Resilient File System*.

22. Click on the **HyperV** volume so that we can look at its details. On the volume details page, we should see a property for **Path**. Make a note of this as we're going to need it later. We can also see that our 100 GB disk consumed 400 GB of disk space:

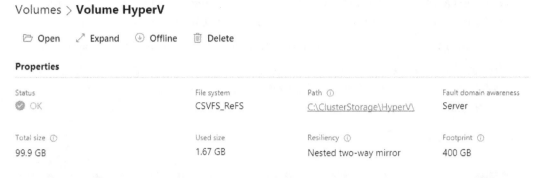

Figure 13.40 – Volume properties

23. Well, this is all great so far – but why is this in the Hyper-V chapter? I'm glad you asked. Still in the Windows Admin Center, click on the **Virtual machines** menu item, under **Compute**.

24. Once it's loaded, move over to the **Inventory** tab. Right now, there should be nothing there – we installed Hyper-V and configured the networking, but we never actually did anything with it. But it certainly looks as though we can create VMs in our cluster from here. However, we're not *quite* ready for that yet. There's one more thing we need to do – we need to tell Hyper-V to use our shared storage.

25. Click the **Settings** button at the bottom-left corner of the page. Once the **Settings** page has loaded, click the **General** option under **Hyper-V Host Settings**.

26. Any setting we change here is going to be applied to all the servers in our cluster, which is exactly what we want. **Virtual Hard Disks Path** is still set to the default location. We need to change this. Click **Browse**.

27. Using the file browser, navigate to the path we recorded in the volume properties. Mine is C:\ClusterStorage\HyperV\.

28. Create a new folder called Virtual Hard Disks. Once created, select that folder and click **OK**.

29. Repeat this process for **Virtual Machines Path**, but instead of creating a `Virtual Hard Disks` folder, create a `Virtual Machines` folder.

30. You should now have both your **Virtual Hard Disks** and **Virtual Machine** paths pointing to the nested resiliency volume. Click **Save**:

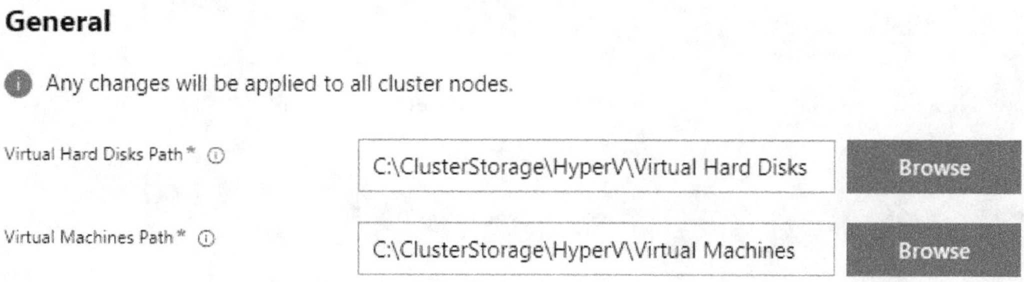

General

ⓘ Any changes will be applied to all cluster nodes.

Virtual Hard Disks Path * ⓘ

| C:\ClusterStorage\HyperV\Virtual Hard Disks | | Browse |

Virtual Machines Path * ⓘ

| C:\ClusterStorage\HyperV\Virtual Machines | | Browse |

Figure 13.41 – Configuring VM storage to use the nested volume

31. Once saved, return to the **Compute | Virtual Machines | Inventory** screen of Windows Admin Center.

32. Let's create our VM. Click the **New** button.

33. Fill in the **New VM** screen with the details for your VM. Don't worry too much about which host you're creating it on – we're going to experiment with this later. Also, don't forget to click the **Add** button under **Storage** to add a virtual disk to your VM.

34. Once you're ready, click the **Create** button.

35. Your VM is now being created. Notice that we haven't used the traditional Hyper-V management tool we've been using in this chapter so far at all. That's because *creating* VMs in a failover cluster *must* be done at the cluster level – not at each individual host.

> **Tip**
> Managing VMs in a clustered environment can be done in many ways. I suggest using the Windows Admin Center for all your VM management, but you can also use PowerShell. The Hyper-V console can also be used for changing basic settings or adjusting settings on the Hyper-V hosts themselves

36. Once your VM has been created, it will show up in the inventory list. Tick the checkbox next to your VM and click **Start**:

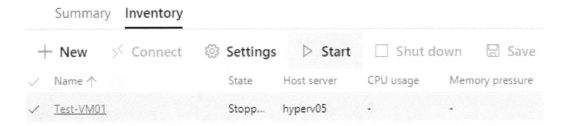

Figure 13.42 – Starting the VM

37. Note that the host server is hyperv05. That indicates that hyperv05's CPU and RAM is being used to run this VM. If you wish, you can use your Hyper-V console to connect to hyperv05 and open the console of your VM. It works as normal!

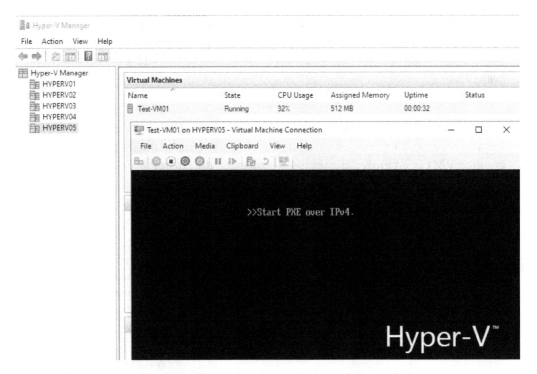

Figure 13.43 – The clustered VM shows up in the normal Hyper-V Manager now

38. But what happens if we restart `hyperv05`? Let's find out. Back in PowerShell, run `Restart-Computer -ComputerName hyperv05` (don't forget `-ComputerName`; otherwise, you will restart your own computer).

> **Important**
>
> If both of your servers are running at full capacity, this might end poorly. This configuration only works if neither your servers run at more than 50% capacity – that way, the other server will always have enough capacity to take on the workload of the first if needed. You can also pre-emptively move VMs between hosts using the **Move** option in the Windows Admin Center.

39. Once the server has started restarting, click the refresh button back in Windows Admin Center. What is the host server for your VM now? If everything has worked correctly, your VM should now be running on `hyperv04`:

Virtual machines

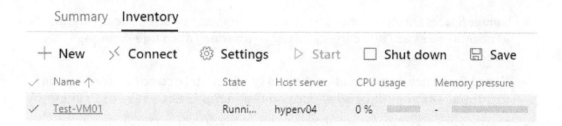

Figure 13.44 – The VM now running on hyperv04

How it works...

What we've done here is a very quick and simple lab of Nested Storage in Storage Spaces Direct and used it to host highly available Hyper-V VMs. It's an excellent proof of concept for an exciting new technology that's been introduced with Windows Server 2019.

However, it is not without its pitfalls. The situation we've created here *may* not be suitable for your production environment. It requires Windows Server Datacenter Edition and Storage Spaces Direct requires 10 gigabit networking and a reasonable amount of fast storage. It really needs SSDs to be used to its full potential. And as you may have noticed, it was a fair amount of work to get up and running, even in this experimental lab.

However, if you have the correct environment, Storage Spaces Direct and Nested Resiliency is an excellent, low cost, high performance, shared-nothing approach to VM high availability.

See also

There is a lot of additional reading you should undertake before implementing Storage Spaces Direct and Nested Resiliency in production:

- Storage Spaces Direct overview: `https://docs.microsoft.com/en-us/windows-server/storage/storage-spaces/storage-spaces-direct-overview`

- Nested Resiliency documentation: `https://docs.microsoft.com/en-us/windows-server/storage/storage-spaces/nested-resiliency`

- Clearing drive configuration before enabling Storage Spaces Direct: `https://docs.microsoft.com/en-us/windows-server/storage/storage-spaces/deploy-storage-spaces-direct`

- ReFS: `https://docs.microsoft.com/en-us/windows-server/storage/refs/refs-overview`

14
Containers and Docker

I'm sure by now you've heard of **virtual machines**. If you're reading this book in order, we've just finished a whole chapter on them. However, some of you might have also heard about this technology called **containers** or a tool called **Docker** and are wondering how they are different to virtual machines. What purpose do they serve? And aren't they a Linux thing, not a Windows thing?

Virtual machines and containers are conceptually related. Virtual machines take what used to be a physical thing (an actual server, installed on a rack) and turn it into isolated software (for example, Hyper-V). Containers do the same thing for applications – they take something that used to be installed on an operating system and isolate it in its own environment.

Think of the typical process you might go through when your business buys a new piece of software. Typically, you receive an installable EXE file. You run the installer and it then expands into being hundreds or thousands of files installed in your operating system with dozens of registry keys. Sometimes, once a piece of software is installed, it can never be fully removed. Upgrading the software involves scheduling a maintenance window, taking the software offline, running an upgrade program, waiting for the upgrade to run, and sometimes restarting your server.

Now, think about the process of when someone gives you a virtual machine that they want to be deployed. You take the virtual machine image and you deploy it on your virtualization host. Done. It's fully self-contained and it doesn't encroach on any other part of the host. When you're done with it, you delete the virtual machine. If someone sends you a new version of the virtual machine, you deploy it and then you delete the old one.

The virtual machine method is much neater, isn't it? Typically, this is a single file (a virtual hard drive), completely self-contained. But there's an overhead – you're shipping an entire operating system. That operating system needs patching, licensing, a security review, and maintenance. You might have 30 or 40 copies of the same operating system running inside Hyper-V, each virtual machine running a single application. It sure is neat and tidy, but it's also wasteful.

Containers, at their essence, are virtualized applications. A container is an entirely self-contained image (like a virtual machine is), but it just contains the bare minimum of what's required to run the application. It generally does not contain a complete operating system; it just contains the minimum operating system files and application files needed to make the application work. When an application upgrade is needed, you just stop the old container and start the new container.

So, what is Docker and how does it fit into this picture? Containerization is a concept, just like virtualization is. Docker is the container technology that Windows implements, in the same way that Hyper-V is the virtualization technology that it implements. Docker is an open source containerization project and, at the time of writing, it's the most common containerization in the wild. And since you're on Windows, Docker is the only containerization technology Windows supports. The Linux world does have more choice, but for now, you can consider the words container and Docker interchangeable.

For the first time in this book, we're also going to look at some Microsoft Azure functionality. This introduction is already long enough, so we'll go into more detail about that when we get to that recipe.

Well, that's a large preamble. Let's look at what recipes we're going to cover in this chapter:

- Configuring your server to run container images
- Running your first container image
- Running commands inside a container
- Creating and customizing your own container image
- Upgrading a container
- Productionizing a running container
- Changing the container networking
- Deploying a container to Azure

Configuring your server to run container images

As is the way with almost everything in this book so far, we need to install the Docker feature on Windows before we can start. However, unlike all the previous things we've done in this book, the Docker installation requires additional steps, rather than just the typical `Install-WindowsFeature` that we've been doing so far.

Getting ready

We have a Windows Server 2019 server joined to the domain. Mine will be called `container01`. The server must have internet access.

How to do it...

From your Windows Server 2019 server, do the following:

1. Open **PowerShell** as an administrator,

2. Run the `Install-Module DockerMsftProvider` command. This is going to instruct PowerShell to install the `DockerMsftProvider` module, which is located in the PowerShell Gallery. The PowerShell Gallery is a Microsoft store that contains PowerShell modules that have been submitted by the community.

3. You will be prompted to install something called NuGet. NuGet is the tool PowerShell uses to install modules from the internet – accept NuGet by typing Y and pressing *Enter*.

4. You will now be prompted to install a module from an untrusted repository. This is because by default PowerShell does not trust any repositories, even its own official one. Type Y and press *Enter*:

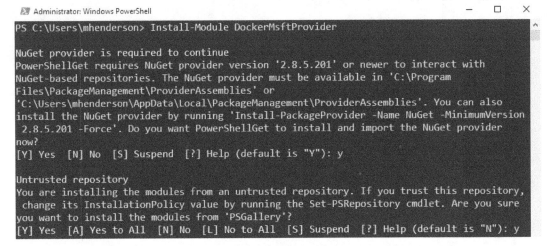

Figure 14.1 – Installing DockerMsftProvider from the PowerShell Gallery

5. After a few moments, you should be back at the PowerShell prompt. We now need to install Docker. We can do this with `Install-Package -Name docker -ProviderName DockerMsftProvider`. You will need to accept the security warnings when prompted.

6. We now need to install the Docker feature for containers. This one we do with the `Install-WindowsFeature` cmdlet, which we've seen a lot in this book; that is, `Install-WindowsFeature Containers -Restart`:

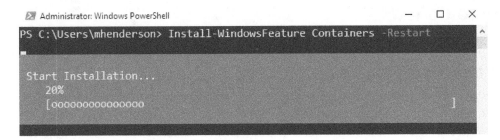

Figure 14.2 – Installing the Windows containers feature

7. We've now installed the containers feature and its management tools. This has also installed Docker for us.

8. Once the server has restarted, we need to do a quick test to make sure it works. Run `docker run hello-world:nanoserver`. Your server will then connect to a service called Docker Hub over the internet, which contains thousands of Docker images. Download the `hello-world` container and then run it. If your test is successful, it should look like this:

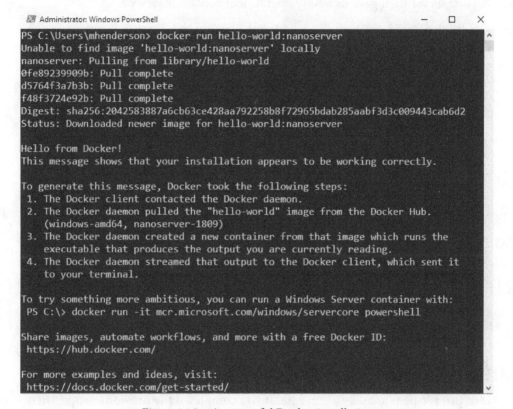

Figure 14.3 – A successful Docker installation

> **Tip**
>
> You can also use containers on supported versions of Windows 10. The installation process is different to what's in this book, but if you get Docker Desktop installed on your Windows 10 machine, everything else in this chapter can be done on your local Windows computer as well!

How it works...

We've just done a few things that we haven't seen before, so let's look at them in a bit more detail.

First, we installed something from the PowerShell Gallery. The PowerShell Gallery is a repository of thousands of PowerShell modules that you can install, and there's a lot of useful things in there. We installed the Docker provider, which we then used to install Docker itself. However, Docker can't do anything on its own – it is just a tool to interface with the container service in Windows. Installing the Windows containers feature and rebooting our server then gave us a fully operational container service.

Finally, we implemented `docker run`. Using this command, Docker connected to Docker Hub (which is its own repository of Docker images) and downloaded everything it needed to run the `hello-world` container. The `hello-world` container then executed and explained itself in a bit more detail to get the container running.

> **Important Note**
> You'll see the terms Docker image and Docker container used in this chapter quite a lot. An image is a template from which the container is created. An image can be copied, used by another image, and uploaded to a container registry. A container is what is created when you use an image.

See also

- `DockerMsftProvider` in the PowerShell Gallery: `https://www.powershellgallery.com/packages/DockerMsftProvider/1.0.0.8`

- The `hello-world` image on Docker Hub: `https://hub.docker.com/_/hello-world`

Running your first container

The title of this recipe is actually a small lie. If you completed the previous recipe, then you have actually already run your first container! Except that container didn't really do anything useful – it just printed out some information. So, instead of just doing something that's not particularly useful, let's take a look at how we can actually do something useful with containers.

Getting started

This recipe picks up right where our previous one left off. We have a Windows Server 2019 server that has containers and Docker installed. We will be doing this recipe from that server.

How to do it...

On our Windows Server 2019 machine, do the following:

1. If you haven't already, on your Windows server, load **PowerShell** as an Administrator.

2. The following command will make Docker download and run our first useful container. This is going to just be a vanilla IIS container that will serve up a default IIS installation for us. It may take a while – at the time of writing, the image is about a 2.5 GB download. The good news is that large parts of containers are reusable, so the next time we need to do something that uses the IIS container, you may not have to pull the whole image down again:

```
docker run -d -p 8000:80 --name my-test-site mcr.
microsoft.com/windows/servercore/iis
```

This results in the following output:

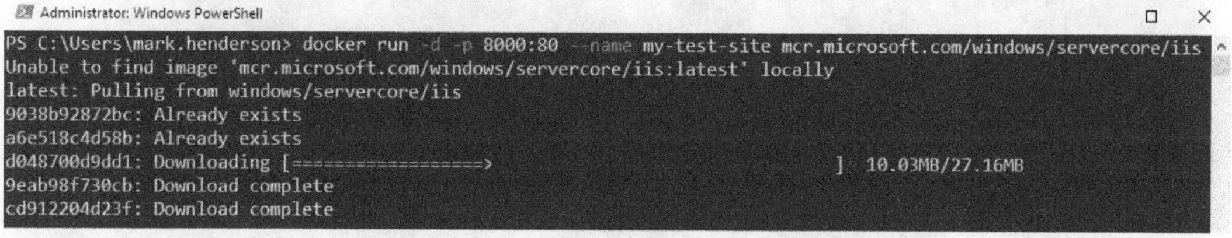

Figure 14.4 – Pulling the IIS image down. The exact text you will see on your screen may differ from this screenshot slightly

3. Once the image has been downloaded, Docker will run it. While it's downloading, let's break down the command we just ran:

   a. `docker`: This is the executable name we're running.

   b. `run`: This instructs docker to run a container.

   c. `-d`: Stands for detached. This tells Docker that this container we're running should run in the background. Otherwise, we wouldn't get our PowerShell prompt back, and the container would stop running when we closed PowerShell.

   d. `-p 8000:80`: This publishes port `80` in the container to port `8000` on our local machine.

   e. `--name my-test-site`: This gives the container a name. All running containers are assigned a unique ID, but by giving the container a name, we don't have to look the ID up later.

f. `mcr.microsoft.com/windows/servercore/iis`: This is the path to the image that we want to use. `mcr.microsoft.com` is Microsoft Container Registry.

4. You should now be back at the PowerShell prompt, after a long ID has been printed out on the screen. It also looks like nothing has happened – but it has. The container has started running in the background. Open a web browser and browse to your server on port `8000`; for example, `http://localhost:8000`, or from another computer, `http://container01:8000`:

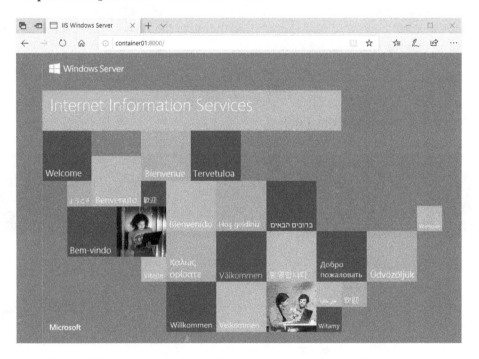

Figure 14.5 – Browsing to our container server to see the running container

5. You should see the default blank IIS installation page. This page is being served by IIS coming out of that container. Notice that we didn't install any roles or modify anything on our Windows server itself – apart from running that Docker command.

6. Let's validate that this is, in fact, coming from our container. On your Windows Server machine, run `docker ps`. In the Unix and Linux world, `ps` is the command for showing which processes are currently running (a bit like Windows Task Manager). Because Docker originated in the Linux world, a lot of its commands and output follow the Linux naming scheme.

7. You should see a bunch of text on your console that probably doesn't make a huge amount of sense. This is the list of Docker containers that are currently running, which image they are running, and a few other pieces of information. The important things we have here is the container ID (the first item in the line, 12 characters long) and the last item on the line, which in our case is my-test-site:

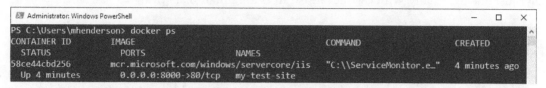

Figure 14.6 – The output of Docker ps

8. Let's stop this image. You can do this in one of two ways: with docker stop my-test-site, using the name we gave our image earlier, or with docker stop [container id] (in my example, docker stop 58ce44cbd256). This will tell Docker to stop running that container.

9. Refresh your web browser that had the default IIS page open. It should now not respond.

How it works...

We ran docker run and saw how Docker did everything for us – downloading the image and starting it for us. We took a brief look at what the command we actually ran did.

You may be wondering why that container was so large, when IIS itself is fairly small. That's because we downloaded a Windows Server Core image as part of that container. This is one of the downsides of running containers on Windows – containers are larger than on Linux. Some Linux containers are barely bigger than the programs themselves – only a few megabytes. To this end, some containers use Windows Nano to make our Windows containers a much more bearable size. Windows Nano is a *very* cut-down version of Windows that is heavily tailored to running applications that have been released with .NET Core. However, it's not all bad news – once you have downloaded the base Windows Server Core container, every other container that also relies on it will not have to download it again. This is because Docker uses a clever way of layering the container images, which means large parts of them can be reused later.

Throughout these recipes, you will also see more Docker commands that use shorthand that you may not recognize, such as ps and rm. Again, this is because of Docker's roots in the Linux world. Linux takes a lot of its commands from Unix, and many of those Unix commands are older than I am. For example, the Unix ps command first showed up in 1973, so there's a lot of history and inertia behind the command scheme that Docker uses – it's just one that many Windows administrators are unfamiliar with.

Running commands inside a container

Containers are a different kind of abstraction that take some getting used to. They're not really designed to be interacted with in the same way you would interact with a virtual machine. Containers are not domain-joined (although your container host might be), and they lack a lot of the bells and whistles we take for granted when using a normal operating system. But you *can* still run commands inside a container if you need to – which is particularly useful for troubleshooting.

Getting started

You need a Windows Server 2019 machine that has a container running. The previous recipe, *Running your first container*, can help you achieve that.

How to do it...

On your Windows Server machine, do the following:

1. Open **PowerShell** as an Administrator if you haven't already.

2. Let's see which containers are currently running. Run docker ps to do so.

3. Hopefully, you have at least one container that is in the running status. Take a note of either its container ID or its name – we'll be using them in the next few commands. I will be using name, which for me is my-test-site.

4. Let's run a basic command inside our container. We can do this by using the docker exec command. The format for the command is docker exec [container] [command]. [container] can be either the container name (my-test-site) or the container ID (in my case, f217fde45943). The container ID is going to change every single time the container is restarted, but the container name can be consistent across restarts. So, let's see what our container thinks its hostname is. Let's run docker exec my-test-site hostname:

Administrator: Windows PowerShell
PS C:\Users\mark.henderson> docker exec my-test-site hostname
f217fde45943

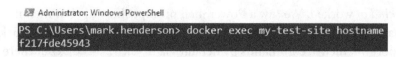

Figure 14.7 – Docker exec showing the container hostname

5. The container believes that its hostname is `f217fde45943`. It's no coincidence that it thinks its hostname is the same as the container ID. Let's try something a little bit more complicated; that is, `docker exec my-test-site powershell` `` `$ENV:ComputerName``. Note the backtick before the `$` sign. If we missed that part, our *local* PowerShell would think that command was for *it*. By putting the backtick in there, PowerShell *escaped* the `$` character and passed it through to docker:

Administrator: Windows PowerShell
PS C:\Users\mark.henderson> docker exec my-test-site powershell `$ENV:ComputerName
F217FDE45943

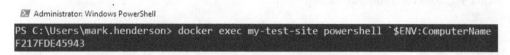

Figure 14.8 – Docker exec running PowerShell

6. The good news is that PowerShell also confirms that the container's hostname is the container ID. What exactly did we do with that command, though? Well, we told the container to start PowerShell and then print out `$ENV:ComputerName`, which is the PowerShell version of printing an environment variable that contains the computer name.

7. You can use `docker exec` to run all sorts of one-off commands like this. But what if you wanted to do something more complicated, such as get an actual prompt inside the container? Let's try something – we know that we have PowerShell inside our container, as we just used it. So, what happens if we run `docker exec my-test-site powershell`?

Administrator: Windows PowerShell
PS C:\Users\mark.henderson> docker exec my-test-site powershell
Windows PowerShell
Copyright (C) Microsoft Corporation. All rights reserved.
Try the new cross-platform PowerShell https://aka.ms/pscore6
PS C:\>
PS C:\Users\mark.henderson>

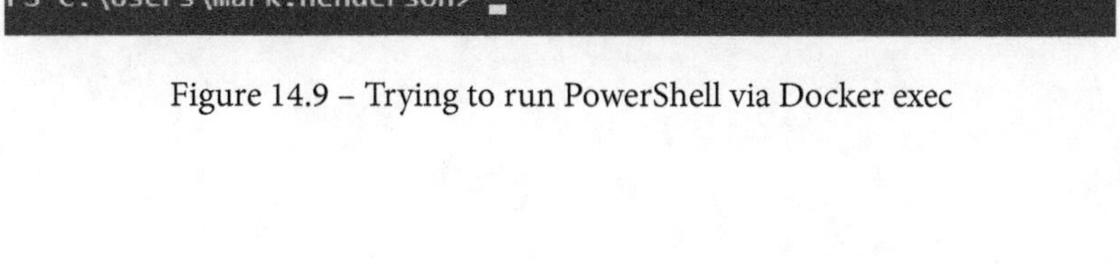

Figure 14.9 – Trying to run PowerShell via Docker exec

8. Well, it *kind of* worked. We saw a PowerShell prompt show up, but then it immediately just dumped us back at our local prompt. This is because Docker does not support *interactive* commands by default via `docker exec`. But there is a flag we can add to our command: `-i` allows interactive programs to be run. There is also `-t`, which attaches a console to the command (`-t` is short for TTY, which is the Linux term for a console). Let's try using `docker exec -it my-test-site powershell`.

9. And voila! We have a PowerShell prompt inside our container. You can do anything you would normally do with PowerShell – run a script, modify files, import modules, and so on. When you're done with PowerShell, run `exit` or press *Ctrl + C* to return to your local prompt.

> **Tip**
> Not all containers you will find on Docker Hub contain PowerShell exactly like we've seen here. If the container is using PowerShell 6 or 7, then the command is `pwsh`, not `powershell`. A lot of containers just do not ship with PowerShell at all – in that case, you can still use `cmd`. If it's a non-Windows container, you might want to also check for `sh` or `bash`, the two most common Linux shells.

How it works...

`docker exec` can be used to run single commands inside your containers. This is very useful when you just need to get a single piece of information out of the container (for example, print the contents of a log file). Although not a default option, you can also start an interactive prompt inside the container for more complicated tasks, such as uploading a debug log to a web server or triggering a change inside the container itself.

It is tempting to do configuration changes via an interactive prompt inside a container, but that's not really what the console is there for – it's for debugging and troubleshooting. As soon as that container stops running, everything you've done in there will be lost, so there's no point in changing anything and expecting it to be permanent. We will look at how to make permanent changes in *Productionizing a running container*.

Creating and customizing your own container image

Hopefully, by now, you're excited about the possibilities of containers. Maybe you're thinking about some of the existing applications you've got and how you might distribute them via containers. Wouldn't it be nice for your developers to just send you a complete container that you can just spin up without having to worry about any of the installation issues?

Although creating your own container images is not something every system administrator will have to do in their lifetime, I find it's very helpful to understand what goes into making a container image in the first place. This will help you understand what's going on behind the scenes when you're using someone else's images, or if your own developers need assistance with theirs.

Getting started

For this recipe, you'll just need a Server 2019 machine that has containers configured on it and an internet connection. That's it!

How to do it...

From your Windows Server 2019 machine, do the following:

1. Create a directory that we're going to work in. It can be stored anywhere – it doesn't really matter. I'm going to be using `C:\Containers\IIS-Container\`.

2. Open **Notepad**. If you have a different text editor you would prefer to use, you can also use that.

3. Enter the following text. We'll come back to this later to explain exactly what is going on in this file:

```
# escape=`
FROM mcr.microsoft.com/windows/servercore:1809

RUN powershell -Command `
    Add-WindowsFeature Web-Server; `
    Invoke-WebRequest -UseBasicParsing -Uri
"https://dotnetbinaries.blob.core.windows.net/
servicemonitor/2.0.1.10/ServiceMonitor.exe" -OutFile
"C:\ServiceMonitor.exe"
```

```
RUN powershell -Command New-Item -Type Directory -Path
C:\InetPub\NewWebsite
```

```
RUN powershell -Command Set-Content C:\inetpub\
NewWebsite\default.htm -Value 'Congratulations, you
are viewing our new website, served from our docker
container!'
```

```
RUN powershell -Command Remove-Website -Name 'Default
Web Site'
```

```
RUN powershell -Command New-Website -Name 'NewWebsite'
-PhysicalPath C:\inetpub\NewWebsite\
```

```
EXPOSE 80/tcp
```

```
ENTRYPOINT ["C:\\ServiceMonitor.exe", "w3svc"]
```

4. Save this file in the directory you created in *step 1*. It must be named `Dockerfile` – exactly that, with no filename extension.

5. Open **PowerShell** as an administrator.

6. Change to the directory you created in *step 1*. In my case, that's `cd C:\ Containers\IIS-Container`.

7. Run `docker build -t my-iis-site:dev .` – this could take a few minutes. The `-t` command tells Docker to tag the resulting image. Using this tag, we can find it again later. The dot on the end tells docker to look in the current directory.

> **Important Note**
>
> If you receive an error message stating `no matching manifest for windows/amd64`, that's because the version of Windows you are running is not compatible with the base container image we're using. Try changing the `FROM` line in the Dockerfile so that it ends in `:1903` and see whether that fixes the issue. This is because the base container you're using needs to be compatible with your current version of Windows. It's also for this reason that you can't run Linux containers on Windows Server (although you can on Windows 10 due to Docker Desktop shipping with a compatibility layer) and Windows containers on Linux.

8. While that's building, let's go through what we did with that code we saved in the Dockerfile. To see what else you can do with a Dockerfile, look at the *See also* section of this recipe for links to the Docker documentation:

    a. `# escape=`` `: This is a trick we can use in Docker. Normally, the escape character for Docker is \ (as it is everywhere in Linux). However, PowerShell uses ` as an escape character. We're going to be mixing PowerShell in with our Dockerfile, so it makes life a whole lot easier if we use the same escape character for both.

    b. `FROM`: This command tells Docker that we're going to be using whatever image follows for the following commands. We're going to be using the Server Core 2019 image for our container. Depending on what you're containerizing, you can also choose from Windows Server Nano or the full Windows Server edition. If you are having issues running this container, try changing the version at the end of the line to `1903` or one of the other tags on the Windows Server Core image (see the *See also* section of this recipe for more details).

    c. `RUN`: This tells Docker that whatever comes next, run it inside the container. We have several `RUN` statements here, and if you completed *Chapter 5, Internet Information Services*, you may even recognize most of the PowerShell commands. The series of `RUN` commands we used here installs IIS, downloads a file called `ServiceMonitor` (we'll get to this in a moment), creates a directory, makes a file called `Default.htm` in that directory, then configures IIS to serve out of that directory.

    d. `EXPOSE`: This tells Docker that we have a service that is going to be running on port `80` – in our case, IIS.

    e. `ENTRYPOINT`: This is the command that Docker will run when the container starts. Because Windows services are a different concept to what Linux uses (and what Docker expects), this is a workaround. This program starts and monitors the service that you specify, allowing you to treat a Windows service the same way you would in Linux. This allows Docker to operate properly. We have told Docker that when the container starts, it needs to monitor the `w3svc` service (which is IIS).

9. When your container finishes running, you should see an output showing everything that happened, along with a message telling you that the image was successfully built and tagged:

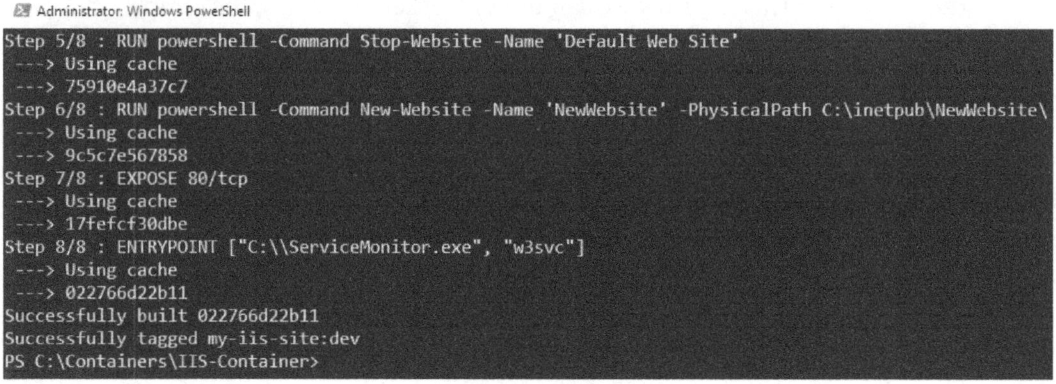

```
Administrator: Windows PowerShell

Step 5/8 : RUN powershell -Command Stop-Website -Name 'Default Web Site'
 ---> Using cache
 ---> 75910e4a37c7
Step 6/8 : RUN powershell -Command New-Website -Name 'NewWebsite' -PhysicalPath C:\inetpub\NewWebsite\
 ---> Using cache
 ---> 9c5c7e567858
Step 7/8 : EXPOSE 80/tcp
 ---> Using cache
 ---> 17fefcf30dbe
Step 8/8 : ENTRYPOINT ["C:\\ServiceMonitor.exe", "w3svc"]
 ---> Using cache
 ---> 022766d22b11
Successfully built 022766d22b11
Successfully tagged my-iis-site:dev
PS C:\Containers\IIS-Container>
```

Figure 14.10 – The output of a successfully built container

10. We can now run our container. We can do that with `docker run -d -p 80:80 my-iis-site:dev`.

11. If you get an error from Docker saying `Ports are not available`, then you probably still have another container running that is using port 80. There's two ways around this: one is using `docker ps` to see which containers are currently running, and then using `docker stop` to stop the container that's using port 80. The other way is to use a port other than port 80 for your container. We will look at how to do that in the *Changing the container networking* recipe. Then, try running the container again.

12. Once the container is running, try browsing to `http://localhost` – you should now see the website we just created being served!

Congratulations, you are viewing our new website, served from our docker container!

Figure 14.11 – Our IIS site being served from a container that we built

13. There is no reason for you to stop here. Any command that you would normally use to configure software on a local machine can probably be thrown into the Dockerfile as a `run` command to install an SSL certificate, copy additional files into the image, and so on. It is also common to take someone else's completely off-the-shelf production image (for example, the Microsoft IIS image), use that in your `FROM` command, and then customize it to your liking.

How it works...

In this recipe, we built our first Dockerfile, and essentially recreated the demonstration IIS image that we used back in the *Running your first container image* recipe – except this time with our own content. We saw how Docker takes the Dockerfile and builds a container, and then we saw how to run the container that we just made using the tags that we assigned.

Truthfully, you would not typically build a container on a Windows Server machine itself. Docker containers are often built by continuous delivery pipelines that developers use, or, if built by hand, they are generally built on a developer's machine. They are then published to what's called a *container registry* (Docker Hub is an example), and then you just execute the appropriate `docker run` command on your Windows server. However, building the container itself is still an important process to learn!

The process of publishing your Docker images to a container registry so that they can be distributed and reused is out of the scope of this book, but I strongly recommend you read up on it if you want to start doing this yourself.

See also

- The Dockerfile reference documentation: `https://docs.docker.com/engine/reference/builder/`
- The Windows Server 2019 Server Core docker image: `https://hub.docker.com/_/microsoft-windows-servercore`

Upgrading a container

As we all know, software changes. Nothing is forever, and containers are the same. Eventually, one of your Docker containers is going to need upgrading. Thankfully, this is fairly simple with Docker and can be done with minimal downtime – assuming you run the right commands in the right order. You may be able to banish hour-long downtimes for good! Wouldn't that be nice?

Getting started

We'll be using our Windows Server 2019 server that has the container functionality installed on it.

How to do it...

We've been tasked with installing a container that's running a piece of software called MongoDB, so let's do that now on our Windows server:

1. If **PowerShell** is not already open, open PowerShell as an Administrator.

2. Let's pretend that we've been tasked with installing a database called MongoDB. We can get that up and running easily with the following command:

    ```
    docker run -d -p 27017:27017 --name mongodb mongo:3.6-
    windowsservercore
    ```

    > **Important**
    >
    > This recipe is demonstrating how to perform an upgrade, not how to deploy MongoDB. You typically would not actually run MongoDB like this as MongoDB requires more configuration before it's actually useful.

3. Note how large the MongoDB container is, and how long it took to download before it started running. Depending on how much of the container you already have, it could have been anywhere up to 5.7 GB.

4. Let's validate the version of MongoDB that we're running. We can use `docker exec` to get MongoDB to show us which version it's running:

    ```
    docker exec mongodb mongod --version
    ```

    This will result in the following output:

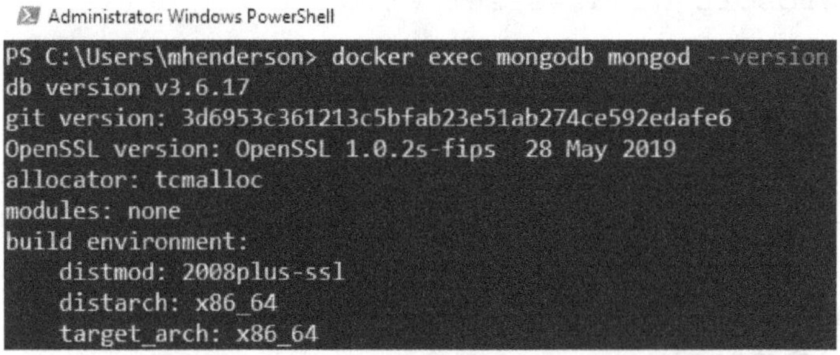

    Figure 14.12 – docker exec showing us the MongoDB version

5. We now receive instructions that we need to upgrade our running version of MongoDB to v4.2. The simplest way of doing this would be to stop the current MongoDB container and start it again, changing the version number in the `docker run` command. But that would mean minutes of downtime while the new server downloads.

6. Before we do anything to the existing container, what we will do is use the `docker pull` command to download the container image before we need to run it. The full command we will use is as follows:

```
docker pull mongo:4.2-windowsservercore
```

7. Notice that this download is a *lot* smaller. You only have to download a gigabyte or so – not exactly small, but not the 5 GB of the initial download. This is because Docker detected that many parts of this new container were the same as the previous container, so it reused them:

```
Administrator: Windows PowerShell
PS C:\Users\mhenderson> docker pull mongo:4.2-windowsservercore
4.2-windowsservercore: Pulling from library/mongo
65014b3c3121: Already exists
eac6fba788c9: Already exists
442da5a04696: Already exists
2cd1d4721643: Pull complete
6f67966d3a47: Pull complete
4e3f18459245: Pull complete
ff28a577006c: Downloading   31.1MB/455.6MB
c88cd1efbb2c: Download complete
d1eb8768e3e3: Download complete
bdc5f1e7a5e6: Download complete
```

Figure 14.13 – docker pull downloading the image and showing that certain parts of the container already existed from our previous MongoDB image

8. Once the image has finished downloading, we're ready to perform our upgrade. The way we'll do this is by stopping the currently running MongoDB container, removing it, and starting a new one. We can chain these commands together so it's still just one line of code:

```
docker stop mongodb; docker rm mongodb; docker run -d -p
27017:27017 --name mongodb mongo:4.2-windowsservercore
```

9. Docker will then stop our existing MongoDB container and start up a new one. The total downtime for MongoDB will be a few seconds. Let's validate that our upgrade was successful:

```
docker exec mongodb mongod --version
```

This results in the following output:

```
Administrator: Windows PowerShell                                    —   □   ×
PS C:\Users\mhenderson> docker stop mongodb; docker rm mongodb; docker run -d --restart=alw
ays -p 8081:8081 --name mongodb mongo:4.2-windowsservercore
mongodb
mongodb
117a2c83dc95eaaa2e1a789ec1ebe724bf2d14ca66404f90d47bcffff0e2eeb1
PS C:\Users\mhenderson> docker exec mongodb mongod --version
db version v4.2.6
git version: 20364840b8f1af16917e4c23c1b5f5efd8b352f8
allocator: tcmalloc
modules: none
build environment:
    distmod: 2012plus
    distarch: x86_64
    target_arch: x86_64
```

Figure 14.14 – The output of our docker upgrade and docker logs commands
showing the updated MongoDB version

How it works...

By using docker pull to download the container image before we needed it, we saved valuable time during our maintenance window. You can perform docker pull at any time – if the upgrade is happening at 9 p.m., you could download it at 9 a.m., or even the day before.

This process, however, still had a few moments of downtime. In a lot of deployments, that's fine. But you may have heard about companies that upgrade their containers daily, or even dozens of times a day, as their developers release new versions. There's no way they're taking even a few seconds of downtime a dozen times a day... are they? The short answer is no. They typically use a container orchestration service to manage this process for them. The most well known is called *Kubernetes*. Kubernetes (and most container orchestration tools) does a lot of things around Docker to make upgrades have an even smaller (effectively zero) downtime during container upgrades – but there are literally entire books written about container orchestration, so we won't be going into it here.

Productionizing a running container

So far in this chapter, we've learned how to get containers up and running, and even how to build or customize container images. But in the previous recipe, I noted that you wouldn't actually want to run MongoDB in production in the way that I described. You may be wondering, why is that?

There are a few reasons. Firstly, containers are, by design, ephemeral – this means every time you restart a container, it's back to the state it was originally in. This is probably fine for something like a web server – but it's not fine for a database server. Imagine losing all your data every time you restarted your server! Secondly, we're not passing any configuration through to our containers. A lot of containers are designed to run with just ephemeral storage. This is not persistent, so how do we configure the software inside the container? There are other things we have to figure out if we're going to keep our software running reliably inside containers.

Getting started

We need our Windows Server 2019 server that has containers configured on it.

How to do it...

We're going to run through various concepts around Docker, and near the end of this recipe, we're going to implement them. We're going to productionize a multiplayer server for an extremely popular game called Minecraft. If you've got younger kids, or if you play Minecraft yourself, you might find this recipe quite useful:

1. The first thing you may have noticed if you've been following this chapter over a period of time is that containers do not survive a restart of the server. This isn't particularly useful for a service that you need to keep high uptime on. Imagine if, after doing Windows u restart. The other options are no, on-failure, and unless-stopped. You can read pdates, you had to log into each server and start all its containers every time. The good news is that `docker run` has a `--restart` flag. Using this flag, we can tell Docker under what circumstances we want the container to be restarted. I find that `--restart=always` is the most useful as this will restart the container if it stops running for *any* reason – a container crash *or* a server restart. The other options are `no`, `on-failure`, and `unless-stopped`. You can read more about what each of these does by looking at the *See also* section of this recipe.

2. Containers are designed to not have any persistent storage. Ideally, every container that starts up would pull its configuration from a database and set itself up when it starts and would never need to talk to any files that are stored on the container host. Unfortunately, life is never that simple – so `docker run` does let you mount what they call a volume to your container. We can use `docker volume create [volume-id]` to create a new volume and `docker run --mount` to attach the volume to our container. Anything that is written to that volume will survive a container restart and can be moved into a new container (for example, during an upgrade).

3. Volumes are fine for storing data that a container creates itself, but what about getting configuration settings into a container in the first place? Some containers use something called a `bind mount command` to get a directory from the local docker host mounted in the container, but another common method is using *environment variables*. Using `docker run --env`, we can pass through as many environment variables as we need to. Which variables you need will depend on the container – most should come with documentation telling you what you need to do.

4. You may have noticed that you also can't tell what a container is doing at any given point in time. There's no obvious log file that's produced, and errors that are outputted by the container look like they disappear into oblivion. Although you can use `docker exec` to get a shell into a container, that may not tell you everything you need to know. Fortunately, Docker has `docker logs` to show you the output of a container. `docker logs [container-id]` will show you the output of what your container has been saying. `docker logs -f [container-id]` will keep outputting the log file to your console until you press *Ctrl + C*.

5. OK, now that we've gone through some of those things, let's put them into practice. Let's do something a little bit different this time: run a Minecraft server. Start by opening **PowerShell** as an administrator.

6. Let's start our Minecraft server as we have been doing everything in this chapter so far – without any productionizing:

```
docker run -d -p 25565:25565 sunghwan2789/minecraft-
server:windowsservercore-1809
```

7. Once again, we're just dropped back to our desktop. Let's see whether the container is running:

```
docker ps
```

This results in the following output:

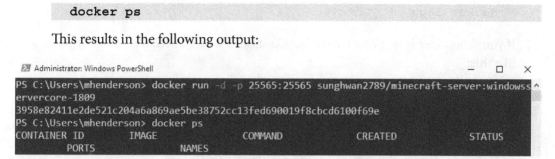

Figure 14.15 – docker run followed by docker ps shows that our container is not running

8. Our container is not running. Let's use the `logs` command we just read about to see whether we can find out why. We were given a long container ID after `docker run`, so we'll use that:

```
docker logs
3958e82411e2de521c204a6a869ae5be38752cc13fed690019f8cbcd
6100f69e
```

This results in the following output:

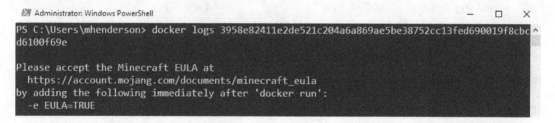

Figure 14.16 – docker logs showing that the container is missing some configuration data

9. So, we need to pass through an environment variable saying we accept the **End User License Agreement (EULA)**. I'm going to assume for the purposes of this recipe that you are willing to accept the EULA, so we need to use the environment command. Our startup command will now look like this:

```
docker run -d -p 25565:25565 --env EULA=TRUE
sunghwan2789/minecraft-server:windowsservercore-1809
```

10. Let's see what our container is doing now. Let's use the -f option with docker logs so that the log will update us in real time:

```
docker logs -f 90dfc74
```

11. If your container is working correctly, you should see a bunch of messages that look like this:

```
[17:40:46] [Server-Worker-2/INFO]: Preparing spawn area:
80%
[17:40:46] [Server-Worker-1/INFO]: Preparing spawn area:
84%
[17:40:47] [Server-Worker-2/INFO]: Preparing spawn area:
88%
[17:40:48] [Server-Worker-2/INFO]: Preparing spawn area:
90%
[17:40:48] [Server-Worker-1/INFO]: Preparing spawn area:
94%
[17:40:49] [Server-Worker-2/INFO]: Preparing spawn area:
99%
[17:40:49] [Server thread/INFO]: Time elapsed: 19626 ms
[17:40:49] [Server thread/INFO]: Done (38.272s)! For
help, type "help"
[17:40:49] [Server thread/INFO]: Starting remote control
listener
[17:40:49] [RCON Listener #1/INFO]: RCON running on
0.0.0.0:25575
```

12. Your Minecraft server is now running. You can connect to it using the Minecraft game if you want to! But for now, press *Ctrl + C* to exit the logs.

13. Now, let's restart our server with Restart-Computer.

14. Once the server has restarted, open **PowerShell** as an administrator and run docker ps. You should notice that there are no containers currently running.

```
docker run -d -p 25565:25565 --env EULA=TRUE
--restart=always sunghwan2789/minecraft-
server:windowsservercore-1809
```

16. Something that's not completely obvious from the logs is that Minecraft is generating a whole new game map each time it starts. This is because when we restarted the container, it lost all its data. Your players will not be happy if their hard work is lost every time the server restarts! The documentation for this container said that the map data is stored at `C:\Data`, so let's attach a volume there. Stop the current Minecraft server with `docker stop [container-id]`, and then attach a volume to it:

```
docker volume create minecraft
```

```
docker run -d -p 25565:25565 --env EULA=TRUE
--restart=always --mount source=minecraft,target=c:/data
sunghwan2789/minecraft-server:windowsservercore-1809
```

This results in the following output:

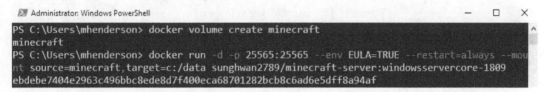

Figure 14.17 – Creating a docker volume and then attaching the volume to our container

17. Once the container has started, we can run `docker inspect minecraft` to see some metadata about our volume. We want to pay attention to the `source` property. This will tell us where Docker is storing the files that are going into this volume. Mine has gone to `C:\ProgramData\docker\volumes\minecraft\_data`.

18. Open a Windows Explorer window and browse to that location. You should see the Minecraft data sitting in it:

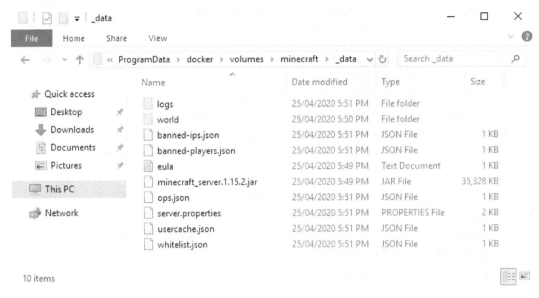

Figure 14.18 – Our Docker volume data

19. Let's put all our productionizing to the test now. Let's restart our server one last time with `Restart-Computer`.

20. Once the server has restarted, log in, open **PowerShell** as an Administrator, and run `docker ps`. You should see your Minecraft server sitting there, ready to be played.

How it works...

Docker is a very flexible tool – it has a lot of customizable features and options for how containers should behave. In this recipe we looked at the most useful ones – ensuring the containers survive a restart, setting configuration via environment variables, using persistent storage, and reading the server logs. We took those options and progressively increased the reliability of our Minecraft server until it was stable and reliable enough for us to use in production.

You may also want to research another Docker tool called *Docker Compose*. It's outside the scope of this book, but it allows you to configure not just a single container, but rather define an entire environment of multiple containers (perhaps you have a Redis server, a MongoDB server, and a web server all required for the same application) and how they interact with each other.

See also

- `docker run`: https://docs.docker.com/engine/reference/run/
- The `docker restart` flag: https://docs.docker.com/config/containers/start-containers-automatically/
- `docker logs`: https://docs.docker.com/engine/reference/commandline/logs/
- `docker Compose`: https://docs.docker.com/compose/

Changing the container networking

We've seen a lot in this chapter about how to get our containers working smoothly and reliably. But what we haven't looked at is how to configure the networking. We've been using the -p flag, but what does it do? And what else can we do with our container networking?

Getting started

We need our Windows Server 2019 server that's running containers.

How to do it...

Follow these steps to change the container networking:

1. On your Windows server, open **PowerShell** as an Administrator.

2. We don't need to do anything complicated to demonstrate this recipe, so let's just start by running the test IIS site:

   ```
   docker run -d -p 8000:80 mcr.microsoft.com/windows/servercore/iis
   ```

3. This starts our IIS container and makes it accessible on port 8000. You can browse to it with http://localhost:8000.

4. But what if we didn't want it running on port 8000? After all, that's not a particularly convenient port if we're going to be directing users' browsers to it. That's where the -p flag comes in. -p stands for *publish* and it tells Docker which ports we want to publish. The first part, 8000, is the local port we want to use. The second part, 80, is the port inside the container we want to publish. So, we're publishing the container's port 80 on our local port 8000.

5. Now, let's start our test IIS site on port 80, which is a much more convenient place to run it:

```
docker run -d -p 80:80 mcr.microsoft.com/windows/
servercore/iis
```

6. We now have our IIS test site running on port 80. Go ahead and browse to http://localhost and see whether it works. You can also browse to your server from elsewhere on the network and see the site running.

> **Tip**
> By default, the software inside your server will use the DNS settings from your host. But if you have multiple network adapters in your server, you might want different containers to use different DNS servers. We can do this with the --dns flag, like this: **docker run -d -p 80:80 --dns 8.8.8.8** mcr.microsoft.com/windows/servercore/iis.

How it works...

Docker abstracts away most of the complexities of running software, but it brings with it some new complexities. One of those is the way it deals with networking. We've gone through some of the basic, most commonly used options for configuring container network, and these cover the majority of cases.

There are more complex networking commands that can be used; for example, the docker network set of commands. You can read more about them in the *See also* section.

See also

- Docker container networking: https://docs.docker.com/config/containers/container-networking/
- Docker network overview: https://docs.docker.com/network/
- docker network commands: https://docs.docker.com/engine/reference/commandline/network/

Deploying a container to Azure

This is an interesting topic to be putting in a book about Windows Server 2019. Why are we talking about Microsoft Azure suddenly? What even is Azure? Azure is Microsoft's cloud platform, similar to Amazon Web Services and Google Cloud Platform. As it's run by Microsoft, it is heavily focused on the Windows side of things. I'm including it here because containers are often a gateway into cloud services. If you have containers running well on-premises, why not try running them in Azure instead? Especially if these are internet-facing services. The opposite might also be true – you might have containers running in Azure that you want to move on-premises.

It's important to note that Azure is not free. Azure does offer free trials and credits, but if you're not careful, you might end up with some charges on your account. Because of that, I'm *not* going to be taking you through the process of signing up for Azure in this book. I'm going to assume that you already have appropriate access to an Azure account.

Getting started

You're going to need a Windows 10 computer and a Microsoft Azure account. A copy of the game Minecraft is useful, but not required.

How to do it...

On our Windows 10 computer, follow these steps:

1. The first thing we need to do is install the PowerShell module for Azure. Start **PowerShell** as an Administrator and run the following command:

    ```
    Install-Module Az
    ```

    This results in the following output:

    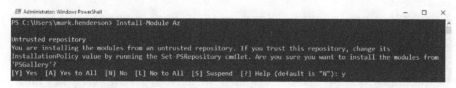

    Figure 14.19 – Installing the Azure CLI via PowerShell. It took
    about 5 minutes to download and install.

2. Let's get started by logging into Azure:

    ```
    Connect-AzAccount
    ```

3. This will open a login page, asking you to log into your Azure account. Once you have logged in, the window will close:

Figure 14.20 – Logging into Azure via PowerShell. For privacy reasons, I have removed some personal details from this screenshot

4. Everything in Azure must be organized into resource groups. This is just a way of collecting all your things for a project together in one place. We can create a resource group for our testing like this. You should specify a location that's close to where you physically are:

```
New-AzResourceGroup -Name PacktCookbook -Location
AustraliaEast
```

5. If you don't know which location you should choose or what the different codes are, you can find out by running az account list-locations:

```
Get-AzLocation
```

6. Now that we have our resource group, we're going to do the work to recreate our Minecraft server from earlier, as that seems like the kind of thing, we might want running in Azure for our friends to access. The first thing we need to do is create the storage for the volume we're going to assign to the container. The name of the storage container needs to be globally unique, so if the name you've chosen is already in use, try a different name:

```
New-AzStorageAccount -Name packtcontainerstorage
-ResourceGroupName PacktCookbook -Location AustraliaEast
-SkuName Standard_LRS
```

7. Once the storage account has been created, we need to get the access key for it. This access key is what will allow Azure to use this storage in our container:

```
Get-AzStorageAccountKey -ResourceGroupName PacktCookbook
-Name packtcontainerstorage
```

8. This command will give you two keys (`key1` and `key2`). Make a note of one of these:

Figure 14.21–Example access keys for the storage account

9. Now, we need to create a file share for our container to mount. I'll call mine `minecraftdata`. You will need to use the account key you just copied from the previous step:

```
New-AzStorageShare -Name minecraftdata -Context
(New-AzStorageContext -StorageAccountName
packtcontainerstorage -StorageAccountKey
A9o3qrXq6Eam63p9sCQo+kM2N9XLDcXSO9Z/
nke4ZLqsDr+o+iem9LnzTO7xOBDtsrWpQwLl9MI9AZ0u6a0eKA==)
```

10. And with that, we're ready to create our server. This command is a long one as we're putting together everything from the previous steps:

```
$credential = New-Object System.Management.
Automation.PSCredential -ArgumentList
"packtcontainerstorage", (ConvertTo-SecureString
-String "A9o3qrXq6Eam63p9sCQo+kM2N9XLDcXSO9Z/
nke4ZLqsDr+o+iem9LnzTO7xOBDtsrWpQwLl9MI9AZ0u6a0eKA=="
-AsPlainText -Force)
```

```
New-AzContainerGroup -ResourceGroupName PacktCookbook `
```

```
  -Name minecraftserver `
```

```
  -Location australiaeast `
```

```
  -DnsNameLabel minecraft-server-packt-cookbook `
```

```
  -Image itzg/minecraft-server `
```

```
  -AzureFileVolumeShareName minecraftdata `
```

```
  -AzureFileVolumeMountPath "/data" `
```

```
  -AzureFileVolumeAccountCredential $credential `
```

```
  -Port @(25565) `
```

```
  -EnvironmentVariable @{"EULA"="TRUE"}
```

Here's what the running container will look like:

Figure 14.22 – Our container is now running on Azure

> **Important Note**
>
> The keen-eyed among you may have noticed that the Minecraft container image we used here is not the one we used previously. That's because Azure has a few limitations on running Windows containers – one of them being that we can't attach storage volumes. So, we've switched to a Linux container just for this example. However, everything else is still the same, and it illustrates how similar Windows and Linux are when it comes to running containers – if I hadn't pointed it out, you may never have noticed.

11. This command may take quite a while to run. Once it's finished, let's check that it's all working OK:

```
Get-AzContainerInstanceLog -ResourceGroupName
PacktCookbook -ContainerGroupName minecraftserver
```

12. You should see logs indicating that the server has started and is listening for connections.

13. The next few steps are optional, and only required if you own the game Minecraft (or maybe you have a child or a niece or nephew who does). We were given an IP address in the output of our `New-AzContainerGroup` command, so if you have the Minecraft game, let's connect to it! If you own **Minecraft**, load it up.

14. Our server is running Minecraft `1.15.2`, as indicated by our container logs, so make sure you've got your game launching that version.

15. Once Minecraft has loaded, click **Multiplayer**, then **Add Server**:

Figure 14.23 – Minecraft running 1.15.2

16. Give the server whatever name you wish and enter the IP address that was shown after `New-AzContainerGroup`, under **Server Address**. Then, click **Done**:

Figure 14.24 – Adding our container server to Minecraft

17. Click on your new server, then **Join Server**, to start playing!

Figure 14.25 – Our server showing up in the Multiplayer list. Note the server description

18. Once you are done with the server, to make sure you don't keep paying for it in Azure, run `Remove-AzContainerGroup` to delete the server:

```
Remove-AzContainerGroup -ResourceGroupName PacktCookbook
-Name minecraftserver
```

19. Let's also delete the storage account so that we don't have to pay for that anymore either:

```
Remove-AzStorageAccount -ResourceGroupName PacktCookbook
-Name packtcontainerstorage
```

How it works...

As you can see, the Azure PowerShell container commands for running containers are different to the Docker commands. However, there is a lot of similarity between them as well – we set environment variables, specified container images, and published ports.

We did have to go through some extra hoops to attach storage to our container. This is down to the nature of cloud services, though – although they allow a lot of flexibility, they are not always the simplest things to configure.

> **Important Note**
> Make sure you delete your Minecraft server and storage accounts if you do not plan on keeping the server! Check *steps 18* and *19* of this recipe for how to do this.

15
Desired State Configuration and Automation

In this book so far, we've seen a lot of different ways of configuring our Windows servers—via the Server Manager, via the Admin Center, via PowerShell commands. **Desired State Configuration** (**DSC**) is yet another way of configuring our servers—but this one is perhaps the most powerful. DSC can be used to configure dozens, hundreds, or even thousands of servers in an identical fashion.

Sounds like Group Policy, right? There are similarities between the way DSC and a **Group Policy Object** (**GPO**) operate, but unlike Group Policy, DSC can be used to configure literally any part of your server. In addition to doing things that a GPO can do, such as setting power profiles and configuring Windows Update settings, DSC can also install virtually any piece of software, create directory structures, and do countless other things. It combines the concepts of Group Policy with the power of PowerShell.

DSC also manages what's called **configuration drift**. If a setting on a server gets changed by a process or a user, DSC will undo the change and put it back. If you have 1,000 servers that are all meant to be configured in a certain way, it's almost guaranteed that some of them will get changed by something or someone in the future.

DSC can also be combined with other tools such as Azure, and many configuration management platforms (such as Puppet) use DSC under the hood for part of their configuration. Another advantage of DSC is that it's all PowerShell under the hood, which means you can commit your files into a version control repository (commonly, a Git repository) and see who made what changes to the DSC configuration over time. Because DSC is PowerShell code, you can also use DSC in conjunction with change control procedures and change management auditing systems if your organization has them.

We won't be going deep into the bowels of DSC in this book—there are books you can purchase that spend hundreds of pages going deeply into it—but we will be going through the process of looking at the kinds of features DSC brings and what we can do with them.

In this chapter, we will be covering the following recipes:

- Making your first DSC
- Adding additional roles to DSC
- Using complex resources
- Converting a GPO to DSC
- Pushing a DSC configuration to multiple servers
- Using Azure DSC automation

Making your first DSC

Throughout this chapter, we're going to continue refining our DSC until we have something that resembles what you might find in production for a web server. Getting DSC installed on your servers is not something we need to do—Windows Server comes with the required DSC functionality out of the box.

DSC is broken up by configurations. By defining a configuration, we tell DSC what we want a specific part of the server to look like. A server might apply multiple configurations—one for setting the server's power policy, another one for setting its system path, and another one for installing specific roles.

DSC works by taking the configuration you've designed and compiling a file called a **MOF** (short for **Managed Object Format**) file. These MOF files contain all the information DSC needs to know about a server so that it can be applied—so, when you get to the step in these recipes about compiling a MOF file, that's what it's for.

Let's begin by creating a basic configuration, and then work our way up from there!

Getting ready

We'll be completing this recipe on a freshly configured Windows Server 2019 server. The server is domain-joined.

How to do it...

On your Windows Server 2019 machine, do the following steps:

1. Open **Windows PowerShell ISE**. If you prefer to use a different editor (such as **Visual Studio Code (VS Code)**), you are free to use that; however, because **Integrated Script Environment** (ISE) ships with every Windows Server machine, we will be using it for the moment:

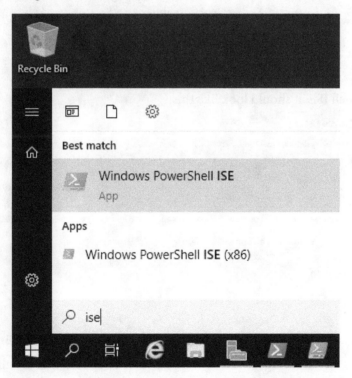

Figure 15.1 – Opening Windows PowerShell ISE as administrator

2. Click the **New Script** icon on the toolbar (or go to **File | New**).

3. This server is going to be a web server, so the logical thing to start with would be to install **Internet Information Services (IIS)**. So, let's create a DSC configuration that does exactly that. Enter this into our new script:

```
Configuration PacktWebServer {

    Import-DscResource -ModuleName
PsDesiredStateConfiguration

    Node 'localhost' {
        WindowsFeature WebServer {
            Ensure = "Present"
            Name   = "Web-Server"
        }
    }
}
```

In PowerShell ISE, it should look like this:

Figure 15.2 – Our basic DSC configuration in Windows PowerShell ISE

4. This creates a DSC configuration called `PacktWebServer` that installs the Web Server role. Let's take a look at this in a bit more detail.

    A `Configuration` is just what it sounds like—a configuration. A `Configuration` can contain a lot of information—nodes, Windows features, registry settings, **Windows Management Instrumentation (WMI)** settings, programs—virtually anything that can be managed by PowerShell can be present inside a `Configuration`.

The `Import-DscResource` line imports the basic DSC resource cmdlets, which we will be able to use later on.

The `WindowsFeature` line is telling DSC to configure a Windows Feature. The name `WebServer` that comes after it can actually be anything we want. Ours is called `WebServer` for ease of identification, but we could just have easily called it `IIS` or `SamsTomatos` if we wanted to.

Inside `WindowsFeature`, we have two properties. The `Ensure` property is common to almost all DSC resources, and tells DSC what we want to do with this resource. `Present` is the one you'll see used the most, and it checks that the feature is installed. You can also specify `Absent`, which will cause DSC to remove the Windows Feature. Other resources may support other values for the `Ensure` property.

The `Name` property is the name of the Windows Feature (or Features) we want installed. We've just specified `Web-Server` here, which is the internal name for the IIS feature. You can get the list of available options here by running `Get-WindowsFeature` in PowerShell.

5. Once you've understood what each part of the file is doing, we need to save the file. The DSC file should live in its own directory, so I'm going to save mine to `C:\DSC\PacktWebServer.ps1` (you will need to create the DSC directory).

6. Now, start PowerShell as administrator and CD into the `C:\DSC\` directory we just created.

7. We now need to import our DSC file that we just wrote. We do this in PowerShell by *dot-sourcing* it. We can do this by running `.  .\PacktWebServer.ps1`.

8. It will look like nothing happened, but our DSC file has now been loaded into our PowerShell session. If we now just execute `PacktWebServer` (the name of our configuration), DSC will compile our configuration:

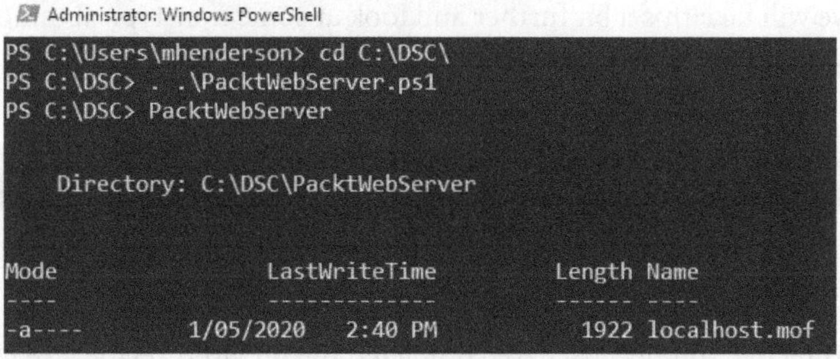

Figure 15.3 – Importing and compiling our PacktWebServer DSC configuration

9. You should see an output saying that a file called `localhost.mof` now exists in a subdirectory called `PacktWebServer`, from where you ran the command. In my case, this is in `C:\DSC\PacktWebServer\`.

10. We're now ready to apply our DSC configuration. Run `Start-DscConfiguration -Path .\PacktWebServer\ -Wait -Verbose`.

11. DSC should now go to work, installing the `Web-Server` Windows role. If you had skipped the `-Wait` and `-Verbose` flags when running the command, this would have all happened invisibly in the background. We will go into what this is actually doing in more detail in the next recipe. Once it has finished, you should be able to browse to `http://localhost/` to see the default IIS page.

How it works...

Using the Windows PowerShell ISE, we created our first DSC configuration to install the `Web-Server` role onto our machine. We compiled a `MOF` file (which is a compiled DSC resource) and applied it to our server.

Right now, this seems a lot more work than using Group Policies or PowerShell, or even using the **graphical user interface (GUI)** just to get IIS installed—and you're right: DSC doesn't really make much sense for doing single-time small tasks such as this on a single server.

However, over the course of this chapter, we are going to be expanding a lot on the power of DSC. We haven't even scratched the surface of how scalable and flexible DSC can be—this was just a small taste of what's to come.

Adding additional roles to DSC

So far, we've not seen anything particularly special about DSC. You could be forgiven for thinking that it is just another (very complicated) way of installing basic Windows roles. In this recipe, we will take this a bit further and look at some non-typical things we can do with DSC: we're going to configure our entire web server, and we're going to do it all using DSC providers.

We've already configured this web server several times in this book: we did it via the IIS console, then via PowerShell, then again as a container. Now, we'll do it via DSC.

Getting ready

To carry out this recipe, you need to have completed the previous recipe. We will be using the same Windows Server 2019 machine and building on its DSC configuration.

How to do it...

On your Windows Server machine, do the following:

1. If not already open, open `C:\DSC\PacktWebServer.ps1` in **Windows PowerShell ISE**.

2. We should have our previous simple DSC configuration present:

```
Configuration PacktWebServer {

    Import-DscResource -ModuleName
PsDesiredStateConfiguration

    Node 'localhost' {
        WindowsFeature WebServer {
            Ensure = "Present"
            Name   = "Web-Server"
        }
    }
}
```

3. Multiple times in this book, we have configured a basic IIS site, so if you've done those chapters, hopefully you'll recognize some of the things we're about to do. To interact with IIS via DSC, we need a module called `xWebAdministration`. The first thing we need to do is make that module available to our configuration. Add another `Import-DSCResource` line to add this module directly underneath the existing one:

```
Import-DscResource -ModuleName xWebAdministration
```

4. When we install IIS, we get a default website running on port `80`, so the next thing we want to do is get rid of that default website. We can do this with `xWebSite`, which is part of the `xWebAdministration` module. Inside the `Node 'localhost'` section of the configuration, we can add the following:

```
xWebSite RemoveDefault {
    Ensure = "Absent"
    Name = "Default Web Site"
}
```

5. This uses the xWebSite resource. We've named our instance RemoveDefault (you can name it anything you want). Note that we've sent the Ensure property this time to Absent, which will tell DSC to remove the resource named Default Web Site instead of adding it.

6. Now, we need to add the content for our new website. We'll do this using the File resource—DSC can make sure that the contents of a file are always the same. We can use that resource to set the contents of our default.htm file. Add this just below the xWebSite resource we just created:

```
File WebsiteDefault {
      Ensure = "Present"
      DestinationPath = "C:\inetpub\NewWebsite\Default.
htm"
      Contents = "Congratulations, you are viewing our new
website, configured by DSC!"
}
```

> **Important note**
>
> This example shows how you can set the contents of a file with DSC, but you would not distribute an entire website by setting the contents of each file in DSC. Instead, you could tell DSC to copy the files from a network share or configure IIS to point directly to a share—perhaps a share that is hosted by a Scale-Out File Server?

7. Now that we have our content, we can create our new website in IIS. We do this using the xWebSite resource again, but this time, we set the Ensure property to Present and define a few more properties:

```
xWebSite NewSite {
      Ensure = "Present"
      Name = "New Website"
      PhysicalPath = "C:\inetpub\NewWebsite\"
      State = "Started"
}
```

8. You should now have a DSC configuration that looks like this:

```
Configuration PacktWebServer {

    Import-DscResource -ModuleName
PsDesiredStateConfiguration
    Import-DscResource -ModuleName xWebAdministration

    Node 'localhost' {
        WindowsFeature WebServer {
            Ensure = "Present"
            Name   = "Web-Server"
        }

        xWebSite RemoveDefault {
            Ensure = "Absent"
            Name = "Default Web Site"
        }

        File WebsiteDefault {
            Ensure = "Present"
            DestinationPath = "C:\inetpub\NewWebsite\
Default.htm"
            Contents = "Congratulations, you are viewing
our new website, configured by DSC!"
        }

        xWebSite NewSite {
            Ensure = "Present"
            Name = "New Website"
            PhysicalPath = "C:\inetpub\NewWebsite\"
            State = "Started"
        }
    }
}
```

9. Save this file as `C:\DSC\PacktWebServer.ps1` (overwriting our old file).

10. If not currently running, open **PowerShell** as **administrator** and `cd` into `C:\DSC`.

11. We now need to dot-source our new DSC configuration. Do that again with the following:

```
. .\PacktWebServer.ps1
```

12. You will probably get an error stating **Could not find the module 'xWebAdministration'**. The good news is that DSC modules can be installed as easily as any other PowerShell module, by running the following code:

```
Install-Module xWebAdministration
```

You should get the following output:

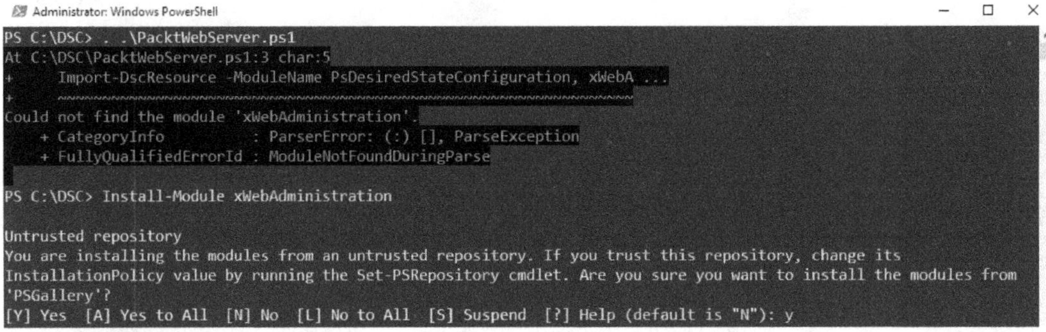

Figure 15.4 – Importing the failing DSC module, followed by installing the correct PowerShell module

13. Let's try loading our module again:

```
. .\PacktWebServer.ps1
```

14. Once done, we generate our updated MOF files by just invoking the command `PacktWebServer` (which is the name of our DSC configuration).

15. And finally, we apply the DSC resource, the same as we did previously:

```
Start-DscConfiguration -Path .\PacktWebServer\ -Wait
-Verbose
```

You'll get the following output:

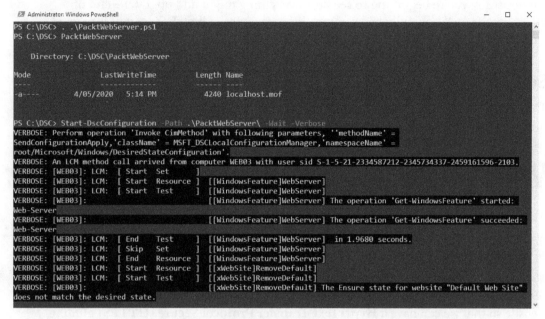

Figure 15.5 – Importing, compiling, and applying our DSC configuration

16. You should see a lot more output on the screen this time. Once it's finished, you
    should be able to browse to `http://localhost` and, instead of seeing the default
    IIS site, you should see our test site:

Congratulations, you are viewing our new website, configured by DSC!

Figure 15.6 – Viewing our DSC configured site

How it works...

We have built on the foundation we set in the first recipe in this chapter by showing how
you can control IIS directly from DSC without having to know any IIS-specific PowerShell
code. The format of the resources used for managing IIS is virtually identical to the one
for managing a file and managing Windows resources. This is not by accident—DSC is
designed so that virtually every resource has a common set of properties such as `Ensure`
and `Name`. Some resources have a lot more properties you can set and some have very few,
but they all operate in essentially the same manner.

You might still be thinking that this is all a rather complicated way of doing basic tasks, but hopefully you're beginning to see how everything might add up. By the end of this chapter, you'll hopefully have a much bigger picture of how DSC can fit into your daily life.

See also

The xWebAdministration DSC module: `https://github.com/dsccommunity/xWebAdministration`

Using complex resources

So far, we've kept our DSC fairly simple—install this role, write this file, remove this website. If only life were always that simple! Often, we need to have DSC do things that are far more complicated than that, so in this recipe, we're going to look at some of these more complex operations.

The first thing we're going to do is have DSC request a certificate from our internal **certificate authority** (**CA**), and then, we're going to use that certificate in our IIS website so that we can have a **HyperText Transfer Protocol Secure** (**HTTPS**) binding. This will show how we can order resources in DSC, as well as use some of the more complex resources.

Getting ready

You'll need your Windows Server 2019 server we've been using for all this chapter's recipes, and you'll also need a working Windows CA to request certificates from. If you need to build one of these, have a look at *Chapter 4, Working with Certificates*.

How to do it...

On your Windows Server 2019 server, do the following:

1. If not already open, open `C:\DSC\PacktWebServer.ps1` in **Windows PowerShell ISE**.

2. We should have our previous simple DSC configuration present. Refer to the previous recipe to see what it should look like now.

3. We're going to use a DSC module called `CertificateDsc`. This is what we're going to use to request and install a certificate from our CA. Let's add another `Import- DscResource` line below our current two. Also, feel free to run `Install-Module CertificateDsc` in an administrative PowerShell prompt to save yourself from having to do this later:

```
Import-DscResource -ModuleName CertificateDsc
```

4. `CertificateDsc` provides a resource called `CertReq`. We can use this resource for requesting a certificate from a Windows CA. We have a CA called `CA01` that we're going to use to request our certificate from, and the template we're going to use is just called `WebServer`. Add this resource to our DSC file inside the `Node 'localhost'` section:

```
CertReq SSLCert
{
        CAServerFQDN         = "ca01.ad.cookbook.packt.com"
        Subject              = "web03.ad.cookbook.packt.com"
        KeyLength            = "2048"
        ProviderName         = '"Microsoft RSA SChannel
Cryptographic Provider"'
        CertificateTemplate  = "WebServer"
        AutoRenew            = $true
        FriendlyName         = "SSL Certificate for IIS"
        KeyType              = "RSA"
        RequestType          = "CMC"
}
```

5. This is going to request a **Secure Sockets Layer (SSL)** certificate from our `ca01. ad.cookbook.packt.com` CA.

> **Tip**
> You may notice that we hardcoded the name `web03.ad.cookbook. packt.com` as the certificate subject. This is fine for this case, but it does make this resource problematic if you were installing this DSC configuration on multiple web servers. This wouldn't be very useful as they would all have a certificate with the subject of `web03`. We'll come back to how to fix this in a later recipe.

6. Now that we've generated our certificate, we need to tell IIS to use it. In our DSC configuration, locate the `xWebSite NewSite` resource that we created earlier. Inside that resource, we're going to add a `BindingInfo` section that will tell IIS to use the certificate we've requested. The entire resource should look like this:

```
xWebSite NewSite {
    Ensure = "Present"
    Name = "New Website"
    PhysicalPath = "C:\inetpub\NewWebsite\"
    State = "Started"
    DependsOn = "[CertReq]SSLCert"
    BindingInfo = @(
        MSFT_xWebBindingInformation{
            Protocol = "HTTPS"
            Port = 443
            CertificateSubject = "web03.ad.cookbook.
packt.com"
        }
        MSFT_xWebBindingInformation{
            Protocol = "HTTP"
            Port = 80
        }
    )
}
```

7. Let's run through the changes we made here:

    `DependsOn`—This tells DSC to only run this resource if the `SSLCert` resource (with the type of `CertReq`) succeeds. This is because we don't want IIS to try to bind to a certificate that doesn't exist yet. This also means that if our certificate request fails, DSC will not create our new website. This is good behavior because then, we won't be creating a broken website.

    `BindingInfo`—This tells DSC to ensure that our website has two bindings—one binding for HTTPS, using the certificate subject that we used to generate our certificate, and one for **HyperText Transfer Protocol (HTTP)** so that the website can still be accessed over unencrypted means. `@()` is the syntax in PowerShell for an array, and `MSFT_xWebBindingInformation` is the type of item we're putting in the array.

8. You should now have a DSC configuration that looks like this:

```
Configuration PacktWebServer {

    Import-DscResource -ModuleName
PsDesiredStateConfiguration
    Import-DscResource -ModuleName xWebAdministration
    Import-DscResource -ModuleName CertificateDsc

    Node 'localhost' {
        WindowsFeature WebServer {
            Ensure = "Present"
            Name   = "Web-Server"
        }

        xWebSite RemoveDefault {
            Ensure = "Absent"
            Name = "Default Web Site"
        }

        File WebsiteDefault {
            Ensure = "Present"
            DestinationPath = "C:\inetpub\NewWebsite\
Default.htm"
            Contents = "Congratulations, you are viewing
our new website, configured by DSC!"
        }

        xWebSite NewSite {
            Ensure = "Present"
            Name = "New Website"
            PhysicalPath = "C:\inetpub\NewWebsite\"
            State = "Started"
            DependsOn = "[CertReq]SSLCert"
            BindingInfo = @(
                MSFT_xWebBindingInformation{
                    Protocol = "HTTPS"
```

```
                        Port = 443
                        CertificateSubject = "web03.
ad.cookbook.packt.com"
                    }
                MSFT_xWebBindingInformation{
                    Protocol = "HTTP"
                    Port = 80
                }
            )
        }


        CertReq SSLCert
        {
            CAServerFQDN        = "ca01.ad.cookbook.
packt.com"
            Subject             = "web03.ad.cookbook.
packt.com"
            KeyLength           = "2048"
            ProviderName        = '"Microsoft RSA
SChannel Cryptographic Provider"'
            CertificateTemplate = "WebServer"
            AutoRenew           = $true
            FriendlyName        = "SSL Certificate for
IIS"
            KeyType             = "RSA"
            RequestType         = "CMC"
        }
    }
}
```

9. Let's go through the process of applying our DSC configuration again. In a
    PowerShell administrator prompt, start by dot-sourcing the file. If you get an error
    about a missing module, run `Install-Module CertificateDsc`:

    ```
    . .\PacktWebServer.ps1
    ```

10. Then, compile the MOF:

    ```
    PacktWebServer
    ```

11. Then, apply the following:

```
Start-DscConfiguration -Path .\PacktWebServer\ -Wait
-Verbose
```

12. You should now be able to browse to `https://web03.ad.cookbook.packt.com` (note that `https://localhost/` will throw a certificate error as `localhost` is not on the certificate):

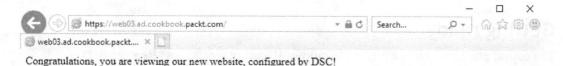

Congratulations, you are viewing our new website, configured by DSC!

Figure 15.7 – Accessing our website over HTTPS – note the protocol
and the padlock in the browser address bar

How it works...

Hopefully, you're now starting to see the benefits of DSC. With very little effort, we were able to go from a zero configuration to a full IIS website configured with SSL. If you have already read *Chapter 4, Working with certificates*, you might remember that we did not go through the process of requesting a certificate via PowerShell or the command line—that's because doing certificate requests that way is, frankly, a nightmare and very difficult to scale. However, we were able to do it easily with DSC.

Once our module was written, it took only seconds to apply the configuration. We were able to tell DSC to wait for certain steps to finish before starting other steps, and the order that the DSC resources are in the file is not the order in which they are executed.

You can chain a lot of resources this way. If you were copying your website from a file share, you could add the copy resource to the DependsOn property for the website resource. DSC would then request and import the SSL certificate at the same time as the files were copying, but it would wait for them both to finish before creating and starting the website. If we needed custom firewall rules, we could have DSC create them only after the website had already been started.

You can end up with very deep dependencies this way, ensuring that you never ship a half-configured or partly broken service.

Converting a GPO to DSC

DSC is all very well, but if you're an organization that has decades of history on Windows Server, then chances are you have a lot of things hidden away in GPOs. We looked at these back in *Chapter 10, Group Policy*. They are a great way of doing mass configuration, but they lack much of the finesse of DSC. After all, the GPO scheme is 20 years old now.

If you're looking to replace some of your old GPOs and extend them with DSC, the good news is that PowerShell has a way we can get started with this.

Getting ready

The easiest place to do this from is a Windows 10 computer that has **Remote Server Administration Tools** (**RSAT**) installed. Instructions on how to do this can be found in *Chapter 1, Learning the Interface*, in the *Administering Server 2019 from a Windows 10 machine* recipe.

How to do it...

From our computer running Windows 10 with RSAT, do the following:

1. Open **PowerShell** as **administrator**.

2. We need to decide which Group Policy we want to convert to DSC. Back in *Chapter 7, Remote Desktop Services* we created a GPO for our **Remote Desktop Services** (**RDS**) servers called `Enable GPU processing`. This is the GPO I want to convert for this recipe.

3. The first thing we need to do is take a backup of our current GPO—hence why we need a computer with RSAT installed. Taking a backup of our group policies can be done like this (assuming that `C:\GPO Backups` exists):

```
Backup-GPO -Name "Enable GPU processing" -Path 'C:\GPO
Backups\'
```

This will give us the following output:

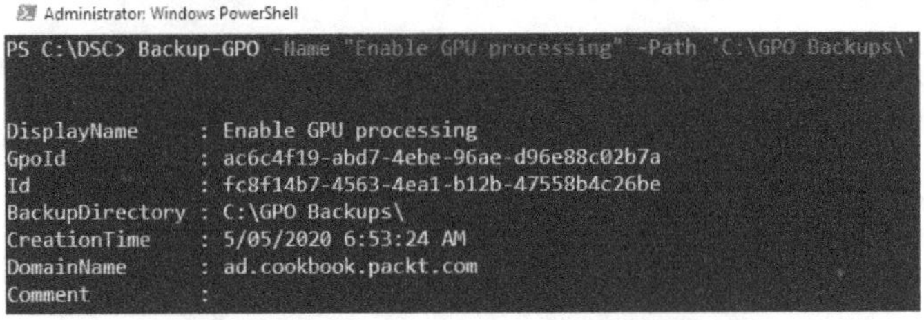

Figure 15.8 – Taking a GPO backup

4. As the GPOs back up, a list will be printed with an ID number. Keep a note of the ID number for the GPO you want to convert.

5. We now need to install a PowerShell module called `BaselineManagement`:

```
Install-Module BaselineManagement
```

6. Once the module has been installed, we need to import the module into our PowerShell session:

```
Import-Module BaselineManagement
```

7. In PowerShell, change to a directory where you want to save the resulting DSC files. I'm in `cd C:\DSC`.

8. It's time to convert our Group Policy. We can do this with the `ConvertFrom-GPO` cmdlet. The path we need to specify will be using the ID number from the `Backup-GPO` cmdlet earlier. In my case, my command is the following:

```
ConvertFrom-GPO -Path 'C:\GPO Backups\{FC8F14B7-4563-
4EA1-B12B-47558B4C26BE}\' -OutputConfigurationScript
```

We'll get the following output:

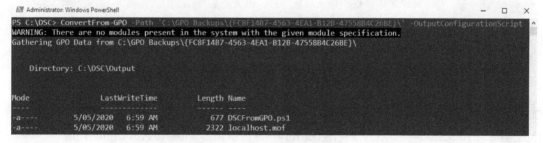

Figure 15.9 – Converting a GPO to DSC

9. The output from the command should be a list of files the command has created. It should create a directory called `Output` and inside that, create a PS1 file. Open that PS1 file in **Windows PowerShell ISE**.

10. The code my GPO has produced looks like this:

```
Configuration DSCFromGPO
{
        Import-DSCResource -ModuleName
'PSDesiredStateConfiguration'
        Import-DSCResource -ModuleName 'AuditPolicyDSC'
```

```
        Import-DSCResource -ModuleName 'SecurityPolicyDSC'
        # Module Not Found: Import-DSCResource -ModuleName
    'PowerShellAccessControl'
        Node localhost
        {
            Registry 'Registry(POL): HKLM:\SOFTWARE\
    Policies\Microsoft\Windows NT\Terminal Services\
    bEnumerateHWBeforeSW'
            {
                ValueName = 'bEnumerateHWBeforeSW'
                ValueType = 'Dword'
                Key = 'HKLM:\SOFTWARE\Policies\Microsoft\
    Windows NT\Terminal Services'
                ValueData = 1


            }
        }
    }
    DSCFromGPO -OutputPath 'C:\DSC\Output'
```

11. We can see that the converted GPO simply sets a registry key for us. Simple! We can now take that configuration and apply it directly or—more likely—copy the resource that was created and put it into another DSC configuration for use there!

How it works...

The `BaselineManagement` PowerShell module provides a few useful utilities for creating DSC resources from various non-DSC sources. It can also convert policies built by Azure Security Center and Microsoft's **Security Compliance Manager** (**SCM**). I also find the tool useful for looking inside various Group Policies to see what they're actually doing under the hood.

We find ourselves in a bit of a strange time with configuration management on Windows. It arguably has one of the oldest and most mature tools —GPO. But by shipping a new tool, DSC, Windows puts the administrator (that is, you) at an interesting crossroads. Do you go down the path of GPO, the tried and, true, and trusted method, even though it can be inflexible? Or, do you go down the road of the new and shiny technology (DSC) and accept that some people won't be willing to learn a new technology?

By being able to convert GPOs to DSCs down the path, we can ensure that if you do go down the GPO path, you can come back to DSCs later on; or, if you have a decade of existing GPOs to deal with, you can recreate them in DSC and retire the GPOs if need be.

Pushing a DSC configuration to multiple servers

So far, we've seen various things we can do with DSC, but we've been doing them all on the server itself, and we've been doing it with a bunch of long-winded commands. In this recipe, we'll look at how we can apply a DSC configuration to multiple servers at the same time, and how we can do it from our Windows 10 machine so that we don't need to log on to each one of our servers manually to apply it.

Getting ready

For this, you'll need a Windows 10 computer and at least two servers to apply the DSC configuration to. We've been using a server called web03 for the previous recipes, so I'm going to extend this to web01 and web02 as well—for a total of three servers.

It's important that the servers you choose to do this on are not running anything for production, as this could potentially remove or break production websites running the servers.

How to do it...

To complete this recipe, we will need to do steps on both our Windows 2019 Server and Windows 10 desktop:

1. The first thing we need to do is grab the DSC work we've been doing already from our Windows Server and move it onto our Windows 10 machine. That way, we don't have to repeat all our hard work from scratch. Copy C:\DSC from our Windows Server 2019 machine, on which we did the previous recipes, to C:\DSC on our Windows 10 machine.

2. Open **PowerShell** as **administrator**.

3. We now need to install the DSC resources that we're using. Because we're building on the work we did in the previous recipes, the modules we need are xWebAdministration and CertificateDsc. We can install them with the following code:

```
Install-Module xWebAdministration, CertificateDsc
```

This command will give us the following output:

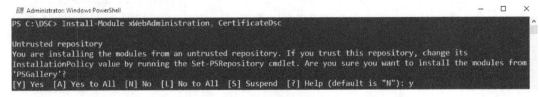

Figure 15.10 – Installing the required DSC modules

4. Open `C:\DSC\PacktWebServer.ps1` in your favorite editor. I'll be using **Windows PowerShell ISE** as it's installed on every Windows 10 machine, but you might like to use VS Code, Notepad++, or any other editor you prefer.

5. The first thing we're going to do is make this DSC configuration load itself when we dot-source it. At the very bottom of our file, add a line that just reads `PacktWebServer`—this will tell PowerShell to compile the module every time we dot-source it:

Figure 15.11 – Adding the configuration name to the end of the PS1 file

6. Now, scroll back up the DSC configuration until you come to the line `Node 'localhost'`. Now that we're on our Windows 10 machine, we don't want to apply this to ourselves—we want to apply this to our web servers. Change this line to read as follows:

```
Node 'web03' {
```

7. Save the file and switch back to **PowerShell**.

8. Change into the DSC directory—in our case, `cd C:\DSC`.

9. Let's dot-source our DSC configuration the same way as we did before:

```
. .\PacktWebServer.ps1
```

10. You should notice that instead of nothing happening, this time you're immediately presented with the list of MOF files—and this time, there's no `localhost.mof`; we now have `web03.mof`:

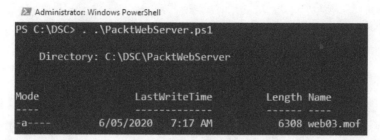

Figure 15.12 – Dot-sourcing the DSC configuration-generated web03.mof automatically

11. We'll now apply this DSC configuration, but this time we'll specify `-ComputerName web03` in our command:

```
Start-DscConfiguration -Path .\PacktWebServer\
-ComputerName web03 -Wait -Verbose
```

12. This time, DSC is running on our Windows 10 machine, but it's pushing the configuration out to `web03`. Let's see what happens if we try pushing our configuration out to one of our other web servers, `web02`:

```
Start-DscConfiguration -Path .\PacktWebServer\
-ComputerName web02 -Wait -Verbose
```

This command will give us the following output:

```
Administrator: Windows PowerShell                                                                    —  □  ×
PS C:\DSC> Start-DscConfiguration -Path .\PacktWebServer\ -ComputerName web02 -Wait -Verbose
Start-DscConfiguration : The computer-specific MOF file for computer web02 does not exist in the current directory.
At line:1 char:1
+ Start-DscConfiguration -Path .\PacktWebServer\ -ComputerName web02 -W ...
+ ~~~~~~~~~~~~~~~~~~~~~~~~~~~~~~~~~~~~~~~~~~~~~~~~~~~~~~~~~~~~~~~~~~~~~~~~~
    + CategoryInfo          : NotSpecified: (:) [Start-DscConfiguration], ArgumentException
    + FullyQualifiedErrorId : System.ArgumentException,Microsoft.PowerShell.DesiredStateConfiguration.Commands.StartDs
   cConfigurationCommand
```

Figure 15.13 – Trying to apply DSC to a node that doesn't exist yet

13. You will receive an error saying that no MOF file was found for `web02`. This is fixed easily enough—back in your editor that has the DSC configuration open, find the line for `Node` and make it read like this:

```
Node @('web01','web02','web03') {
```

The edit to the line should look like the example in *Figure 15.14*:

Figure 15.14 – Adding multiple nodes to a configuration

14. Back in PowerShell, if you dot-source the file now, you should see that three MOF files are created: web01.mof, web02.mof, and web03.mof:

```
. .\PacktWebServer.ps1
```

15. Now, let's try applying our configuration again:

```
Start-DscConfiguration -Path .\PacktWebServer\
-ComputerName web02 -Wait -Verbose
```

> **Important**
>
> If you receive an error stating that a DSC resource was not available, this could be because of a mismatch between your version of PowerShell and/or the DSC modules on your Windows 10 machine versus what's on your Server 2019 machine. Running Install-Module xWebAdministration, CertificateDsc on your web02 and web03 machines should fix this, but does defeat the point of pushing a DSC configuration. We'll look at another way of doing DSC that doesn't involve this in the next recipe.

16. The DSC configuration has now been applied to both web02 and web03 web servers. We should now have two identically configured web servers. Try it out! Visit https://web02.ad.cookbook.packt.com in your web browser:

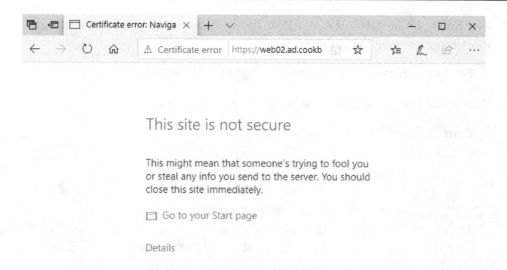

Figure 15.15 – Browsing to web02 over HTTPS causes a certificate error

17. Oh no. We now have two *identically configured servers*. That means they both have a certificate with the name of web03 in it—which is obviously wrong for our web02 server. The good news is that we can fix this! Pop back into your editor with the DSC configuration open.

18. Because a DSC configuration is very closely related to a normal PowerShell function, we can include almost any PowerShell code we need in it. So, underneath the very first line, which reads Configuration PacktWebServer {, we can add a parameter, like this:

```
param(
    [string[]] $NodeName
)
```

19. And we can switch our Node line to read like this:

```
Node $NodeName  {
```

20. We now need to change our configuration to use the NodeName parameter where we used the name web03. There should be two places: the IIS binding and certificate request. Change both those lines to use "$NodeName.ad.cookbook.packt.com" instead of "web03.ad.cookbook.packt.com".

21. And finally, on the last line of our DSC configuration, change the line that reads `PacktWebServer` to the following:

```
PacktWebServer -NodeName @('web01','web02','web03')
```

22. Your entire DSC configuration should now read as follows:

```
Configuration PacktWebServer {
    param(
        [string[]]$NodeName
    )
    Import-DscResource -ModuleName
PsDesiredStateConfiguration
    Import-DscResource -ModuleName xWebAdministration
    Import-DscResource -ModuleName CertificateDsc

    Node $NodeName  {
        WindowsFeature WebServer {
            Ensure = "Present"
            Name   = "Web-Server"
        }

        xWebSite RemoveDefault {
            Ensure = "Absent"
            Name = "Default Web Site"
        }

        File WebsiteDefault {
            Ensure = "Present"
            DestinationPath = "C:\inetpub\NewWebsite\
Default.htm"
            Contents = "Congratulations, you are viewing
our new website, configured by DSC!"
        }

        xWebSite NewSite {
            Ensure = "Present"
            Name = "New Website"
```

```
            PhysicalPath = "C:\inetpub\NewWebsite\"
            State = "Started"
            DependsOn = "[CertReq]SSLCert"
            BindingInfo = @(
                MSFT_xWebBindingInformation{
                    Protocol = "HTTPS"
                    Port = 443
                    CertificateSubject = "web03.
ad.cookbook.packt.com"
                }
                MSFT_xWebBindingInformation{
                    Protocol = "HTTP"
                    Port = 80
                }
            )
        }


        CertReq SSLCert
        {
            CAServerFQDN        = "ca01.ad.cookbook.
packt.com"
            Subject             = "web03.ad.cookbook.
packt.com"
            KeyLength           = "2048"
            ProviderName        = '"Microsoft RSA
SChannel Cryptographic Provider"'
            CertificateTemplate = "WebServer"
            AutoRenew           = $true
            FriendlyName        = "SSL Certificate for
IIS"
            KeyType             = "RSA"
            RequestType         = "CMC"
        }
    }
}

PacktWebServer -NodeName @('web01','web02','web03')
```

23. Let's pause for a moment to go through what we've just done.

    We added a parameter to our DSC configuration called `NodeName`. This parameter accepts an array of names. We use those names in our `Node` section. This means that the configuration is no longer tied to a predefined set of server names, and we can refer to the server name in our configuration via the `$NodeName` variable.

    Because we now have `$NodeName` inside our configuration, we swapped out any references to web03 to `$NodeName`. This means that every MOF file that is generated will have the correct reference to the correct computer name in it.

24. Dot-source our DSC configuration again. You should still have three MOF files generated at the end of it:

    ```
    . .\PacktWebServer.ps1
    ```

25. And let's re-apply the DSC configuration for web02:

    ```
    Start-DscConfiguration -Path .\PacktWebServer\
    -ComputerName web02 -Wait -Verbose
    ```

26. Let's also browse to our server in our internet browser again: `https://web02. ad.cookbook.packt.com/`. The connection should succeed this time.

27. Let's validate this again by pushing out to web01 this time:

    ```
    Start-DscConfiguration -Path .\PacktWebServer\
    -ComputerName web01 -Wait -Verbose
    ```

28. If everything goes according to plan, you should now have three web servers, all serving identical web pages, each with its own working SSL certificate.

How it works...

This recipe got a bit complicated, but it got complicated for a good reason. If I had just jumped straight into the final form of our DSC configuration, you may not have understood why we structured the configuration the way we did. I don't blame you if, right now, you're feeling that this is all just too complicated, and you want to stick with GPOs.

However, I implore you: if you're feeling confused or despairing, please try not to. We've gone on a bit of a roller coaster in this recipe (and this chapter), but now that you know about using parameters in DSC configurations, in the future we can just go straight there. Imagine how confused you would be if we had started at this place, rather than worked our way up to it.

Now that you know about using parameters in configurations, it's tempting to parameterize a lot of things —and this is fine, to an extent. However, if you do end up making very complex DSC resources, you might want to look into DSC's ConfigurationData functionality.

In the next recipe, we're going to take a look at using DSC with Microsoft Azure, which is where DSC can really come alive.

See also

DSC's ConfigurationData functionality: https://docs.microsoft.com/en-us/powershell/scripting/dsc/configurations/configdata?view=powershell-7

Using Azure DSC automation

The examples we've seen so far in this chapter have all involved us pushing a configuration out to a server. Every time the configuration changes, we have to manually apply the configuration to the server again. By using Microsoft Azure to manage the DSC for us, we get a lot more flexibility and options for DSC. For one, we don't need to push the configurations out any more—each server will reach out to Azure and pull its configuration down, so when a configuration changes, you don't need to touch each server to apply the new configuration. Also, if you have a simple configuration, you can apply that configuration to hundreds of servers by just compiling it once. Another neat feature is that you can assign a configuration to a server with the click of a button—no more needing to know our full list of servers beforehand.

As a bonus, Azure provides us with a neat dashboard that we can use to see whether our servers are up to date with their configurations or not.

Getting ready

To do this recipe, you're going to need an Azure account. Azure is not a free service, although Microsoft usually has some method with which you can get free credits for lab purposes, such as experimenting with the topics in this chapter. As such, we're not going to walk you through the process of getting an Azure account—but you must have an active Azure account to complete this recipe.

The only other things we need are our Windows 10 and Server 2019 machines that we'll be configuring via DSC. In this case, I'll be using web01, web02, and web03.

How to do it...

On your Windows 10 computer, do the following:

1. Open your web browser and browse to `https://portal.azure.com`, and log in to your Azure account.

2. Once logged in, click the **Resource groups** button on the left-hand side of the page. Everything in Azure must be organized into a resource group, so let's create one for our DSC.

3. On the **Resource groups** page, click the + **Add** button:

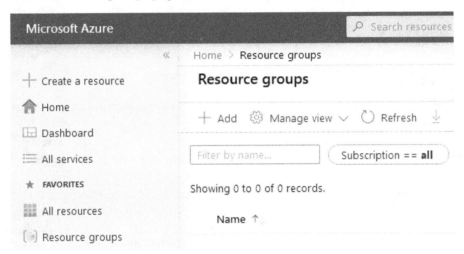

Figure 15.16 – The Azure Resource groups page, showing the + Add button

> **Important**
>
> These screenshots were all accurate at the time this chapter was written. However, Azure regularly updates its web portal, so what you see in your Azure portal when you're following this recipe might be different from what is shown in this book.

4. The **Create a resource group** screen appears. You will need to give your resource group a name and select a region. The region you select should be one that is close to your servers. I am naming mine `PacktCookbook` and selecting the region of **(Asia Pacific) Australia Central** as that's my closest region:

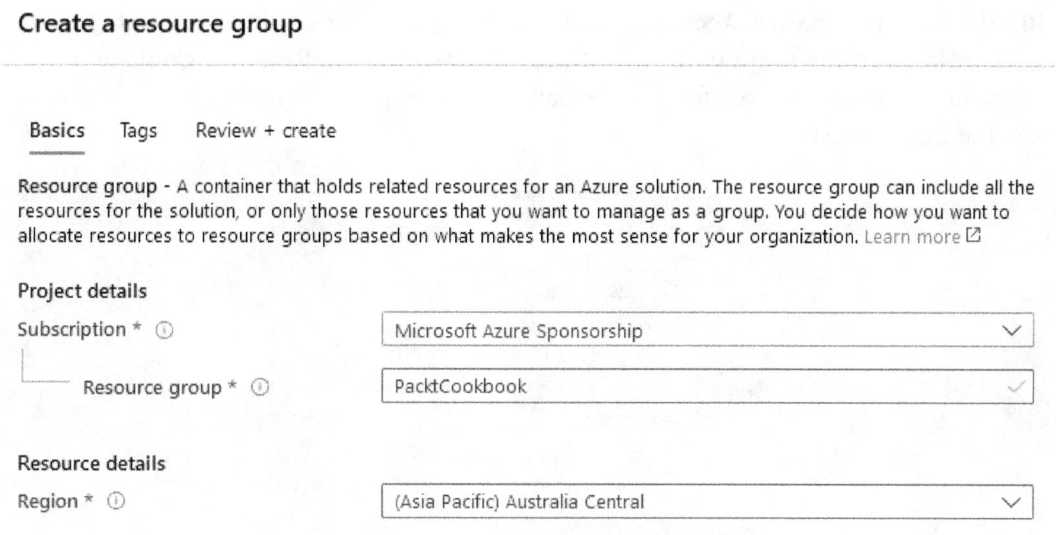

Create a resource group
Basics
Tags
Review + create
Resource group - A container that holds related resources for an Azure solution. The resource group can include all the resources for the solution, or only those resources that you want to manage as a group. You decide how you want to allocate resources to resource groups based on what makes the most sense for your organization. Learn more
Project details
Subscription *
Microsoft Azure Sponsorship
Resource group *
PacktCookbook
Resource details
Region *
(Asia Pacific) Australia Central

Figure 15.17 – Creating our resource group

5. Once you've named your resource group and selected your region, click **Review + Create**. Once the validation passes, click **Create**.
6. Your resource group will take a few moments to be created. Click **Refresh** in the **Resource groups** list to see if it's finished. Once your resource group shows up, click on it.
7. DSC in Azure is managed through Azure's **Automation** functionality. Once you're in your resource group, click the **+ Add** button.
8. In the search box of the **New** screen, type `Automation` and press **Enter**.
9. You should now have the **Automation** resource screen. Click **Create** to create a new **Automation** resource:

Automation
Microsoft
Automation
Save for later
Microsoft
Create

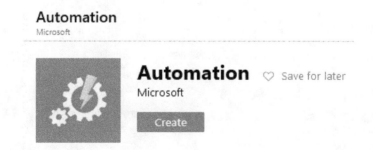

Figure 15.18 – Creating an Automation resource

10. The **Add Automation Account** screen should open. Enter anything you want for the **Name** option (I'm calling mine `PacktDSC`). Select the **Resource group** and same **Location** you used for your resource group. You can leave the rest as default. Then, click **Create**:

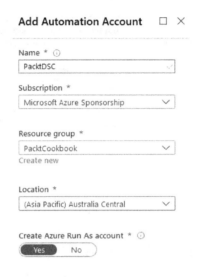

Figure 15.19 – Adding our Automation account

11. The Automation account may take several minutes to create. Once it's finished, you should be able to access the Automation account by viewing your resource group again. An Automation account should create several resources:

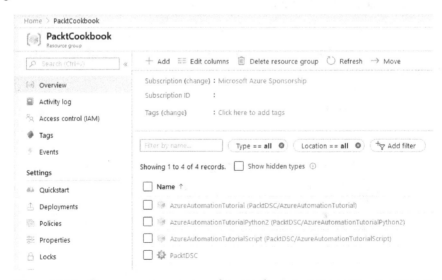

Figure 15.20 – Our resource group now showing the Automation account resources

12. Click on your Automation account. In our example, it is called **PacktDSC**. This will open the Automation account's default screen.

13. Once in the Automation account, in the left-hand navigation, scroll down until you find **Account Settings | Keys**. Click on **Keys**.

14. In this screen, you will have a **Primary access key** and a URL. Make a note of both of these, as we'll need them in a moment:

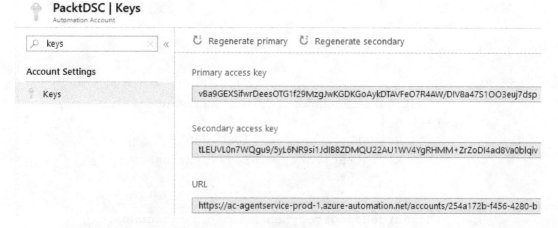

PacktDSC | Keys
Automation Account

🔎 keys ✕	«	↻ Regenerate primary ↻ Regenerate secondary
Account Settings		Primary access key
🔑 Keys		vBa9GEXSifwrDeesOTG1f29MzgJwKGDKGoAykDTAVFeO7R4AW/DIV8a47S1OO3euj7dsp
		Secondary access key
		tLEUVLOn7WQgu9/5yL6NR9si1JdIB8ZDMQU22AU1WV4YgRHMM+ZrZoDI4ad8Va0blqiv
		URL
		https://ac-agentservice-prod-1.azure-automation.net/accounts/254a172b-f456-4280-b

Figure 15.21 – The access keys and URL for our Automation account

15. Once that's done, click the link for **State Configuration (DSC)** in the navigation. You should see the *DSC* dashboard, showing no nodes and no configurations.

16. OK—the Azure configuration for DSC is complete—*for now*. Now, we need to get some computers checking in to Azure!

17. How do we get our servers to use Azure for DSC management? By using DSC, of course! On your Windows 10 machine, open your favorite PowerShell editor. For this example, I'll be using **Windows PowerShell ISE**.

18. To configure DSC with DSC itself, we need to generate a DSC **meta-configuration**. Don't worry too much about what this means—the configuration for Azure DSC can essentially be copied and pasted. Create a file called C:\DSC\ EnableAzureDSC.ps1 and put this content in it:

```
[DscLocalConfigurationManager()]
Configuration EnableAzureDSC
{
    param
    (
```

```
            [Parameter(Mandatory = $True)]
    [String]$RegistrationKey,

            [Parameter(Mandatory = $True)]
    [String[]]$ComputerName
        )


    Node $ComputerName
    {
        Settings {
            RefreshMode = 'Pull'
        }


        ConfigurationRepositoryWeb AzureAutomationState
Configuration {
            ServerUrl       = "[DSC-URL]"
            RegistrationKey = $RegistrationKey
        }


        ResourceRepositoryWeb AzureAutomationState
Configuration {
            ServerUrl       = "[DSC-URL]"
            RegistrationKey = $RegistrationKey
        }


        ReportServerWeb AzureAutomationState
Configuration {
            ServerUrl       = "[DSC-URL]"
            RegistrationKey = $RegistrationKey
        }
    }
}
```

19. To be frank, this recipe is going to be quite long, so we're not going dissect
    every single thing in this configuration. But you must replace the part of the
    script with [DSC-URL] with the URL you copied earlier on from the **Keys**
    page. In my example, the URL is https://ac-agentservice-prod-1.
    azure-automation.net/accounts/254a172b-f456-4280-b22c-
    a1b9b57dffcc, but yours will be different.

20. Once that PowerShell file has been saved, open a **PowerShell** prompt.

21. Change into the directory where we just saved our file. In my case, that's `cd C:\DSC`.

22. We need to dot-source our DSC configuration, the same as we have for all our previous DSC configurations:

```
. .\EnableAzureDSC.ps1
```

23. Because this DSC configuration does not automatically invoke itself (as we have done in previous recipes), we need to generate the MOF files by hand. The reason we've done this is because we don't want to store our access keys in the script itself—that's not something you should just leave lying around in unsecured scripts. To generate our MOF files this time, we'll use the following:

```
EnableAzureDSC -ComputerName web01,web02,web03
-RegistrationKey [Registration-Key]
```

This command should give us the following output:

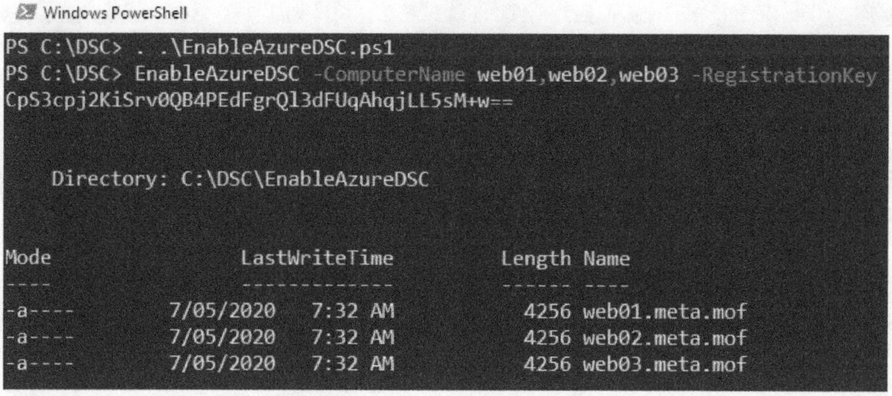

Figure 15.22 – Generating our metadata MOFs (don't forget to use your registration key, not mine!)

24. We now have three MOFs, but they're slightly different this time—they have `.meta.` in the middle of their filename. That's because these configurations don't contain any DSC resources; they contain the configuration for DSC itself. That means we invoke them differently:

```
Set-DscLocalConfigurationManager -ComputerName
web01,web02,web03 -Path .\EnableAzureDSC\ -Verbose
```

25. After a moment, PowerShell should drop you back at the prompt. When it does, pop back into your web browser that has the Azure portal open.

26. It should still be open to the **State Configuration (DSC)** dashboard. Click **Refresh**, and your servers should now be showing up:

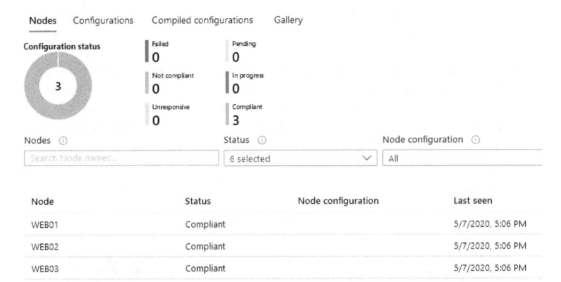

Nodes   Configurations   Compiled configurations   Gallery

Configuration status

Failed	Pending
0	0

Not compliant	In progress
0	0

Unresponsive	Compliant
0	3

(3)

Nodes ⓘ

Search Node names...

Status ⓘ

6 selected ⌄

Node configuration ⓘ

All

Node	Status	Node configuration	Last seen
WEB01	Compliant		5/7/2020, 5:06 PM
WEB02	Compliant		5/7/2020, 5:06 PM
WEB03	Compliant		5/7/2020, 5:06 PM

Figure 15.23 – The Azure DSC portal now showing our servers reporting in via DSC

27. You'll notice that Azure can tell us a lot of information about our servers—how many are compliant with their configuration; how many are in the progress of applying; when DSC last checked in; and, importantly, the Node configuration, which for our servers is currently blank. That means that although our servers are checking in to Azure DSC, it's not doing anything with them yet. That's because we haven't configured Azure with any of our DSC configurations.

28. So, earlier, when I said we were done with the Azure configuration for the moment—well, it didn't last long. There are more things we need to configure now. Just as we had to perform Install-Module on our local computers when we pushed modules out to our servers, those same modules need to be imported to Azure. In your Automation account in the Azure portal, find **Shared Resources | Modules Gallery** on the navigation. Click on **Modules gallery**:

Figure 15.24 – Modules gallery

29. We've used two modules so far—xWebAdministration and
    CertificateDsc. In the search box, type xWebAdministration and
    press *Enter*.

30. Locate the xWebAdministration module and click on it. Then, click the
    Import button at the top of the page.

31. Now that the module is importing, return to the **Module gallery** and import the
    CertificateDsc module.

32. Before we add our configurations into Azure, we need to make some small
    changes. Open up the PacktWebServer.ps1 DSC configuration we were using
    earlier on in this chapter.

33. Make the following changes:

    Under File WebsiteDefault, find the Contents parameter and change
    this so that it reads Congratulations, you are viewing our new
    website, configured by DSC from Azure!. This way, we'll know when
    DSC has done its job, as our website configuration will change.

    Remove the last line of the DSC configuration, which should have been
    PacktWebServer -NodeName @('web01','web02','web03'). This
    is because we are going to use Azure to compile our configurations, not our local
    PowerShell instance.

34. Save the DSC configuration. I'm calling mine C:\DSC\PacktWebServer-
    Azure.ps1.

35. Switch back to the Azure portal and go to the **Configuration Management | State
    Configuration (DSC)** page in the navigation.

36. This time, click the **Configurations** button at the top of the **DSC** dashboard:

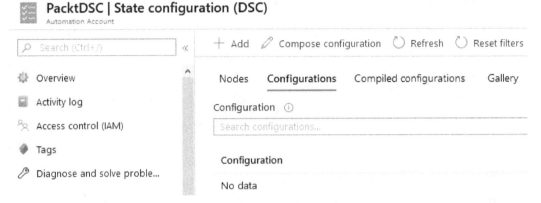

Figure 15.25 – The DSC configurations screen

37. Click + **Add**.

38. Under the **Configuration** file, upload the DSC file we just saved—C:\DSC\
    PacktWebServer-Azure.ps1. Feel free to give the DSC module a description
    if you wish.

39. Click **OK**, and the DSC will upload. Once it has uploaded, click the **Refresh**
    button in the Azure portal, and you should see the PacktWebServer
    configuration show up:

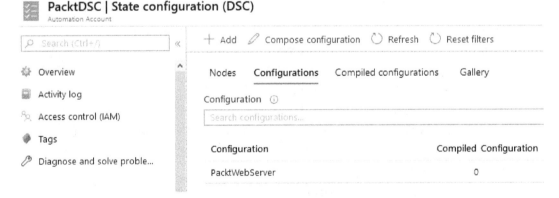

Figure 15.26 – Our PacktWebServer configuration showing up

40. Click on the PacktWebServer configuration to view its details.

41. Just as we had to do on our local PowerShell instance, we now need to have Azure
    create our MOF file so that we can apply it to our nodes. Click the **Compile** button
    in the top bar:

Home > PacktCookbook > PacktDSC | State configuration (DSC) > **PacktWebServer**

PacktWebServer
Configuration

⚙ Compile   ⬆ Export   🗑 Delete

Resource group...   : PacktCookbook

Location   : Australia Central

Subscription ID   :

Last published   : 5/7/2020, 5:52 PM

Figure 15.27 – The PacktWebServer DSC configuration in the Azure portal

42. **Start Compilation Job** will now be asked which **NODENAME** to compile for. This is because this is the parameter that we have in our DSC document. Our three nodes are web01, web02, and web03. The Azure portal requires an array to be defined a bit differently from what we'd normally do, so enter ['web01', 'web02', 'web03']. Our filled-in field should look like this:

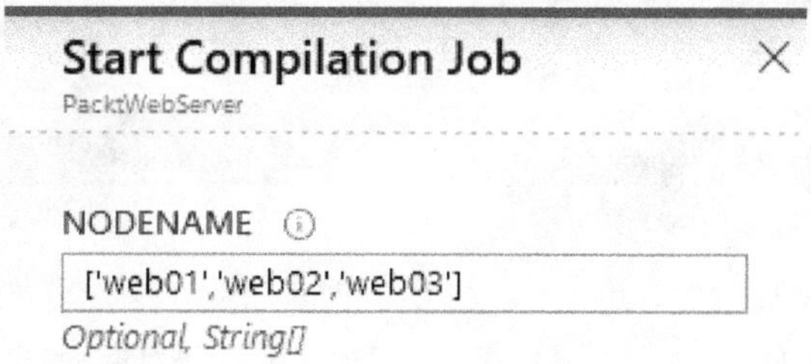

Start Compilation Job   ✕
PacktWebServer

- -

NODENAME ⓘ

['web01','web02','web03']

Optional, String[]

Figure 15.28 – Entering our NodeName parameter in the Azure portal

43. Click **OK** and a complication job should now appear in the configuration screen. This can take a few minutes to finish. Once it has finished, if you click the **Node configurations** tab, you should see three configurations—one for each web server:

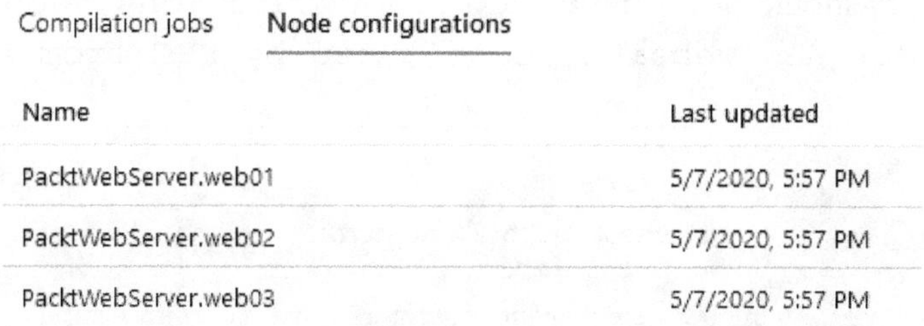

Compilation jobs   **Node configurations**

Name	Last updated
PacktWebServer.web01	5/7/2020, 5:57 PM
PacktWebServer.web02	5/7/2020, 5:57 PM
PacktWebServer.web03	5/7/2020, 5:57 PM

Figure 15.29 – Node configurations tab showing the three compiled nodes

44. Return to **State configuration (DSC)**, and on the dashboard, click the **Nodes** tab.

45. Click on our first node, **WEB01**.

46. In the node details, click **Assign node configuration**.

47. In the list of available configurations, choose **PacktWebServer.web01**, and then click **OK**.

48. Return to the **Nodes** dashboard and repeat this for **WEB02** and **WEB03**, selecting the appropriate configuration each time.

49. The node status should change to **Pending** and the **Node configuration** should now have the correct web server configuration against it.

50. Within a few minutes, the **Status** column should change to **In progress** and then **Compliant**:

Figure 15.30 – The Nodes dashboard showing nodes in different statuses

51. Once the web servers are compliant, browse to them from your Windows 10 machine. They should now print the text `Congratulations, you are viewing our new website, configured by DSC from Azure!`:

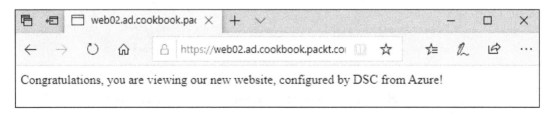

Figure 15.31 – Our local web server showing that it has pulled its new configuration down from Azure

Now, every time you upload and compile a new configuration to Azure, every server will automatically pick up that configuration within a matter of minutes and apply it automatically. It's a fair amount of work to get the first configuration out, but every subsequent configuration will be much easier!

How it works...

We've just walked through what seemed like a complicated process—and to be frank, the initial Azure configuration is more complex than what we've done so far. However, this is one of the less complicated methods of deploying a DSC pull server! It's also one of the most reliable.

If we were not using DSC to generate certificate requests, this process would be even simpler. We complicated things for ourselves by using a configuration that needed compiling once for each individual server. If we didn't need to use the $NodeName argument, then we could have just compiled this once and applied the same configuration to every server.

The other reason this was a bit slower and more complicated than it could have been was because we did all this via the web console. If we had done this via PowerShell, it would have involved substantially fewer steps—however, I felt that at this point, the web console makes the process a lot clearer than if we had stuck purely to PowerShell. There are completely native ways of doing all these steps in PowerShell—creating the Automation account, uploading and compiling configurations, and assigning configurations to nodes. If you have a development pipeline for DSC, it would not be too difficult to hook the Azure Automation side up to it to have your configurations re-uploaded and re-compiled every time they changed.

It's worth noting that Azure is not the only tool that offers DSC integration—other configuration management platforms do so as well. Three of the major configuration management tools—Puppet, Ansible, and Chef—support embedding DSC resources into their configurations as well. So, if your company has an existing configuration management platform running for their Linux infrastructure, it's very possible that you can extend that to your Windows infrastructure now as well.

16
Hardening Your Infrastructure

Windows Server 2019 is more secure than any previous version of Windows Server. Right out of the box, you have a good anti-virus and anti-malware service (which we looked at in previous chapters). Although everyone's environment is different and has different needs, there are certain security requirements that are fairly common to most environments, and that's what we're going to look at in this chapter.

It's usually not good enough to just stop at the default security configuration. The default configuration in Windows (and frankly almost every operating system) aims to strike a balance between ease of configuration and being secure out of the box. But once you've got your servers configured with the services and roles that they require, there are further security steps that we can take.

There are also other Windows features that we can use to help enhance our security; for example, configuring Windows Server Update Services and using Desired State Configuration to disable outdated and insecure Windows protocols. Active Directory itself comes with a number of useful features for making recovery from security incidents and mistakes easier as well.

With that in mind, let's undertake a brief overview of the things we're going to cover in this chapter:

- Using Group Policy to enforce a password policy
- The Microsoft Security Compliance Toolkit
- Using Desired State Configuration to enforce sensible defaults
- Disabling outdated services and protocols
- Delegating Active Directory permissions
- Enabling the Active Directory Recycling Bin
- Using System Monitor to identify security issues
- Windows Server Update Services
- Using BitLocker for drive encryption

Using Group Policy to enforce a password policy

In most networks, your password is the only thing that lies between a hacker and access to your network. People will choose bad passwords if we let them. We know this – that's why a lot of websites and companies have password policies such as this: A minimum of 8 characters, one uppercase letter, one lowercase letter, one special character, and you have to change your password every month. However, modern research tells us that password policies like this are actually detrimental – they force users into creating passwords that are difficult for humans to remember, but are easy for computers to guess.

The best current practices around what constitutes a good password policy changes from time to time, and it is currently different to the default Windows policy. So, let's have a look at how we can change the password policy so that if best current practices change again in the future, we can keep up with the times.

Getting started

You'll just need a Windows 10 computer with RSAT installed. If you're not familiar with group policies, I suggest going over *Chapter 10, Group Policy* before attempting this recipe.

How to do it...

On your Windows 10 computer with RSAT installed, perform the following steps:

1. Click on **Start** and open **Group Policy Management**.

2. Navigate to **Forest | Domains | Your Domain | Group Policy Objects**.

3. Right-click on **Group Policy Objects** and choose **New**.

4. Give your GPO a name. I'll call mine simply `Password Policy`.

5. Locate your new password policy GPO in the list of **Group Policy Objects**. Right-click on it and choose **Edit**:

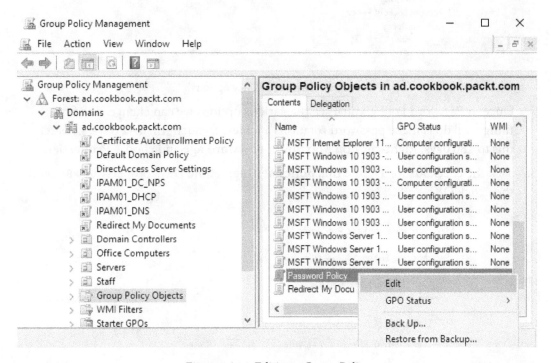

Figure 16.1 – Editing a Group Policy

6. In the Group Policy Management Editor, navigate to **Computer Configuration | Policies | Windows Settings | Security Settings | Account Policies | Password Policy**:

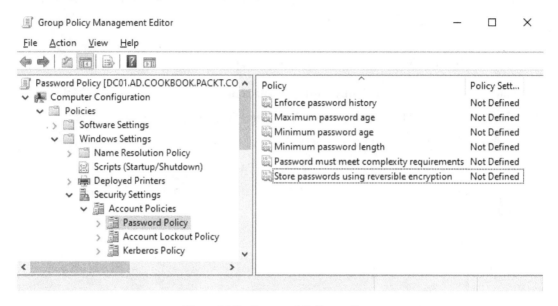

Figure 16.2 – Password Policy options

7. Once in Password Policy, you'll see the various options we can change. The first thing we'll do is make password rotations a lot less frequent than 42 days. Let's set this to 180 days. Right-click on **Maximum password age** and choose **Properties**.

8. Tick the checkbox for **Define this policy setting**, set the **Days** property to 180, and then click **OK**:

Figure 16.3 – Setting the maximum password age to 180 days

9. GPO will now warn you that it's going to change another setting – the minimum password age. If you're not comfortable with this change, then you can manually undo it by editing **the Minimum password age** setting in the same way we just did.

10. We're now going to set the minimum password length to 14 characters. Right-click on **Minimum password length** and choose **Properties**.

11. Check the box for **Define this policy setting** and change the password to be 14 characters. Then, click **OK**.

12. Finally, we're going to disable the complexity requirements. Windows does not let us fine-tune complexity requirements – only toggle them on or off. You may not want to do this specific step, depending on your company's policies. Right-click on **Password must meet complexity requirements** and then click **Properties**.

13. Check the box for **Define this policy setting** and then check the box for **Disabled**. Then, click **OK**:

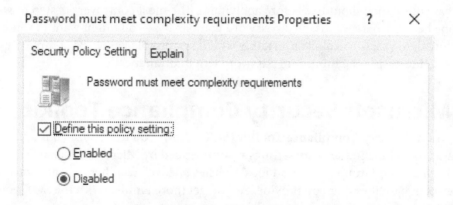

Figure 16.4 – Disabling the password complexity requirements

14. We'll now change our account lockout policy. Navigate to **Computer Configuration | Policies | Windows Settings | Security Settings | Account Policies | Account Lockout Policy**.

15. There are three settings we can change here – **Account lockout duration, Account lockout threshold, and Reset account lockout counter after**. Using the same process as we just did for the password options, I'm going to set the **Account lockout** threshold to 10. This will automatically set the other two properties for us.

16. You can now close the Group Policy Management Editor and return to the Group Policy Management screen.

17. I want this policy to apply to everyone in the company, so right-click on your domain in the Group Policy Management screen and choose **Link an existing GPO…**.

18. Locate the policy we just finished editing, `Password Policy`, and click **OK**.

19. When users' computers next update their group policies (typically within 90 minutes), the new password policy will be applied and the next time they change their password, it will have to conform with the new policy.

How it works...

We used the Group Policy functionality in Windows Server to set a password policy that is quite different from the default Windows policy. However, you should take care in following the exact policy I set out in this book in your production network. Password policies are not something you should take lightly, and probably not something where you should just accept the advice of something you read in a book somewhere. Think sensibly about what your policy should be before applying it. The most controversial step in what we've done here is where we disabled password complexity – you might want to think twice before doing that. You almost certainly would not disable password complexity without also increasing the minimum password length dramatically.

The Microsoft Security Compliance Toolkit

The Microsoft **Security Compliance Toolkit (SCT)** allows you to analyze your systems against a series of baseline security settings recommended by Microsoft. It analyzes settings such as your Group Policy and local policies to check whether they are consistent with a series of baselines that you provide. As you get more familiar with the SCT, you may start to create your own baselines to reference against.

Getting started

For this, you'll need a Windows Server 2019 server. Any previously configured Windows 2019 Server will do. We've built a lot of servers over the course of this book, so I'm going to choose my server, `web01`, to run the compliance toolkit against. We'll also need a Windows 10 computer with RSAT tools installed for doing some Group Policy imports.

How to do it...

On your chosen server, do the following:

1. The first thing we need to do is to download SCT. The toolkit can be downloaded by using your search engine to search for `Microsoft security toolkit download` or visiting `https://www.microsoft.com/en-us/download/details.aspx?id=55319`. There are several components to download – you will need to grab **PolicyAnalyzer.zip** and the **Security Baseline** for your version of Windows.

> **Tip**
> There are multiple versions of the Microsoft Security Toolkit security baseline – make sure you get the one that's appropriate for your version of Windows.

2. Once the toolkit has been downloaded, extract it somewhere onto your server. Your security baseline directory should end up looking like this:

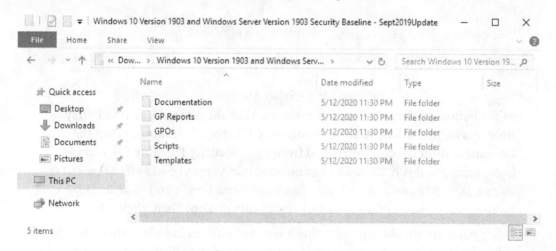

Figure 16.5 – The Security Toolkit directory

3. Once **PolicyAnalyzer** and **Security Baseline** have been extracted, browse to the **PolicyAnalyzer** directory and start the `PolicyAnalyzer.exe` program:

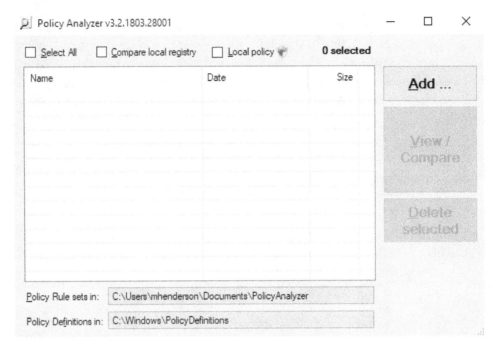

Figure 16.6 – Policy Analyzer

At the bottom of the Policy Analyzer screen, click the directory next to **Policy Rule sets in**, this will allow us to change this directory. You should select the **Documentation** directory extracted from your **Security Baseline** ZIP archive. In my example, this is `C:\Users\mhenderson\Downloads\Windows 10 Version 1903 and Windows Server Version 1903 Security Baseline - Sept2019Update\Documentation`. Then, click **OK**.

4. Policy Analyzer should now be listing a series of policies in its list. This is the list of baselines that we can compare our server to. There will likely be policies that do not apply to your server – for example, Windows 10 policies, or Domain Controller policies. Put a tick next to the policy that has **MemberServer** in its name. Mine is called `MSFT-WS v1903-MemberServer-FINAL-Sep2019Update`, but yours might be different.

5. Also tick the box at the top of the window that says **Local policy**. This tells Policy Analyzer to include our current servers' configuration in its analysis:

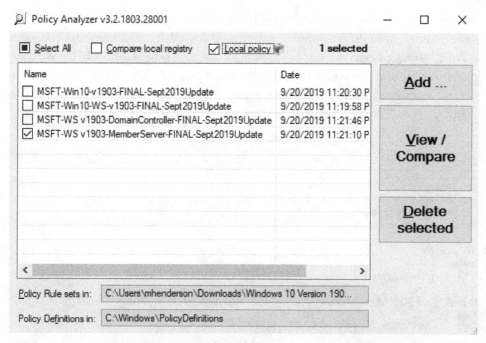

Figure 16.7 – Policy Analyzer with MemberServer and Local policy checked

6. Click the **View/Compare** button.

7. Policy Viewer will now show the results of all the settings it discovered and audited. It's probably a long list. We can filter this down to just the interesting parts by going to the **View** menu and choosing **Show only Conflicts**:

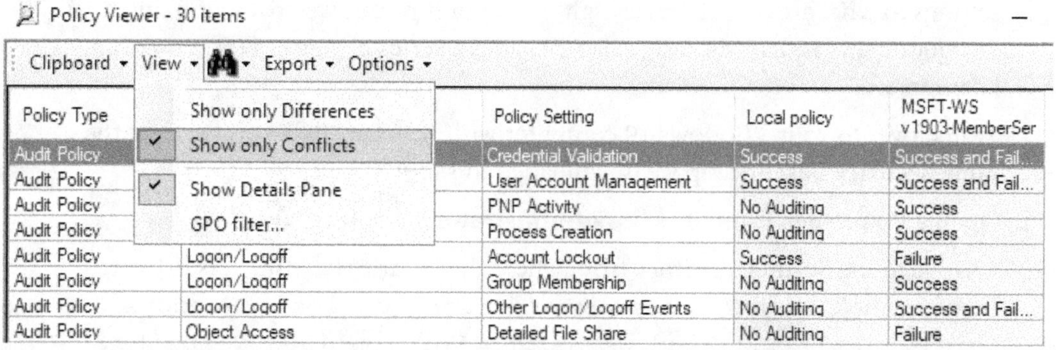

Figure 16.8 – Selecting Show only Conflicts in the View menu

8. Now, the list of items in Policy Viewer is only showing the settings on our server that are different to the baseline we selected. If you click on an item, the bottom half of Policy Viewer describes what the setting does, and how it differs between your local machine and the policy baseline. For example, if I select the item for **System Access | MinimumPasswordLength**, Policy Viewer tells me that my local password length is set to **7**, but the security baseline says it should be **14**:

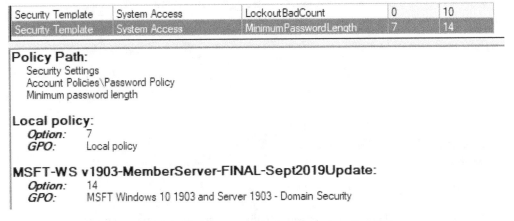

Figure 16.9 – The MinimumPasswordLength policy differs

9. I can also see that **System Access | LockoutBadCount** (the number of times an incorrect password can be entered before the account is locked out) is currently set to 0, when the baseline suggests it should be 10.

10. It is great to know that the baselines provided by Microsoft are suggesting different settings to what are on the server right now, but how can we go about fixing this? The good news is that Microsoft also provides a series of starter GPOs that can be imported.

11. Switch over to your Windows 10 computer with RSAT installed and extract the same **Security Baseline** zip we downloaded in *step 1*.

12. Open a **Powershell** prompt as the **administrator**.

13. Change to the **Scripts** directory from where the security baseline was extracted. In my example, this is `C:\Users\mhenderson\Downloads\Windows 10 Version 1903 and Windows Server Version 1903 Security Baseline - Sept2019Update\Scripts`.

14. Run the `Baseline-ADImport.ps1` script:

```
.\Baseline-ADImport.ps1
```

15. The script will now start to import a series of baseline Group Policy Objects into your Active Directory environment. It does not enable them or link them anywhere though, so you have a chance to modify them before applying them.

16. If you open the Group Policy Management tool and navigate to the Group Policy Objects view, you will see a series of new policies with names such as *MSFT Windows Server 1903 - Member Server*. You can now edit, link, and enable those policies as required. For more information on using group policies, refer to *Chapter 10, Group Policy*, of this book.

How it works...

Using the Microsoft SCT is a great way to check that what you've specified as security requirements are actually being applied to your servers. In this recipe, we just took the example Microsoft baseline requirements and ran a comparison against them, but if your environment grows large enough, you may want to define your own security baselines.

The inclusion of Group Policy objects to get you started on the road to compliance is also a nice inclusion from Microsoft. It means you don't have to go and define hundreds of individual security settings yourself – you can start from their baselines and modify them as required. You may want to be careful about just applying the Microsoft supplied baselines without spending time reviewing what's in them first. The last thing you want to do is break some existing functionality in your network because you applied a GPO you didn't understand!

Using Desired State Configuration to enforce default configurations

We've just seen how we can use the SCT to check whether our security configurations are in line with a set of recommendations, and we've seen that the security toolkit comes with some group policies that we can use as a starting point for getting our security configurations up to speed. However, in the previous chapter of this book, we went through a new technology called **Desired State Configuration (DSC)**.

In this recipe, we're going to build on the foundations laid by our chapter on DSC by taking the security baselines offered by the security toolkit and including them in our DSC configuration.

Getting started

You'll need a Windows 10 machine for completing this recipe. You will also need to have completed the previous recipe and completed *Chapter 15, Desired State Configuration*, in this book. I'm also going to be referencing the recipe from this latter chapter on using Azure for our DSC, but that is optional.

How to do it...

Using your Windows 10 computer that we used in *Chapter 15, Desired State Configuration and Automation* (so that it has your existing DSC web server configuration on it), perform the following steps:

1. Make sure that you have downloaded and extracted the Microsoft SCT ZIP file. Mine is extracted to `C:\Users\mhenderson\Downloads\Windows 10 Version 1903 and Windows Server Version 1903 Security Baseline - Sept2019Update\`.

2. Open a **PowerShell** prompt.

3. Change to your DSC directory. Mine is `C:\DSC`.

4. We're now going to convert the Windows Server baseline GPO provided by the security toolkit into a generic DSC configuration. We can do that with the `ConvertFrom-GPO` cmdlet. The GPO GUID for the Windows Server 2019 baseline in my example is `{61F0BC30-2A4C-4B8C-92F2-9442FE6DEB9F}`, but yours may be different depending on whether the security toolkit has been updated by the time you complete this recipe:

    ```
    ConvertFrom-GPO -Path "C:\Users\mhenderson\Downloads\
    Windows 10 Version 1903 and Windows Server Version 1903
    Security Baseline - Sept2019Update\GPOs\{61F0BC30-2A4C-
    4B8C-92F2-9442FE6DEB9F}" -OutputConfigurationScript
    ```

This will give us the following output:

Figure 16.10 – Converting the security baseline GPO to DSC

5. You should now have a directory called Output. Rename this directory to SecurityBaseline. This is just so we don't forget what the directory contains.

6. Using your favorite editor, open the DSCFromGPO.ps1 file that is inside the SecurityBaseline directory. I'll be using PowerShell ISE:

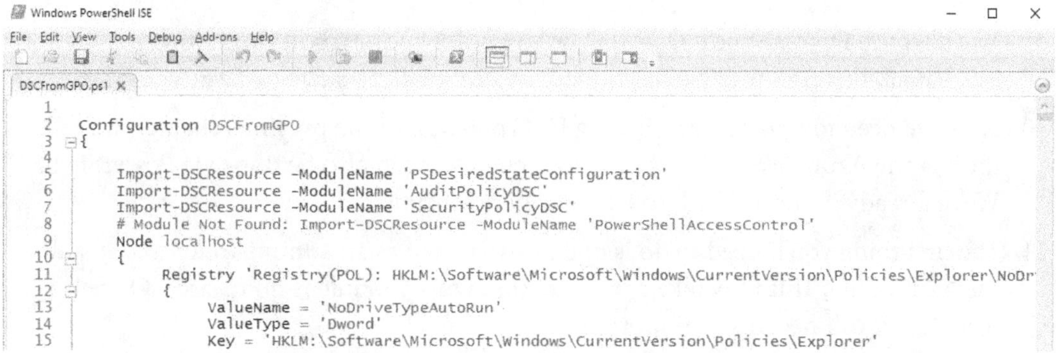

```
Windows PowerShell ISE                                                              −   □   ×
File  Edit  View  Tools  Debug  Add-ons  Help

DSCFromGPO.ps1  X
  1
  2   Configuration DSCFromGPO
  3  {
  4
  5       Import-DSCResource -ModuleName 'PSDesiredStateConfiguration'
  6       Import-DSCResource -ModuleName 'AuditPolicyDSC'
  7       Import-DSCResource -ModuleName 'SecurityPolicyDSC'
  8       # Module Not Found: Import-DSCResource -ModuleName 'PowerShellAccessControl'
  9       Node localhost
 10       {
 11           Registry 'Registry(POL): HKLM:\Software\Microsoft\Windows\CurrentVersion\Policies\Explorer\NoDr
 12           {
 13               ValueName = 'NoDriveTypeAutoRun'
 14               ValueType = 'Dword'
 15               Key = 'HKLM:\Software\Microsoft\Windows\CurrentVersion\Policies\Explorer'
```

Figure 16.11 – The converted GPO in DSC format

7. From here we have a few options. If you have a mature DSC environment, or an existing configuration management system such as Puppet, Chef, or Ansible, you might want to take this DSC configuration and insert it into your existing configuration management as a module. However, for the purposes of this recipe, I'm going to assume you have nothing more than the recipes we've already done in this book. This means that we should *also* open up our DSC file that we used for configuring our web servers, C:\DSC\PacktWebServer-Azure.ps1.

8. Once you have both DSC configurations open, copy and paste everything inside the Node portion of the converted GPO in DSCFromGPO.ps1 to the bottom of the Node portion of PacktWebServer-Azure.ps1:

```
Windows PowerShell ISE                                                              −   □   ×
File  Edit  View  Tools  Debug  Add-ons  Help

DSCFromGPO.ps1   PacktWebServer-Azure.ps1.ps1  X
 52               AutoRenew          = $true
 53               FriendlyName       = "SSL Certificate for IIS"
 54               KeyType            = "RSA"
 55               RequestType        = "CMC"
 56           }
 57
 58           Registry 'Registry(POL): HKLM:\Software\Microsoft\Windows\CurrentVersion\Policies\Explorer\
 59           {
 60               ValueName = 'NoDriveTypeAutoRun'
 61               ValueType = 'Dword'
 62               Key = 'HKLM:\Software\Microsoft\Windows\CurrentVersion\Policies\Explorer'
 63               ValueData = 255
 64
 65           }
```

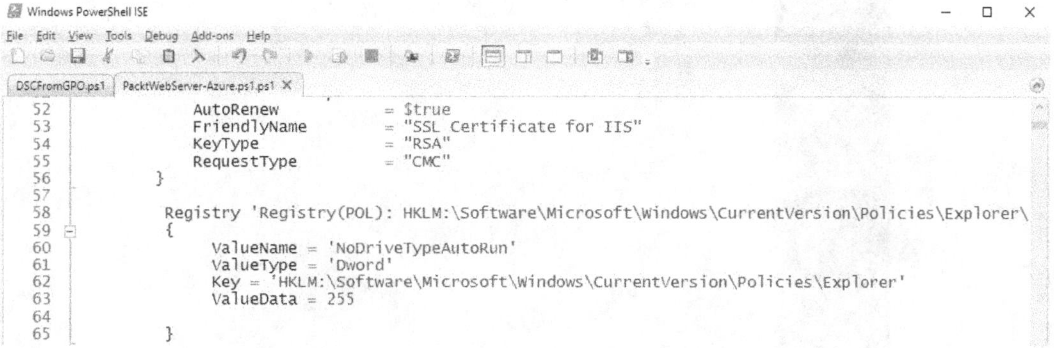

Figure 16.12 – Copying one DSC configuration into the other

> **Important**
>
> You might want to take this time to look through everything that this DSC
> configuration is now doing. There's a lot to go through, but you should always be
> aware of what you're applying before you make changes in production. Testing
> this DSC resource against a non-production machine would also be a good idea.

9. You also need to copy and paste the `Import-DSCResource` lines from
    `DSCFromGPO.ps1` into the same place in `PacktWebServer-Azure.ps1`.

10. Now, we need to update our running DSC policies. In the previous chapter, we did
    this via the Azure Web UI, but I mentioned that it can also be done via PowerShell.
    We're already in PowerShell, so let's stay here for now.

11. The first thing you'll need to do is open **PowerShell** as an administrator and install
    the `Az` module. This may take a while as the Azure module is quite large. Once it's
    installed, it will need to be imported:

```
Install-Module Az
Import-Module Az
```

12. Once the `Az` module has been imported, we need to log in to Azure. We can do this
    with the following command:

```
Connect-AzAccount
```

This command will open the **Sign in** page:

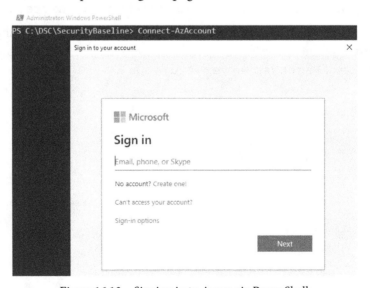

Figure 16.13 – Signing in to Azure via PowerShell

13. Now that we're logged in to Azure, we're going to generate our DSC configurations – but we're going to add an extra step over what we did before. We'll also dissect this command in a moment. In `C:\DSC`, execute the following command:

```
. .\PacktWebServer-Azure.ps1
```

```
PacktWebServer -NodeName 'web01','web02','web03' |
ForEach-Object { Import-AzAutomationDscNodeConfiguration
-AutomationAccountName PacktDSC -ResourceGroupName
PacktCookbook -ConfigurationName PacktWebServer -Path
$_.FullName -Force }
```

This will give us the following output:

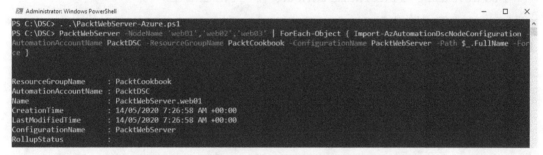

Figure 16.14 – Uploading our MOF files directly to Azure

14. Let's break apart that second command:

a. `PacktWebServer -NodeName`: This is the same as what we were normally doing back in *Chapter 15, Desired State Configuration and Automation*. It will create three MOF files – one for each node.

`|` is the PowerShell pipeline operator and is one of PowerShell's most useful features. It takes whatever the output of the first command is and passes it to the second. The output of our first command is a list of the three MOF files, so that's what will be passed to the next command.

b. `ForEach-Object { }`: This tells PowerShell to take each object on the pipeline (whatever came before the `|`) and run whatever comes next on it. This is also often shortened to the PowerShell shorthand, `%`.

c. `Import-AzAutomationDscNodeConfiguration`: Back in the previous chapter, we went through the process of laboriously clicking through the UI to upload a DSC configuration and generate node configurations for each configuration. This PowerShell cmdlet bypasses all that work by letting us upload our MOF files directly to Azure.

d. -AutomationAccountName: This is the name of our automation account from *Chapter 15, Desired State Configuration and Automation.*

e. -ResourceGroupName: This is the name of our resource group from Chapter 15.

f. -ConfigurationName: This is the name of our DSC configuration for the web servers from Chapter 15.

g. -Path: This is the path to our DSC MOF.

h. $_: This represents the item currently on the pipeline. In this case, it's a PowerShell object that represents the MOF file. We want to get the path of the file, so we're using its FullName attribute – $_.FullName.

i. -Force: Don't ask for confirmation.

15. Once that command finishes – it might take a while – DSC will then start pushing out the new configuration to your web servers. You can check the DSC dashboard in the Azure portal to confirm this:

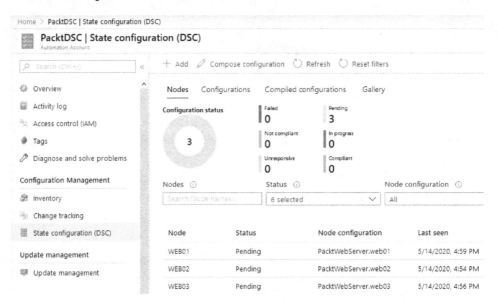

Figure 16.15 – Checking the DSC dashboard shows that our three web server nodes are now pending DSC updates

How it works...

DSC can be used to configure any number of features for a server, and it's great that Microsoft provides us with some baselines that we can use for this configuration.

There are a lot of other things we could have done in this security baseline as well; things such as ensuring that the Windows Defender service is running, or that Windows Updates are configured. You might even have existing GPOs for Windows Updates that you could convert to DSC.

Once you have enough complex DSC configurations, you'll probably want to start creating reusable DSC modules. Although beyond the scope of this book, there are plenty of books and documentation about how to do this.

Disabling outdated services and protocols

Microsoft has always had a focus on backward compatibility. It's for this reason that Active Directory domains still control options for enabling compatibility with Windows NT 4 – an operating system that was released in 1996. In recent times, Microsoft has taken to disabling certain very old protocols for security reasons – and with very good reason. Most of them are no longer used, and if they are used, then they shouldn't be. Microsoft even curates a naughty list of devices that use its 30-year old file-sharing protocol SMB (`https://aka.ms/stillneedssmb1` and `https://aka.ms/StopUsingSMB1`).

In this recipe, we're going to look at how we can use DSC to ensure that SMB1 is disabled and stays disabled. You can also use DSC to ensure that other various Windows features that you either do or don't want are installed or uninstalled.

Getting started

You should have completed *Chapter 5, Desired State Configuration*. We will be doing this work from our Windows 10 machine that we've been doing all our DSC work from so far.

How to do it...

On your Windows 10 computer, perform the following steps:

1. Open the DSC configuration we've been working with so far in your favorite editor. I'll be opening `C:\DSC\PacktWebServer-Azure.ps1` in **PowerShell ISE**.

2. Add the following `WindowsService` configuration somewhere in your Node configuration:

```
WindowsFeature DisableSMB1 {
    Ensure = "Absent"
    Name = "FS-SMB1"
    IncludeAllSubFeature = $true
}
```

3. That's it! Once you push your DSC configuration out to each of your machines, this will ensure that if the SMB1 protocol is enabled, it will be disabled, and if anyone enables it in the future, DSC will undo the change.

4. If you've been following the Azure process for publishing DSC, then the process is the same as all the other occasions: dot-source the configuration, generate the MOFs, and upload the MOFs to Azure (these are exactly the same commands we ran in the previous recipe):

```
. .\PacktWebServer-Azure.ps1
PacktWebServer -NodeName 'web01','web02','web03' |
ForEach-Object { Import-AzAutomationDscNodeConfiguration
-AutomationAccountName PacktDSC -ResourceGroupName
PacktCookbook -ConfigurationName PacktWebServer -Path
$_.FullName -Force }
```

How it works...

This is probably the smallest recipe in this book, but that's no accident. Nor is it laziness on behalf of the author, or yourself. It's because we've put so much work into making sure that our Windows environments are easily managed and configured that making important changes like this becomes incredibly simple.

With one small block of code, you can disable an outdated, dangerous protocol in minutes across your entire fleet of servers – assuming you've put in the work to get them onto DSC in the first place.

Delegating Active Directory permissions

Have you ever seen a company where almost everyone has Domain Admin access? Anyone who has been in this industry for long enough will respond with a resounding YES. Some companies hand out Domain Admin rights to anyone who asks for it, usually because the user needs to do something that's slightly more powerful than the default user and the administrators don't know how to delegate Active Directory permissions. Sometimes, it's a vendor who comes along and hasn't bothered to do their research into exactly which Active Directory permissions their software needs in order to do the job.

For example, if you have a helpdesk individual who needs to be able to change a user's name, but not create accounts or change user passwords, then why would you give that person Domain Admin? But a lot of companies do, simply because they don't know the power of Active Directory's delegation.

Getting started

For this, we'll need our Window 10 machine with RSAT installed. We will also need two Windows 10 accounts – your normal Domain Admin account that you've been using so far in this book, and a second normal account to which we can delegate some access.

In this example, I am using the following two accounts:

- `mhenderson`: My Domain Admin account

- `aivancic`: The person to whom I need to delegate some Active Directory permissions

How to do it...

On your Windows 10 computer with RSAT, perform the following steps:

1. Open **Active Directory Users and Computers**.

2. In this example, we want to give the user `aivancic` permission to reset the passwords for everyone in our organization. Right-click on the OU that contains your user accounts (mine is under `ad.cookbook.packt.com/Staff`), and then choose **All Tasks | Delegate Control…**:

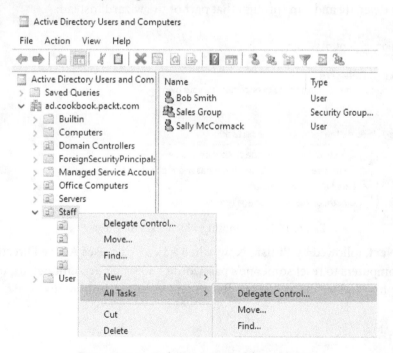

Figure 16.16 – Delegating control from an OU

3. Click **Next**, and on the **Users** or **Groups** screen, click **Add…**.

4. Type in the username or group we want to delegate to. In this case, I'm delegating to a specific person, so I'm going to enter `aivancic` in the object name field.

5. Click **OK** and the person's name should now appear in the **Users or Groups** screen:

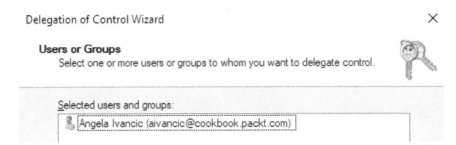

Figure 16.17 – Adding a user to delegate to

6. Click **Next** and you'll come to the **Tasks to Delegate** screen. This screen comes with some very useful common defaults. I find that these defaults cover my needs about 75% of the time – and what do you know, **Reset user passwords** and **Read all user information** is right there in that list. Those match my needs exactly, so I'm going to tick those two boxes. If you need more complex permissions, click **Create a custom task to delegate** and run through that part of the wizard instead:

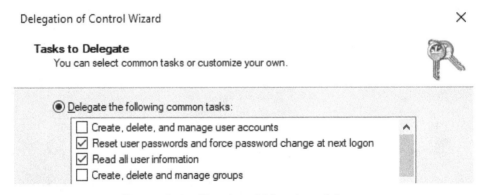

Figure 16.18 – Choosing which tasks to delegate

7. Click **Next**, followed by **Finish**. Now, when `aivancic` uses Active Directory Users and Computers to reset someone's password or see their account details, they will be able to – and we didn't have to give them Domain Admin to do it!

How it works...

Active Directory has a very fine-grained permissions system. If you chose the **Create a custom task to delegate** option, you would see literally dozens of different permissions you can choose from. You may have to fine-tune permissions based on trial and error if you have an application where you don't know what permissions it needs, but it's very rare that you actually have to assign Domain Admin to an application.

Enabling the Active Directory Recycle Bin

We just walked through the task of delegating access to Active Directory to certain users, but that's not without its own risks. What if the user goes and does something silly like deleting a user, instead of moving them? Because that would never happen to *you*, would it?

The Active Directory Recycle Bin has been around for a long time – since Windows Server 2008 R2 in fact. But it's not something that I see in use all that often, which leads me to believe that a lot of systems administrators are just not aware of its existence. It's also not turned on by default, which doesn't help.

Let's take a look at how we can make use of it.

Getting started

You'll need your Windows 10 computer with RSAT installed. That's it!

How to do it...

On your Windows 10 computer that has the Active Directory RSAT tools installed, perform the following steps:

1. Open **PowerShell**.
2. Run the following command:

```
Enable-ADOptionalFeature -Identity 'Recycle Bin Feature'
-Scope ForestOrConfigurationSet -Target 'ad.cookbook.
packt.com' -Server dc01
```

This will give us the following output:

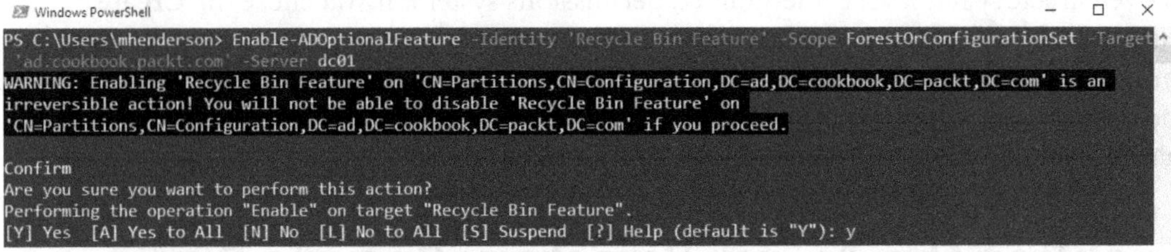

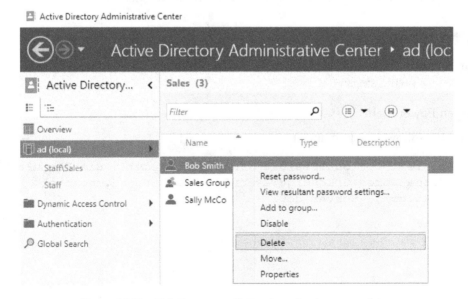

Figure 16.19 – Enabling the Active Directory Recycle Bin

3. That's it! End of recipe? Not quite – let's take a look at how we can use the Recycle Bin and restore things from it. Open **Server Manager**.

4. If you haven't already done so, add your domain controllers to **Server Manager** by going to **Manage | Add Servers…**.

5. Once you have your domain controllers listed in **Server Manager**, right-click on one of your domain controllers and go to **Active Directory Administrative Center**. This is a new tool that we haven't seen so far in this book. This is an alternative way of interacting with your Active Directory contents without using the **Active Directory Users and Computers** screen.

6. Once **Active Directory Administrative Center** has loaded, we need to "accidentally" delete something. I'm going to go to **Staff | Sales** and "accidentally" delete **Bob Smith**:

Figure 16.20 – Deleting a user that we're going to recover later

7. We now get an email from the helpdesk manager, who was contacted by Bob Smith's manager, asking why he can no longer log in. Bob's manager also mentioned that Bob thought he had been fired but nobody had told him yet. Oops. Let's get Bob's account back as quickly as possible.

8.   Go back to the home screen of **Active Directory Administrative Center**.

9. You should see an OU listed for **Deleted Objects**. Double-click on that.

10. Bob Smith's account should be listed in there. Right-click on Bob and choose **Restore**:

Figure 16.21 – Restoring a user from the Deleted Objects OU

11. Bob's account should now be back where it belongs, in the Sales OU, and Bob can get back to work as normal.

How it works...

Normally, if you delete an object from Active Directory, it's almost unrecoverable. In some circumstances, it could be done, but it was very difficult. By enabling the Active Directory Recycle Bin, you give yourself a grace period of 180 days (by default) to restore any deleted items.

However, the Deleted Objects OU doesn't show up by default in the **Active Directory Users and Computers** screen – so we used the Active Directory Administrative Center to restore the object instead.

Using System Monitor to identify security issues

In this chapter, we've spent quite a bit of time looking at how to prevent things going wrong; using compliance checklists; delegating appropriate permissions; disabling old services and protocols. Earlier in this book, we also looked at using Windows Defender for anti-malware and crypto-ransom protection. But we haven't yet looked at things we can use to figure out what went wrong in the event that our planning wasn't effective.

System Monitor (Sysmon) is tool that, once installed, logs a lot of additional information about your system to your Windows Event Log. It is a very powerful tool when it comes to tracking down what went wrong and where and is very useful in the event that something security-wise does go wrong with your systems. If you have systems that log events to a central location, then you have even more power at your fingertips.

Getting started

All you'll need for this is a Windows Server 2019 machine on which to install Sysmon.

How to do it...

On your Windows Server 2019 machine, follow these steps:

1. The first thing we need to do is download Sysmon. It is published under the Microsoft System Internals suite of tools and can be downloaded at `https://docs.microsoft.com/en-us/sysinternals/downloads/sysmon`.

2. Sysmon can also accept an optional configuration file to tell it what to monitor. Thankfully, an anonymous (but very well known) security expert who goes by the name *SwiftOnSecurity* released a comprehensive open source Sysmon configuration we can use to get started. This can be downloaded from `https://github.com/SwiftOnSecurity/sysmon-config`:

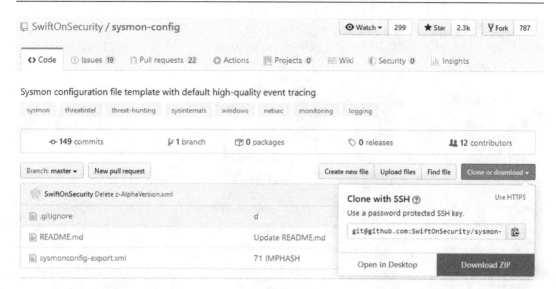

Figure 16.22 – Downloading SwiftOnSecurity's Sysmon configuration from GitHub

> **Tip**
> If you are not familiar with downloading from GitHub, the process for this
> file is quite simple. Click the green button for **Clone or download** and then
> choose **Download ZIP**. This will download all the files present in the GitHub
> repository.

3. Before we copy these files to our Windows Server, let's take a look at the
    configuration that we're going to be installing. After all, it's not usually a great idea
    to blindly install any random thing you find on the internet. Extract the contents of
    the `sysmon-config` download and open `sysmonconfig-export.xml`.

4. You will find therein *a lot* of XML. Thankfully, it begins with a very comprehensive
    README section. Have a read through the README and then take a look at
    various parts of the file. You may not understand a lot of it to begin with, but if you
    decide to add your own monitoring, or perhaps remove some of the monitoring in
    the configuration, this can give you a good understanding of what a configuration
    file should look like.

5. Now that you have Sysmon and sysmon-config downloaded, copy them onto your Windows Server 2019 server and extract them somewhere. I have extracted mine to `C:\SysMon`:

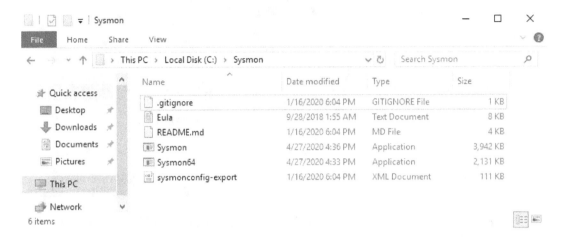

Figure 16.23 – The downloaded and extracted Sysmon files and configuration

6. Open **PowerShell** as the administrator.

7. Change to your Sysmon directory – mine is `cd C:\Sysmon`.

8. To install Sysmon, run the following command. Once this is done, you should have a message indicating that Sysmon has been started:

```
sysmon.exe -accepteula -i sysmonconfig-export.xml
```

This will give us the following output:

```
PS C:\Sysmon> .\sysmon.exe -i sysmonconfig-export.xml


System Monitor v11.0 - System activity monitor
Copyright (C) 2014-2020 Mark Russinovich and Thomas Garnier
Sysinternals - www.sysinternals.com

Loading configuration file with schema version 4.22
Sysmon schema version: 4.30
Configuration file validated.
Sysmon installed.
SysmonDrv installed.
Starting SysmonDrv.
SysmonDrv started.
Starting Sysmon..
Sysmon started.
```

Figure 16.24 – Installing Sysmon with our configuration

9. Now, we need to check that Sysmon is working. Click **Start** and open **Event Viewer**.

10. Once the event viewer is opened, navigate to **Applications and Services Logs | Microsoft | Windows | Sysmon | Operational**.

11. You should already see some logs flowing in. Because Sysmon logs so many things, including DNS queries, you should be seeing things such as process creation and DNS queries. On their own, these are not particularly useful, but in the event of reconstructing an event that happened in the past, they can provide some invaluable insight.

12. Let's now take a look at the DNS queries our server has been making. In **Event Viewer**, click the **Filter Current Log…** link on the right-hand side of the screen.

13. Select **Event ID**, enter 22, and then click **OK**:

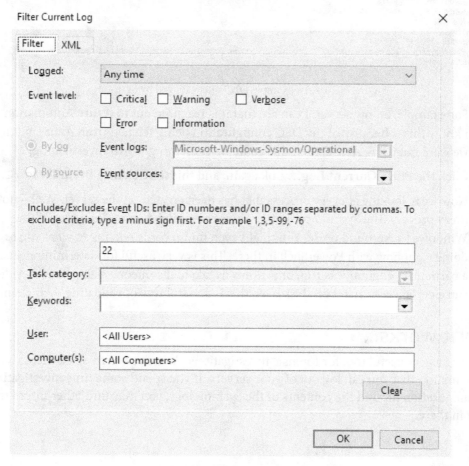

Figure 16.25 – Filtering the event log

14. You should now only see events that match ID number 22 in the view. These are all the DNS queries that the server has been making:

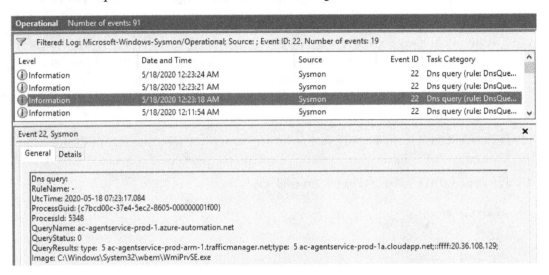

Figure 16.26 – An example DNS query logged by Sysmon

15. For example, on my server, I can see that it is reaching out to Azure Automation. I know this is because of my DSC configuration being fetched from Azure, but if we were not using Azure, then this could be something worth investigating.

16. Click the **Filter Current Log…** link again, and this time change **Event ID** to 11.

17. Now we're looking at every process that has been created on the server. Well – not every process. The Sysmon configuration we are using does exclude a lot of the Windows background noise. You might even find records relating to what you're doing right now with PowerShell in there. This is very useful for determining when a particular program was run, or action was taken. If someone claims that they didn't run a certain command on the server, this is a useful way of validating their claims.

How it works...

Sysmon is a very useful tool for forensic investigations. As we've briefly seen, there's a lot of information that you can log out of your servers. If you spend some time investigating the configuration file and the contents of the Sysmon logs, you may find other interesting things in there.

Sysmon is at its most useful when it's combined with a central logging system. Some such tools are called **SIEMs – Security Information and Event Management**. One duty of a SIEM is to ingest all of the event logs from all your servers and provide an easy way to query all of them at once. Then, you can look for patterns across all your servers or determine whether particular events are isolated.

Once you have the information you need to be collected from your Sysmon events, you may be able to put further protections in place to stop them from happening again.

Windows Server Update Services

Software updates are just a fact of life. Every administrator has to deal with them regularly – whether it's regular updates on your personal operating system, enterprise software that has software releases, or even updating the maps in your automobile's satellite navigation system.

When you have even two or three computers in your office, you'll also know some of the pain of managing Windows Updates for the desktop version of Windows such as Windows 10. Throw in a few servers and you're either very busy once a month doing updates and restarts, or you're never patching at all.

Windows has long provided a tool called **Windows Server Update Services (WSUS)**, which can be used to help alleviate some of that pain, and that's what we're going to take a look at in this recipe. WSUS is generally installed in each physical location where you have computers or servers, and it acts as a go-between between your computers and the Windows Update service. This means that you only need to download the updates from the internet once, and that you can control which updates get released when for different services in your network.

Quite frankly, managing Windows Updates could be an entire chapter on its own (maybe in the next edition of this book perhaps?), so in this recipe, I'm just going to walk you through how to get Windows Server Update Services up and running, and getting your Windows computers talking to it.

Getting started

You'll need a fresh Windows Server 2019 server that's joined to your domain. You'll want to make sure it has enough disk space to store your required Windows Updates. Modern Windows Updates can be quite large in size, so several hundred gigabytes might be required for a production system.

You'll also need a Windows 10 computer with RSAT installed so that we can create a Group Policy.

How to do it...

On your fresh Windows Server 2019 machine, perform the following steps:

1. The first thing we need to do is install the WSUS role onto our Windows server. Open **PowerShell** as the administrator.

2. The Windows feature we need to add is called `UpdateServices`. We can add it with the following command:

```
Install-WindowsFeature UpdateServices
-IncludeManagementTools
```

3. Once the feature has finished installing, click **Start** and open **Windows Server Update Services**.

4. You will now be prompted to complete the WSUS installation. Tick the box for **Store updates locally**. For the content directory path, enter where you want the updates to be saved. I only have a single hard disk, so I'll be using `C:\WSUS`:

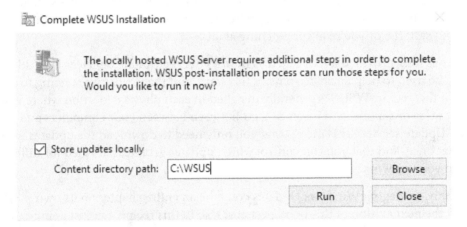

Figure 16.27 – Initial configuration of the WSUS service

5. Click **Run**. WSUS will now complete its installation. This may take a few minutes. Once it has finished, click **Close**.

6. You will now have a new wizard – the **Windows Server Update Services Configuration Wizard**. Read the *Before you begin* section, and then click **Next**.

7. Decide if you want to join the Microsoft Update Improvement Program, and then click **Next**.

8. On the **Choose Upstream Server** screen, we need to choose where to download our Windows Updates from. You can synchronize downloads between multiple servers if you need to, but as this is our first WSUS server, we'll just leave it on **Synchronize from Microsoft Update** and click **Next**.

9. If your network uses a proxy server, enter it on the **Proxy Server** page. Otherwise, just click **Next**.

10. We now have to connect to our upstream update server (in our case, Microsoft Update) to continue the configuration, as it needs more information from the internet. Click **Start Connecting**. This may take several minutes, depending on your internet connection speed:

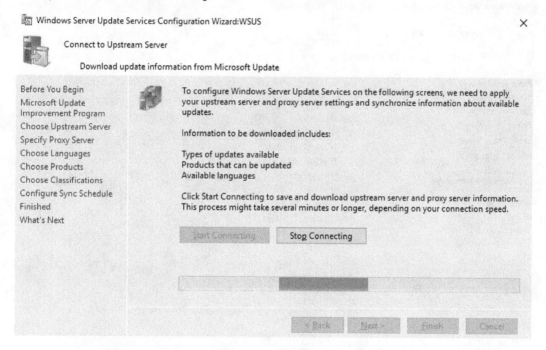

Figure 16.28 – Connecting to upstream server

11. Once it's finished, click **Next**.

12. You'll now be asked which languages you want to download. This can increase your download size dramatically, so make sure you only select the languages that are in use in your network. I'm only using English, so I'm leaving mine as the default setting and then clicking **Next**.

13. You now need to select which products you want to download updates for. You should only select products that are actually in use in your network, otherwise you'll waste disk space and downloads downloading updates that are never going to be used. By default, all Windows products are enabled. Again, this default is fine for my network, but it may not be for yours. Confirm that you've ticked the products you need, and then click **Next**.

14. Next, you need to select which classifications of updates you want to download. At this point, you may not know which ones you need, so feel free to tick **All Classifications** and click **Next**:

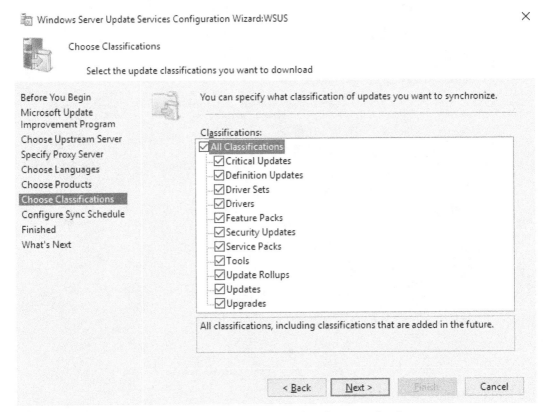

Figure 16.29 – Synchronizing all classifications of updates

15. You can now choose a synchronization schedule. If you leave this as manual, you'll need to trigger your WSUS updates by hand each time. To avoid this, choose **Synchronize automatically**. For the synchronization time, choose a time when your network will not be busy. I typically choose midnight. One synchronization per day is generally all you need, unless you're downloading updates for products that have updates released more frequently.

16. On the final page, choose if you want WSUS to download all the updates right now with the **Begin initial synchronization** checkbox. If you tick that box, WSUS will kick off a synchronization job when you finish the wizard. If not, it will wait until the schedule you set on the previous page. The first synchronization can take hours, so be prepared for a lengthy wait.

17. Click **Next**, and then **Finish**.

18. The Update Services dashboard will now appear. There's nothing much to see right now as nothing is using this WSUS server:

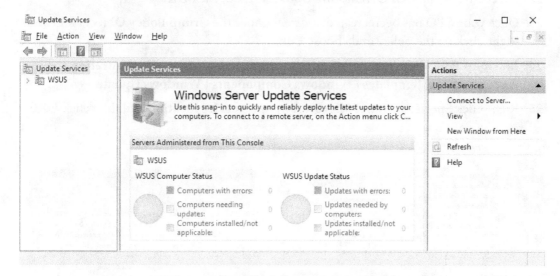

Figure 16.30 – The default WSUS dashboard

19. While we're waiting for the initial synchronization to complete, now would be a good time to configure our Group Policy to tell Windows clients to connect to our WSUS server. Switch over to your Windows 10 system with RSAT.

20. Once in your Windows 10 system, click **Start** and then open **Group Policy Management**.

21. I want this WSUS policy to apply to every single computer in my entire domain – be it Windows Desktop or Windows Server. Therefore, I'm going to right-click my domain and choose **Create a GPO in this domain, and Link it here…**:

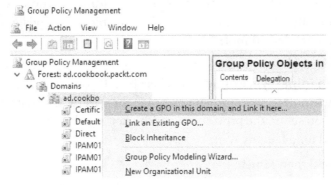

Figure 16.31 – Creating a new GPO

22. I'm calling my new GPO **Windows Updates**. Then, click **OK**.

23. Once your GPO has been created, locate it under the **Group Policy Objects** folder. Right-click on the policy and choose **Edit**.

24. In **Group Policy Management Editor**, navigate to **Computer Configuration | Administrative Templates | Windows Components | Windows Update**.

25. Right-click **Specify intranet Microsoft update service location** and then click **Edit**:

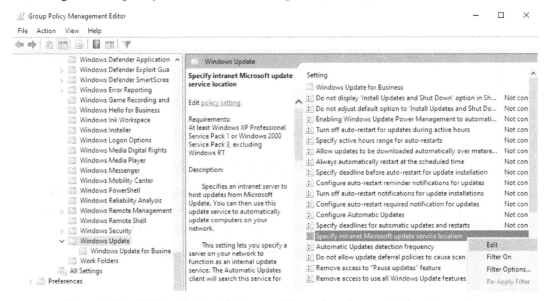

Figure 16.32 – Editing the Specify intranet Microsoft update service location setting

26. Change the option to **Enabled**.

27. For the intranet update service setting and the intranet statistics server setting, enter `http://[your-wsus-server]:8530`. I'll be setting mine to `http://wsus.ad.cookbook.packt.com:8530`:

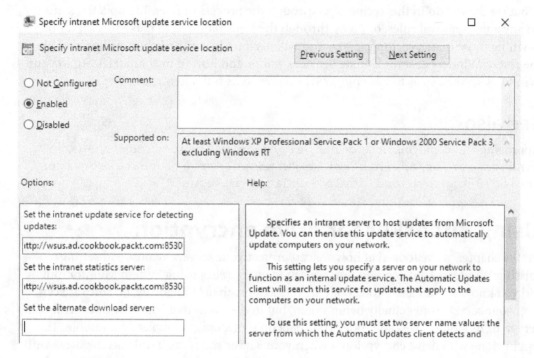

Figure 16.33 – Specifying the intranet Microsoft update service location

28. Click **OK** and close this GPO.

> **Tip**
> You might want to also look at the options for **Configure Automatic Updates**. You might have one policy for desktop machine installation and reboot at, say, 3 a.m., once updates are released, and another policy for your servers where they download updates but do not install them.

29. As your Windows machines update their GPOs, computers will start to check in to our WSUS server. If you switch back to your WSUS server, click the **Refresh** link on the right-hand side of your dashboard and see whether the **Computers** number under **Server Statistics** has gone up from zero. Additionally, under **Synchronization status**, you'll be able to see how far through your synchronizations are.

How it works...

In this recipe, we went through the process of installing the WSUS service, getting it configured, and configuring a Group Policy to get Windows machines checking in with the service.

What we did *not* do in this recipe is go through the process of releasing updates, setting up any auto-approval rules, or going through the steps required to make this server be anything more than a caching server. You will need to do some further reading on how the rest of Windows Server Update Services works, and how to push updates out to your Windows servers, so as to use your WSUS server to its full potential.

See also

Approving and deploying updates: `https://docs.microsoft.com/en-us/` `windows-server/administration/windows-server-update-services/` `deploy/3-approve-and-deploy-updates-in-wsus`

Using BitLocker for drive encryption

In this chapter, we've looked at how we can protect your servers against bad settings, missing Windows Updates, and how we can identify issues using System Monitor. But did you know we can also protect our servers against theft? Obviously, no software can stop your server from actually being stolen, but in the event that someone does steal your server, or its storage, we can render your data on that storage completely unusable. This can be done with drive encryption – when your server starts up, it unlocks the drive with a special key, known only to that server. If your disk is ever stolen, it won't be able to be unlocked as it will be missing the key. And if the entire server (with its key inside it) is stolen, if the person that stole it doesn't have an administrator password to your computer, they still won't be able to get any data off it. Microsoft calls this BitLocker.

To execute drive encryption well, your server needs to be equipped with a device called a **Trusted Platform Module (TPM)**. This is a small physical chip inside the server (sometimes embedded in the CPU itself) that holds the encryption keys for the disks. If the chip is ever removed, or put in a different server, it wipes itself, rendering the keys useless. This is particularly important for servers that contain sensitive private information, such as payroll servers or database servers that hold customer information.

Getting started

You'll need a physical Windows Server 2019 server for this recipe, and that server needs to be equipped with a TPM.

How to do it...

On your Windows Server, perform the following steps:

1. Open **PowerShell** as the administrator.

2. We then need to install the BitLocker windows feature with the following command:

```
Install-WindowsFeature Bitlocker -Restart
```

3. Once your server has restarted, log in again, click **Start**, and open **Manage BitLocker**:

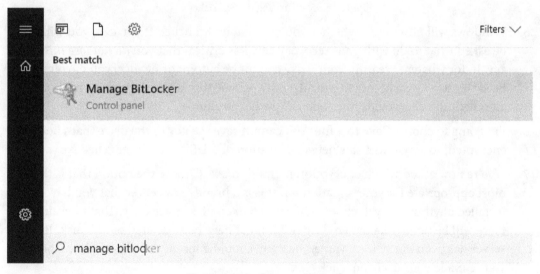

Figure 16.34 – Manage BitLocker

4. You will now be presented with a list of drives on which you can enable BitLocker. If you want to enable the automatic unlocking of any BitLocker-protected drive, you must turn BitLocker on for your boot drive. Click **Turn on BitLocker** for your C drive:

Figure 16.35 – Turning on BitLocker

5. Windows will now verify whether you can enable BitLocker. If you can, you will be asked what to do with your recovery key. It is critical that you *do not lose this key*. If, for whatever reason, your drive cannot be automatically decrypted, you will need this key to get access to your data. If you lose this key and the drive cannot be automatically decrypted, *your data will be lost forever.*

6. I'm going to choose **Save to a file**. You cannot save the key to the drive that's being encrypted, so save it to a safe network location or a USB stick. Then, click **Next**.

7. You're now asked which encryption method to use. Choose the option that is the most appropriate for your situation – if this is a brand-new server that you haven't installed anything on yet, choose **Encrypted used disk space only**. That's because there will be no private data hiding in files that have been deleted off the disk. If this server has been in use for a while, then you should encrypt the entire drive. Once you've made your decision, click **Next**.

8. For the encryption mode, there is really no reason to choose **Compatible mode**. The only time you should choose that mode is if you are going to need to read this encrypted disk on an older version of Windows. I'm going to leave mine on **New encryption mode** and then click **Next**.

9. BitLocker will now ask you if you want to run a system check. I strongly recommend that you do this, as it will validate the fact that the encryption can be automatically unlocked before starting the encryption process. Tick **Run BitLocker system check** and then click **Continue**.

10. Reboot your server.

11. When the server boots next time, it will begin encrypting the drive in the background. You can confirm this by going to **Manage BitLocker** and checking the encryption status:

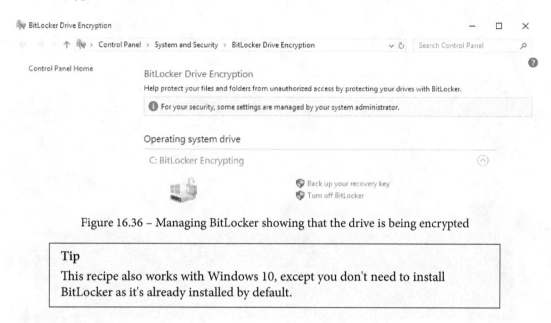

Figure 16.36 – Managing BitLocker showing that the drive is being encrypted

> **Tip**
> This recipe also works with Windows 10, except you don't need to install BitLocker as it's already installed by default.

How it works...

BitLocker is an essential tool for securing physical servers that contain private data. The modern solid state drives that ship with servers also typically have encryption support built in, meaning that encryption has virtually no performance penalty. Once upon a time, encryption took a serious performance hit, but with modern SSDs, it's barely measurable.

By encrypting your drives with BitLocker, you ensure that any physical theft of your hard drives – or even accidentally shipping a hard drive back to a manufacturer before wiping it – doesn't result in any of your sensitive data being exposed.

However, it is absolutely critical that you do not lose your BitLocker recovery key. If you lose that, then your data could very well be locked forever, and you'll be restoring from backups. On that note though, are your backups encrypted? Backup servers are a common target for thieves looking to steal corporate data, as stealing one set of hard drives can provide you with the data from dozens or even hundreds of servers. So maybe your backup storage servers are the ideal place to start?

Other Books You May Enjoy

If you enjoyed this book, you may be interested in these other books by Packt:

Mastering Windows Server 2019 – Second Edition

Jordan Krause

ISBN: 978-1-7898-045-342

- Work with the updated Windows Server 2019 interface, including Server Core and Windows Admin Center

- Secure your network and data with new technologies in Windows Server 2019

- Learn about containers and understand the appropriate situations to use Nano Server

- Discover new ways to integrate your data center with Microsoft Azure
- Harden your Windows Servers to help keep the bad guys out
- Virtualize your data center with Hyper-V

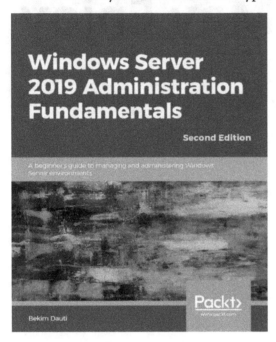

Windows Server 2019 Adminsitration Fundamentals

Bekim Dauti

ISBN: 978-1-83855-091-2

- Grasp the fundamentals of Windows Server 2019
- Understand how to deploy Windows Server 2019
- Discover Windows Server post-installation tasks
- Add roles to your Windows Server environment
- Apply Windows Server 2019 GPOs to your network
- Delve into virtualization and Hyper-V concepts
- Explore ways to tune, maintain, update, and troubleshoot Windows Server 2019
- Study relevant concepts in preparation for the MTA 98-365 exam

Leave a review - let other readers know what you think

Please share your thoughts on this book with others by leaving a review on the site that you bought it from. If you purchased the book from Amazon, please leave us an honest review on this book's Amazon page. This is vital so that other potential readers can see and use your unbiased opinion to make purchasing decisions, we can understand what our customers think about our products, and our authors can see your feedback on the title that they have worked with Packt to create. It will only take a few minutes of your time, but is valuable to other potential customers, our authors, and Packt. Thank you!

Index

C

D

W

CPSIA information can be obtained
at www.ICGtesting.com
Printed in the USA
BVHW021242200723
667496BV00012B/79